American Dreams *and* Nazi Nightmares

Brandeis Series in American Jewish History, Culture, and Life

Jonathan D. Sarna, Editor
Sylvia Barack Fishman, Associate Editor

For the complete list of books in this series, please see www.upne.com and www.upne.com/
series/BSAJ.html

American Dreams
and
Nazi Nightmares

Early Holocaust Consciousness and
Liberal America, 1957–1965

KIRSTEN FERMAGLICH

Brandeis University Press
WALTHAM, MASSACHUSETTS

PUBLISHED BY UNIVERSITY PRESS OF NEW ENGLAND
HANOVER AND LONDON

Brandeis University Press
Published by University Press of New England,
One Court Street, Lebanon, NH 03766
www.upne.com
© 2006 by Brandeis University Press
Printed in the United States of America
5 4 3 2 1

This book was published with the generous support of the Koret Foundation.
An earlier version of chapter 2 was originally published in *American Jewish History*
91, no. 2 (June 2003): 205–32.

Library of Congress Cataloging-in-Publication Data
Fermaglich, Kirsten Lise.
American dreams and Nazi nightmares : early Holocaust consciousness and
liberal america, 1957–1965 / Kirsten Fermaglich.
    p.   cm. — (Brandeis series in American Jewish history, culture, and life)
Includes bibliographical references and index.
ISBN-13: 978–1–58465–548–0 (cloth : alk. paper)
ISBN-10: 1–58465–548–8 (cloth : alk. paper)
1. Holocaust, Jewish (1939–1945)—Moral and ethical aspects.
2. Holocaust, Jewish (1939–1945)—Psychological aspects.
3. Psychohistory. 4. Elkins, Stanley—Criticism and interpretation.
5. Friedan, Betty—Criticism and interpretation.
6. Milgram, Stanley—Criticism and interpretation.
7. Lifton, Robert Jay, 1926–—Criticism and interpretation.
I. Title. II. Series.
D804.7.M67F47 2006
301.092'273—dc22   2005035959

For my parents,

Lois and Danny Fermaglich

And for Jon

CONTENTS

ACKNOWLEDGMENTS

It is a really good thing that book acknowledgments are not like the Academy Awards ceremony. Because I'm sure the music would start playing on me before I'd even mentioned my graduate adviser, and I definitely wouldn't get time to thank my husband. Also, I would be seriously underdressed.

The first person who must be thanked for helping me to complete this manuscript in a timely fashion is Raphael Benjamin Fermaglich Gold, who knew just when to shut up.

A number of institutions provided me with the funding necessary to research and write this book. Fellowships from the Graduate School of Arts and Sciences at New York University and the Graduate School of Arts and Sciences at Harvard University enabled me to conduct my research. The American Jewish Archives and the Feinstein Center for American Jewish History at Temple University awarded me additional funds for research. And funds from the Internal Research Grant Program, the Kussy Scholarship, and the History Department at Michigan State University have allowed me to conduct additional research, as well as to complete the writing of this book.

Librarians and archivists at a number of institutions eased the research process considerably. Librarians at the Manuscripts and Archives Division at Yale University, at the Schlesinger Library, Radcliffe Institute at Harvard University, and in the Rare Books and Manuscripts Collection at the New York Public Library were attentive and helpful. I am particularly grateful to archivist Melanie Yolles at the New York Public Library for organizing and helping me to view materials that had been until then unused. Librarians at New York University's Bobst Library, Harvard University's Widener and Lamont Libraries, and the Michigan State University library also facilitated my research.

The subjects of this book, as well as their family members, associates, and administrative assistants, have been critical to my research process. I thank Aaron Aronow, George Bellak, Stanley Elkins, Betty Friedan, Robert Jay Lifton, and Joel Milgram for generously giving their time and energy to submit to several long interviews. Moreover, Betty Friedan and Robert Lifton deserve thanks for making their personal files available to scholars, as does Alexandra Milgram, who has made her late husband's papers accessible. I am truly grateful to these men and women for allowing me to pry into their own and their loved ones' lives.

My graduate adviser, Lizabeth Cohen, was a crucial presence in the development of this book. She consistently and enthusiastically supported my work, even as I veered farther and farther from her own field of research. Hasia Diner, Thomas Bender, Jeffrey Shandler, and Stephen J. Whitfield offered important criticism of my work while I was a graduate student; I am particularly grateful to Hasia Diner for her comments on parts of the manuscript as it neared completion.

Many others have helped me in private discussions and at conferences with both intellectual and practical matters as this project developed, including Andrew Heinze, Karla Goldman, Laura Levitt, Peter Novick, Riv-Ellen Prell, Alex Sagan, Rona Sheramy, Michael Staub, Beth Wenger, and James Edward Young. Thomas Blass was generous enough to speak with me about his own work on Stanley Milgram, and to give me several important references for my own work. Daniel Horowitz offered kind reassurance on my research on Betty Friedan. And attendees at the Scholars Conference on American Jewish History in June 2002 helped me to redirect and shape my argument at a crucial stage in the writing of this book.

I owe my editor at Brandeis University Press/University Press of New England, Phyllis Deutsch, a debt of gratitude. She has enthusiastically encouraged my work since I first approached her several years ago, and she has shepherded this book through the publication process with both speed and sensitivity. Comments from Jonathan Sarna and Pam Nadell made the manuscript immeasurably better. And copy editing by Will Hively and technical assistance from Richard Pult and Jessica Stevens helped me to focus on the details that I typically overlook.

I have been tremendously fortunate to have become a member of the History Department and the Jewish Studies program at Michigan State University as I revised and completed this manuscript. My friends and colleagues (past and present) at MSU have provided a genuinely collegial and supportive environment to develop this mansucript. I am particularly indebted to colleagues who read and commented on parts of my chapters, or even (God help them) the entire manuscript: Daina Ramey Berry, Katie Dubois, Laurent Dubois, Lisa Fine, Ethan Segal, Gabriela Soto Laveaga, Keely Stauter-Halsted, and Kenneth Waltzer. Marc Bernstein, Maureen Flanagan, Steve Gold, Dagmar Herzog, Michael Koppisch, Joyce Ladenson, Leslie Moch, Sayuri Shimizu, Susan Sleeper-Smith, Tom Summerhill, and Steve

Weiland offered valuable professional advice along the way, as well as kind words and thoughtful concern for my well-being. Bets Caldwell, Shawn McBee, and Janet Roe-Darden provided crucial administrative help. Two chairs of the MSU history department, Lewis Siegelbaum and Mark Korn-bluh, have been instrumental in providing me with advice, encouragement, support, and most importantly, professional leave that allowed me time to finish the book.

Several reading groups—at New York University, at Harvard, and at Michigan State—have supported and nourished my work, imposing dead-lines on me, reading my work critically, and letting me cry on their collective shoulder. Katie Barry, Neil Maher, and Deb Michals at NYU, and Mindy Morgan, Anna Pegler-Gordon, and Stephen Rohs at MSU, deserve special and heartfelt thanks.

In addition to my colleagues and formal reading groups, I have been lucky enough to have had generous friends who have, throughout the years, read and commented informally on my work, offered suggestions and advice, attended my conference panels, laughed at my jokes, and in general, made my academic life much less solitary: many thanks to Dan Bender, Dina Berger, Jeremy Buchman, Aleisa Fishman, Dale Fulcher, In-dira Gesink, Liora Gubkin, Elizabeth Hatcher, Christine Levecq, Mary Lewis, Keren McGinty, Alex Molot, Sara Pugach, Mark Roseman, and Jane Roth-stein. Amy Hay deserves special mention as a friend, research assistant, and dedicated reader of the manuscript as it progressed.

Thanks go too to those generous friends and family members who pro-vided me with comfortable beds and refrigerators for the peanut butter and jelly sandwich to take to the archive next day: Hasia and Steve Diner; Mark and Lorrie Appleton; Fran and Ron Sunter; Elizabeth Hatcher; and Lewis Fermaglich, Rob Avery, and Lisa Sieckhaus. Kirsten Danis and Bob Kolker deserve special thanks not only for offering me the keys to their Brooklyn apartment, but for their consistent support, generosity, and love (not to mention brownies).

I would not have been able to complete this book without my family. My extended family, including Pearl Gelber; Sandy Schaare; Jeff, Marci, Sho-shanna and Ian Ruff; Fran, Ron, Jared, and Brian Sunter; Linda, Jay, An-drew, Shari, Rachel, and Joshua Gold, has been a constant source of sup-port and affection. It pains me to realize that neither Gene Fermaglich nor Ben Gelber, who kept track of my progress better than anyone, will be able to appreciate the completion of this work.

My immediate family has been a source of inspiration. My brother, Lewis, has provided me with psychology textbooks, several beds to crash on in New Haven, and fine instruction in the art of horseshoe playing. He has been a terrific sounding board for both intellectual and emotional concerns, and he amazes me with his remarkable capacity for empathy. My father, Danny, told me his own version of history in long, nighttime car rides when I was nine and sparked my interest in the field, although I am quite certain I would be fired if I ever repeated his stories in a classroom setting. His enthusiasm, his boundless energy, and his passion for life and for people has been a model for my own life and work. My mother, Lois, read every word of this book and even more remarkably, offered me honest opinions on them. She even came up with the title. Her dedicated support for this project was matched only by her loving support for me as a person. I hope that some day I will be as loving, as empathetic, and as generous a mother as she has been.

There are both too few and too many words to describe how Jonathan Gold has helped bring this book to life. He has been my chef, my chauffeur, my critic, and my conscience. He has cared about this project as if it were his own—and in many ways, it is. I can think of no way to thank him adequately, other than to promise that, when it is his novel being completed, I will be the one who vacuums the living room.

American Dreams *and* Nazi Nightmares

Introduction

ON MARCH 17, 2002, the Jewish Museum in New York City opened the controversial art exhibit Mirroring Evil: Nazi Imagery/Recent Imagery, featuring recent artwork that combined imagery evoking the Nazi regime with imagery from contemporary media culture. One artist, for example, superimposed a portrait of himself holding a Diet Coke can onto a famous Margaret Bourke-White photograph of liberated concentration camp inmates at Buchenwald. Another artist created Zyklon B poison gas canisters decorated with the designer labels of Tiffany, Hermes, and Chanel. For months before the exhibit's opening, a number of Holocaust survivors' groups, historians, politicians, and Jewish leaders unsuccessfully pressured the Jewish Museum to cancel the exhibit. Impassioned editorials for and against the exhibit filled the pages of such Jewish journals as the *Forward* and the *Jewish Week*. Ultimately, about one hundred survivors, yeshiva students, and politicians picketed the exhibit opening; and a number of individuals and insitutions, including the American Gathering of Jewish Holocaust Survivors, participated in a boycott of the museum.[1]

The controversy surrounding Mirroring Evil should not have been terribly surprising to the museum's curators or to most Americans living in the beginning of the twenty-first century. We are accustomed to a culture in which the Holocaust occupies a sacred space. It has become normal for Jews, scholars, and survivors to protest Holocaust representations they believe trivialize Jewish extermination—especially artistic or intellectual works that somehow wrench Nazi destruction out of its historical context and connect the Holocaust to contemporary American life, as did many of the artists of Mirroring Evil.

Forty years ago, however, many Americans would have been much more surprised to encounter this controversy. Far from occupying a sacred space in American culture, "the Holocaust" did not, for practical purposes, exist in Americans' vocabulary until the late 1960s. Americans, to be sure, were familiar with the Nazi extermination of millions of Jews. Newspapers, magazines, and newsreels had reported this extermination both during and after the war, and books such as Anne Frank's *Diary of a Young Girl* (1952) had insured that images of Jewish persecution remained in American media during the 1950s. Nonetheless, American mainstream scholarship and journalism had not yet labeled the persecution and extermination of Jews as a discrete narrative with a name.[2] Consequently, Americans felt much more free to represent the symbols we now associate with the Holocaust—concentration camps and SS storm troopers, for example—very differently from the ways now considered acceptable and intellectually legitimate.

American Dreams and Nazi Nightmares explores images of Nazism used by American academics and journalists between about 1957 and 1965 in ways that readers today may find disturbing. During this time, which I call the "turn of the 1960s," a number of influential American Jewish writers developed elaborate social-scientific analogies between Nazi German concentration camps and American society. In 1959, for example, historian Stanley M. Elkins compared Nazi concentration camp victims to black slaves in the United States in order to understand how ordinary human beings might become slaves who did not revolt. Journalist Betty Friedan suggested in *The Feminine Mystique* (1963) that American women's suburban homes were "comfortable concentration camps," because suburban women, like concentration camp inmates, participated in their own oppression. Between 1960 and 1962, psychologist Stanley Milgram ran a series of experiments demonstrating that ordinary people, when pressed by figures of authority, would be willing to administer life-threatening shocks to subjects. The experiments were explicitly designed to reproduce the psychology of Nazi death camps. And psychiatrist Robert Jay Lifton sought to understand the lasting trauma of historical disaster by comparing Hiroshima survivors to concentration camp survivors, first briefly in a 1964 article and then more extensively in his 1967 book, *Death in Life*.

Given contemporary understandings of the Holocaust, these analogies between Nazi Germany and American life may seem shocking or simply invalid for today's readers. The survivors, scholars, and Jewish leaders who protested *Mirroring Evil* might similarly have attacked such analogies had they been developed in the final years of the twentieth century. During the turn of the 1960s, however, the intellectuals who created these analogies believed that their imagery was entirely appropriate and natural. Their readers, moreover, did not find these representations of the camps particularly shocking but instead found them intellectually engaging and politically meaningful. Indeed, some of these representations of Nazi destruction had significant impact on American politics and culture, in ways far removed from our contemporary understanding of the Holocaust. Americans' understandings of Vietnam veterans' troubles after the war, for example, were shaped by Robert Jay Lifton's portrait of survivors. *American Dreams and Nazi Nightmares* explores how the distinct culture of the turn of the 1960s made these analogies between Nazi and American life seem particularly natural and appropriate for their creators and audiences, as well as how those analogies have shaped intellectual and political thought in the United States even in our own era.

The Flourishing of Holocaust Analogies at the Turn of the 1960s

The social-scientific analogies developed by Stanley Elkins, Betty Friedan, Stanley Milgram, and Robert Jay Lifton reflected a significant trend in American cultural life.[3] A substantial number of American Jewish figures between 1957 and 1965 used extended comparisons between the United States and Nazi Germany in order to address their fears of bureaucracy, alienation, and conformity in modern mass society.

To be sure, Americans made comparisons between American political life and Nazi society earlier than 1957. Throughout the 1940s and 1950s, men and women of different political persuasions had used brief, angry rhetoric that compared various components of American politics to the travesties of the Nazi German regime: one *Newsweek* magazine reader in 1945, for example, suggested that Jersey City's corrupt machine politics had made it a Nazi "concentration camp," while a *Time* magazine reader called America's occuption of Germany a "super-Buchenwald policy."[4] American Jews on the left, moreover, used rhetorical strategies that compared Nazi racial policies with those in the United States in the late 1940s and early 1950s.[5] However, systematic analogies grounded in social-scientific theory, comparing the psychological and social dehumanization of Nazi Germany to the conformist, bureaucratic, and technocratic mass society of the United States, have been more rare and more limited to the turn of the 1960s.[6]

In addition to Elkins, Friedan, Milgram, and Lifton, sociologist Erving Goffman, in his book *Asylums* (1961), explored the concept of "total institutions" by comparing the closed environments of the mental asylum and the prison to that of the Nazi concentration camp.[7] Psychologist Lawrence Kohlberg analyzed Adolf Eichmann's 1961 testimony to illustrate the universal nature of his stages of moral education among children.[8]

These influential social-scientific analogies mirrored a larger trend within American popular culture during the same era to use representations of Nazi Germany as extended artistic images of dehumanization. The years between 1957 and 1965 saw a proliferation of Nazi camp imagery in American literature, film, and theater, developed primarily by Jews. The stage directions of Arthur Miller's play *After the Fall* (1964) called for the "blasted stone tower of a German concentration camp" to remain onstage throughout all the action, most of it taking place in the head of the American protagonist, Quentin.[9] Edward Lewis Wallant's novel *The Pawnbroker* (1961) compared the devastation of Sol Nazerman in Nazi concentration camps to the poverty and humiliation of the Puerto Ricans with whom Nazerman lived and worked in Spanish Harlem after the war; the film version of *The Pawnbroker* (1964), directed by Sidney Lumet, visually emphasized these comparisons between Nazi camps and Spanish Harlem.[10] And in director Stanley Kubrick's popular 1964 film, *Dr. Strangelove or: How I Learned to Stop Worrying and Love the Bomb,* actor Peter Sellers played the title character, a maniacal inventor of a nuclear doomsday machine, as a man unable either to control his mechanical hand from giving a "Heil Hitler" salute or to refrain from calling the American president "Mein Fuhrer," in a thick Germanic accent.[11] In all these works between 1957 and 1965, the Nazi regime was not the subject itself, nor was it a brief metaphor or rhetorical flourish; it was instead part of a substantial comparison that lasted throughout the entirety of the work of art and that shed light on the brutality of ordinary American life.

The turn of the 1960s was a distinct time that both fostered and welcomed these sorts of extended comparisons between American society and Nazi Germany.[12] Popularly, most Americans see the 1950s and the 1960s as discrete eras with radically different sensibilities. We remember the 1950s as an era of conformity, innocence, and repression and the 1960s as a time of radicalism, chaos, and liberation. Understanding the years between 1957 and 1965 as a distinct time period helps us to break down this simplistic dichotomy. There were important continuities between these decades that allow us to think about the history of the post-World War II United States in different ways.[13] Thinking about the turn of the 1960s as a distinct era also helps us to understand the changes that contributed to the very real differences between these two decades: the turn of the 1960s served as a bridge that transformed the quietism of the early McCarthy years into the angry radicalism that dominated headlines in 1968.

The four men and women whose work this book will examine—Stanley Elkins, Betty Friedan, Stanley Milgram, and Robert Jay Lifton—all developed and published their comparisons between Nazi Germany and American society initially during the turn of the 1960s. During this era, readers excitedly and even unquestioningly embraced these comparisons. To be sure, the impact of these analogies, particularly those designed by Stanley Milgram and Robert Jay Lifton, was by no means limited to the turn of the 1960s. Throughout the 1960s and 1970s, authors such as Milgram and Lifton published their works in new formats, exposed their ideas to new readers, and audiences continued to read, discuss, and consider their comparisons between American and Nazi life. Nonetheless, the ways in which Milgram and Lifton interpreted and explained their ideas changed after the turn of the 1960s. Then, too, readers' responses to their works, particularly by the early 1970s, were markedly different from those at the turn of the 1960s, as the political and intellectual climate in the United States changed substantially. Exploring the ways that these academics reshaped their comparisons in the late 1960s and early 1970s, and the ways that readers' responses to their analogies changed during this later era, will help us to understand the distinct nature of the turn of the 1960s, the time that initially made these comparisons seem natural and even obvious.

The exceptional nature of the turn of the 1960s was partly the result of political change. During the onset of the Cold War immediately after World War II, most Americans had been persuaded—or coerced—to join a national consensus that sang the praises of American democracy in contrast with the evils of Nazi Germany and Soviet Russia, evils that were equated by the popular concept "totalitarianism."[14] This environment sharply discouraged any special attention to Nazi atrocities, or any comparisons between American inequity and Nazi racism.[15]

In the late 1950s, however, this consensus began to crack, and the Cold War changed shape: American leaders redoubled their efforts to fight the Soviet Union, but they began to believe that domestic reform, not ideological conformity, was the best way to win the war. In 1957, for example, white mob violence against black students in Little Rock, Arkansas, and the Soviet launching of the first Sputnik satellite, led Americans to question their position as the "leader of the free world," thus opening up important space for domestic dissent and support for domestic reform.[16] Supreme Court decisions after 1956, moreover, weakened McCarthyism's stranglehold on American public discourse and made dissent easier.[17] As a result, in 1959 and 1960, sit-ins at segregated lunch counters, boycotts of civil-defense drills, and public protests against the House Un-American Activities Committee faced weakened opposition and demonstrated for American audiences the existence of political alternatives to the Cold War ideological consensus. As this consensus came under attack, the analogy between communism and fascism embodied by the word "totalitarianism" lost some of its hold on American discourse, and intellectuals began quietly to compare American domestic and foreign policy to that of Nazi and communist regimes with few repercussions.[18]

At the same time that the domestic Cold War changed its focus, liberalism became the dominant political ideology in the United States in the years between 1957 and 1965. Tainted during the early 1950s by McCarthyite suggestions of treason, liberals at the end of the decade capitalized on the nation's unease after Sputnik and Little Rock and successfully presented their ideology, one that trumpeted domestic reform and economic growth as the solution for renewed national character. By 1958, liberal politicians had won important seats in the midterm congressional elections, and by 1960 and 1964, they had recaptured the White House. Although conservative ideology flourished at the grass roots during this era, liberals were dominant on the national level and were, in fact, fairly successful in marginalizing the rising conservative movement.[19]

The dominance of liberalism at the turn of the 1960s determined the political causes that motivated writers to compare American society to the Nazi regime, while it also sparked their enthusiasm for making those comparisons. Liberals championed a multitude of issues at the turn of the 1960s: articles on education and prison reform, on New Deal and prolabor legislation, on the improvement of women's lives, and on opposition to capital punishment all filled the pages of liberal journals like the *Nation* and the *New Republic* during this era. The two issues that dominated the liberal imagination, however, were civil rights for African Americans in the South and a nuclear test-ban treaty with the Soviet Union. Although liberals were not necessarily supporters of nuclear disarmament and some exhibited substantial hypocrisies regarding racism, particularly in the North, the evils of institutionalized racism in the South and the unimpeded nuclear arms race galvanized and unified almost all liberals, including Stanley Elkins, Betty Friedan, Stanley Milgram, and Robert Jay Lifton.[20] Elkins's, Milgram's, and Lifton's comparisons between American society and Nazi Germany were substantially shaped by these popular liberal issues.

Moreover, as liberalism became the dominant ideology in the United States, its political style shaped American public discourse substantially. On the one hand, this liberal style revolved around rational efficiency and toughness: liberal academics such as Stanley Elkins, for example, eschewed "moral attitude" and sought measured, institutional means for reform.[21] On the other hand, however, many young liberals at the turn of the 1960s were highly optimistic about progress and were enthusiastic, earnest, and idealistic in their opposition to moral evils like segregation and in their support for a ban on nuclear testing: "I'm horrified by the word 'cool,'" Betty Friedan told a *Life* magazine reporter in 1963. "What I think you're supposed to be is passionate, fanatic, and crusading."[22] Friedan's enthusiasm reflected the idealism of thousands of other liberals. That enthusiasm and idealism helps to explain many liberals' passionate embrace of Friedan's analogy between Nazi concentration camps and American suburban homes, as well as similar analogies by other social critics during this era.

Liberals' optimism was sparked in part by the rise of activism among young people at the turn of the 1960s. An upsurge in radicalism in antinuclear politics and civil rights activism changed American politics during this era, and liberals, for the most part, greeted this trend with tremendous enthusiasm and empathy, sometimes profoundly identifying themselves with young radicals. "All of us ought to ask ouselves: 'How can I help these young courageous Christians?'" wrote one *Nation* reader about the southern sit-ins in 1960.[23] Activists and liberals supported many of the same morally compelling causes at the turn of the 1960s—particularly African American civil rights and nuclear test ban—and they inhabited a common political world distinctively marked by appeals to moral conscience, faith in universalism, and calls for personal responsibility and social commitment.

It was this shared political atmosphere that encouraged liberal writers such as Stanley Elkins and Stanley Milgram to see their work as part of the civil rights or antinuclear movements, while participants in the Berkeley Free Speech Movement of 1964 and civil rights attorneys unhesitatingly used the obedience experiments and *Slavery* as part of their own radical efforts.[24] To be sure, this identification between activists and liberals should not be exaggerated. Liberals' willingness to compromise within the political system and their emphasis on rational debate distinguished them from activists' physical activism, radical commitments, and emotional political culture, and these differences would ultimately become sharper and more difficult to ignore after 1965. But at the turn of the 1960s, appeals to the "Human Race," the "dignity and decency of men," "our obligations to each other as moral human beings," and "the responsibility of the individual" peppered the political ideals of both liberals and activists, and created an environment in which careful social-scientific analogies between Nazi Germany and American life seemed productive for both liberal academics and radical activists.[25]

Thus engaged by ideals of social commitment and conscience, liberals supported emerging radical protests against segregation and nuclear proliferation, even if liberals themselves rarely engaged in civil disobedience or supported fundamental restructuring of the American political or economic system. Liberal intellectuals were more likely to question Cold War dogma by quietly—but publicly—deemphasizing the comparison made between the Soviet Union and Nazi Germany in the political model of "totalitarianism" and by finding instead compelling similarities between Nazi Germany and the United States—which by the early 1960s appeared in liberal eyes less a glorified democracy than an imperfect nation that required significant political reform. These social-scientific comparisons between Nazi and American society were generally enthusiastically received both by liberals and by radical activists. Important political trends at the turn of the 1960s—the reshaping of the Cold War, the rise of liberalism, and an upsurge in political radicalism—thus had significant impact on liberal intellectuals such as Stanley Milgram and Betty Friedan, contributing to the creation and popularity of their analogies between Nazi Germany and American life at the turn of the decade.

Intellectual and cultural trends at the turn of the 1960s similarly shaped the works of Milgram and Friedan, as well as their reception by readers. Many of these cultural trends were not entirely new but instead continuations of the dominant intellectual paradigms at the height of the Cold War. Intellectuals at the turn of the 1960s were still, for example, preoccupied with the dangers posed to an individual in a mass society that had featured so prominently in works such as David Riesman's *Lonely Crowd* (1950), William Whyte's *Organization Man* (1956), and C. Wright Mills's *Power Elite* (1956) and *White Collar* (1951).[26] All of these books' concerns about conformity, bureaucracy, and the dangers of a world shaped more by consumption than production were products of the intellectual environment that developed in the wake of World War II, when the nation began to shift to a service economy and fears of the mass societies of Nazism and Stalinism were at their height. The loss of individual rationality at the hands of the organization, the crowd, or the collective dominated liberal intellectual thought at a time when the economy itself had become more organized and intellectuals assumed that the "people" were, in fact, emotional, atomistic men easily manipulated and controlled. At the turn of the 1960s, Vance Packard's portrait of advertisers in *The Hidden Persuaders* (1957), Daniel Boorstin's description of the political process in *The Image* (1961), and Stanley Elkins's depiction of slaves dehumanized by the plantation in *Slavery* (1959), among many other works, continued to revolve around these intellectual preoccupations.[27]

Linked to the era's preoccupation with the dangers of mass society for individual autonomy was an emphasis on universalism. Intellectual approaches that valued group attachments to or identification with racial, class, or ethnic communities were severely out of fashion in the United States after 1945, while the often unstated but sometimes loudly trumpeted assumption that individuals of all backgrounds were the same "under the skin" was widespread throughout the worlds of academia, art, and film. This universalistic perspective, it has become commonplace to note, ignored differences among racial and ethnic groups and subtextually presumed a male and middle-class perspective, thus ignoring gender and class differentiation as well.[28] In the immediate postwar period, universalism had been exemplified best in works such as *The Family of Man* (1955) and *Sexual Behavior in the Human Male* (1948) that fundamentally ignored racial difference.[29] At the turn of the 1960s, universalism was reflected in a flood of popular books, plays, and movies including *Black Like Me* (1961, film 1964), *To Kill a Mockingbird* (1960, film 1962), *A Patch of Blue* (1965), and *West Side Story* (1957, film 1961), which did address racial divisions but ultimately emphasized the arbitrary nature of racial categories and the possibilities for universal human connections beyond race.[30] As both civil rights and peace activists insisted that their work was intended to benefit the "human race," they clearly heightened the relevance of universalism for many in the United States.

The emphasis on race and ethnicity as important markers of identity and community that would come to preoccupy liberal intellectuals from the end of the 1960s through the 1990s was not fashionable at the turn of the 1960s. Only after the late 1960s did intellectual comparisons between American and Nazi society begin to focus primarily on the Nazis' marginalization, persecution, and destruction of Jews. Liberal intellectuals of the early 1960s such as Stanley Elkins and Betty Friedan were much more engaged by the problems of alienation and conformity than they were by the issues of race or ethnicity, and that engagement was reflected in the sorts of comparisons they developed. The intellectual and cultural paradigms of universalism and the dangers that mass society posed to individual autonomy were crucial in shaping analogies between Nazi Germany and U.S. society at the turn of the decade.[31]

Still another cultural trend at the turn of the 1960s informed social-scientific writers such as Friedan and Lifton as they developed comparisons between Nazi German and American life: a spirit of cultural transgression that shaped the works of many academics, artists, writers, and filmmakers throughout the years between 1957 and 1965. Rejecting the

cultural insistence on normality, sanity, and maturity that had dominated American life in the early 1950s, by 1957, American thinkers had
begun to question these categories and even to invert them.[32] Paul
Goodman's *Growing Up Absurd* (1960) and Erving Goffman's *Asylums*
(1961), for example, powerfully argued that it was behavior produced by
adjustment to a meaningless, bureaucratic institution that was crazy, not
the juvenile delinquency or mental illness that psychiatrists labeled as
abnormal.[33] And in their classic novels *Catch-22* (1961) and *One Flew
Over the Cuckoo's Nest* (1962), authors Joseph Heller and Ken Kesey highlighted the meaninglessness of sanity in the insane worlds of military
and mental institutions.[34]

As the examples of Kesey and Heller suggest, black humor informed
much of the cultural transgression at the turn of the 1960s. Transgressing
traditional boundaries between reality and fiction, and between good and
evil, and breaking the conventions of both art and polite society, artists during
this era dramatized horror by ridiculing its banality.[35] In *Dr. Strangelove,* Stanley Kubrick heralded the end of the world with the love song: "We'll meet
again / don't know where don't know when / but I know we'll meet again
some sunny day."[36] John Frankenheimer's *Manchurian Candidate* (1962) featured a nightmarishly funny scene of brainwashing, in which vicious Communist Chinese generals became tea-drinking old ladies at a garden lunch-
eon.[37] Using ridicule, irony, and satire rather than serious, reasoned debate to
represent important political and social positions flouted traditional conventions of discourse. *Dr. Strangelove,* for example, elicited angry reviews from
some critics dismayed by Kubrick's "sportive speculation about a matter of
gravest consequence."[38] Artists who used black humor also transgressed
Cold War political boundaries: the McCarthyite politician of *The Manchurian
Candidate* became a communist plant, and the American spy in Kurt
Vonnegut's *Mother Night* (1961) became a Nazi.[39] Although these transgres-
sions might have seemed amoral or politically confused to some critics,
many liberal and radical viewers at the turn of the 1960s recognized and responded to their moral commentary and spirit of rebellion.

This spirit of cultural transgression and political inversion also shaped
works such as Stanley Milgram's obedience experiments and Betty
Friedan's *Feminine Mystique,* as well as their reception by readers. Men and
women on the left at the turn of the 1960s enthusiastically welcomed subversions of traditional Cold War dichotomies between communism and
capitalism, between totalitarianism and democracy, and between insanity
and sanity. These subversions did not equate democracy with totalitarianism, nor did they call for a total revolution and fragmentation of artistic or

political forms, as would political activists and artists by the late 1960s.[40] Instead the cultural spirit at the turn of the 1960s urged political and social reform. Artists and academics flouted conventions in the hope of reviving American democracy as a humane system that recognized individual dignity and integrity. This spirit of cultural transgression, just as much as that of intellectual universalism or political liberalism, shaped the zeitgeist of the turn of the 1960s and fostered an environment in which readers perceived analogies between Nazi Germany and American society as thrilling and instructive.

In addition to the political, intellectual, and cultural trends that made the years between 1957 and 1965 a distinct era, social transformations that integrated Jews more fully into a newly important academic and professional class became substantial and visible during the turn of the 1960s, further encouraging the development of analogies between Nazi concentration camps and American society.

These social transformations were not new in 1957. The numbers of Americans engaged in professions that revolved around educational status, communication, and analysis began expanding rapidly after World War II, forming what some scholars have called a New Class: a class of people whose work involved the production and dissemination of knowledge rather than the production of goods or the accumulation of capital.[41] As it grew in size, this New Class also democratized along ethnic and religious lines. Good numbers of the men and women who entered the ranks of educators, administrators, technicians, and communicators during this postwar era were Jews whose families had experienced significant discrimination in the years before the war, in the form of university admissions quotas and employment denial.[42] The entry of these men and women into the New Class was facilitated by federal funding from the GI Bill of Rights and the Federal Housing Administration after the war, as well as changing American attitudes about race that began to redefine descendants of European immigrants as "white," permitting them access to a new social and intellectual milieu.[43]

Although these changes all began in the wake of World War II, it was at the turn of the 1960s that Jews entering the New Class reached a critical mass and began to attract comment from both Jewish and non-Jewish observers. In 1963, for example, the president of the American Historical Association publicly expressed anxiety about the influx of "urban bred," "lower middle-class," and "foreign" young practioners into the historical profession.[44] And beginning at the turn of the 1960s, a host of publications, dissertations, and articles in the Jewish press, as well as programs developed by Jewish communal groups, began to address the problem of "runaway Jewish intellectuals" who had become newly integrated into academia and seemed to have detached themselves from organized Judaism.[45] Indeed, Stanley Milgram was one of the subjects for a sociology dissertation on this new subculture of Jewish academics.[46]

As Jews entered the New Class, they brought with them different preoccupations and life experiences that followed from their backgrounds. These preoccupations and experiences shaped their research and writing agendas, as well as changing the larger professional discourse. For example, the presence of Jews on college faculties discouraged other academics from using Christianity as a pertinent framework for their work, thus encouraging a "de-Christianized," secular intellectual conversation throughout academia.[47] On a smaller scale, many Jewish historians of the United States at the turn of the 1960s viewed the Populists of the nineteenth century through the framework of eastern European pogroms.[48]

Most significantly, the Nazi destruction of European Jewry played an important role in a number of young Jewish professionals' understanding of the world at the turn of the 1960s. Many of the American Jews who became professionals during this era were members of the same generation, men and women who were born in the 1920s and 1930s and came of age during an era in which antisemitism became more prominent in the United States and more vicious and deadly in Europe. These men and women grew up in the shadow of Hitler, understanding very well from conversations with family and friends, and from the news media, that Jews throughout the world were threatened, and that their options as young men and women seeking professional and social acceptance in the United States might be limited by their Jewish background. The rise of this generation to prominence in academia, journalism, and the arts at the turn of the 1960s further helps to explain the proliferation of Nazi imagery during that era.

The works of Betty Friedan, Stanley Elkins, Robert Jay Lifton, and Stanley Milgram reflect the combination of political, intellectual, cultural, and social change that helped to make the turn of the 1960s a distinct era. These four Jewish writers all participated in the spirit of liberal social reform and cultural transgression that dominated the turn of the 1960s, while they all were also preoccupied with dehumanization, alienation, and conformity, typical concerns of intellectuals in the 1950s. Their entry into academia and journalism reflected the ways in which Jews both became integrated into—and helped to shape—the intellectual culture of this era. Although Friedan, Elkins, Lifton, and Milgram formed no close personal or professional ties, their work at the turn of the 1960s, and their coming of age in the United States in the 1920s and 1930s, having been born within twelve years of one another, made them a significant generational cohort with similar preoccupations and assumptions. Any of the other artists or academics who developed comparisons between Nazi and American life, including Erving Goffman, Stanley Kubrick, and Arthur Miller, could easily have been selected (and were in fact considered) as subjects for this book, but Elkins, Friedan, Milgram, and Lifton provide a useful window on the increasing significance of Jews in academia at the turn of the 1960s, as well as on the lasting influence that analogies between American and Nazi life have wrought in American political, intellectual, and cultural life.

Particularly Jewish Analogies?

As the above discussion suggests, although they were not directly or openly connected to issues of antisemitism or Jewish life, analogies between Nazi Germany and American society were the products of a predominantly Jewish cohort of men and women. This is a paradox that requires more examination.

Jewish writers such as Stanley Milgram were not simply more interested in exploring the Cold War problems of conformity and alienation than they were in addressing the late 1960s issues of race or ethnicity. In their published works at the turn of the 1960s, Jewish writers and artists who compared American society to Nazi concentration camps remained virtually silent on the subject of Jewish destruction in Nazi Europe altogether. Stanley Elkins's analogy between concentration camp victims and slaves, explained in a 50-page chapter, purposely emphasized that the camp inmates to whom he referred came from a wide variety of racial, ethnic, and class backgrounds, mentioning Jews only three times.[49] Erving Goffman's 120-page portrait of "total institutions" offered only two very brief anecdotal mentions of Jews as a subset of prisoners in Nazi concentration camps.[50] Betty Friedan's description of the "comfortable concentration camp" made no mention of Jews at all, nor did Stanley Milgram's 1963 article describing his experiments. Only Edward Wallant, of all the Jewish men and women I have identified who developed analogies between Nazi Germany and American society during the turn of the 1960s, emphasized the Jewish background of Nazi victims.

This substantial pattern of eliding the subject of Jewish victims might suggest that these intellectuals' Jewish backgrounds had nothing to do with their works at all, or with their interest in the symbolism of the Nazi concentration camps. Or this pattern might suggest that Jews—along with other Americans—were unfamiliar with the details of Jewish extermination under the Nazis. A brief examination of non-Jewish artists who developed similar extended comparisons between American life and Nazi Germany at the turn of the 1960s, however, demonstrates not only that Americans were indeed familiar with the Nazi extermination of European Jewry but that there were striking differences between the works of Jewish and non-Jewish writers, differences that suggest that the Jewish background of intellectuals such as Betty Friedan may have been significant in their work.

A number of prominent non-Jews did compare aspects of American life with features of Nazi German society at the turn of the decade. In 1962, Sylvia Plath wrote "Mary's Song," "Lady Lazarus," and "Daddy," the three poems that have come to be called her "Holocaust poems" because they compare her pain as a woman, living with the brutality and viciousness of men, with the pain of Jews in Nazi Europe. In *Mother Night* (1961), Kurt Vonnegut described the life of fictional American spy Howard W. Campbell, Jr., who was imprisoned in Israel, waiting to stand trial for his work during the war as a Nazi propagandist who spewed antisemitic rhetoric over the radio. Vonnegut's novel of the absurd linked together the crimes of Americans and the crimes of the Nazis during the war, making them indistinguishable from one another.

Neither Sylvia Plath nor Kurt Vonnegut was of Jewish ancestry. Both created metaphors that were very different from many of the comparisons developed by Jewish academics, intellectuals, and artists at the same time. Plath and Vonnegut openly and readily addressed in their works the Jews murdered in Hitler's Europe. Plath explicitly compared herself to a suffering Jew under the Nazis throughout her three poems. In the poem, "Daddy," for example, Plath envisioned a railroad engine "chuffing" her off like "a Jew to Dachau, Auschwitz, Belsen" and imagined that she had begun to talk like and even become a Jew.[51] At the same time, Vonnegut's Howard Campbell interacted guiltily with Jewish Auschwitz survivors and described himself as "a shrewd and loathsome anti-Semite."[52] Both Plath and Vonnegut made clear to their readers that the Nazis had exterminated millions of Jews.[53]

In contrast with Plath and Vonnegut, American Jews such as Friedan, Elkins, and Milgram were peculiarly elusive, even cryptic, in their published work about the murders of millions of Jews in Nazi-occupied Europe. Even as these men and women constructed artistic and intellectual analogies that used the symbolic language of Nazi destruction of European Jewry—concentration camps, gas chambers, genocide—they carefully avoided mentioning Jews at all.

This pattern suggests that, by avoiding the subject of Jews altogether, Jewish intellectuals and artists may actually, ironically, have talked about the Nazi destruction of European Jewry in a way that was "Jewish." This is not to say that these men and women believed that their works were expressions of their Jewish identities; for the most part, they emphatically did not. This is also not to say that there exists an essential "Jewishness" that these writers were expressing in their analogies. There is no such Jewish essence. Instead, what I am saying is that the peculiar silences found in *The Feminine Mystique*, in *Asylums,* in *Slavery,* and in other famous works reflected a long tradition of Jewish intellectuals eliding Jewish subjects in their work.

A number of historians have described the ways that Jewish writers, artists, intellectuals, and political activists in the United States, since at least the 1920s through the present day, have continually deemphasized their own Jewish background while they have identified vicariously with other marginal groups. According to various scholars, this tradition of elision and vicarious identification has included, among many others, Al Jolson's blackface, Felix Frankfurter's championing of anarchists Sacco and Vanzetti, the work of Jewish activists such as Michael Schwerner and Andrew Goodman in the civil rights movement, and the writings of Jewish feminist scholars such as Judith Butler and Eve Kosofsky Sedgwick, who have explored the subjects of gay men and drag performance.[54]

Given this substantial history of Jews vicariously identifying with other marginalized people while deemphasizing their own Jewish background, it makes sense to view men and women such as Betty Friedan and Stanley Elkins within that historical context. This is not to say that being Jewish determined the life and work of intellectuals such as Stanley Elkins at the turn of the 1960s. It should be obvious that a host of factors shaped their lives, and their identity as Jews was not necessarily the most important of these factors. Moreover, as the example of Edward Wallant suggests, there were other Jews at the turn of the 1960s who talked more vocally about Jewish murders under the Nazi regime. There was not only one Jewish way of talking about the Holocaust during this era.[55] Nevertheless, the long history of American Jewish intellectuals choosing not to discuss Jewish matters, while supporting other marginal groups, suggests strongly that Stanley Elkins's silence regarding the Nazi destruction of European Jewry, even as he made the symbolism of concentration camps central to his seminal work on African American slavery, needs to be explored as a *part* of Jewish intellectual tradition, not a radical *disassociation* from that tradition.[56]

American Dreams and Nazi Nightmares demonstrates that Stanley Elkins and other members of his cohort saw themselves as Jews because of their birth, and because of the antisemitism that surrounded their coming of age in the 1930s and the 1940s, both in the United States and in Europe. This secular Jewish identity informed, though it did not wholly direct or shape, these intellectuals' perceptions of Nazi genocide and their decisions to reproduce symbols of that genocide in their work.

The predominant models for examining Jewish identity do not address this particular type of secular Jewish identity, and thus they do not help us to examine men and women such as Lifton or Friedan. Sociologists have typically described Jewish identity as an expression of ritual behavior and social networks that can be quantified and evaluated.[57] By contrast, scholars in cultural studies have recently urged us to consider Jewish identity as a more fluid, less well-defined entity that individuals continually construct in relationship to history, power, and culture.[58] As mostly nonpracticing, unaffiliated Jews, however, intellectuals such as Betty Friedan did not engage in most of the ritual behavior that sociologists use to determine Jewish identity, nor did they consciously construct their Jewish identities as they developed analogies between Nazi camps and U.S. society. Instead, they saw their Jewishness as a marker of difference with which they were born, and for which they might face discrimination, hostility, or even violence, but a marker that they would not deny or attempt to escape.[59] More subtle models of Jewish identity should help us understand the large numbers of American Jews who have been unaffiliated and nonpracticing yet have still been shaped by ideas about Jewish "descent," both because they willingly identified themselves as Jews and because others—both Jews and antisemites—identified them as Jews.[60]

Some scholars have criticized Jewish intellectuals who focused on other marginal groups for turning their back on American Jewish communal life. Others have charged that Jewish academics such as Stanley Elkins denigrated other marginal groups in an effort to become "white." Still other historians have suggested that Jews' vicarious interest in marginal groups represents an inherent Jewish liberalism or sympathy for the underdog.[61] My work does not seek to echo any of these authors' arguments. Instead, I believe that the works of intellectuals such as Stanley Elkins reflect the liminal, ambivalent position of Jews in American society as both "insiders" and "outsiders." Unlike in Europe, where Jews have traditionally played the role of the "other," in the United States, this marginal status has typically been forced on people of color, permitting American Jews by the 1960s to integrate fully, with only a few impediments, into high levels of American economic and cultural life. At the same time, however, lingering antisemitism and Jewish self-definition have continued to make American Jews feel like outsiders, like a marginal group possibly faced with extinction. This strange blend of comfort and unease, of insider status and outsider fears, has marked American Jewish life throughout the twentieth century, particularly in the post-World War II years.[62]

Importantly, however, American Jews have rarely emphasized this ambivalence. Instead, they have traditionally sought to synthesize American and Jewish concerns, "to ensure that Judaism and Americanism reinforce one another."[63] This "cult of synthesis" has appeared throughout American Jewish history, in folk art and holiday celebrations, as well as in intellectual and religious leaders' pronouncements, as Jews attempted to legitimize their home in America. Rather than perceiving Jewish fears of marginality as dissonant with their American success, for example, Jewish intellectuals such as Horace Kallen, Louis Brandeis, and Will Herberg instead advocated that the United States identify as a pluralistic nation that is a home for marginal groups, thus making outsiders into insiders. In this way, Jews were able in the twentieth century to translate the fears of a Jewish minority into concerns for the larger American mainstream.[64]

The analogies of Stanley Elkins, Betty Friedan, Stanley Milgram, and Robert Jay Lifton offer readers a poignant lens into these American Jewish tendencies toward ambivalence and synthesis. *Slavery*, *The Feminine Mystique*, the obedience experiments, and *Death in Life* made their creators' careers, giving them upward mobility from their ordinary middle-class backgrounds into an intellectual elite. These men and women became insiders in the American intelligentsia through analogies drawing on the ultimate experiences of Jews as outsiders in Nazi-occupied Europe. Yet, the wholly natural and unselfconscious way in which all these men and women injected Nazi concentration camps into their ambitious works on American life suggests that they were not motivated to explore the paradox between their own American dreams and Nazi nightmares but instead that they had synthesized the two and interpreted their Jewish fears of Nazi society as fundamental concerns for the larger American mainstream to address. The title of this book, *American Dreams and Nazi Nightmares*, reflects the strange dissonance—and the powerful synthesis—between success and fear in these intellectuals' lives, works, and political ideals, as well as in American Jews' lives more broadly in the postwar era.

Early Holocaust Consciousness

The proliferation of, and enthusiasm for, extended comparisons between Nazi Germany and American society at the turn of the 1960s, developed primarily by Jewish artists and intellectuals, is a subject that few historians have explored in depth. Some historians studying the 1960s in America have noted the impact of Nazi imagery on all Americans' political consciousness during that era, but these historians have done so only briefly, in passing, and they have rarely noted the years between 1957 and 1965 as a particular era during which that imagery flourished.[65]

Moreover, scholars who have explored the impact of the Holocaust on American Jews, and especially on Jewish intellectuals, have typically emphasized Jewish reticence in discussing the Holocaust before the Six-Day War in 1967, as well as the Holocaust's strong impact on American Jewish identity and support for Israel after 1967.[66] Peter Novick has recently harshly criticized American Jews for their uses of the Holocaust since the late 1960s and especially after the Yom Kippur War of 1973.[67] However, regardless of whether they have been supportive or critical of the ways that many American Jews have connected the Holocaust to American Jewish identity and to Israel, most scholars have assumed that these post-1967 connections represent the only ways that American Jews have thought about the Holocaust, the only type of Holocaust consciousness that might exist.[68] Historians have only recently begun to describe discourse surrounding the Holocaust before 1967 as significant, or to consider the variety of ways in which American Jews have interpreted and used the Holocaust to address non-Jewish subjects.[69]

If we look more closely at the turn of the 1960s, however, it becomes clear that the Nazi destruction of European Jewry became a dominant presence in discussions of world events, in film, and in literature between 1957 and 1965, in a way that it had not been since the end of World War II. This is not to say that Jewish mass murder had not been a part of political, intellectual, religious, or artistic discourse during the late 1940s or 1950s. Jewish groups protested former Nazi artists who performed in the United States in 1948 and 1949, Anne Frank's diary became a popular book for both adults and teenagers after it was published in the United States in 1952, and Leon Poliakov's *Harvest of Hate* became one of the first standard historical works on Nazi destruction in 1954. Jews of all denominations, moreover, developed prayer books, sermons, and music to commemorate the Nazi destruction in the decade after World War II.[70]

In the years between 1957 and 1965, however, representations of Nazi destruction multiplied, while they also increasingly moved from the margins to center stage in American public discourse. To a large extent, this change was a result of contemporary events. Prosecutions of former Nazi concentration camp commanders in 1958 and a wave of neo-Nazi vandalism in West Germany from 1959 to 1960 shocked American journalists and led to growing press attention to the nation's Nazi past.[71] Even more spectacularly, the Israeli capture of Adolf Eichmann in 1960 and his trial in 1961 to 1962, as well as his execution in 1962, propelled Nazi genocide to the forefront of American public discussion. Newspapers featured Eichmann's capture on their front page, television stations broadcast his trial daily into millions of viewers' homes, and news documentaries, television dramas, movies, and books about the Nazi bureaucrat proliferated in the wake of the trial.[72] Eighty-four percent of Americans surveyed in 1961 had heard of the Eichmann trial.[73]

It was not simply press coverage of world events that placed Nazi destruction at the forefront of American public discourse, however. Both before and after the Eichmann trial, the best-seller lists, movie houses, and theaters in the United States were dominated by American literature and film that described Nazi extermination. Leon Uris's novel *Exodus* (1958), for example, became the biggest best seller since *Gone With the Wind,* and the film version in 1960 sold out in New York for months after it opened.[74] *The Rise and Fall of the Third Reich* (1960), by journalist William Shirer, won enthusiastic reviews from critics, became a Book-of-the-Month Club selection, and remained on best-seller lists for months.[75] The film *Judgment at Nuremberg* (1961), directed by Stanley Kramer, sparked controversy and garnered praise, ultimately receiving nominations for eleven Academy Awards.[76] And German playwright Rolf Hochhuth inspired international controversy with *The Deputy* (1963), a play criticizing the Pope for not having explicitly condemned the extermination of six million Jews. Although there was no violence in the United States, as there had been in France and Switzerland, the New York production of Hochhuth's play in 1964 inspired pickets, angry community forums, and heated coverage in American newspapers and magazines.[77]

Many of these writers and artists placed Nazi mass murder in frameworks that reflected the prevailing political, cultural, and intellectual trends of the turn of the 1960s. A number of key works provided sharp criticisms of Cold War ideology. Abby Mann's script for *Judgment at Nuremberg,* for example, criticized the political pressure placed on American judges because the U.S. government needed the Germans as allies in the Cold War. The script was clearly critical of this anticommunist moral expediency, and indeed, conservative critics believed that the film might endanger the U.S. relationship with West Germany.[78] Conservatives were also angered by William Shirer's argument that the atrocities of the Third Reich had their origins in German history, as well as in the German people's "lust for power and domination," "contempt for democracy and individual freedom," and "longing for authority, for authoritarianism."[79] Shirer's and Mann's criticisms of German history and the German people for their part in Nazi mass murder clearly reflected the ways that liberals were questioning the Cold War at the turn of the 1960s.[80]

Perhaps even more importantly, creators and reviewers of works such as *Judgment at Nuremberg* and *The Deputy* understood one of the most pervasive themes of the turn of the 1960s as being central to the Nazi destruction of European Jewry: the responsibility of individuals to act according to their consciences. Rolf Hochhuth himself, as well as most contemporary reviewers of *The Deputy*, for example, repeated consistently that the play was less an indictment of the Catholic Church than a call for responsibility: "The real message of this play," Hochhuth told the *New York Times*, "is the individual's moral responsibility in the face of evil."[81] The central question of *Judgment at Nuremberg*, similarly, according to reviewers and creators alike, was "Who is responsible?" and the answer, for many, was "all of us."[82] "Conscience," "morality," and "responsibility" were among the central concepts many journalists, reviewers and artists used to grapple with representations of Nazi annihilation during this era.[83]

The work of the early 1960s that most famously struggled with conscience, moral responsibility, and the Nazi destruction of European Jewry was Hannah Arendt's *Eichmann in Jerusalem* (1963). Reporting on the Eichmann trial for the *New Yorker* magazine, Arendt developed two central arguments that created a storm of controversy throughout the world. First, Arendt observed, Eichmann was far from a sadist or a vicious antisemite; indeed, he was simply a bureaucrat. "The trouble with Eichmann," Arendt concluded, "was precisely that so many were like him, and that the many were neither perverted nor sadistic, that they were and still are, terribly and terrifyingly normal."[84] This devotion to bureaucracy, to pleasing his superiors, and to keeping the organization running smoothly had shaped Eichmann's conscience, allowing him to abdicate his moral responsibility and commit mass murder. Moreover, Arendt charged, Jewish leaders too had become a part of the Nazi bureaucratic regime, agreeing to organize and police their own people and ultimately facilitating the Jews' extermination: the cooperation of Jewish leaders, she argued, signaled the "totality of the moral collapse the Nazis caused . . . not only among the persecutors but also among the victims."[85] The construction of an immense bureaucratic apparatus had blinded Germans as well as Jews, allowing them all to relinquish their moral responsibilities as human beings and to collaborate in a system of mass murder.

Arendt's ideas provoked an uproar among both Jewish and non-Jewish intellectuals and among Jewish leaders in the United States and abroad.

The Council of Jews from Germany released a statement condemning Arendt, while the B'nai Brith Anti-Defamation League (ADL) sent out memorandums to its regional offices and national committees denouncing the philosopher's *New Yorker* series.[86] Local American Jewish newspapers printed articles critical of Arendt's work with headlines such as "Self-Hating Jewess Writes Pro-Eichmann Series For New Yorker Magazine."[87] National newsmagazines, scholarly journals, and daily newspapers published reviews and articles about *Eichmann in Jerusalem,* and the *New York Times Book Review, Partisan Review,* and *Commentary* printed running series of opinion pieces and ardent letters to the editor on both sides; the *New York Times* reported receiving well over one hundred letters regarding its review of Arendt's book.[88]

Arendt's defenders applauded the brilliance with which she had penetrated the fundamental problems of the era: the problem of moral responsibility and conscience, and the dangers of bureaucratic blindness that still threatened Americans. "[S]he demonstrates, with great incisiveness . . . that genocide can be reduced to an almost purely mechanical bureaucratic routine," praised Robert G. Hayden. "It is a warning against complacency and inaction in the face of tyranny."[89] Many supporters were particularly aware and pleased that Arendt's formulation had contemporary relevance; if Eichmann was not a vicious antisemite but a bureaucrat, then he resembled nothing more than an American general proposing the internment of Japanese American citizens, or a U.S. senator contemplating nuclear policy.[90] Arendt's formulation thus had significant contemporary political meaning for her audiences in the early 1960s, a meaning the philosopher herself addressed when she warned that the threat of using nuclear weaponry to eliminate "superfluous populations" in an era of population explosion and labor automation "should be enough to make us tremble."[91]

Suggesting the crucial nature of this discourse in the early 1960s, Hannah Arendt's detractors also used the language of responsibility and conscience. They were resistant, however, to the ways in which Arendt had described responsibility and conscience; rather than identify responsibility, she had seemed to evade it by implicating victims and exculpating criminals. "At the final moment of responsibility the individual chooses and if his choice is inhuman he is guilty," one reader of the *New York Times* argued.[92] For Arendt's detractors, innocent Jewish victims should not have been enclosed within a vicious circle of responsibility for the crimes of the Nazis, nor should Eichmann's responsibility for his murderous antisemitism have been erased or reduced to the simple banality of a bureaucrat. The controversy surrounding Arendt's *Eichmann in Jerusalem* thus demonstrates the ways that the discourse of moral responsibility and conscience, as well as the power of bureaucratic imagery, were central to early Holocaust consciousness at the turn of the 1960s.

During those same years two other prominent scholars of Nazi atrocities similarly emphasized the Nazi regime's bureaucratic machinery of death. Raul Hilberg's historical monograph *The Destruction of the European Jews* (1961) received praise for its extensive research and portrait of murderous bureaucracy.[93] And in *The Informed Heart* (1960), Bruno Bettelheim, a former inmate of Dachau and Buchenwald, emphasized the devastating dehumanization of his fellow prisoners in the Nazi system, continuing the arguments of his widely read and influential 1943 article in the *Journal of Abnormal and Social Psychology*.[94] In both the earlier article and the 1960 book, Bettelheim described the victims of Nazi concentration camps becoming a part of the SS system: the Nazis' "slow process of personality disintegration," he argued, had essentially succeeded in reducing "not only free men, but even the most ardent foes of the Nazi system . . . from their position as autonomous individuals."[95] Bettelheim offered grim portraits of concentration camp inmates who had been so infantilized and emasculated by Nazi brutality that they came to admire their captors and enforce SS rules themselves. In their works at the turn of the 1960s, both Bettelheim and Hilberg, like Arendt, emphasized the Nazi bureaucracy's ability to erase its victims' individual autonomy.

Arendt, Hilberg, and Bettelheim, perhaps the three best-known scholars writing on the Nazi concentration camps at the turn of the 1960s, thus all described Nazi extermination as the product of a bureaucratic machine that dehumanized all individuals and implicated them in their own and others' destruction. This perspective sparked anger and controversy within the Jewish community and ultimately led to a new perspective on Nazi destruction by the late 1960s and early 1970s that emphasized antisemitism and Jewish genocide, but many Americans—both Jews and non-Jews—during the turn of the 1960s were deeply persuaded by these scholars' interpretations of Nazi destruction as a site for understanding bureaucratic domination and dehumanization.

As the above description suggests, early Holocaust consciousness not only existed before the events of the Six-Day War but was also a qualitatively different sort of consciousness from the one that most scholars have emphasized. The works of Stanley Elkins, Betty Friedan, Stanley Milgram, and Robert Jay Lifton, explored in the chapters that follow, help us to consider the distinct period of Holocaust consciousness at the turn of the 1960s. Rather than expressing their personal Jewish identity or justifying Israeli military policy or expressing an obligation to remember the past, in the ways that Americans today expect, a number of American Jewish thinkers at the turn of the decade publicly emphasized the evils of Nazi concentration camps as a means of expressing prevalent intellectual concerns with bureaucracy, alienation, and conformity and of criticizing American society from a liberal perspective.[96] And during a distinct era in American history shaped by a spirit of social commitment and cultural transgression, American readers—both Jews and non-Jews—were inspired and engaged by these uses of Nazi concentration camps, not repelled or insulted. Indeed, during this era, in part because of works such as *The Feminine Mystique* and the obedience experiments, Nazi concentration camps became, for many liberal readers in the United States, appropriate and valuable symbols for exploring inhumanity in an American landscape.

"One of the Lucky Ones"

Stanley Elkins and the

Concentration Camp Analogy in Slavery

IN 1959, the University of Chicago Press published *Slavery: A Problem in American Institutional and Intellectual Life,* the doctoral dissertation of a young historian named Stanley M. Elkins. Among other contentions, Elkins argued that slave owners in the American South had maintained absolute power over their slaves and that this power had effected a psychological change in the enslaved people, turning them into childlike "Sambos" who came to depend on and even admire their masters as parental figures. Elkins's provocative thesis was almost wholly based on recent psychological studies of Nazi concentration camp inmates, who, he said, had experienced an analogous form of oppression and had responded to this oppression with infantilism, even to the point of becoming devoted to their oppressors, the SS guards.

Some contemporary readers may not be terribly shocked by Stanley Elkins's comparison. At the turn of the twenty-first century, comparisons between slavery and the Holocaust have become quite familiar for many Americans, as blacks and Jews have talked a great deal about the historical traumas of their respective racial groups, sometimes in the form of a quasi competition in which each group suggests that its own suffering deserves greater sympathy. In this environment, the comparison between slaves and concentration camp inmates seems very familiar.[1]

On the other hand, Elkins's portrait of degraded and childish slaves may shock some contemporary readers. Many readers have been offended by the portraits that Elkins presented. Moreover, Elkins's reliance on the stereotype of "Sambo," and his lack of primary evidence from slaves themselves, represented flawed and problematic historical scholarship. Most historians have rejected Elkins's ideas, although the Elkins thesis has remained an important chapter in the historiography of black slavery.[2]

In 1959, however, many readers viewed Stanley Elkins's comparison between concentration camp inmates and slaves as innovative and daring, not as ahistorical or offensive, and certainly not as part of a well-worn or distasteful competition, or an attempt to "trivialize" the destruction of European Jewry. Rather than examining Stanley Elkins's analogy solely through the lens of current political and historical assumptions, it is important to recognize its origins and significance in its own era. By exploring the comparison between concentration camp inmates and slaves in its own time period, and through the lens of American Jewish history, the Stanley Elkins analogy can help us to think anew about the history of American Jews, the history of the 1960s, and the significance of the Holocaust in American intellectual and political history in the postwar era.

To be sure, Elkins's text was published in 1959, and historians have rarely mentioned *Slavery* as a significant part of the 1960s.[3] Similarly, Elkins's significance for American Jewish life or for representations of the Holocaust is not at first obvious. The historian did not connect his work to the subject of Jews. He scarcely mentioned Jewish genocide and purposely emphasized that the concentration camp inmates to whom he referred came from a wide variety of racial, ethnic, and class backgrounds, mentioning Jews only a few times.[4] Moreover, he did not refer to his own Jewish background, either in *Slavery* itself or in any of his subsequent efforts to defend his work.

Nonetheless, Elkins's analogy helps to tell a larger story about how American Jews in the immediate postwar years understood the Nazi destruction of European Jewry and, perhaps even more importantly, how they believed that that destruction was linked to their own protected lives in the United States. Then, too, Elkins's analogy suggests the ways that Jewish history has participated in, and helped to shape, intellectual life in the United States in the twentieth century. Finally, the sharp contrast between receptions of Elkins's *Slavery* in 1964 and 1965 and those in the late 1960s and 1970s illustrates the distinctly liberal zeitgeist that prevailed at the turn of the 1960s.

Slavery was actually a set of three interlocking essays about American slavery, all of which challenged contemporary scholarship and urged a new perspective on the institution, one that emphasized comparative study of slavery and disdained moralistic approaches to the subject.[5] The first essay compared slavery in the United States with slavery in Latin America, arguing that the latter was constrained by the powerful institutions of the Spanish Crown and the Catholic Church, while the former allowed capitalism to operate virtually unconstrained, with only public sentiment limiting the harshness or severity of a master's behavior. As a result, Elkins noted, Latin American slavery was far less harsh, with many more gradations of freedom and slavery, while North American slavery was a "closed system" that gave the master absolute power over the slave, denying slaves any recourse to other powerful religious or political institutions and thus denying their fundamental humanity. The third essay argued that, because American culture was so devoid of institutions, the abolitionists who confronted slavery saw it as an individual sin, an instance of personal guilt, that needed to be expunged entirely and immediately, rather than a problem that might be addressed through institutions such as the political party or the church.

The linchpin holding together the first and third essays was the second one, "Slavery and Personality," in which Stanley Elkins introduced and elaborated the comparison between American slaves and Nazi concentration camp inmates as a means of explaining the consequences of the "closed" nature of American slavery. Ultimately, Elkins argued, because American slavery, like the Nazi regime, permitted no alternative institutions to recognize slaves as human, plantations reduced grown men to irresponsible, passive, corruptible children, very much like the concentration camp inmates described in contemporary literature.

Elkins introduced his chapter by arguing that the stereotype "Sambo" had been a real personality type among black slaves. Relying on southern lore—primarily the records of slaveholders—Elkins first devoted several pages to describing Sambo: he was "docile but irresponsible, loyal but lazy, humble but chronically given to lying and stealing; his behavior . . . full of infantile silliness and his talk inflated with childish exaggeration."[6]

Although Elkins knew that this portrait of black slaves was highly offensive, he believed that his description of Sambo might be acceptable if he rejected the notion that Sambo was childlike *because* he was black.[7] The historian justified his work by arguing that it would aid in the "strategy, now universally sanctioned, of demonstrating how little the products and consequences of slavery ever had to do with race."[8] Rather than describing slaves as a racial group, Elkins argued at length that the Africans enslaved in America were descendants of "cultural traditions essentially heroic."[9] Using the work of anthropologist Melville Herskovits, as well as historical works on Africa, the historian described dignified warriors, intact family structures, and complex political hierarchies in the tribal cultures of the Gold Coast and Dahomey, and finally concluded that "something very profound" must have intervened to transform these brave African men into "a society of helpless dependents."[10] That profound thing was power. By disputing the biological racism of the Sambo stereotype, Elkins believed that he could legitimately explore the universal ways that power can transform brave, even "heroic," men into children.

In order to probe this relationship between power and personality, Elkins focused not on American slave plantations but on Nazi concentration camps. Relying on contemporary literature on the camp, especially that of former prisoner Bruno Bettelheim, Elkins described the process by which Nazis had incarcerated, tortured, and dehumanized their prisoners. Again, he deemphasized the racial nature of Nazi ideology, emphasizing instead that concentration camp internees represented a cross section of European society and that the Nazis' absolute power over inmates led to the disintegration of their personalities. Inmates quickly and painfully learned that the SS guards had absolute power over their bodies. Eating and even defecation were wholly controlled by the guards, privacy no longer existed, and the threat of death was both unpredictable and omnipresent. In order to adjust to this terrifying environment, former inmates reported that their minds had split their degraded public "selves" from their real, private "selves" and then, in order to survive, they had adopted new standards of public behavior, including extreme selfishness, a craving for inconspicuousness, and, most surprisingly, a reversion to childlike behavior. Inmate discussions centered on excretory functions rather than sexual impulses, which had mostly disappeared because of hunger. Relationships became unstable, like those of adolescents, and braggadocio and dishonesty, without shame, were commonplace.[11]

Perhaps most shocking was the ultimate culmination of this childlike behavior: *"Only very few prisoners escaped a more or less intensive identification with the SS,'"* Elkins wrote, quoting directly from Elie Cohen, a physician who had survived Auschwitz.[12] Longtime or old prisoners who had successfully adjusted to the system sewed their uniforms to resemble those of SS guards, took pride in their ability to stand at attention during roll call, and continued to follow nonsensical rules long after the SS guards themselves had abandoned them. Prisoners even adopted the political ideas of the Nazis and mimicked their extreme violence against other prisoners. "To all these men," Elkins concluded, "reduced to complete and childish dependence upon their masters, the SS had actually become a father symbol. . . . The closed system, in short, had become a kind of grotesque patriarchy."[13] The few cases of rebellion, the scarcity of suicides, and the absence of intense hatred toward the SS even after liberation, Elkins said, provided the most compelling evidence of the degree to which the personalities of the concentration camp inmates had been fundamentally altered.[14]

After describing the impact of the Nazi concentration camps, the historian then relied on several different psychological theories to explain the prisoners' reactions to their internment. Using Freudian theory, Elkins explained that, because of extreme shock and "infantile regression," prisoners had acquired new superegos, with new values personified by the SS guard.[15] Relying on the "interpersonal theory" of Henry Stack Sullivan, which claimed that individuals' personalities are formed in order to please "significant others," Elkins concluded that prisoners had had only one, very brutal, significant other—the SS guard—and thus had molded their personalities, even internalizing his attitudes, to please him. In the related theory of role psychology, Elkins noted, scholars posited that individuals' personalities are established through playing various social roles. Since the concentration camp forced prisoners into dependency in every way, this dependency became the defining aspect of their personalities. It was only when inmates found some other role to play, such as in the camp underground, that they were able to resist their oppressors and maintain their humanity.

Using all three of these theories (Freudianism, interpersonal theory, and role theory), Elkins attempted to argue that the personality alteration experienced by concentration camp inmates was a social-scientific process that would occur in almost any individual in an extremely patriarchal and unfree culture. Thus Africans enslaved on American plantations in the eighteenth century—who were dependent for sustenance on one significant other and father figure, their master; who were cut off from all other forms of authority; and who were denied any social roles other than "slaves"—must have experienced personality changes similar to those of European concentration camp inmates in the twentieth century.

Since modern discussions of slavery and the Holocaust typically highlight racism, it is probably surprising to contemporary readers to note that Stanley Elkins's analogy said virtually nothing about racial persecution. Again, Elkins hardly mentioned Jews as camp inmates at all, and he made special efforts, as discussed above, to argue that "Sambo" was not necessarily black. Instead, the historian emphasized that "the very cultural diversity among the African tribes involved in the slave trade [made] it impossible to generalize at all" about enslaved peoples, just as he emphasized that the concentration camps of the 1930s "formed a cross-section of society which was virtually complete: criminals, workers, businessmen, professional people, middle-class Jews, even members of the aristocracy."[16] Even the extermination of European Jews did not alter, according to Elkins, the concentration camps' polyglot prisoner system: "The basic technique [of victimization] was everywhere and at all times the same."[17] Stanley Elkins thus purposely deemphasized the specific racial elements of both systems to demonstrate the universal ability of absolute power to decimate individual personality.

If he deemphasized race as a category of persecution, Elkins at the same time subtextually stressed the gendered nature of slavery and the concentration camps. The historian's portraits of Africans before their enslavement were unquestionably portraits of *men:* "The typical West African tribesman was a distinctly warlike individual; he had a profound sense of family and family authority; he took hard work for granted . . . he might have had considerable experience as a political or military leader."[18] Even aside from his use of the male pronoun, unexceptional in 1959, Elkins's language of familial authority, discipline, work, and war clearly identified slaves in their former lives as men. Once enslaved, these men lost that familial authority; they no longer had the power to discipline their children or even to protect the mothers of their children. Enslaved men took on characteristics that Elkins labeled childlike but that can also easily be seen as feminine: "obedience, fidelity, humility, docility, [and] cheerfulness."[19] Without patriarchal power, having become absolutely dependent on the master, slaves, coded as male by Elkins, developed passive personalities that led them to serve their masters, rather than to resist.

Elkins's concern with the masculinity of slaves was mirrored by his description of concentration camp inmates. Although Elkins did read the works of two female concentration camp survivors, and he included one brief footnote about the internal physical exams women were forced to endure before entering the camps, for the most part, Elkins relied on Bruno Bettelheim's descriptions of powerless men in the concentration camps.[20] Camps such as Dachau, Elkins explained, punished inmates who displayed any "bravado" or performed "any heroics"; concentration camps made it impossible for men to imagine providing for their wives and children, while also depriving them of their status as workers and professionals and even destroying their sexual capacities.[21] Their sexual impotence only symbolized their larger emasculation, made clear by the willingness of these men, "when commanded by their masters, [to] go to their death without resistance."[22] Elkins's decision to deemphasize the race of slaves and inmates, while subtly emphasizing their gender as men, suggested his interest in masculinity as a sign of individualism, unhampered by race or class.

ELKINS'S ANALOGY WAS HIGHLY UNUSUAL for the era (and indeed for today). Historians do not, as a rule, develop arguments about historical events using analogous situations, social-scientific theory, and virtually no specific primary evidence. For a Ph.D. candidate, this strategy was tremendously daring—and is worth closer observation. What led Elkins to develop his peculiar analogy, one that introduced Nazi German concentration camps into a book about American slavery?

It seems logical to turn to Elkins's Jewish origins as a possible explanation for his unusual historical strategy, and indeed several scholars have suggested that Elkins's analogy was motivated by his Jewish background.[23] Elkins himself, however, was disinclined in early interviews to connect his Jewish origins with his use of concentration camps. In his 1997 book, Daryl Michael Scott reported, for example, that Elkins "has rejected any link between his [Jewish] identity and his [concentration camp] imagery."[24] In 1986, August Meier and Elliott Rudwick, relying on their interview with Elkins, denied that the concentration camp analogy was motivated by the historian's interest in Jewish experience.[25] In these interviews, Elkins tended to emphasize to interviewers that his intellectual interest was slavery and that his use of the concentration camp analogy was merely an expediency: "I chose the concentration-camp analogy because it was dramatic, because it was fresh in our memories, and because it got around the problem of race."[26] Elkins's insistence that his analogy "got around the problem of race" is ironic, given the racial uproar that surrounded *Slavery* in the late 1960s, but the historian's claim suggested that he did not consciously see his analogy as being connected to his own Jewishness.

We should not take these published insistences to be the last word on the significance of Elkins's Jewish background, however. In the interviews discussed above, Elkins may have felt more pressured to emphasize his objective interest in the field of slavery. In more recent interviews, he has been open to discussing the possibility that his Jewish upbringing might have shaped his concentration camp analogy. Indeed, during the more recent interviews, he volunteered that his Jewishness had "sensitized" him to the example of the concentration camps.[27] To be sure, many other intellectual and personal influences were at play in the development of *Slavery*. To limit the origins of Elkins's complex intellectual ideas solely to ethnic background would be reductionist. At the same time, however, it would also be a mistake to ignore the ways that Elkins's experiences as a Jewish boy growing up in the shadow of Hitler in the 1930s, his serving in the U.S. military in the 1940s, and then his becoming a history graduate student in the first generation of Jewish scholars to attain significant numbers in American academia in the 1950s may have played a role in the historian's understanding of the camps and their significance for intellectual inquiry.

Many of Stanley Elkins's key memories of growing up Jewish in the 1930s were of antisemitism. Indeed, his very sense of being Jewish was determined to some extent by that antisemitism. Born in 1925, the son of second-generation eastern European Jews, Elkins grew up in a middle-class Jewish home in Brighton, a neighborhood in Boston where many upwardly mobile Jews lived, separate from the working-class Jewish neighborhoods of Mattapan and Dorchester.[28] Elkins's father, Frank, was a salesman who eventually worked his way up to owning a dress factory in the neighborhood around Kneeland Street, a business district with primarily Jewish proprietors in the garment industry. Elkins's mother, Frances Reiner Elkins, was from a well-educated Jewish family that had been a part of an early pre-Zionist experiment in New Jersey. Her father died young, however, and Frances went to work in a factory at the age of sixteen.[29]

Consistently throughout interviews, Stanley Elkins referred to his Jewish identity as something that was a "given." By "given," he meant, on the one hand, that he did not perceive his Jewish background to have been as rich a cultural or religious experience as it could have been. Elkins insisted that he had missed "the really ethnic life of Boston" that he believed was extant in the working-class neighborhood of Dorchester. He seemed to regret too that his family did not possess a "good social-democratic-cum-communist" Jewish background. Although Elkins's grandparents were Orthodox and spoke Yiddish, his immediate family was not observant, and Elkins could not speak Yiddish well. Elkins says he "was bar mitzvahed as a matter of course," but he did not continue in his Jewish education, nor did Jewish ritual play an important part in his daily life.[30]

On the other hand, by calling Jewishness "given," Elkins was speaking proudly of his connections to the Jewish community and his open Jewish identity. He noted with satisfaction that he was one of the first professors when he began teaching at Smith College, in the early 1960s, to join the local synagogue, and he contrasted himself a number of times with other Jews he had known as an adult who had tried to "escape" from Jewishness by hiding their origins: "It never entered my mind that I could be anything but Jewish." Elkins's pride in maintaining his identity surely reflected the fact that his family was part of a tight-knit Jewish community in Brighton, a community in which Elkins found all his close friends and in which he engaged in most of his social activities, including Boy Scouts and dating: "As a high school kid I just took it for granted that all the girls I would go with would be Jewish. You know, it was a fairly tight ethnic community." Identifying as Jewish and socializing with other Jews was something that Elkins took for granted as "given."[31]

Elkins's use of the word "given" to describe his Jewishness also hints at the antisemitism that he faced as a Jewish boy growing up in Boston in the 1930s. Indeed, his primary memories of growing up Jewish were of a general atmosphere of violence and discrimination, and his use of the word "given" makes clear that it was difficult to be Jewish in this kind of atmosphere. "[Jewishness] certainly . . . wasn't anything you'd escape from; there was no place to go. . . . My Jewishness was kind of a given, and . . . there wasn't an impossible amount of antisemitism, but that was a given." For Elkins, that antisemitism was reflected in the voice of Father Coughlin on the radio, in stories of colleges discriminating against Jews in admissions, and in the family's general understanding that Elkins's aunt couldn't get certain jobs because she was Jewish. The presence of German Jewish refugees from Hitler in his neighborhood added further to Elkins's general understanding of the salience of antisemitism.[32]

Perhaps most consistently in Elkins's memory, being Jewish in Boston in the 1930s meant facing physical violence. He, his friends, and the male members of his family seem to have been constantly aware of and on guard against attacks by non-Jews: "My Jewish orientation in part was formed by, you know, guys looking to make trouble."[33] Elkins's father, who had fought in the Bowery in New York as a young man, broke someone's jaw in a fight over an antisemitic comment, and in the next generation Elkins's brother and friends consistently defended the young Stanley in fights. Groups of non-Jews jumped or insulted Elkins more than once: "My experience was, you gotta watch it because these guys'll get you," he remembered, though he noted that not all non-Jews had been antisemites or violent by any means.[34]

Historical accounts confirm Elkins's memories of violent antisemitism, particularly directed toward men, in Boston during this era. Tensions among white ethnics in Boston, always strong, were particularly high in the 1930s and 1940s, as international conflict and the economic pressures of the Depression affected the segregated neighborhoods of the city. Conflict between Irish and Jewish communities was particularly intense as more upwardly mobile Jews moved into the formerly Irish neighborhoods of Roxbury, Dorchester, and Mattapan. Father Charles Coughlin, famous for his radio attacks on "international bankers," was particularly popular in Irish Catholic neighborhoods in the city; indeed, Boston's mayor, James Michael Curley, called the city "the most Coughlinite city in the United States."[35] During the 1930s and 1940s, newspapers in Boston reported attacks on Jews living near Irish neighborhoods, some of them appearing organized by gangs, particularly those associated with Coughlin supporters. The B'nai B'rith Anti-Defamation League recorded frequent battles between Irish and Jewish teenage boys in Boston begun as a result of antisemitic baiting and/or violence. And like Elkins, in interviews and memoirs, many Jewish men who were teenagers in Boston between the 1930s and the 1950s, including conductor Leonard Bernstein and journalist Nat Hentoff, have remembered antisemitic violence suffered at the hands of young non-Jewish, frequently Irish, men.[36]

In this environment of frequently violent antisemitism, intensified by news reports of events in Nazi Germany, the masculine ethos that Stanley Elkins internalized from his family was one that demanded self-defense: "Discrimination was a kind of given for me as I was growing up and it was intensified by . . . everything that was going on in Germany, and it's something you have to be prepared to fight against. My old man would do it very directly, but I just didn't have that ability. But it was, 'you got to defend yourself.'"[37] As this quotation makes clear, Elkins remembered with some admiration his father's pugnacious style in the face of antisemitism, and his father's skill as a fighter, while he denigrated his own ability to defend himself similarly. Explaining that he "never got in a fistfight that [he] won," Elkins noted several times that he needed to rely on bigger, tougher friends and family members to help him in fights against antisemitic toughs: "You hope your friends are bigger than they are. . . . I had a big big brother, and he was always very helpful."[38] Although Elkins felt that he "couldn't aspire" to his father's confrontational abilities, he seems to have admired them, and to have internalized an ethos that demanded physical confrontation, especially on the part of men.

Antisemitic stereotypes, particularly those of Jewish men as passive weaklings incapable of fighting, played a strong role in Elkins's perceptions of himself and of his father: "There was a kind of negative image, Jews won't fight, or something like that, which in the case of my father was utterly ridiculous; he'd fight on the drop of a hat. I couldn't aspire to his qualities in that respect." Instead, Elkins labeled himself as a teenager, "a nice Jewish boy," a stereotype that reifies the Jewish man as a passive weakling: "The nice Jewish boy doesn't make trouble, he certainly doesn't get into fights."[39] Several times in one interview, the historian referred to the stereotype of the eastern European Jew who cowers from armed service.[40]

The stereotype of the weak or feminized Jewish man is a product of centuries of victimization: Jewish men were constructed as "others," often faced with substantial violence from non-Jews, and legally prevented from participating in traditional masculine activities, such as bearing arms.[41] The weak Jewish man was not only a stereotype imposed by non-Jews, however, but also a constructed ideal within medieval and early modern eastern European Jewish culture, as rabbis consciously sought to reject Gentile male ideals and to construct instead a different model of Jewish manliness that was gentle and scholarly.[42] In the nineteenth century, white European and American men experienced a crisis in gender roles in the wake of modernization and attempted to establish a new virile white masculinity that distinguished their healthy, athletic, even violent bodies from the weak, passive, degenerate bodies of "others": people of color, women, and Jews.[43] Many secular Jewish men at this time sought to separate their own bodies from the scientific labels of homosexuality and femininity accumulating during this era and instead to make themselves "Muscle-Jews," either as Zionists or as active participants in sporting, gangster, or military culture in their adopted nations.[44]

Given the significance of the stereotype of the weak Jewish man in Stanley Elkins's imagination, as well as the significance of the larger cultural project of "Muscle-Jews" in the modern era, it is not surprising that Elkins's own time in military service, from 1943 to 1946, loomed large in his description of his life as a Jewish man. In Elkins's recounting, the army provided an escape from the antisemitism he had encountered on the streets of Boston. Although he did encounter some anti-Jewish attitudes in the army, the historian remembers the army as an institution that gave him a new masculine identity, that of an American soldier, without forcing him to abandon his Jewishness: "[Being a soldier] became a new identity which didn't require I give up my old identity." Perhaps even more importantly, the army offered an escape from antisemitism because it allowed Jews like himself to challenge the stereotype of Jewish men by becoming good soldiers. Speaking fifty-five years after he had joined the army, Elkins still clearly took pleasure in describing his own skills as a soldier, particularly in handling weapons; in two separate interviews, he related in detail how to play the "Chicago piano," a complicated machine-gun maneuver. The military environment, he explained, was able to change him "from a nice Jewish boy to a relatively good infantryman." This challenge to Jewish stereotypes was clearly both about Jewishness and about masculinity. In addition to "tak[ing] the Ost Juden stereotype and turn[ing] it on its head," Elkins very literally saw his development as a soldier as a "rite of passage" and a "transition to manhood."[45]

This challenge to Jewish stereotypes was not only effective in changing Elkins's sense of himself as a Jewish man and in silencing antisemitism among his fellow American soldiers; it also offered the future historian terrific emotional satisfaction in fighting German troops, particularly as news of the concentration camps emerged. Understanding that Germans were massacring innocent Jews infuriated and galvanized him as a soldier, allowing him to see himself as a Jewish man fighting back against the Germans: "you . . . had the opportunity to hit back; you could shoot Germans, to put it bluntly. That was my line of work," he remembered. Knowing that he was fighting Nazis made the war morally simple for him as a Jewish soldier: "One was very clear why one was there, if you know what I mean. It was a clear-cut war, especially for the Jewish boys." And being Jewish, knowing that he was fighting Nazis, made him savor even more the strength of the American army as the tide turned against the Germans:

> We were not in the regiment that broke the German lines, but we were right behind them, and we came out of the mountains, down into the valley, and as far as your eyes could see, the roads were packed with American trucks jammed with infantry and tanks, artillery and I do remember, I honestly remember this, [thinking,] you murderers, you arrogant murdering bastards, we're going to tear you to pieces. And we did. . . . It was a fairly simple experience emotionally.[46]

Being a Jew in the U.S. Army fighting Nazis, particularly after he had felt unable to fight back against violent antisemitism as a teenager in Boston, gave Stanley Elkins a strong sense of power.[47]

After the war, during his years in college and graduate school in the late 1940s and 1950s, Elkins encountered an intellectual environment that resonated with, and helped him make sense of, his early experiences with antisemitism, his ethos of self-defense, and his surprise and satisfaction with the changes that the army had wrought within him. Perhaps the most important intellectual trend during this era was environmentalism, or the belief that culture, rather than biology, shapes individual behavior. Environmentalism had begun as a movement with the pathbreaking work of anthropologist Franz Boas in the early twentieth century, and by the end of World War II, it was the dominant intellectual trend in the social sciences. Influential works such as Ruth Benedict's *Patterns of Culture* (1934) and Gunnar Myrdal's *American Dilemma* (1944) had helped to make the biological concept of race an intellectual anachronism, while advertising the power of culture to shape human behavior and to explain differences between social groups.[48] After the Nazis had made racial explanations for behavior anathema in the wake of World War II, environmentalism reigned supreme in American academic institutions.

As an undergraduate at Harvard in the late 1940s, Elkins took an influential class with historian Oscar Handlin, whose future Pulitzer Prize–winning book, *The Uprooted* (1951), would portray immigrants with few cultural resources of strength, buffeted and ultimately transformed by the storms of a fluid American environment.[49] As a graduate student at Columbia in the

1950s, Elkins studied with Robert K. Merton, the important sociologist who was at the forefront of functionalism, the dominant sociological theory in the postwar era. Functionalists like Merton emphasized the power of social structures, relationships, and institutions over individual human agency and prided themselves on a "tough-minded" perspective that emphasized that individuals had less power over their actions than they believed.[50] Years later, when struggling to name his specific intellectual influences, Elkins noted his classes with Handlin and Merton and emphasized the general trend of environmentalism that had hung heavily "in the air" during his graduate school days.[51]

Elkins's attraction to environmentalism was not due simply to the fact that environmentalism was popular or that it was the strongly held belief of his teachers and mentors in the immediate postwar era, however. In interviews, Elkins continually connected his personal experiences in the army and with antisemitism to his powerful interest in environmental explanations for behavior: "if you've gone through an experience of a dramatic change in environment, and you recognize that this has an impact on personality, you're sort of cued for an environmental explanation."[52] Throughout his interviews, Elkins described the "dramatic change in environment" he had experienced in three different examples, and all three of those examples centered on Elkins's early experiences of antisemitism and the dramatic impact that World War II had on that antisemitism.

Understandably, one of the dramatic changes in environment Elkins pointed to several times was his own dramatic transition in the army from a "nice Jewish boy" to a good soldier:

> Okay, I personally was raised by a fairly protective Jewish mother. I was not very athletic, I certainly wasn't very pugnacious, I never won a fistfight in my life. I go into the army and I discover that I have a fair amount of stamina, I can stand up to the long marches, lo and behold I'm a good rifle shot. . . . I was a good machine gunner in addition to this, and I was sort of intrigued by the fact that I had sort of changed my personality. . . . you're conscious of the fact that fairly intensive training can make some relatively significant changes in behavior.[53]

Although Elkins mentioned a few other examples of environmental change that he had witnessed in the army—for example, the personality differences he had observed between his Italian American friend and that friend's Italian cousins—it was the dramatic change in his own life as a Jewish man that he spoke about again and again in his interviews.[54]

Yet another substantial change in environment that Elkins pointed to several times was the increasingly unfashionable nature of antisemitism after World War II, a dramatic shift, he believed, from the discrimination and hatred that had so dominated his life in the 1930s:

> If you went to college, say one of the Ivy League schools, in the 1930s . . . you took a certain amount of antisemitism; I certainly did when I was growing up. If you went to college after the war, it may have existed, but it was very much out of fashion, it was very much out of fashion. . . . Now, that change had occurred within a generation. And certainly the experience that my children had growing up was utterly different than the one I had growing up in Boston; it was significantly different. And so again I'm sensitized to changes in environment.[55]

The shift away from a dominant environment of antisemitism toward an environment of tolerance or acceptance had significant impact on Elkins, permitting him to see changes in his own life and helping him to understand, perhaps, his own professional trajectory, his transition from an ordinary Jewish boy to a member of an academic elite that had excluded Jews until very recently.

Historians' descriptions of the declining acceptability of antisemitism in postwar America generally coincide with Elkins's memories.[56] To be sure, antisemitism still did exist during these years, and Elkins still encountered unkind words, even in graduate school. Describing his relationship with close friend and coauthor Eric McKitrick, for example, Elkins noted that McKitrick had poked fun at romanticized portraits of the Jewish ghetto of eastern Europe and had asked him why the "pushy Jews" that he'd known all his life didn't show up in that ghetto.[57] Although McKitrick's joke might seem a clear example of anti-Jewish prejudice, Elkins did not describe his friend's comment as an example of antisemitism. Instead, Elkins seems to have interpreted the graduate school environment—where he could succeed, become friends with an elite Gentile man such as McKitrick, and face none of the public humiliation he had faced as a young man—as a space remarkably cleansed of hatred, a space that enabled him to take on a new personality as a confident intellectual.[58]

Finally, Elkins pointed repeatedly to a third shift in environment that World War II had enabled, and to which Elkins's experiences in the military had sensitized him: the changed personality of Jews in the new state of Israel. Several times in interviews, without being posed any specific questions about Israel or Zionism, Elkins brought up independently his fascination with the military training of Israeli soldiers, in order to illustrate the power of the environment in shaping personality. He described being particularly impressed by an article in an infantry journal that he had read in either the late 1940s or early 1950s describing Israeli military training: "I knew the old East European stereotype about Jews in the military . . . but then you've got the Israelis, and the Israelis were a glorious example of the grandchildren of these Ost Juden suddenly becoming the best soldiers in the Western World. And you were very conscious of the fact that you change the environment dramatically, you change the personalities."[59] The military prowess of the Israeli army thus vindicated and supported Elkins's theories of environmentalism. Israeli military might belied the Jewish stereotypes that Elkins had grown up with, demonstrating that those stereotypes were malleable and changeable, the product of circumstance, just as Elkins's own experience in the U.S. Army had demonstrated that the stereotype of the "nice Jewish boy" was dependent on the circumstances of his upbringing, not representative of his inherent qualities as a Jew.

It is particularly telling that throughout his interviews, Elkins continually referred to the power of the Israeli military as evidence of environmentalist theory, rather than as a source of ethnic pride or nationalist pleasure. To be sure, Elkins seems to have derived a good deal of emotional satisfaction from Jewish military prowess in Israel, but his emphasis was never on the righteousness of Zionist theory or the necessity for Jewish "toughness." Israel, for Elkins, was proof of the power of the environment to change the stereotype of the "nice Jewish boy."[60]

All three of Elkins's illustrations of a powerful environment indicate the ways that his personal experiences as a Jew and a soldier in World War II shaped his intellectual understanding of human behavior and social change when he was in college and graduate school. Understanding this fundamental grounding for Elkins's environmentalism should help readers to understand a bit better how and why Elkins developed his controversial analogy between Nazi concentration camps and American slavery.

First, as Elkins has noted, being Jewish "sensitized" him to the subject of Nazi concentration camps, making the subject emotionally powerful and immediate: "I had a feeling of what it would amount to, what it would be like to have these animals in complete control," he explained.[61]

Perhaps even more significantly, however, the terrifying experience of the concentration camps, as described by Bruno Bettelheim, provided for Elkins a dramatic and compelling proof for environmentalism. Bettelheim's influential article, "Individual and Mass Behavior in Extreme Situations," to which Elkins had first been introduced as an undergraduate by a friend, provided him with much of this proof. Bettelheim's portrait of a concentration camp environment making its inmates into willing slaves offered Elkins two crucial messages, both of which he was enthusiastically prepared to receive. The first of these messages was that a powerful environment could shape personality. The second message was that the commonly held stereotype of Jewish victims marching passively to their death in Nazi-occupied Europe was incorrect; people of any nationality or religion, not only Jews, could become passive participants in their own destruction. "You see, Bettelheim is an enormous relief for any doubts that you might have," Elkins explained in one of his interviews, "because it happens to everybody; it doesn't just happen to Jews."[62] Given Elkins's description of Bettelheim's work as an "enormous relief," it is not surprising that the article made enough of an impression on him as an undergraduate for him to "file it away in his memory" and to draw on it again in graduate school, when he had become interested in the question of slavery.[63]

Bettelheim's portraits of passive concentration camp inmates contrasted, moreover, with Stanley Elkins's own triumphant success as an American soldier, further demonstrating for Elkins the power of the environment. When asked how being Jewish had sensitized him to the concentration camp imagery, Elkins responded: "There were stories of Jewish [passivity,] you know, they didn't fight back, and I would get deeply annoyed with these because they couldn't. I was very conscious of that. . . . I mean I was very conscious of the fact that I was one of the lucky ones and that I was given a chance to fight back on good terms."[64] Although Elkins may have been imagining that his current consciousness was also present in the 1950s, given the preoccupation in his interviews with antisemitism, self-defense, and environmental transformation, it seems almost certain that these issues occupied Elkins's subconscious mind when he wrote *Slavery*.[65] If not consciously then at least unconsciously, Elkins was playing out in his head, as he developed his controversial analogy between Nazi concentration camps and American slave plantations, the stark contrast between his own fortune as a Jew in the U.S. Army and that of the Jews trapped in Nazi camp machinery.

Indeed, some of Stanley Elkins's language in *Slavery* suggests that he believed that his position as a Jew struggling with the legacy of Nazism helped him to understand the experiences of African American slaves. In his effort to distinguish his work from the most recent monograph on slavery, Kenneth Stampp's pathbreaking *Peculiar Institution*, Elkins argued that Stampp's portraits of defiant black workers did not accurately present slavery from the viewpoint of the slave. He charged that it was "morally a little callous" for scholars such as Gunnar Myrdal and Kenneth Stampp, "white men who knew nothing of what it meant to be reared in slavery," to assume that African slaves would have responded with ideal rebelliousness and courage to such a coercive social system. "What [Stampp] didn't appreciate that I did appreciate . . . is the impact of this system on the people who experienced it," Elkins remembered in a recent interview.[66]

Elkins's language, both in his book and in his interviews, is suggestive. To be sure, he was a graduate student anxious to distinguish himself from the important scholars in the field, but in a work that disdained "moralizing," it is particularly interesting that he referred to his antagonists as "morally a little callous." By pointing out Stampp and Myrdal's whiteness and their ignorance of the experience of slavery, and by implying that he, Elkins, better appreciated that experience, Elkins may have been subtly invoking or at least drawing on his own Jewish origins as a source of authority for his understanding of slavery. And indeed, in an interview, when asked how his Jewish origins might have influenced his writing of *Slavery*, Elkins testified that he had felt that his Jewishness "gave me a certain degree of insight into the experience of African Americans because I had experienced discrimination—not much—but enough so I knew what it felt like."[67] To be sure, none of this emphasis on Jewishness was overt in the text of *Slavery* itself, and Elkins's testimony may have been an effort to impress or please this interviewer; as far as I know, he has not told any other interviewer that his Jewish experiences led him to sympathize with racism against African Americans. But evidence at least suggests that Elkins may have unconsciously interpreted his own understanding of antisemitism as a source from which he could draw to write about black slavery.

Like his Jewish background, Stanley Elkins's political liberalism shaped the dramatic analogy between concentration camp victims and slaves. To be sure, Elkins did not necessarily define himself as a liberal in 1959 or see himself as an ally of civil rights reformers. In a recent interview, he described himself as being in a "conservative phase" when he wrote *Slavery*, one that reflected the political sensibilities of the 1950s.[68] Moreover, his criticism of the "reforming zeal" of abolitionists and his provocative use of the term "Sambo," even though (or perhaps because) that term had recently been the subject of student protests at Queens College, suggested that he felt a certain amount of distance from liberal reformers championing civil rights in the 1950s.[69]

Nonetheless, Elkins's viewpoints clearly reflected a number of crucial liberal trends in the 1950s. For example, historian Daryl Michael Scott has convincingly argued that Elkins's portrait of slavery destroying African

Americans' personalities was an example of the "damage liberalism" that governed much of mainstream racial thinking in the decades following World War II. From the 1940s through the early 1960s, as Scott has described, both black and white liberal social scientists frequently used imagery that emphasized the psychological damage wrought on blacks by racial discrimination in order to justify top-down social policies, such as integration, to white audiences.[70] In advocating for integration, E. Franklin Frazier, for example, emphasized the "pathology" of lower-class black families and their children segregated in urban ghettos, while Kenneth and Mamie Clark, in their famous experiments used in *Brown v. Board of Education, Topeka, Kansas*, described the toll that racism took on black children's self-esteem.[71] Knowing that middle-class white Americans in the 1950s valued intact personalities and mental health, social scientists emphasized that racism prevented blacks from attaining this all-important psychological well-being. By developing this argument, academics such as Frazier and the Clarks hoped that they would be able to create political support for federal policies that aided black Americans. Stanley Elkins's portrait of psychologically damaged slaves fit this model of liberalism perfectly.

Daryl Scott has also contended convincingly that Elkins's discomfort with activism reflected an "elitist, statist" brand of liberalism that governed mainstream thinking in the 1950s. Many American liberals had been shaken by the mass fervor of Nazism and Stalinism in the 1940s and had come to see mass democratic action as a dangerous threat to liberty, rather than a means of preserving it. Activists, these statist liberals believed, were dangerous extremists, whose passions needed to be channeled through mainstream institutions such as the Democratic party, the welfare state, or the university in order to maintain individual liberties.[72] For Elkins, this political philosophy was shaped by his personal history. The future historian had become disillusioned with radicalism while working with communists on the Henry Wallace campaign in 1948.[73] The historian's jabs at activists at Queens College in the 1950s, and at abolitionists in the antebellum era, make more sense when one understands the elitist and statist ideology of liberalism at the time.

Then, too, Elkins's insistence on objective, value-free social-scientific inquiry, rather than "moralizing," was part of a larger postwar liberal interpretation of science as the repository of liberty in the Western democracies. Indeed, Elkins's professor, Robert Merton, in his 1938 essay "A Note on Science and Democracy," played an important role in constructing the prevailing belief that science was inherently democratic, in part because of its "disinterestedness," which prevented individuals or groups from shaping or abusing scientific results for their own interests.[74]

Stanley Elkins's environmental understanding of race offers further evidence of his liberalism. In the 1950s, biological racism was under attack in academia, but it had not been extinguished. Indeed, only one decade earlier, the historical literature on slavery had still been dominated by the racist work of southerner Ulrich B. Phillips, who was convinced of black biological and cultural inferiority. Phillips argued that African Americans had been contented in their lives as slaves and that the institution of slavery had been mild, kind and civilizing.[75] Stampp's *Peculiar Institution* had been written to supplant Phillips's racist work, and although Elkins suggested that Stampp's antiracism was "polemic," Elkins, too, firmly and continually rejected Phillips's biological racism, noting, for example, that the southern historian's "assumptions of Negro inferiority . . . had been fully discredited by modern science."[76] Elkins rejected, moreover, Ulrich Phillips's contempt for African culture. *Slavery* described an African culture that was sophisticated, diverse, proud, and independent, not servile or depraved. Although he was perhaps too sanguine about his belief that the biological concept of race had been consigned to the intellectual dustheap, Elkins established his liberal credentials by clearly rejecting biological racism.

Perhaps most strikingly, Elkins offered a devastating criticism of Phillips's portrait of slavery that had significant implications in contemporary racial politics in the 1950s. Instead of offering southern nostalgia for a civilizing institution that had treated its captives with the utmost kindness, Stanley Elkins presented a nightmarish vision of American slavery by comparing it to the recent horrors of the Nazi concentration camps. Simply by making that analogy, Elkins offered a clearly provocative position, one that corresponded much better to liberal demands for civil rights than it did to conservative southern support for segregation in the 1950s. Indeed, southern practitioners of "massive resistance" were more likely to view federal troops, not their own slave-owning ancestors, as totalitarian analogues.[77] Uninterested in the rights of the southern states or slaveholders, Elkins offered a moral condemnation of slavery as an institution that, even at its mildest, was inherently harsh because it destroyed the human personality. The position was far more valuable for liberals than for conservatives in the 1950s.

Importantly, in more recent writings and interviews, Elkins has noted that his own argument was far more liberal than he was willing to acknowledge in 1959. In 1975, he referred to *Slavery* as part of a larger "damage" argument that existed among liberals in the 1950s and "crested" in the early 1960s. Elkins further identified himself with the "abolitionists" such as Stampp who attacked Ulrich Phillips's work: "I was a bit lofty about the need for value-free judgments, and I had some hard things to say about moralizing abolitionists. But for practical purposes I was one of them."[78] Although Elkins viewed his work as an academic treatise, not advocacy for social policy, he did believe that his environmental approach could help to explain problems in the black community.[79] Indeed, as *Slavery* became a political document in the early 1960s, as we shall see below, put to use by both white liberals and black activists in the cause of civil rights, Elkins supported a number of those causes. For example, when he heard that NAACP lawyers had used *Slavery* to defend a young black activist on trial for sitting in at a restaurant, Elkins said, "Needless to say I was enjoying every bit of it." And when Daniel Patrick Moynihan adopted Elkins's argument in *Slavery* to support federal programs for African Americans in the controversial Moynihan report, Elkins supported those programs as "good old-fashioned New Deal" and "imminently sensible."[80] The liberalism of the turn of the 1960s was clearly reflected in Stanley Elkins's work.

GIVEN THE INTENSE PUBLIC SCRUTINY that *Slavery* would undergo in the next two decades, it is perhaps surprising that in its first several years, between 1959 and about 1962, the book remained quite unknown. In general, the initial reception of Elkins's book was lukewarm. It sold only about 1,800 copies in hardback in its first four years of publication and its reviews were extremely mixed, with critics and opponents quite evenly split.[81] Indeed, reviewers who liked Elkins and those who attacked him frequently made many of the same comments. Although they were frequently impressed by the historian's "boldness" or "originality," and praised him for his ability to ask important questions, readers also criticized his reliance on the Sambo image and his absence of hard data.[82] Perhaps because the University of Chicago Press decided to publish Elkins's 1959 dissertation as a book without demanding any revisions, a number of reviewers, moreover, commented on the book's "infelicitous style."[83] In any event, the book was reviewed almost exclusively in the scholarly press during these early years, and reviewers' perspectives revolved entirely around the academic questions that Elkins had addressed.

Virtually no academics protested initially that Elkins's concentration camp analogy misrepresented or dishonored Jews in the camps, a reaction one might assume would follow such a comparison in today's intellectual milieu. Indeed the word "Jew" appeared in no early reviews of Stanley Elkins's work. Only one critic, historian David Donald in the *American Historical Review,* criticized the "poor taste" of the concentration camp analogy, and Donald did not make clear exactly what he thought was in poor taste: the use of the camps at all, or comparing American slavery to Nazi terror.[84]

Then, too, only one reviewer, librarian Abraham Barnett, questioned that the concentration camps had indeed corrupted their victims in the way Elkins described: he called the infantilization process of the camps "alleged."[85] No reader protested that the internees' experience in the Nazi camps had been a unique one that could not be compared. The only Jewish journal I have found that reviewed Elkins's *Slavery* during its first years of publication was *Commentary*, where Nathan Glazer published a glowing review that validated the author's concentration camp analogy and praised his "fruitful" comparative approach.[86] And the *American Jewish Yearbook* from 1959 to 1962 recorded no protests or complaints against Elkins's work.[87]

Perhaps most strikingly, neither Elkins's critics nor his supporters dwelt at length on the Nazi analogy at all, even when they embraced that analogy. Only a few initial readers actually attempted to analyze in any depth Elkins's comparison between the experiences of African slaves and European concentration camp inmates.[88] Elkins has remembered being surprised by this lack of scrutiny because he had anticipated that he would receive more criticism based on a close examination of the two institutions.[89] Instead, most reviewers described the concentration camp analogy in more or less detail and then labeled that analogy with one of a number of adjectives such as "striking," "original," "provocative," or "daring," without elaborating on whom Elkins was provoking or what he had actually dared to do.[90] Historian John William Ward offered perhaps the most tantalizing suggestion of what was "daring" about Elkins's comparison, noting that the historian "runs an obvious risk in bringing together two such emotionally laden situations," but Ward did not pursue this thought, and so the reader was still not clear what Ward thought Elkins risked: anger from blacks? anger from white southerners? anger from Holocaust survivors? disapproval from the academic community? competition between blacks and Jews? all the above? Ward left it entirely unclear.[91]

The initial reception of *Slavery* demonstrates that the American intellectual community at the turn of the 1960s perceived the Nazi destruction of European Jewry through a conceptual framework very different from the one scholars use today. Stanley Elkins's use of concentration camps as an "extended metaphor" for slavery led to no discussion of Jews, Jewish extermination, or the uniqueness of the Holocaust, nor any recorded protests from concentration camp survivors or Jewish scholars.[92] Given this absence, it seems highly unlikely that academics believed that Elkins's ideas would provoke anger from Jews or survivors of the camps. Instead, it is more likely that academics believed that white southerners might be the ones offended.[93] And although John Ward's contention that it was risky to compare these two "emotionally laden" subjects may sound today like a veiled reference to what one scholar has called the "big-time martyr ratings contest" between African Americans and Jews, no other reviewer even hinted at the existence of such a competition.[94] Indeed, some adjectives used by reviewers, most obviously "original" and "ingenious," strongly suggested that these academics did not take a comparison between concentration camps and slavery for granted, in the way that discussions of blacks and Jews do today in contemporary America.[95] Instead, by using adjectives such as "provocative" and "daring," these academic reviewers demonstrated the ways that Elkins's analogy was perceived by many as intellectually exciting and full of promise, a way of thinking anew about old material.[96]

The excitement with which some intellectuals responded to *Slavery* was equaled and even exceeded by mainstream readers and critics when the book moved out of its small academic orbit. After 1962, the growing civil rights movement catapulted the issue of slavery into the mainstream of American society, and with it Stanley Elkins's book. Responding to a growing interest in black history on campuses and in the mainstream press, Grosset and Dunlap published *Slavery* in paperback in 1963. Over the next several years, Elkins's book sales and publicity shot up dramatically. Sales averaged about 25,000 copies a year, as professors grasped for books to assign on the black experience and reviewers such as Michael Harrington, William Styron, and Norman Podhoretz warmly recommended Stanley Elkins's work to the general audiences of the *Village Voice,* The *New York Review of Books,* the *Washington Post,* and the *New York Herald Tribune.*[97] And the theses put forth in *Slavery* began to spread beyond its pages, as writers such as Howard Zinn and Charles Silberman, who wrote for broad educated readerships, relied on the historian's ideas in their own works.[98]

Once again, I found virtually no recorded criticism from Jewish audiences regarding Elkins's comparison between 1963 and 1965.[99] Some of the historian's greatest supporters—Glazer, Podhoretz, Zinn, and Silberman, for example—were Jewish. And an editorial in the *Jewish Advocate,* a Boston newspaper, called Stanley Elkins's book "brilliant," and called for readers to heed "its important message."[100] Few Jews at the turn of the 1960s seem to have been offended by Elkins's use of concentration camps to talk about African American slavery.

One Jewish lay reader did protest the portrait of degraded concentration camp inmates that Elkins had painted: Elkins remembered that an ordinary Jewish man kept sending him postcards and clippings of brief articles about Jewish militancy during the war: "He kept saying Jews will fight back."[101] This man was most likely sensitized to Elkins's argument by the concurrent angry debate in the Jewish community over similar images of

Jews complicit with their own deaths in Raul Hilberg's *Destruction of European Jews* and Hannah Arendt's *Eichmann in Jerusalem*. Although it is significant that this ordinary man took such passionate exception to Elkins's portrait, it is even more significant that, given the existence of the ongoing emotional debate among Jewish intellectuals, so few followed this man's lead, and none at all protested the comparison between blacks and Jews.

As they were persuaded by the arguments of Stanley Elkins's book, public intellectuals such as Harrington, Styron, and Silberman adopted the historian's concentration camp analogy as a part of their own intellectual infrastructure. They repeated Elkins's comparison between slaves and camp inmates without criticism, analysis, or even significant comment. Socialist Michael Harrington, for example, in his review of *Slavery*, used the testimony of "the survivors of Buchenwald" to explain the degradation that had scarred African Americans' experience in America and to argue that blacks deserved justice for these wrongs. Harrington did not praise or even draw special attention to Elkins's analogy here; he simply used the comparison as "scholarly confirmation of a political point."[102] *Fortune* reporter and Columbia University economics lecturer Charles Silberman devoted almost twenty pages of his book on race relations, *Crisis in Black and White*, to repeating Elkins's argument in *Slavery*, with about half of those pages dedicated solely to spelling out the historian's concentration camp analogy. Although Silberman did briefly note that "there are risks in any such comparison," the reporter did not explain those risks, nor did he criticize or praise Elkins for taking them. Instead, Silberman simply reiterated the historian's descriptions of the parallels between Nazi camp inmates and American southern slaves in order to help further his argument that African Americans suffered a "problem of identification," as well as economic and political disfranchisement, that needed to be overcome by activism.[103] Novelist William Styron's reviews in the *New York Review of Books* offer perhaps the best example of the ways in which Stanley Elkins's concentration camp analogy was ingested and delivered back to a general reading audience. Styron casually used the historian's comparison between Nazi camps and southern plantations to help him illustrate the evils of slavery, claiming, for example, that the Black Laws of antebellum Virginia, "even now, read like the code of regulations from an inconceivably vast and much longer enduring Nazi concentration camp."[104] For all these famous writers, Elkins's comparison between inmates and slaves was not an intellectual innovation to be lauded or attacked or even explored further; it was embraced wholeheartedly as a truth, as confirmation of a larger political ideology.

The years between about 1963 and 1965 offered an intellectual and political environment in which Stanley Elkins's ideas, including his concentration camp analogy, were warmly heralded as the historical grounding for liberal ideology and government programs designed to aid black Americans. Elkins's attacks on slavery and his environmental explanations for black contemporary problems appealed tremendously to northern white liberals such as Silberman and Zinn. Even Harrington, a socialist, was able to see within Elkins's descriptions of Buchenwald survivors justification for "a policy of social compensation" that would subvert mainstream America's assumption that blacks were seeking "special favors."[105] Young white southern liberals such as William Styron were particularly attracted to Elkins's thesis because it offered them a "ready-made manual" to argue with segregationist southern whites and to rebel against the racism of the established southern system.[106] Finally, there is some evidence that young black students, as well as white liberals in both the North and the South, appreciated Elkins's descriptions of the horrors of slavery—including the analogy to concentration camps—because they powerfully condemned whites for the enslavement and oppression of blacks.[107] Liberalism was in full flower in the United States during the turn of the 1960s, and Elkins's work powerfully tapped into the swelling support for liberal policies and ideology, while shaping liberals' understanding of the degree and nature of the oppression of blacks.

Perhaps the best example of the extent to which Elkins's theses were a part of, and helped to define, the political zeitgeist of the turn of the 1960s was the way that *Slavery* was embraced by political operatives in Washington, D.C. In 1965, Stanley Elkins's concentration camp analogy actually became a part of national public policy debate. Writer Nathan Glazer, whose glowing review of *Slavery* had first appeared in *Commentary* in 1960, had shown the book to his friend and coauthor, then Assistant Secretary of Labor Daniel Patrick Moynihan.[108] Moynihan, like Glazer and many other white liberals in 1963 and 1964, viewed Stanley Elkins's theories as valuable historical explanation for the continuing poverty of African American neighborhoods and families. According to Elkins, Moynihan was so impressed by *Slavery* that he recommended it to other political staffers in Washington.[109] Particularly disturbed by the relationship between black unemployment and black female-headed households, perhaps because his father had been absent in his own family, Moynihan believed that government policy regarding African Americans needed to go beyond issues of civil rights and address issues of employment and economic resources.[110] Working with two staffers, the secretary developed a seventy-eight-page internal memorandum, "The Negro Family: The Case for National Action," and presented it to a small number of officials in the White House and the Department of Labor in March 1965.

Stanley Elkins's work did not play a major role in what came to be called the "Moynihan report," but it did play a significant minor role. In the report, Moynihan described the damage, or "pathology," that liberals at the time, both black and white, generally agreed existed in the black community, and he offered several chapters of statistics, pie charts, and bar graphs pointing to the high frequencies of illegitimate births, female-headed households, unemployment, and welfare among African Americans to explain the nature of this "pathology."[111] In one chapter on the "roots of the problem," which included urbanization and the wage system, Moynihan pointed first to slavery and used only Stanley Elkins's *Slavery* to verify his argument, even though his staff had researched a wide variety of historical texts on slavery.[112] Elkins's comparison between Nazi concentration camps and American slave plantations became a central piece of evidence for Moynihan as he attempted to portray slavery's impact on black men's roles as workers and as fathers: "The profound personality change created by Nazi internment . . . was toward childishness and total acceptance of the SS guards as father figures—a syndrome strikingly similar to the 'Sambo' caricature of the Southern slave." That childishness and dependence had "lowered the need for achievement" among black men, and had thereby helped to contribute to the matriarchal family structure that currently contributed to black "pathology," according to Moynihan.[113] Although "The Negro Family" emphasized contemporary causes of the disintegration of the black family, such as unemployment and poverty, it did offer a historical perspective on slavery that was wholly reliant on Stanley Elkins's theories, particularly the concentration camp analogy.

Moreover, that historical perspective, and indeed the specific analogy between slavery and concentration camps, performed a crucial function in Moynihan's argument. A prevailing school of social science theory at the time, "acculturation theory," espoused by scholars such as sociologist Phillip Hauser and historian Oscar Handlin, argued that African Americans were essentially an immigrant group much like other immigrant groups, such as Irish or Jewish Americans, who had also experienced discrimination. To solve the "Negro problem," these scholars argued, blacks simply needed to "acculturate" to the urban American environment, to be taught by more established migrants how to behave in the city.[114] For example, in *The Newcomers,* Oscar Handlin wrote optimistically about the possibilities for African Americans and Puerto Ricans to assimilate into American urban life: "The experience of the past offers a solid foundation for the be-lief that the newest immigrants to a great metropolis will play as useful a role as any of their predecessors. They themselves need only show the will and energy, and their neighbors the tolerance, to make it possible."[115] Moynihan's purpose in "The Negro Family" was quite explicitly to argue against this "acculturation" school, to argue that African Americans were different and needed more than simply "tolerance." Instead, he viewed his report as a "case for national action," or affirmative action, as it would come to be called.[116] Indeed, Moynihan cowrote the famous June 1965 speech given by Lyndon Johnson to establish public support for federal programs to help African Americans escape poverty and attain genuine equality: "You do not take a person who, for years, has been hobbled by chains and liber-ate him, bring him up to the starting line of a race and then say, 'you are free to compete with all the others.'"[117] In order to make the controversial argument that black Americans needed affirmative action, which was la-beled "preferential treatment" by detractors, Moynihan felt compelled to demonstrate that there were historical differences between African Ameri-cans and other immigrant groups, most notably enslavement, that might make black experience in the United States qualitatively different.[118] Stan-ley Elkins's frightening portrait of plantation life served this purpose.

By repeating Elkins's concentration camp analogy, moreover, Moynihan may have believed that the specific image of Nazi evil could encourage his readers to embrace a liberal alternative that they might not otherwise have considered. Moynihan did not need to include Elkins's analogy; he could have relied on black sociologist E. Franklin Frazier's description of slavery destroying black families to make his point on its own.[119] The fact that the assistant secretary of labor specifically chose to repeat Stanley Elkins's com-parison between Nazi camps and American slavery suggests the power he believed that Nazi imagery contained. Then, too, the emphasis in "The Negro Family" on the fact that "concentration camps molded the equivalent [Sambo] personality pattern in a wide variety of Caucasian prisoners" sug-gests that Moynihan thought the example of white European degradation would encourage his mostly white audience of political elites to appreciate the need for affirmative action.[120]

There is some circumstantial evidence, moreover, that Moynihan may have been hoping that the subtextual reference to Jews in the concentration camp analogy would provide a valuable comparison for his readers. At the turn of the 1960s, an intellectual trend emerged in which intellectuals, many of them Jews, compared Jewish religious and social achievement in the United States with what they believed was a hollow and stigmatized black cultural and family life.[121] Daniel Moynihan may have been attempting to address this intellectual trend in his report. In a syndicated column published before the Moynihan report was officially made public, journalists Roland Evans and Robert Novak hinted that this discussion within the Jewish community had contributed to Moynihan's thinking: "Moynihan believes that the public erroneously compares the Negro minority to the Jewish minority. When discriminatory bars were lowered, Jews were ready to move. But the implicit message of the Moynihan Report is that ending discrimination is not nearly enough."[122] By describing the concentration camps' devastating impact on their inmates, who were implicitly understood by many Americans to be Jewish, Moynihan may have been hoping that he could undermine his audience's assumptions about Jews and thus avoid the invidious comparison between Jewish success in America and black "pathology."

In the Moynihan report, as in the works of Silberman and Styron but with even broader impact on American society and culture, Stanley Elkins's comparison between Nazi inmates and southern slaves was used excitedly, and without analysis or criticism, as raw data to explain contemporary urban and racial issues and to justify liberal government policies. The symbol of the Nazi concentration camp, through the lens of Stanley Elkins's theories, thus helped to shape the ways that at least some white Americans interpreted the problems of African Americans at the turn of the 1960s; perhaps more importantly, policy-makers such as Daniel Moynihan believed that the image of Nazi inmates might push some Americans to look favorably on liberal government policies such as affirmative action.

Ultimately, however, those liberal ideas faced significant scrutiny and attack, as the alliance between liberals and radicals that had shaped the turn of the 1960s cracked. In 1965, changing political strategies among African American activists and intellectuals, as well as in the Johnson White House, led to a storm of public controversy over the Moynihan report. Made public after the Watts uprisings in August 1965, "The Negro Family" initially won the approval of white liberals and outlets of the mainstream press. The Catholic magazine *America,* for example, called for "every Congressman . . . to take home with him a copy of the Moynihan report, study the alarming facts contained in it, and be prepared to do something to remedy the situation when he gets back to his desk."[123] The report soon provoked angry responses, however, from black activists such as James Farmer and whites on the left such as psychologist William Ryan, who charged Moynihan with a "new form of subtle racism" that blamed victims of oppression for their own misery.[124] Critics believed that Moynihan's portrait of damaged black families and emasculated black men exposed African Americans to ridicule and contempt, deemphasized the central problems of discrimination and racism in black lives, and ignored the brave activism that had propelled the civil rights movement to success in the preceding five years. As liberalism came under attack from the left and "Black Power" became an important slogan for the civil rights movement in the late 1960s, Moynihan's emphasis on dehumanized black men, shaped in part by Stanley Elkins, fell precipitously out of favor.

Elkins's concentration camp analogy did not disappear immediately or entirely from American intellectual and cultural thought, however. Indeed, one group of black intellectuals—black psychiatrists and psychologists—continued to embrace Elkins's comparison wholeheartedly and even unquestioningly through the late 1960s and 1970s.

These psychological professionals were comfortable with the idea that blacks might be psychologically unhealthy, with poor self-esteem and self-destructive tendencies resulting from extreme oppression under slavery. Psychiatrists William H. Grier and Price M. Cobbs, for example, built their famous analysis of "black rage" around the assumption that the tendency of slavery to infantilize black men, described by Stanley Elkins, had left a legacy of psychological "deformity" among modern black men: "Slavery required the creation of a particular kind of person, one compatible with a life of involuntary servitude. The ideal slave had to be absolutely dependent and have a deep consciousness of personal inferiority . . . he was instilled with a sense of the unlimited power of his master. Teachings so painstakingly applied do not disappear easily."[125]

Grier and Cobbs legitimized Elkins's concentration camp analogy, noting the "bizarre reactions" of Jews under the terrors of Nazi persecution and claiming that these Jews' tendency to identify with their aggressors was seen commonly "in its milder forms . . . in contemporary America" among black citizens.[126] One black psychoanalyst was even more enthusiastic about the concentration camp analogy than Grier and Cobbs. Charles Pinderhughes wrote that he "felt indebted" to Stanley Elkins for having humanized and personalized the experience of slavery for readers: "The vivid imagery associated with the incarceration and murder of millions of Jews superimposed upon the slave experience offered an illusion of a history brought to life for consideration as it might have been."[127] For black psychologists attempting to treat troubled black patients, Elkins's thesis of psychological damage under oppression struck a chord, and his use of concentration camp imagery made this damage dramatic, emotional, and understandable. Moreover, these black psychologists popularized Elkins's ideas for tens of thousands of ordinary American readers. *Black Rage* was a best-selling book that went into ten printings in two years, was offered by the Negro Book Club, and became part of the Library of Urban Affairs; its ideas were condensed, syndicated, and serialized for major newspapers by the United Features Syndicate.[128]

Far from disappearing entirely from the American intellectual scene, as the attacks on the Moynihan Report might suggest, Stanley Elkins's concentration camp analogy thus continued to linger on that scene throughout the 1970s, shaping and formulating the ways that many Americans perceived African American history and life. By the end of its last printing in 1976, *Slavery* had sold about 350,000 copies, a number far greater than the sales figures of most historical monographs, clearly indicating that it was being assigned, read, and debated not only among a small group of historians but among a much wider range of readers, students, and educators.[129]

On the whole, however, even as Stanley Elkins's influence lingered in American culture throughout the late 1960s and the 1970s, it was the controversy surrounding his concentration camp analogy that dominated both historians' and popular understandings of his work. In the wake of the political struggles over Moynihan's "The Negro Family," American historians in the late 1960s and early 1970s began to research and publish articles critiquing Elkins's work, particularly his extended analogy between concentration camps and plantations. The bulk of those historical criticisms echoed criticisms from civil rights leaders who had responded to Moynihan's report. Rather than understanding slaves as infantilized men who participated in their own oppression, as concentration camp inmates supposedly had, historians in the late 1960s and early 1970s developed a new paradigm for understanding African American slaves: they were now seen as resisters, whose very survival through the autonomous mechanisms of culture and family had kept them healthy, cohesive, and moral.

Nonetheless, these historians did not entirely abandon or forget Stanley Elkins's comparison between slave plantations and concentration camps. Indeed, the new paradigm of slave resistance was in part grounded on new images in the American mainstream illustrating Jewish resistance in the concentration camps; the use of these images was clearly a direct response to Elkins's ideas. In the black left-wing journal *Freedomways,* for example, librarian Ernest Kaiser argued that new works such as Yuri Suhl's *They Fought Back* and Jean-François Steiner's *Treblinka,* as well as John Hersey's 1950 novel *The Wall* and other historical works on the Warsaw ghetto uprising, "exploded" the "myth of Jewish dehumanization and submission in German concentration camps" that had been "ostensibly documented" by

Bruno Bettelheim's work. This literature, Kaiser claimed, showed that "Jews resisted even under such bestial circumstances."[130] Another historian substituted the newly circulating description of resistant Jews for a description of resistant slaves. John Blassingame claimed that the "most apt characterization of the [African American] slave's behavior" came from descriptions of German Jews under Nazi oppression in Jewish historian Lucy Dawidowicz's "magnificent book," *The War against the Jews:* "They learned not only to invent, but to circumvent; not only to obey, but to evade; not only to submit, but to outwit. Their tradition of defiance was devious rather than direct, employing nerve instead of force."[131] Thus, by the 1970s, some historians of African American slavery accepted and themselves employed a comparison between Nazi concentration camp inmates—who by this time were openly being referred to as Jews—and American slaves, so long as both were understood to have heroically resisted their oppression.

Other historians in the late 1960s and early 1970s rejected the validity of Elkins's analogy between concentration camps and slavery, but in doing so, they reified his comparison. John Blassingame, for example, continued to compare concentration camps and slave plantations, insisting by the end that the slave plantation was a "relatively benign" place compared with the "murderous institution" of the concentration camp.[132] Ernest Kaiser too concluded, after describing Jews' heroic resistance in the camps: "Slaves were under different, less bestial conditions, and their resistance was therefore much greater."[133] With its modern technological efficiency, its policies of brutality and terror, and its goal of Jewish extermination, southern historians who specialized in American slavery concluded that the Nazi concentration camp had far exceeded the capacity to dehumanize possessed by southern plantations. "Slavery," historian Kenneth Stampp concluded typically, "did not ordinarily have anything like as shattering an impact on personality as did the concentration camps."[134] Thus, Stanley Elkins's comparison between Nazi concentration camps and American slave plantations shaped the ways that American historians of slavery approached their work even in the late 1960s and 1970s, when the liberalism that had both shaped and embraced Elkins's comparison had come under attack.

Nonetheless, it was the debate associated with Elkins that many Americans learned about when they heard about his work during this era. Secondary-school and college history students, for example, were probably introduced to Elkins's ideas through a filter of skepticism and controversy. In a 1965 pamphlet written and produced by the American Historical Association to help high school history teachers and college professors teach about slavery, historian Louis B. Harlan described Stanley Elkins's approach to slavery but noted that, although Elkins's work seemed to be backed by "modern behavioral science," a "substantial body of historical evidence" did not support his analogy.[135] In 1979, the high school textbook *The American Experience: A Study of Themes and Issues in American History*, published a selection from the Moynihan report, a rebuttal from William Ryan, and then a detailed discussion of Stanley Elkins's concentration camp analogy as a possible historical explanation for the black experience of slavery and lasting black difficulties in the United States.[136] Stanley Elkins's ideas remained a significant part of American culture after the turn of the 1960s, but Americans generally no longer heralded Elkins's work enthusiastically or used *Slavery* unquestioningly, instead submitting his analogy to scrutiny, probing the controversy over his work, and beginning to consider new ways to think about the devastation of American slavery.

The controversy over Stanley Elkins's concentration camp analogy in the late 1960s and early 1970s may have been intensified by growing tensions between African Americans and Jews during this era, particularly after efforts to decentralize the New York City school system had pitted Jewish teachers against African American students and parents in an angry and ugly conflict in the Brownsville/Ocean Hills section of Brooklyn.[137] Scholars Michael Rogin and Emily Miller Budick have suggested that Elkins and his critics played important roles in the tense interactions between blacks and Jews during this era.[138] Although there is little evidence that Elkins's black readers perceived him as Jewish or addressed his ideas as Jewish, Budick's and Rogin's charges are plausible because Elkins's work was indeed marked by some of the arrogance that African Americans decried when they addressed Jewish perspectives on black life.

For example, in *Slavery*, Elkins had written that the infantilization that he described among camp inmates had been possible "for people in a full state of complex civilization, for men and women who were not black and not savages."[139] The ugly contrast between white "civilization" and black "savage[ry]" can be read as highly offensive.[140] Given the fact that Elkins moved from this statement immediately into a long description of the heroism and complexity of black culture in Africa, however, it is probable that his comment on black savagery was designed either to be ironic or to persuade readers who might believe that black Africans were savage, rather than intended as a legitimate description of his own beliefs about European and African society. Nonetheless, if read out of context, the statement is clearly disturbing. Although no black historians or scholars at the time commented specifically on this sentence, Emily Budick noted that Harold

Cruse had been angered by a similar comparison that characterized Nazi atrocities as worse than those of the Japanese because of the civilized nature of both Germans and Jews.[141]

Much more disturbing, Elkins's use of concentration camp data rather than records of African American slaves themselves, rendered these enslaved black men and women silent and inert, while allowing concentration camp inmates—many of them Jews—to speak for themselves in his text. Elkins's choice of evidence suggested that he, as an American Jew, was attempting to speak for African Americans, which is precisely the accusation that a number of African American activists made of Jewish activists during the late 1960s and 1970s.[142]

Although Elkins's assumptions about race here were certainly unconscious, rather than conscious, and although his portraits of inmates represented them as degraded and passive, not strong or active, the silence of African American voices in *Slavery* is notable and troublesome, particularly given the fact that Elkins did vocalize white southern plantation owners' descriptions of "Sambo." Elkins's use of subtextually Jewish concentration camp inmates to speak for silent African American slaves may certainly have added fuel to tensions between black and Jewish intellectuals in the late 1960s.

Ironically, however, Elkins's portraits of concentration camp inmates also attracted criticism from Jewish intellectuals and Holocaust scholars during the 1970s. In the early 1970s, Holocaust scholars began to criticize Stanley Elkins's portrait of Nazi concentration camps, noting that he had reproduced controversial images of passive camp inmates and ignored the growing literature on Jewish survival and resistance.[143] Perhaps the sharpest reflection of this criticism was visible in the controversy surrounding William Styron's novel, *Sophie's Choice* (1979). Styron, who in 1963 had publicly lavished praise on Stanley Elkins's *Slavery*, had been attracted to Elkins's vision of camp prisoners of all different ethnic backgrounds and had been influenced by Elkins as he made a non-Jewish Polish survivor of Auschwitz central to his novel.[144] Jewish intellectuals castigated the novel, protesting in particular its emphasis upon a non-Jewish Holocaust victim.[145] Although none of these intellectuals specifically pointed to Stanley Elkins's portraits of Nazi concentration camps as the origin of their discontent, their angry responses to *Sophie's Choice* suggested the ways that American Jews' understandings of Nazi destruction had changed by the 1970s. At the same time, however, *Sophie's Choice* became a best-selling book and an Academy Award-winning film that had substantial impact on Americans' understanding of the Holocaust between the 1970s and the 1990s; Stanley Elkins's concentration camp analogy thus continued to remain a significant component of American culture, even as the controversy surrounding his ideas become central to his legacy.

THE HARSH CRITICAL RECEPTION of Stanley Elkins's *Slavery,* and particularly the angry efforts to reject his concentration camp analogy in the late 1960s and early 1970s, illustrate important differences between this later era and the turn of the 1960s. Elkins's portrait of Nazi concentration camps as racially indistinct and dehumanizing had greatly attracted readers between 1959 and 1965. Readers had accepted this analogy during this era so enthusiastically and unquestioningly in part because intellectual frameworks that emphasized universalism, dehumanization, and bureaucracy in the Nazi destruction were so pervasive. By contrast, Elkins's critics in the late 1960s and early 1970s organized around racial definitions of oppression and victimization, and they were offended and infuriated by Elkins's portrait of universal, dehumanized slaves. Then, too, while African American activists and white leftists who protested the Moynihan report in 1965 illustrated the growing hostility that liberalism faced by the late 1960s, the fact that Elkins's comparison between Nazi camps and American slavery became part of Moynihan's efforts to support affirmative action programs in the first place reflected the substantial ways that Americans used Nazi imagery for liberal purposes at the turn of the 1960s. Men and women who rejected Stanley Elkins's portrait of Nazi concentration camps during the late 1960s and 1970s offer us important insight into the crucial differences between the turn of the 1960s and the later half of the decade.

The reception of Elkins's work in the late 1960s and 1970s also illustrates, however, that his ideas continued to wield influence during this era, even as his concentration camp analogy underwent substantial scrutiny and eventually became anathema to many in the historical profession. As liberalism came under attack from the left in the late 1960s and 1970s, American intellectuals and educators found themselves compelled to use Elkins's Nazi analogy even if they were rejecting it, because the comparison was so powerful and the imagery of Nazi camps remained highly relevant for readers. By the end of the 1970s, Stanley Elkins's ideas had encouraged many Americans to view the Nazi concentration camps not as distant sites of terror but instead as a practical symbol for understanding the contemporary United States.

Importantly, Stanley Elkins's use of Nazi camps was shaped by changing dynamics in American Jewish history. Elkins's history as a Jewish boy facing antisemitism in the 1930s, his experiences as a soldier during World War II, and his intellectual growth in the academy in the 1950s—made possible by diminishing antisemitism—all formed a crucial backdrop as he shaped his understanding of Nazi concentration camps and used those camps to help him analyze American slavery. Stanley Elkins's work provides a crucial window on early American Jewish responses to the Holocaust. Then, too, Elkins's work helps us to understand the many hidden and subtextual ways that American Jews have understood themselves as Jews, regardless of their degree of affiliation or religiosity, or even self-identification. The concentration camp analogy also reflects the terrible ambivalence of American Jews' position as both insiders and outsiders in the post-World War II era, as Stanley Elkins sensitively attempted to communicate the suffering of individuals under an oppressive regime while at the same time insensitively substituting voices of Jewish grief for those of black pain.

Finally, Stanley Elkins's work offers insight into the relationship between African Americans and Jews in the United States. Although Elkins's analogy may have contributed to tensions between these two groups in the late 1960s and early 1970s, it is worth noting that debates over Elkins then looked very different from battles between blacks and Jews today, in which partisans compete for the claim of greater suffering, whether of blacks under slavery or of Jews in the Holocaust. Far from demanding that the trauma of slavery be recognized as ten times *worse* than the Holocaust, African Americans in the late 1960s and 1970s resented Elkins's portrait of their degradation in slavery, insisting that the Holocaust demonstrated that blacks had experienced *less intense* suffering and thus had been better able to survive through the existence of their family, culture, and community. Understanding that the current competition over the degree and nature of black and Jewish suffering is not natural or inherent, but that it has been constructed differently by different intellectuals at different times, should help to defamiliarize the subject and encourage more scholars to look more closely at the nature of Jewish and African American public debates.

CHAPTER 2

The "Comfortable Concentration Camp"

The Significance of Nazi Imagery in Betty Friedan's
Feminine Mystique

IN ONE OF THE MOST SHOCKING PASSAGES of her 1963 feminist classic, *The Feminine Mystique*, Betty Friedan claimed that "the women who 'adjust' as housewives, who grow up wanting to be 'just a housewife,' are in as much danger as the millions who walked to their own death in the concentration camps."[1] Friedan went on to explore this analogy for several pages and then, later on in *The Feminine Mystique*, used the phrase "comfortable concentration camps" to refer to suburban homes.[2] The writer also highlighted this expression in excerpts of her book in magazines and newspapers, and in the speeches and interviews publicizing her work throughout 1963.[3] Contemporary readers and reviewers used Friedan's camp imagery either to refute or applaud her work, and the "comfortable concentration camp" was initially one of the more famous phrases repeated from Friedan's best-selling book, along with the "feminine mystique" and "the problem with no name."

Scholars have since castigated Friedan for her inaccuracy and insensitivity in developing the concept of the "comfortable concentration camp." Feminist scholar bell hooks, for example, has charged Friedan with "narcissism, insensitivity, sentimentality, and self-indulgence."[4] Historian Daniel Horowitz called Friedan's comparison "problematic," "trivializing," "careless and exaggerated."[5] And Friedan herself has backed away from her comparison, saying in her recent memoir, "I am ashamed of that analogy . . . The American suburb was no concentration camp."[6] Indeed, in a 2001 interview, Friedan refused to discuss her camp analogy in any detail, repeating several times that she had made an error in judgment.[7]

There is no question, to be sure, that Betty Friedan's analogy was an exaggerated and flawed one, as she herself now recognizes. The Nazi regime publicly confined, starved, and tortured its victims in camps, and selected Jewish victims for mass extermination. This psychological and physical destruction was obviously wholly different from, and much more extreme than, the psychological devastation that was wreaked by suburban homes, which privately confined and socially marginalized middle-class women. Even when taking into account the physical violence that Betty Friedan faced at the hands of her husband in her own home, as well as that experienced by hundreds of thousands of other women, the comparison between suburban homes and concentration camps does not appear to most modern readers to be convincing.[8]

Nonetheless, it is intellectually unsatisfying to dismiss this powerful analogy merely as inaccurate or sensational or to accept Friedan's disavowal of the comparison without probing further. Friedan's analogy offers historians an important window on the impact of the Holocaust on American Jewish thinkers, as well as its impact on the larger American culture. By comparing Nazi concentration camps to American suburban homes in 1963, Friedan demonstrated not only that American Jewish intellectuals were conscious of the devastation of the Holocaust earlier than most historians have recognized but that these intellectuals were also vocal about the Holocaust, using it to shape American public opinion in ways that most historians have thus far overlooked. To be sure, when she wrote her groundbreaking book, Friedan considered herself an "agnostic" Jew, unaffiliated with any religious branch or institution.[9] Her status, however, as an unaffiliated Jew makes her use of the concentration camps only more valuable for study; Friedan's peculiar analogy in *The Feminine Mystique* also allows historians to explore the nature of secular Jewish identity in the United States, and the ways that the Nazi destruction of European Jewry shaped that identity in the years before "the Holocaust" became a fixed narrative with a specific meaning in both American and Jewish life.

To UNDERSTAND THE ORIGINS and significance of Friedan's concentration camp analogy, it is first important to understand it in more detail, as well as its context within the larger book. Betty Friedan's central argument in *The Feminine Mystique* was that, since World War II, American cultural outlets—women's magazines, colleges, and the advertising industry—had exalted the "feminine mystique," a glorified image of women as mothers and housewives in the home. This mystique, she argued, silently stifled women's growth and denied women's humanity by limiting them to their suburban homes and to a life of domesticity. Only by resisting the mystique and breaking out of their lives of domesticity by finding productive work could American women grow as human beings.

In one of her final chapters, titled "Progressive Dehumanization: The Comfortable Concentration Camp," Friedan brought to a horrifying conclusion her argument that domesticity denied women's humanity: she developed a five-page analogy between suburban homes and Nazi concentration camps. To do so, she relied exclusively on Bruno Bettelheim's 1960 book, *The Informed Heart.* As suggested in the introduction and chapter 1, Bettelheim emphasized the psychological dehumanization of inmates in concentration camps, arguing that even more important than the Nazis' physical violence was their psychological violence. Bettelheim claimed that one of the SS's major goals in the concentration camps was to "break the prisoners as individuals, and to change them into a docile mass from which no . . . act of resistance could arise."[10] To this end, the SS purposely "destroy[ed] all personal autonomy" by forcing inmates to become obedient children, who performed useless labor and needed permission even to use the toilet.[11] As their personalities disintegrated, Bettelheim argued, prisoners actually did regress to childhood, lying, boasting, and even becoming inordinately interested in defecation and urination.[12] In the "final adjustment" to the camps, he said, these childlike inmates began to "identify with the enemy," to adopt the values of the SS themselves by terrorizing new prisoners and enforcing SS rules.[13] "[T]he ultimate realization" of SS goals, Bettelheim suggested, was the extermination camp, where prisoners, deprived of all human dignity, chose to commit "suicide" by "[w]alking to the gas chamber."[14]

Betty Friedan liberally borrowed Bettelheim's language and analysis to argue that suburban housewives, like concentration camp prisoners, were dehumanized by their pointless work. Just like Bettelheim's camp inmates, Friedan claimed, suburban women "have become dependent, passive, childlike; they have given up their adult frame of reference to live at the lower human level of food and things. The work they do does not require adult capabilities; it is endless, monotonous, unrewarding."[15] Suburban women, moreover, just like concentration camp inmates, aided in the destruction of their own humanity. By adjusting to the life of a housewife, as Freudian psychologists encouraged, "a woman stunts her intelligence to become childlike, turns away from individual identity to become an anonymous biological robot in a docile mass."[16] In the final stages of docility, Friedan argued, a dependent woman became parasitic, "preyed upon by outside pressures, and herself preying upon husband and children."[17] Just as dehumanized concentration camp inmates internalized the SS guards' values and began to attack other prisoners, American women internalized their inferiority, and they turned their aggression against their loved ones, and against themselves.[18]

IT IS PERHAPS SURPRISING for the current reader to realize that Betty Friedan's striking analogy between women and concentration camp inmates did not refer at all to Jews. Friedan never actually mentioned the destruction of European Jewry in *The Feminine Mystique*. Although Friedan at times conflated "gas chambers" with "concentration camps," referred to prisoners who were "exterminated," and at one point called the destruction of women "genocide," she never mentioned Jews in her discussion of any of these four concepts.[19] Moreover, Friedan did not openly identify herself as Jewish anywhere in her book. *The Feminine Mystique* included only a few passing references to Jews throughout its 365 pages, and none suggested the author's background.[20] Indeed, Friedan had considered herself an unaffiliated, "agnostic" Jew for years when she published *The Feminine Mystique*, and she did not openly address her Jewish background in her activism and writing until the 1970s.[21]

Given all this, is it accurate, fair, or appropriate to consider Friedan's book an American Jewish intellectual's response to the Holocaust? There were certainly other Jewish intellectuals more identified with the Jewish community who addressed the camps through a Jewish lens during the early 1960s.[22] Moreover, shouldn't Friedan's silence about her Jewish background in this book be respected as a signal that she did not consider *The Feminine Mystique* shaped by her ethnic identity?

To be sure, to argue that ethnic identity was the determinative factor in *The Feminine Mystique*'s concentration camp analogy would be overly simplistic and reductive. Many other factors in Friedan's life and work obviously led to her development of the concentration camp analogy, and certainly to *The Feminine Mystique*. But it would also be reductive to assume, simply because Friedan did not openly engage the concepts of Holocaust or Jewish identity in the ways we are most accustomed to seeing those concepts expressed, that Friedan's position as a Jew coming of age during the era of the Holocaust had nothing to do with her peculiar analogy. Friedan's personal experiences and intellectual influences suggest that her background as a Jew during an era marked by the rise of Nazism in Germany played a role in the development of her portrayal of the suburban home as a "comfortable concentration camp." Understanding how Friedan's Jewish roots contributed to her analogy can help us to understand how nonpracticing, nonaffiliated Jewish thinkers conceptualized their Jewish identity in the United States in the 1950s and 1960s, and how the destruction of European Jews affected that Jewish identity.

FRIEDAN HAS TESTIFIED in a recent interview that being a Jew made her particularly sensitive to the subject of Nazi concentration camps.[23] But it was not only the specter of Nazi concentration camps that symbolized Jewish exclusion for Friedan; it was also her own American experience as a Jew in the middle of the country during an era of discrimination. In interviews, speeches, and memoirs, Betty Friedan has emphasized her personal experiences with antisemitism growing up as a Jewish girl in the Midwest in the 1920s and 1930s. Born in Peoria, Illinois, in 1921 as Bettye Naomi Goldstein, Friedan was the eldest child of Harry Goldstein, a Russian Jewish immigrant who owned a successful jewelry store, and Miriam Horwitz Goldstein, a second-generation American Jew whose father had been a doctor and a substantial member of the Peoria Jewish community.[24]

Peoria's Jewish population was small, and the Goldsteins faced significant social discrimination. Harry Goldstein told his daughter that Christian business associates avoided speaking to him or seeing him socially once the workday had finished. With the rise of institutionalized antisemitism in United States in the 1920s, moreover, the Peoria Country Club restricted Jews from joining, and the high school sorority that dominated the adolescent social scene in Peoria rejected Friedan's bid to join.[25]

Miriam Goldstein heightened her daughter's anxiety over the antisemitism the family faced in Peoria. As a second-generation Jew from a socially prominent family, Goldstein saw herself as a local leader in style and fashion. She was ashamed of her husband's accent and immigrant status and dissatisfied by her daughter's looks, in part because she believed Friedan had inherited Harry's prominent, "Jewish" nose. She urged her daughter, unsuccessfully, to get a nose job and insisted that Friedan's rejection from the sorority was not related to her Jewishness, thus intensifying her daughter's feelings of exclusion.[26]

Growing public manifestations of antisemitism in the United States, bolstered by those in Nazi Germany, where anti-Jewish legislation, boycotts, and violence spiraled after 1933, must have strengthened Friedan's feelings of isolation. Political discussions at the Goldstein dinner table emphasized Hitler's persecution of the Jews. "You knew you had to take care of fellow Jews; no one else wanted them. When Hitler was rampant, there were strong discussions," her brother Harry Junior has remembered.[27]

While Friedan was a freshman student at Smith College in 1938, the college president William Allen Neilson urged students to sign a petition calling for the federal government to relax its immigration quotas so that Smith could open its doors to persecuted college-age Jewish girls; Friedan has remembered that, during the debates in her dormitory, most students argued against the petition.[28] National and international images of Jews increasingly isolated and under attack throughout the 1930s thus formed a crucial backdrop to Bettye Goldstein's personal experiences of isolation and exclusion.

While in college, Friedan developed a political and psychological language to help her to interpret the isolation she felt as a Jew. Friedan was a talented psychology student whose professors, including the renowned Gestalt psychologist Kurt Koffka, encouraged her to work with Kurt Lewin at the University of Iowa during the summer of 1940. Lewin, who began his work as a member of the Gestalt school in Germany, is famous for his work on group dynamics, which pushed psychologists to consider the group environments in which individuals' psyches formed and operated.

Lewin was a Jewish refugee from Nazi Germany, and his work was shaped by his anger at Nazism, his fear for—and efforts to rescue—friends and family still left in Europe, and his support for a Jewish state in Palestine.[29] In the late 1930s and early 1940s, the period when Friedan went to work with him, Lewin devoted a series of papers to understanding Jewish group dynamics, Jewish education, and what he called "Jewish self-hatred."

Lewin's theory of group dynamics emphasized that individuals needed to feel secure in their group memberships. Jews in particular, he believed, had difficulty establishing this security, since the group itself had no stable meaning: it was unclear whether Jews were members of a race, followers of a religion, or members of a nation. Moreover, Jews were scattered throughout the Diaspora and, being a minority group everywhere, they received mixed messages of acceptance from dominant nationalities. While some Jews at times were treated virtually the same as members of the dominant group, Lewin argued, this position was unstable; Christians could and would, when it was convenient for them, use Jews as "scapegoats" for their own troubles.[30]

This dependence on the dominant group, and confusion within the minority group, led many Jews to become insecure and to wish to enter the dominant group. These Jews became "marginal men" who "sought to move as far away from the center of Jewish life as the outside majority permits."[31] "Marginal men," Lewin continued, became frustrated because they could not actually enter the dominant group. That frustration, he theorized, led to a "generalized tendency to aggression" that could not be directed against the powerful majority and was thus instead "turned against one's own group or against one's self."[32] Thus self-hating Jews urged their children not to act or look Jewish and sought to silence any conversation on antisemitism, for fear of insulting Christians.

Lewin's ideas seem to have affected Betty Friedan quite deeply: in one interview, she testified that his work had a big influence on her.[33] In an autobiographical paper written in college, she wrote that during the summer at Iowa, she had "learned about life."[34] In an interview much later in life, Friedan stated that her work with Lewin had helped her begin to understand "the dynamics of the anti-Semitic Jew."[35] In the same interview, she claimed that working with Lewin had made her "very strong about Jewish identity."[36] And Friedan told several interviewers that she began to understand herself and her mother as antisemitic Jews because of Lewin's ideas.[37]

Indeed, soon after her summer working with Lewin, Friedan began to analyze antisemitism among Jews in her written work, using her experiences in Peoria and at Smith as models. In 1941, she wrote a short story about antisemitism among Jews titled "The Scapegoat," based on her experiences at Smith. The story describes a group of college girls—including two assimilated Jewish girls—who isolate and ultimately destroy another Jewish girl. Told from the perspective of one of the assimilated Jewish girls, the story ends with the girl's chilling fear that she herself could become the "scapegoat."[38] Clearly, Lewin's description of Jewish antisemitism became an important theme in Friedan's thought during her college years.

After college, Lewin's ideas about Jewish self-hatred still shaped Friedan's work. After graduation from Smith, for example, she gave a talk at her hometown synagogue on Jewish antisemitism and on Nazism titled "On Affirming One's Jewishness."[39] Short stories that she wrote after college continued to incorporate the theme of Jews who rejected their own Jewish backgrounds or who attacked other Jews who seemed "too Jewish."[40] In "A Good Woman Driver," for example, narrator Ruthie describes her mother Blanche as a perfectionist who hated it when someone talked too loudly or served chopped liver, and who blamed their exclusion from the country club on "Daddy's accent and 'Jewish' ways."[41] Friedan seems to have clearly drawn on Kurt Lewin's ideas as she grappled with her family and community as a young adult.

Later interviews, speeches, and autobiographical writings in the 1970s and 1980s similarly suggest that, even much later in life, Friedan continued to interpret her own history as a Jew through Lewin's concept of self-hatred. In one speech, Friedan described Peoria as a place "where you were very marginal as a Jew" and where people "changed their names and did something to their noses." In a 1988 interview, she said she had grown up in "an assimilated, almost anti-Jewish community."[42] In a number of interviews and writings, Friedan continually contrasted her own decision to sign President Neilson's petition for allowing European Jewish girls into Smith with the stark silence of four wealthy Jewish girls in her house who never signed the petition: "They were the type that spoke in whispery voices and became utterly anemic because they did not want to be known as Jews."[43] And in her 2000 memoir, *Life So Far*, Friedan explained that her story "The Scapegoat" was based on her own willingness to watch her housemates at Smith ridicule and exclude another Jewish girl in her class. Writing the story, Friedan believed, had exposed her own self-hatred, while it also "freed [her] . . . from being an anti-Semitic Jew."[44] Lewin clearly offered Friedan a powerful and lasting method of interpreting Jewish antisemitism as a significant component of her own life.

Lewin did not simply offer Friedan a way of understanding antisemitism, however. He offered her a set of ideas about oppression, which she eventually used to understand sexism as well as antisemitism. One of the most striking examples of Lewin's impact is found in this raw passage from a rough draft of *The Feminine Mystique:*

> Mothers, women are such a safe scapegoat, in America. . . . Does anyone know who makes a good scapegoat, when? The Jews made a good scapegoat in Germany because there weren't very many, and they were "different," and enough were rich and brilliant to blame them for your troubles. You could pretend you were solving everything by burning them in furnaces, and getting rid of all that helpless anger, and feel important again. And life could go on anyhow, because there weren't that many Jews, after all.
>
> Mothers made better scapegoats in America . . . [b]ut Americans wouldn't do anything as mean as furnaces. What did it hurt to write those nasty words about the women?[45]

Friedan's reference to Jews isolated because they were "different," "rich," and "brilliant" echoes precisely her descriptions of her own marginalization in Peoria, while her deliberately childlike language suggests her own pain and anger as a Jewish girl. Most significantly, this passage demonstrates how Friedan used one of Kurt Lewin's key concepts, "scapegoat," to link the oppression of Jews and women.

Although this particularly brutal passage was left out of *The Feminine Mystique,* the book still offered clear evidence that Friedan made other links between the oppression of Jews and women, using the ideas of Kurt Lewin. Friedan's understanding of Jewish self-hatred echoed strongly throughout her description of women's self-destruction in chapter 12, "Progressive Dehumanization." Throughout this chapter, particularly in the pages explaining the concentration camp analogy, Friedan described women who had internalized the passivity and dependence expected of them by the feminine mystique. This passivity and dependence paradoxically made them bossy and domineering; they attacked those to whom they were closest, "devour[ing]," beating, or "liv[ing] vicariously" through their children because, as women, they had no personal identities of their own: "The aggressive energy she should be using in the world becomes instead the terrible anger that she dare not turn against her husband, is ashamed of turning against her children, and finally turns against herself until it is as if she does not exist."[46]

This description was similar to Lewin's analysis of the frustrated "marginal" Jew, who internalized the negative attitudes toward Jews in the dominant society and then "turned against [his] own group or against [him]self" because he could not improve his status in society, nor could he fight the dominant group.[47] The similarity between the domineering mother and the self-hating Jew is even more apparent when it becomes clear that Friedan's model for both categories was the same person: her mother, Miriam Goldstein. In Friedan's descriptions, Miriam's frustration with her second-class status in Peoria because of her Jewish background closely resembled her frustration at being forced to quit her job at the Peoria newspaper as the womens' page editor when she married Harry Goldstein.[48] Powerless to improve her status, Miriam instead responded with disdain for her husband's accent and immigrant background, as well as "impotent rage" at his business abilities as his store faced economic trouble in the Depression.[49] The image of Miriam Goldstein encompassed both the self-hating Jew and the domineering mother, suggesting that Friedan used Lewin's concept of the self-hating Jew to analyze the internalized sexism of women.[50]

In a 1988 interview, Friedan acknowledged the connections between Lewin's ideas and *The Feminine Mystique*, agreeing with a reporter who wondered whether her understanding of internalized antisemitism had helped her to understand internalized sexism: "Yes. I think that in a certain sense, my experience as a Jew informed, though unconsciously, a lot of the insights that I applied to women, and the passion that I applied to the situation of women," she replied.[51] Although it may not have been conscious, Friedan's understanding of self-hating Jews, sparked by Kurt Lewin's work, helped her to analyze both herself and her mother, and to make significant links in *The Feminine Mystique* between the oppression of Jews and that of women.

BETTY FRIEDAN'S CONCENTRATION CAMP ANALOGY, however, reflected more than her Jewish roots and her work with Kurt Lewin. Her analogy also reflected her personal experiences and political ideology in the 1950s and 1960s, and the ways that the prevalent discourse about Nazi machinery during that era intersected with those experiences and ideals. Most significant for Friedan in this discourse was the work of the refugee Bruno Bettelheim. The feminist writer read Bettelheim's *Informed Heart* after it was published in 1960 and took copious notes on it. Friedan's unpublished comments on Bettelheim, as well as the published version of chapter 12 in her own book, suggest that reading the Jewish writer's description of his experiences in the Nazi concentration camps resonated sharply not only with Betty Friedan's understanding of Jewishness but also with her personal experiences as a housewife, with her intellectual attraction to existential humanistic psychology, and with her political liberalism.

Unlike in his famous 1943 article on the concentration camps, in the last chapter of *The Informed Heart*, Bettelheim specifically addressed the extermination of Jews in Nazi camps, and he did so, moreover, in a way that resonated with Betty Friedan's understandings of internalized antisemitism. Comparing the enforced passivity of concentration camp victims with the earlier inertia of Jews who had wanted to "go on with business as usual" and who had been unwilling to abandon their possessions to escape to freedom, Bettelheim claimed that "millions of the Jews of Europe . . . could at least have marched as free men against the SS, rather than to first grovel, then wait to be rounded up for their own extermination, and finally walk themselves to the gas chambers."[52] The Austrian refugee's descriptions of submissive, self-destructive Jews in the camps particularly touched Friedan. Several of her unpublished notes on *The Informed Heart* focused on the descriptions of passive Jews walking to their deaths, and an early rough draft of *The Feminine Mystique* quoted one of Bettelheim's descriptions of apathetic bourgeois Jews who could not abandon their possessions and thus went to the gas chambers.[53] Bruno Bettelheim's argument that passive, self-destructive Jews had allowed themselves to be murdered reverberated with Friedan's prior understandings of Jewish self-hatred and internalized antisemitism. Although Friedan deleted all the actual references to Jews in her discussions of concentration camps in *The Feminine Mystique*, her use of the words "genocide," "extermination," and "gas chambers" were not simple mistakes or displays of ignorance; they were clearly influenced by her reading of Bruno Bettelheim and his specific discussion of Jewish mass murder.

Bruno Bettelheim affected Friedan not only because his work resonated with her own understandings of Jewishness, however. *The Informed Heart* also spoke to Betty Friedan's personal experiences as a housewife. Bettelheim's descriptions of concentration camps replicated, in Friedan's mind, the sensation of entrapment and powerlessness that she had experienced as a housewife in the suburbs.

Daniel Horowitz has recently argued that Betty Friedan worked throughout almost all of her life and yet portrayed herself in *The Feminine Mystique* as a woman who "married, had children, lived according to the feminine mystique as a suburban housewife" in order to mask her radical past.[54] Tracing Friedan's history at Smith College as a campus radical on the student newspaper between 1938 and 1942, her brief time as a graduate student in psychology at the University of California, Berkeley in 1942 to 1943; her experiences as a reporter for the left-wing news service Federated Press and the radical union newspaper *UE News* between 1943 and 1952, and then her work as a freelance reporter and community activist in the suburbs of Queens and Rockland County, New York, between 1953 and 1963, Horowitz has convincingly demonstrated that Friedan's past was more radical and her extensive work experience more significant to the construction of *The Feminine Mystique* than the feminist herself has acknowledged.[55]

Nonetheless, Horowitz's argument does not negate Friedan's genuine feelings of entrapment in domesticity. The historian acknowledges that Friedan did feel imprisoned as a housewife for a brief period of time.[56] The feminist writer's notes on Bruno Bettelheim expressed painfully the degree to which Friedan's experience of housewifery—no matter how brief or transitory it was—made her feel confined and desperate. As she took notes on *The Informed Heart,* she juxtaposed those notes with her own commentary on her life as a housewife, creating a notebook with alternating pages describing first suburban, then camp life. For example, one page of notes reads, "In the early 1950s, when the pregnancy of my second child plus other chaotic changes—forced me to define myself as [a housewife], as a great many educated women did . . . I suffered, for a time, the reactions of terror—no future—feelings I had no personality, that I have heard described by so many other women," while the opposing page, with page references to *The Informed Heart,* reads, "No 'spark' in senseless tasks. (These degrading) Psychological fatigue because No 'anticipation of advancement' . . . no planning of time—no end—might fill thinking?"[57] Similarly, in a different series of unpublished notes, Friedan used Bettelheim's concepts, such as the dangers of adjustment and the inital shock of imprisonment, to describe how difficult it was for women like herself, who had been "educated to be people," to "adjust to that definition of themselves as housewives and live within that narrow world of home and children." This adjustment, she argued, was a "drastic break" with their former human identity, and thus it was, "in more ways than one, like entering the concentration camp."[58] Bettelheim's accounts of the camps offered Friedan what she believed were extreme, but parallel, descriptions of her own suffering as a suburban woman.

In her recent autobiography, Friedan wrote that she is now "ashamed" of her comparison because "it denied [her] personal truth": the many happy hours she had spent with her children when she was a suburban housewife, which she then described in her autobiography in some detail. This happy domesticity was understandably an important aspect of Betty Friedan's life as a suburban housewife and mother. But her sensation of entrapment, as noted in her contemporary descriptions, was surely a significant part of her life as well. Given the harsh criticism Friedan received for her analogy, as well as her natural desire to reassure her children of her love, it made sense for her to insist retrospectively that calling her suburban home a "comfortable concentration camp" was a mistake that "denied [her] personal truth" as a mother.[59] But that should not distract us from understanding how and why Bruno Bettelheim's descriptions of concentration camps initially attracted her.

In addition to offering a portrait of concentration camp life that resonated with Friedan's sensation of confinement in suburbia, Bettelheim's descriptions of his efforts to resist victimization in the camps provided Friedan with the sustaining hope that she too could escape her status as a victim. The destructiveness of the camps, Bettelheim explained, had motivated him to observe his fellow prisoners; in order to "protect [himself] from a disintegration of personality," he explained, he had maintained his former interests—psychological observation and analysis—and thus had maintained his self-respect and his humanity.[60]

Unsurprisingly, given Betty Friedan's personal interest in psychology and desire to escape the confinement of her role as a suburban woman, Bettelheim's account of using psychological observation in order to withstand the disintegration of his personality deeply impressed Friedan. The feminist consistently compared her own labors interviewing housewives to Bettelheim's effort to interview fellow inmates. In an early postscript to *The Feminine Mystique* that was never published, for example, Friedan reported that she had finally realized that it was not "detached scientific curiosity nor even writer's nose for a story" that made her want to "study the other prisoners" but instead her need to find her own identity, to become herself and thus escape the "trap" of defining herself as a housewife. In this passage, she echoed Bruno Bettelheim, who had claimed in *The Informed Heart* that it was not "detached curiosity, but vital self interest" that led him to "study [his] fellow prisoners" and thereby survive the camps by preserving his own self-respect.[61] In a different unpublished note, Friedan wrote that she hoped her book would bring "strong relief" to its readers, despite its "depressing content," because she, like Bettelheim, had used an "intellectual defense through understanding" to assure herself and others that they were not helpless in an "oppressive mass society." Bettelheim had used almost identical language in *The Informed Heart* to describe his own readers' "strange relief" at his "intellectual defense through understanding."[62] Friedan clearly saw in Bruno Bettelheim a model of how a victimized person might rely on an "autonomous core of personality," with certain values and intellectual interests, to preserve herself from dehumanization, and even to continue growing, in extreme circumstances.[63]

A contemporary reader might legitimately argue that Betty Friedan was indeed narcissistic and self-absorbed in her willingness to connect her own sense of purposelessness with the terror, starvation, and violence of the concentration camp. But it is important to note that Friedan's decision to link the camps to her own contemporary suburban life was guided by Bruno Bettelheim himself, who, in *The Informed Heart,* used his experience in the concentration camps to comment on the dangers of technology, consumption, dehumanization, conformity, and the loss of autonomy in contemporary American society. "My interest," he noted several times as he discussed the concentration camps and the mass state that was Hitler's Germany, "is not in the importance of this process within a now defunct system, but that similar tendencies are present in any mass society and can be detected to some degree in our own time."[64] Bettelheim compared the technocratic immorality of Nazi physicians in death camps to the modern American glorification of technology and expertise: "Auschwitz is gone," he warned, but "pride in professional skill and knowledge, irrespective of moral implications," still threatened "modern society oriented toward technological competence."[65] And the Viennese refugee further suggested that the American culture of consumption, its devotion to material possessions, might blind Americans to the dangers of mass society and prevent them from protecting their autonomy in the face of encroaching technological and state control, just as "victims of the Nazi state" had "perished under the weight of their earthly possessions."[66]

Bettelheim's criticisms of American mass society, its culture of consumption, its worship of technology and professionalism, and the loss of autonomy in the contemporary age all took their cue from the prevailing discourse in sociological discussions at the turn of the 1960s and, in fact, interwove the image of the Nazi concentration camp with this discourse. In the changing postindustrial economy of the 1950s, a rash of popular sociological books such as David Riesman's *Lonely Crowd* and William Whyte's *Organization Man* had made common the proposition that modern mass society turned white middle-class men into "other-directed" conformists, unable to think for themselves, passively allowing big corporations and government to dominate their lives.[67] Fears of men losing their autonomy and becoming weak, apathetic, and submissive to tyranny dominated discussion among educated middle-class Americans at the turn of the 1960s, and Bruno Bettelheim's work not only borrowed that language but used his experience with the Nazi regime as an example of the crushing impact of mass society on male autonomy and strength. His descriptions of the camps focused almost entirely on men, and they emphasized that a crucial element in the dehumanization of concentration camp inmates was their "emasculation"—their regression to childishness and passivity and the loss of their position as breadwinners and patriarchs in their families.[68]

Bettelheim's connections between male autonomy and life in the concentration camps influenced Friedan and indeed allowed her to turn this prevalent sociological and psychological discourse on its head, pointing out that what men defined as their own victimization they also, in fact, defined as femininity. All the personality traits that male intellectuals such as Riesman, Whyte, and Bettelheim feared developing in men, including the passivity, childishness, weakness, and dependence found in concentration camp inmates, had been used for years to describe women, she pointed out. The specter of "the apathetic, dependent, infantile, purposeless being, who seems so shockingly subhuman," so appalling when applied to men, Friedan noted angrily, "is strangely reminiscent of the familiar 'feminine' personality."[69] If Hitler's camps had tried to destroy European Jews and others by robbing them of their humanity—defined by Bettelheim as their autonomy as workers, their active roles as protectors and breadwinners for their families—then American women who were denied this autonomy and these active roles were similarly being victimized as "less than human," she argued.[70] To an extent that few scholars have recognized, Betty Friedan's concentration camp analogy permitted her to subvert the masculine discourse of liberal sociologists and psychologists for her own purposes: to demonstrate the ways that intellectuals had oppressed women by relegating them to a nonhuman status.[71]

Friedan's description of American suburban homes as "comfortable concentration camps" also offered a subtle, yet powerful, dissent from the Cold War liberalism that had glorified women's domesticity as a means of protecting the United States from the totalitarianism of the Soviet Union. Unlike the Truman and Eisenhower administrations' portraits of suburban homes replete with well-stocked air-raid shelters in the face of a communist atomic attack, Betty Friedan offered an image of the suburban home as a site of totalitarian mass destruction itself.[72] Ridiculing Democratic candidate Adlai Stevenson's claim that a woman's political work as a housewife was to "inspire in her home a vision of the meaning of life and freedom," Friedan suggested that housewives were instead akin to Nazi concentration camp inmates who had been denied their own freedom by being confined to their homes.[73] Friedan thus attacked the pieties of Cold War liberalism by comparing American society to Nazi concentration camps, rather than assuming that American democracy prevented the totalitarian tyranny that both Nazi Germany and the Soviet Union represented.

As Betty Friedan questioned the prevalent discourse of liberal intellectuals in the United States from a perspective more radical than that of many thinkers at the time, one that criticized the ways that male intellectuals had equated "dehumanization" with femininity and that attacked Cold War assumptions about domesticity, she still, however, borrowed many essentially liberal values and beliefs about American society. Although Friedan had been radicalized in college, had engaged in leftist political activity in the late 1930s and early 1940s, and had written for the radical press in the 1940s and early 1950s, by the middle of the 1950s, the feminist writer had backed away from her radicalism, becoming more interested in psychological than in economic interpretations of the world. Perhaps scared by McCarthyite witch hunts around her, and galvanized by her psychotherapy with a sympathetic Freudian analyst in the 1950s, Friedan came to believe that her years as a reporter for the leftist press had diverted her from expressing her true abilities and her authentic self. She began to regret that she had not instead continued in psychology, and she adopted an outlook on the world that was more liberal, focused on the psychological language of the "self" that was popular at the time rather than on economic analyses of inequality.[74] She became particularly attracted to the newly popular existentialist and humanist perspectives of psychologists such as Abraham Maslow, which called for each person to "self-actualize," or fulfill his or her fullest potential, in order to pursue a better world.[75]

The Feminine Mystique reflected this liberal psychological emphasis, as Friedan adopted many postwar liberal thinkers' assumptions that the nation had already solved its significant economic and political problems and that it was now the psychological health and well-being of Americans that needed to be addressed. Friedan's emphasis on middle-class, educated suburban women who were presumably white reproduced the assumption of many liberal intellectuals in the 1950s that the nation was comfortably middle-class, as well as reflecting their lack of interest in or awareness of poor, working-class, and minority populations.[76] And Friedan's solution to the problems of women, her "new life plan for women," did not involve any organized protest or any significant restructuring of the American political or economic system, but instead called for New Deal–like assistance from the state: "a national education program, similar to the GI bill," for women to continue their education and break through the feminine mystique.[77] Friedan's ideology thus was more radical than that of many male liberal intellectuals of the day, but she still employed many liberal assumptions and maintained many liberal goals, which infused the tone of her work.

Betty Friedan's description of suburban homes as "comfortable concentration camps" thus reflected her Jewish background, her personal experiences, her intellectual preoccupations, and her liberal political ideology. The analogy also reflected the tension between her understanding of herself as a persecuted outsider and her hopes of becoming an intellectual insider. By using the psychological language of the self and a liberal discourse that assumed a white middle-class America, Betty Friedan constructed an audience that was white, middle-class, and elite, suggesting her own belonging in that elite. Her decision not to refer at all to her own Jewishness in the text of the book furthered her self-presentation as a member of the white middle class, an insider in the American mainstream. And her descriptions of Nazi concentration camps, gas chambers, and genocide absent any discussion of Jews suggested that Friedan hoped that her readers would not interpret her work to be the special pleading of a Jewish woman but would instead see it as a powerful insider's demand for female humanity, a demand that would resonate with men and women who wielded power in America.

At the same time, Friedan's description of the "comfortable concentration camp" gave voice to her own perception of herself as a damaged outsider who had faced victimization as both a woman and a Jew. Her analogy suggested her sensitivity as a Jew to the horrors of the concentration camps while also reproducing her understanding of the antisemitism and self-hatred that she had experienced throughout her early life. Like Stanley Elkins, Betty Friedan developed an analogy that was shaped by her own understanding of herself as a victim of antisemitism but that was also dominated by her desire to present herself as part of a white, middle-class intellectual elite. That shaky balance between seeing herself as a comfortable intellectual insider and a humiliated outsider was typified in Friedan's description of her angry response to her editor at W. W. Norton, George Brockway, over lunch in 1964, when he tried to sign her second book after *The Feminine Mystique* had become a surprise success: "George, I'm going to another publisher [to publish my next book]. You make me feel Jewish for wanting to sell books."[78] Confident enough to recognize the value of her writing in the publishing world, Friedan nonetheless still saw herself as a Jew who faced stereotypes, public censure, and humiliation.

FRIEDAN'S CONCENTRATION CAMP ANALOGY reflected her ambivalent image of herself as a Jew and an intellectual, and it also had substantial impact on her audience. Readers' reactions to Betty Friedan's "comfortable concentration camp" illustrate the significance of Holocaust imagery in liberal political discourse at the turn of the 1960s. These reactions also demonstrate how Americans' understanding of the Holocaust has changed over time.

Published in February 1963, *The Feminine Mystique* became a best seller within a few months. Excerpted in newspapers and magazines throughout the country, selected as a book of the month by the Book Find Club, and promoted through a nationwide publicity tour unusual for its time, the book became a small phenomenon.[79] Friedan's appearances on television and radio talk shows helped to spark a grassroots storm of controversy throughout 1963 and 1964, as "cocktail parties turned into debate teams" and local civic and religious groups sponsored heated panel discussions.[80]

Reviewers and readers were sharply divided over Friedan's work because they were divided over the place of women in American society. Friedan's image of the "comfortable concentration camp" appeared frequently in Americans' debates over *The Feminine Mystique*, but virtually never as a subject to be debated in its own right. Instead, reviewers and readers focused on women's status in America and debated whether women were oppressed in American society.

Although leftist literature had continued to address women's inequality throughout the 1950s, most mainstream literature during the era assumed that housewives were revered, coddled, and cherished above all other groups. In fact, some commentators actually believed that women were in fact the victimizers of men: housewives, after all, were lazy parasites who had nothing to do all day and expended their energy only by taking men's money and dominating men's lives.[81] To see white middle-class women as oppressed was a large leap for ordinary Americans in the 1950s, who had mostly ignored Simone de Beauvoir's *Second Sex,* even when it was published in English in 1952, and who had used the word "feminism" as an epithet since at least 1945.[82]

To be sure, there was a growing body of popular literature in the 1950s that reported on the dissatisfaction and unhappiness experienced by many women in suburban America, but this literature never described women as victims. Historian Eva Moskowitz, for example, has demonstrated that women's magazines in the 1950s and early 1960s constantly portrayed women who were unhappy with their marriages and encouraged women regularly to monitor their marital dissatisfaction.[83] Friedan herself noted that, in 1960, publications such as the *New York Times* and *Newsweek* had begun to report extensively the unhappiness of suburban housewives and that, "by 1962, the plight of the trapped American housewife had become a national parlor game."[84] These media reports on women's unhappiness, however, usually blamed women's education for making them dissatisfied with their lives, or dismissed women's anxieties by pointing out how privileged they really were, or simply advised women to adjust to their prescribed lot in life. Friedan's argument that white middle-class women were systematically oppressed and treated as less than human was thus quite dramatically different from the prevailing popular discourse on women, and because of that dramatic difference, her work sparked rousing controversy.

Most newspaper and magazine critics responded positively to *The Feminine Mystique,* calling it "brilliant and original," "disturbing and challenging," "stimulating," "insightful," and "devastating."[85] Many of these reviewers, moreover, readily accepted Friedan's description of women as "victims of the feminine mystique."[86] They recognized and agreed with Friedan's argument that society treated women as "functionaries whose jobs are predestined by nature," rather than as real human beings, and they loudly cheered Friedan's insistence that "women are people; therefore individuals."[87]

Critics who liked Friedan's book generally approved of her concentration camp analogy. Several quoted the phrase "comfortable concentration camp," and still more repeated her warning that America was committing "genocide" by "burying women alive."[88] Cynthia Seton "[took] exception to the blanketing overstatement of [the] proposition" that suburban homes might produce effects similar to the effects of Dachau and Buchenwald but declared, "I believe there is more truth than poetry in it."[89] No writers who liked Friedan's work took issue with her concentration camp analogy; they were comfortable with her image of women as a victimized group.

Some critics, in fact, thought that Friedan did not go far enough. Although some testified to their "gratitude and exhilaration" on reading *The*

Feminine Mystique, leftist reviewers complained that, although her analysis of women's problems was accurate, her solutions were "far too simple:" she had focused too much on education and professionalism as a panacea, and she had not dealt with the larger problems of capitalism or male opposition.[90] These critics from the left, however, all approved of Friedan's description of women as an oppressed group in American society; many of them too quoted the concentration camp analogy without negatively commenting on it.

A sizable number of critics, however, rejected Friedan's description of women as oppressed. Reflecting many contemporary observers' claims about women in the 1950s, some reviewers scoffed outright at the notion that women were victims, and not victimizers, of men.[91] Other reviewers did not believe that women were victimizers, but nonetheless believed that American women "never had it so good."[92] If women were unhappy or unfulfilled, it was their own fault. "The fault, dear Mrs. Friedan, is not in our culture, but in ourselves," Lucy Freeman chided in the *New York Times Book Review.*[93] As befitted the consumerist culture of the United States in the post–World War II era, these critics insisted that middle-class women lived easy lives in a society full of comfort and freedom.[94]

Understandably, these critics accorded very little respect to Friedan's concentration camp analogy. One reviewer just repeated the analogy, with an exclamation point at the end, implying that the comparison was so ridiculous that it was beneath discussion.[95] Others assumed that Friedan was exaggerating to make her point, calling it a "wildly provocative statement" designed to "divert attention" from an argument she felt she could not defend.[96] One reviewer insisted that "[n]o matter how stifling or limiting of individual expression the life of suburbia, it ought not to be compared to Hitler's extermination camps!"[97] This reviewer was the only one I found who hinted that the extermination camps themselves were incomparable, but she believed that Friedan should not have compared women to African Americans either.[98]

These critical reviewers were disturbed by Friedan's analogy, but not because they believed that the destruction of European Jews was incomparable. Even among the Jewish newspapers and rabbis who criticized *The Feminine Mystique,* none stated that the camps could not be used as points of comparison.[99] Neither the *Index to Jewish Periodicals* nor the *American Jewish Yearbook* reporting the events of 1963 suggests the existence of any published or organized Jewish opposition to Friedan's book.[100] Indeed, Rabbi Julius Nodel of Temple Shaare Emeth in St. Louis refuted Friedan's argument by instead worrying about the man "confined in his 'concentration camp' of business, factory, office, store or salesman's route."[101] What these reviewers found disturbing was that Friedan believed that American women, who were at the time supposedly the most pampered of all creatures, might be seen as disadvantaged at all.

Like professional reviewers, ordinary readers divided sharply over Betty Friedan's concentration camp analogy. Ordinary men and women were exposed to *The Feminine Mystique* through women's magazines, local newspapers, radio and television programs, as well as word of mouth, and they displayed extreme reactions, both positive and negative. While most reviewers abstractly approached Friedan's arguments, most men and women who wrote to Friedan reacted emotionally and personally, seeing their own lives reflected in her words.

Perhaps the most interesting of these personal responses were those of three people who identified themselves to Friedan as survivors of the Nazi destruction. None of these writers attacked Friedan for desecrating the memory of victims or for appropriating their tragedy for her personal purposes in her concentration camp analogy. One male survivor from Itasca, Illinois, did angrily tell Friedan that if she "had ever lived through more than three years of concentration camps—as this man has—you would be even happy to sweep your floor with a broom, so long as it is your own floor!" This accusation suggested that Friedan lacked authenticity to speak about the concentration camps, but the writer's emphasis was actually on Friedan's lack of gratitude for "how fortunate you American women are." The rest of his letter encouraged unhappy women to go to war with one another: "Pretty soon the world would void of dissatisfied females and peace would finally return."[102] This survivor was less concerned that Friedan had used the concentration camp experience improperly and more angry with her for vocalizing the unhappiness of women in domesticity.

The other two survivors, both female, were far more positive about Friedan's book, and they wrote to Friedan to help her in her work, as did many other women. One survivor from Indianapolis described the details of her life, hoping that she might help Friedan in her future work, and she thanked Friedan for letting her know that "my neighbor-housewives also have problems, as I do." "In spite of my different background," she wrote, "I feel the problem very strongly."[103] The other female survivor, a housewife from Larchmont, New York, called Friedan's theories "fascinating," but she wanted to help Friedan with her "incomplete, not to say incorrect," portrait of passive and destructive camp inmates. During her three years in German concentration camps, including Auschwitz, this woman told Friedan, prisoners had discussed philosophy and religion and protected one another from danger: "We may have looked like subhuman beings but at no time lost our human dignity," she explained.[104] Although she found problems in Friedan's analogy, this survivor engaged Friedan's ideas seriously and openly.

Only a few survivors even bothered, then, to respond to Friedan's concentration camp analogy at all, but their responses were different from the ones we might imagine Friedan would receive today. None insisted that Nazi terror was an inviolable or sacred subject, and two out of three found Friedan's ideas interesting and worthwhile, and hoped that they could help her further.

No other Jewish readers who wrote to Friedan, moreover, suggested that she should not have touched the memory of the camps, or that any comparison using Nazi camps was inappropriate.[105] Reports of Friedan's appearances before Jewish audiences suggest no controversy over her "comfortable concentration camp" imagery.[106] Instead, Friedan's audiences—both Jewish and non-Jewish—all focused entirely on how well her image of Nazi camps fit American women's circumstances.

Many women eagerly embraced Friedan's ideas, believing that her image of dehumanized victims perfectly represented their personal lives. "My entire case history appears on your pages," wrote one housewife.[107] These women often repeated her description of housewives as "victims," or described themselves as "trapped" or "servile."[108] Many readers, moreover, saw Friedan's book as a tool for liberation. One young graduate student thanked Friedan "for setting me free! Really free!" while a housewife in Sioux City, Iowa, similarly cheered that "the cobwebs of guilt have been swept away and what a marvelous free feeling! The release of women from [this] subtle bondage can only be good and right."[109] A substantial number of readers urged that Friedan's book be required reading and reported buying extra copies to lend to friends: "Many, many thanks for saying all you did," wrote one housewife. "I must now rush off to lend it to my fellow prisoners."[110]

A number of women specifically adopted Friedan's concentration camp imagery to reinscribe this image of themselves as victims. "Glory be, I got myself out of it," wrote one Brooklyn mother of her life as a housewife, "and can only shudder when I think of those 'concentration camp' days."[111] A housewife from Towson, Maryland, explained to Friedan, "I live here in Towson, in a 'comfortable concentration camp' or how I call it a 'white ghetto.' I know I have to get out of it."[112] And one woman from Los Angeles testified, "Your poignant analogy of the subtle plight of women and the open dehumanization of Nazi victims in concentration camps made me weep, for it surely points slowly or more quickly to the death of human spirit."[113] Friedan's fans thus were clearly persuaded by her description of housewives as victims, and a number accepted even its most extreme manifestation: the concentration camp analogy.[114]

Not all of Friedan's readers warmed to the image of themselves as victims, however. *McCall's* and *Ladies Home Journal* received extraordinary numbers of letters from women attacking their published excerpts from *The Feminine Mystique*. Writers pronounced themselves "completely appalled" and "thoroughly disgusted" by Friedan's portrait of women as brainwashed, dependent, even parasitic victims.[115] Many ridiculed Friedan's charge that they were psychologically suffering: "Strange, I don't feel the brick wall or the devastating shackles of my frustration," commented one housewife.[116] If they were victimized, these women argued, it was by Betty Friedan, who made "the average housewife and mother feel that she is inadequate, useless, and very uninteresting."[117] To protest this portrait, these women went into great detail portraying themselves as successful, mature, heroes of their families. "Mrs. Friedan should save her pity for those who really need it," wrote one woman, who listed in great detail her accomplishments over twenty-three years of marriage.[118]

For *McCall's* readers, the "comfortable concentration camp" was the most ridiculous of Betty Friedan's claims.[119] "Sizing it all up I say, 'Thank you Lord, for my comfortable, warm concentration camp," wrote one homemaker ironically; another signed her letter, "A Parasite, who has been happily and efficiently running her concentration camp for twenty five years.'"[120] The "comfortable concentration camp" was also the most painful of Friedan's charges. "The 'concentration camp,'" wrote one New Jersey housewife—"could one degrade the home more shamefully than Mrs. Friedan did?"[121] Surprisingly, however, even these angry housewives often gave credence to Friedan's camp analogy, admitting that women not as heroic as they might, in fact, be living in concentration camps: "The woman who has allowed her mind and spirit to be limited to the confines of status symbols, material possessions and drudgery is, indeed . . . living in a concentration camp," allowed one Los Angeles woman "But it is really a prison built of her own narrow desires and self-pity."[122] Thus, even women who were deeply insulted by Friedan's imagery were still willing to employ her symbol of the concentration camp.

The fact that so many housewives engaged with Friedan's concentration camp analogy signifies that Nazi imagery became a part of American political at the turn of the 1960s in a way very different from the one historians usually describe. None of these women believed that the concentration camp was an incomparable or sacred symbol of oppression; indeed, some women critical of Friedan were comfortable using the symbol of the concentration camp themselves to label other housewives. Again, no Jews or camp survivors protested that Betty Friedan's use of the concentration camps had trivialized the Holocaust in the *McCall's* excerpt. Instead, American women—even those who fundamentally rejected Betty Friedan's analogy—were forced to confront her liberal feminist critique of the suburban home as a concentration camp. Rather than thinking about Nazi concentration camps as a justification for the existence of the state of Israel or the capital punishment of Adolf Eichmann, many American women in 1963 were struggling instead, because of Betty Friedan's liberal use of Nazi imagery, with the possibility that the concentration camp might have significant political meaning for their own lives and society. A good number of ordinary readers, as well as professional reviewers, found Friedan's portrait of "comfortable concentration camps" an acceptable, even an impressive description of American women's lives. Even women or reviewers who disagreed with Friedan's perspective felt forced to engage her portrait—to ridicule it, to attack it, or to accept its partial truth. Friedan's analogy thus pushed ordinary readers of *McCall's* and the Book Find Club to consider Nazi concentration camps a significant reference for understanding American life, not simply a political travesty that had occurred in a totalitarian state far away.

To be sure, Friedan's concentration camp analogy had its most substantial impact during the turn of the 1960s. The feminist's comparison between concentration camps and suburban homes does not seem to have had much impact on American intellectual and political culture after the late 1960s. Although *The Feminine Mystique* continued to sell in the millions, and Friedan moved on to greater public fame after she assumed the presidency of the National Organization for Women (NOW) in 1966 and engaged in substantial political activism in the late 1960s and early 1970s, the phrase "comfortable concentration camp" does not seem to have been a important part of the growing popularity of her ideas during these later years. Indeed, the phrase mostly fell out of public consciousness altogether. In an April 1970 speech at Fordham University in New York City, Friedan did note leftists' fears of concentration camps established by the Nixon administration, and joked that they might even be "relatively comfortable concentration camps," provoking laughter from an audience that clearly recognized the phrase from her book.[123] After 1970, however, few news reports on Friedan mentioned "comfortable concentration camps" in her rhetoric, and by the 1990s, many people seemed to have forgotten the phrase as a part of *The Feminine Mystique*.[124]

As Friedan's analogy began to disappear from public view in the late 1960s, the tenuous ambivalence that the analogy had reflected between her insider and outsider status came under attack from new groups of radical, minority, and working-class women. Many members of these new feminist groups did believe that *The Feminine Mystique* was a compelling and fundamental text in the women's liberation movement.[125] Nonetheless, they rejected Friedan's efforts to influence a powerful white middle-class elite, and many were further angered by her portraits of debased victims who collaborated with their oppressors. Women such as Robin Morgan and Roxanne Dunbar argued that Friedan's emphasis on the psychological damage of a comfortable lifestyle and her focus on women who could succeed through careers signaled her middle-class biases and unworkable solutions.[126] These feminists' criticisms were surprisingly similar to those of some housewives who had resented and explicitly rejected her middle-class assumptions about work.[127] Other critics, particularly those from poor or minority backgrounds, attacked Friedan for ignoring the problems of working-class, black, and Latina women.[128] Still others, such as critics from the radical group Redstockings, believed Friedan's psychological language had blamed women for their own oppression and had encouraged individual therapy rather than social action.[129] Neither Betty Friedan's portrait of outsiders who colluded in their own oppression, nor her ambitions to speak to the elite intelligentsia or the powerful white middle class, resonated among radicals after the later 1960s.

NONETHELESS, FRIEDAN'S ANALOGY did have immediate and significant meaning for her readers at the turn of the 1960s, and the power of that phrase during that era suggests that historians need to regard the "comfortable concentration camp" as more than an example of narcissism, carelessness, or exaggeration. Instead, Friedan's Nazi imagery was a product of significant historical forces and personal influences in her life, and that imagery had some impact on American political discussion. A closer look at Friedan's imagery offers us a valuable window into a period of American cultural history.

The "comfortable concentration camp" analogy allows us to explore seriously a period in American culture before the Holocaust became "the Holocaust," thus engaging historical actors on their own terms, rather than criticizing them through frameworks that did not exist in an earlier era. Friedan developed, and readers accepted without protest, her Nazi analogy because the narrative of the Holocaust had not yet been constructed as something distinct and unique, incomparable and incomprehensible. Without that understanding of the event, Americans—including American

Jews and even camp survivors—generally accepted the concentration camp analogy and indeed engaged with Friedan's ideas, rather than rejecting them immediately as inappropriate.

For some American women, moreover, engagement with Friedan's concentration camp analogy was powerful and influential. For these women, the "comfortable concentration camp" was entirely appropriate—the analogy confirmed their understanding of their own experiences. For other women, the concentration camp analogy was degrading and despicable, not because it trivialized the experiences of camp inmates, but because it portrayed housewives as passive and self-destructive victims. Crucially, Friedan's use of the concentration camps came from a politically liberal perspective, and it thus encouraged both political liberalism, as well as conservative reaction, during the turn of the 1960s. Unlike later uses of the Holocaust that may have encouraged Jews to support Israel or to strengthen their Jewish identity, Friedan used the concentration camps to reflect and bolster an American liberalism that was increasingly questioning Cold War dogma and criticizing the inequality of American society.

At the same time, Friedan's liberal use of Nazi camp imagery points out the tension in Friedan's own self-understanding as a Jewish woman who was both an outsider and an insider in American life. Friedan certainly did not write *The Feminine Mystique* as an expression of her Jewishness, but her personal background as a Jewish woman and several key intellectual influences—Jewish refugees Kurt Lewin and Bruno Bettelheim—clearly shaped her portrait of self-destructive women and Nazi concentration camp inmates as victims who colluded in their own oppression. At the same time, Friedan's silence about Jews in Nazi camps, and her silence about racial or class differences among women, suggests that she hoped to speak to the white middle class and the intellectual elite in the United States. This tension between Friedan's sensitivity to potential persecution and her ambitious hopes for power and influence suggests that the author's understanding of herself as a Jew was shaped by the position of Jews in midcentury America as both insiders and outsiders.

CHAPTER 3

"An Accident of Geography:"

Stanley Milgram's Obedience Experiments

Obedience, as a determinant of behavior, is of particular relevance to our time. It has been reliably established that from 1933–45 millions of innocent persons were systematically slaughtered on command. Gas chambers were built, death camps were guarded, daily quotas of corpses were produced with the same efficiency as the manufacture of appliances. These inhumane policies may have originated in the mind of a single person, but they could only be carried out on a massive scale if a very large number of persons obeyed orders.[1]

WITH THIS STRIKING RHETORIC, American social psychologist Stanley Milgram introduced a series of ingenious, but horrifying, experiments to the small professional readership of the *Journal of Abnormal and Social Psychology (JASP)* in 1963. In these experiments, Milgram reported, large numbers of people obeyed orders to push a series of levers that they believed were delivering increasingly painful shocks to a protesting, screaming victim. In the fifteen years that followed the *JASP* article, these experiments became more famous than virtually any other social science research of the postwar era. In addition to the profound respect and heated controversy they sparked in the psychological profession, Milgram's "obedience experiments," as they came to be called, were featured in newspaper and popular magazine articles, discussed on talk shows and in religious sermons, dramatized in theatrical plays and television movies, and included in college and high school curricula. By 1978, the obedience experiments, along with the Nazi imagery that Milgram invoked to describe them, had become an integral part of American life.

Although a recent biography of Milgram has noted his experiments' wide-ranging popular appeal and their influence in the fields of psychology and Holocaust scholarship, Milgram's work has mostly been taken for granted by both Holocaust scholars and American intellectual historians.[2] A number of scholars who study Nazi genocide have referred to Stanley

Milgram's experiments to help them develop their arguments, but they have rarely deconstructed the experiments themselves to explore the scientist's comparison of the Yale laboratory and the Nazi death camps.[3] Even fewer historians of intellectual life in the United States have addressed Milgram's ideas in detail at all. Historian Peter Novick has briefly noted that the obedience study became a part of American culture, and he has argued that those experiments offered Americans excellent lessons about obedience under authoritarian bureaucracy—much better lessons than study of the Holocaust itself could provide.[4] Novick has not, however, examined the comparisons that Stanley Milgram made between the laboratory subjects in his own work and the Nazi destruction of European Jews, nor has the historian explored the significance of the obedience experiments in liberal ideology and radical activism at the turn of the 1960s and afterward. Novick, like many other scholars, ultimately has made little effort to explore the obedience studies within their historical context.

By passing up close historical examination of Milgram's work, scholars have missed a valuable opportunity to explore the importance of Nazi imagery in American intellectual and political life. On the one hand, Milgram's experiments help us to understand early American Jewish reponses to the Holocaust. As a Jewish man whose relatives had hidden from the Nazis and been interned in concentration camps, Milgram constructed his experiments in order to understand Nazi evil. On the other hand, the obedience study helped to introduce and cement the image of Nazi murder as a relevant subject in American political life for many American readers and viewers, both Jewish and non-Jewish. Both excited and horrified by Stanley Milgram's work, ordinary Americans of many different backgrounds were encouraged to see their own lives and political actions through the lens of Nazi Germany.

First, a description of the obedience experiments will help to familiarize readers with their details. Then, this chapter will use Milgram's unpublished and published works from 1960 through 1974 to explore his purpose in designing those experiments and his analysis of their results. The chapter will then uncover in some detail the significance of the psychologist's liberal political sympathies, his intellectual mentors, and his Jewish background in constructing and interpreting his research. Milgram's Jewish background offers particularly interesting insight into the ethical controversy that surrounded his work. Thus, after exploring the significance of Milgram's ethnicity, this chapter will describe the professional ethical debates that surrounded the obedience study beginning in 1964 and the ways that Milgram perceived the ethics of his own behavior.

Finally, this chapter will examine the reception of Milgram's work among the larger American public, paying particular attention to the political interpretations that many in the United States gave the obedience experiments in the 1960s and 1970s.

STANLEY MILGRAM BEGAN DESIGNING his experiments on obedience in 1960 at Yale University, where he had just begun working as an assistant professor. After developing experimental procedures with help from students and then conducting several trial experiments on Yale undergraduates, Milgram received funding from the National Science Foundation in 1961.[5] With the aid of several graduate assistants, he began recruiting residents of New Haven, Connecticut, as subjects, first through a newspaper advertisement and then through mail solicitation, offering to pay them $4.50 for an hour's work. Trials began in the summer of 1961.

The standard experiment proceeded in the following manner. At an appointed time, two subjects arrived at a rather posh laboratory at Yale University. One person was actually a naive subject, the other a confederate hired to play the part of a subject. The experimenter (another actor, not Milgram himself) greeted them and explained that he was studying the effects of punishment on learning. The two people drew slips from a hat, both of which said "teacher," thus ensuring the naive subject's role. With the "teacher" watching, the experimenter strapped the confederate, who was designated the "learner," tightly into a chair, spread electrode paste on his arm in order "to avoid blisters and burns," and then attached an electrode to his wrist, explaining that he would receive a shock every time he answered a question incorrectly. He also told the learner: "Although the shocks can be extremely painful, they cause no permanent tissue damage."[6]

The experimenter then seated the teacher in front of a shock machine in another room, where he could hear but not see the learner. The machine presented thirty levers in a horizontal line, each marked with a voltage from "15V" to "450V," and with designations ranging from "Slight Shock" to "Intense Shock" to "XXX." The experimenter explained that the teacher was to read to the learner a series of word associations, such as "blue—box" or "nice—boy," and then a series of multiple-choice questions testing those associations, such as "blue: sky, ink, box, lamp." The learner was to buzz in his answer. If he got it wrong, the teacher was to give him a shock, and he was to increase the shock level each time.

When the experiment began, the learner answered most questions correctly, but as time went on, he began to get more wrong, forcing the teacher to give what he thought were increasingly powerful shocks. At 75 volts, the learner turned on a tape with a series of his prerecorded responses. First he gave a little grunt, and then several more louder grunts. At 120 volts, he shouted that the shocks were becoming painful, and at 135 volts he groaned with pain. He insisted on being let out of the experiment after 150 volts, with the cry: "Experimenter, get me out of here! I won't be in the experiment any more! I refuse to go on!" At 180 volts, he shouted, "I can't stand the pain," and by 270 volts, he gave an "agonized scream." The learner shouted that he refused to participate any longer after 300 and 315 volts, and thereafter gave no more answers to any questions. He continued to scream until 330 volts, when he simply became silent altogether. The experimenter instructed the teacher to continue with the learning experiment, treating silence as a wrong answer that required another shock. When the teacher had reached 450 volts, the experimenter told him to press this lever two additional times, before cutting off the experiment.[7] Twenty-six out of 40 people, or about 65 percent, continued in this experiment all the way to the end.

Milgram created many variations on his basic trial in order to uncover variables for obedience. He conducted several trials that placed the learner closer to the teacher, including one in which the teacher actually had to force the learner's hand onto a shock plate in order to punish him; about 30 percent of subjects continued this variation until the end. In another variation, in which subjects were required to perform only a helping task rather than actually shocking the learner themselves, 37 out of 40 subjects continued until the end.[8] One variation used women as subjects; their obedience levels were the same as those of men, who were tested in every other variation. After three years, Milgram had tested over 1,000 subjects in twenty-four different variations of the experiment.

Most subjects did not simply press levers unquestioningly. Rather, they turned to the experimenter at various times to protest, pointing out that the learner said he was being hurt, that the learner no longer wished to be in the experiment, that they did not want to be held legally responsible; they often requested that the experimenter go in to check on the learner. The experimenter had a set sequence of "prods" with which he would respond to these protests, firmly, but not rudely:

Prod 1: Please continue, *or* Please go on.
Prod 2: The experiment requires that you continue.
Prod 3: It is absolutely essential that you continue.
Prod 4: You have no other choice, you *must* go on.[9]

Only if one prod was unsuccessful in mollifying the teacher could the next prod be used. If the subject refused to obey after the fourth prod, no matter how many shocks he had already given, the experiment was terminated, and Milgram labeled the subject a "defiant" subject. Those who had protested, but continued to give shocks all the way up to 450 volts, were labeled "obedient" subjects.

Unsurprisingly, given these procedures, Milgram reported high levels of stress among both obedient and disobedient subjects in the experiments: "In a large number of cases the degree of tension reached extremes that are rarely seen in sociopsychological laboratory studies." He noted that subjects were characteristically observed "to sweat, tremble, stutter, bite their lips, groan, and dig their fingernails in their flesh," as well as to laugh uncontrollably in bizarre nervous reactions.[10] In order to alleviate this stress after the experiment was over, Milgram made sure that every subject had a friendly reconciliation with the learner, as well as a reassurance that the learner had not actually been harmed. In follow-up communication, he mailed subjects a report that explained the experiment in detail, and he asked subjects to fill out questionnaires expressing their satisfaction or dissatisfaction with the experiment.[11]

MILGRAM'S ANALYSES OF HIS EXPERIMENTS emerged in a piecemeal fashion. The psychologist first reported his results to the National Science Foundation in 1962, then published his first article on obedience in 1963. He published a number of follow-up articles in the next several years, as well as producing an educational film, *Obedience,* in 1965. Finally, Milgram published the monograph *Obedience to Authority* in 1974. Despite the long time lapse between the initial experiments and his final monograph describing and explaining them, two elements remained consistent throughout Milgram's experimental design and explanations for almost fourteen years: his comparison of the experiments to the situation in Nazi death camps, and his emphasis on the number of subjects who had obeyed.

Although the experiments may have had little to do with Nazi Germany on their surface, the relationship between obedience at the Nazi death camps and at the Yale laboratory dominated Milgram's work from conception to publication. Initially, Milgram had launched the experiments in order to study obedience among Germans, with a clear eye to understanding the destruction of European Jewry during World War II. Influenced by books such as William Shirer's *Rise and Fall of the Third Reich,* which had argued that Nazism had originated in traditional German personality traits,

Stanley Milgram originally intended his obedience experiments to be part of a cross-national comparison of Germans and Americans.[12] "What I wanted to study was those characteristics in the Germans that permitted the history of the Third Reich to unfold," the psychologist remembered in one unpublished note. "I came across many statements which implied that Germans tended to obey orders more conscientious[ly] than Americans."[13] Milgram's initial impulse to develop the experiments was thus clearly guided by his interest in German behavior during World War II.

As he designed his experiments, moreover, Milgram deliberately attempted to create a situation that would approximate that of Germans who had followed orders at the Nazi death camps. The very design of the obedience experiments for Milgram—the command for subjects "to administer pain to others; to hurt them"—was "the laboratory analogue of what happened in the gas chambers, in the concentration camps, and the like."[14] Milgram had purposely created the shock generator to serve as a metaphor of Nazi evil. "Let us stop trying to kid ourselves," Milgram admonished himself in one unpublished note: "what we are trying to understand is obedience of the Nazi guards in the prison camps, and that any other thing we may understand about obedience is pretty much of a windfall, an accidental bonus."[15] Unpublished notes suggest that the example of Nazi destruction ran consistently throughout Stanley Milgram's thought processes as he designed and launched the obedience experiments.[16]

Then, too, as Milgram interacted with grant officers, experiment subjects and research assistants, he communicated to them his analogy between Nazi concentration camps and the laboratory experiments. When explaining his excitement regarding his experiment's progress to an administrator at the National Science Foundation, Milgram reported that he had "once wondered whether in all of the United States a vicious government could find enough moral imbeciles to meet the personnel requirements of a national system of death camps, of the sort that were maintained in Germany. I am now beginning to think that the full complement could be recruited in New Haven."[17] In his debriefing report to experiment subjects, Milgram understandably used much more coded, less harsh language, but he still linked the experiments to the destruction that had occurred in the death camps of World War II: "Many of us were shocked to discover how far men would go in obeying authority during the last war. . . . The experiments you took part in represent the first efforts to understand this phenomenon in an objective, scientific manner."[18] Responses to the questionnaire that Milgram sent out along with his debriefing report make it clear that a number of subjects understood Milgram's code and interpreted their experience using the Nazi comparison, referring to Hitler, Eichmann, and Germany as they considered the experiment's significance.[19] Research assistants, too, absorbed Milgram's comparison of the laboratory to the death camp. Yale graduate student Alan Elms, who worked with Milgram on the obedience experiments, developed a related research project that explored the personality traits of their subjects. Among the topics that Elms—guided by his mentor and co-writer Milgram—asked participants to consider were their feelings about Adolf Eichmann.[20] Stanley Milgram thus encouraged the people contributing to or participating with him in the experiment to view it as an analogue of Nazi evil.

Finally, as he published his results, the psychologist encouraged his readers to link his subjects' obedience to that of Germans who had carried out the Nazi destruction. As noted above, for example, in the first paragraph of his first published article on obedience, Milgram established the value of his work by claiming that "gas chambers were built, death camps were guarded," only because "a very large number of persons obeyed orders."[21] He then continued this argument by quoting C. P. Snow's charge that the German Officer Corps' code of obedience had led it to participate in "the most wicked large scale actions in the history of the world."[22]

It is worth noting that in all these early references to Nazi evil, Milgram made no reference to his own Jewish background or to the Jewish identity of Nazi victims in the gas chambers and death camps. Like Betty Friedan and Stanley Elkins, Stanley Milgram did not talk about Jews openly in his early publications, although he did use language that specifically referred to the Nazi murder of Jews, speaking of "gas chambers," "death camps," and "millions of innocent persons."

Facing professional criticism in 1964 that his laboratory experiments did not approximate the conditions of Nazi Germany, Milgram stepped back slightly from his overt discussion of Nazi Germany for a few years, using the Biblical story of Abraham and Isaac instead to illustrate his argument about obedience.[23] By 1967, however, as the Holocaust began to be labeled openly and specifically as a narrative of Jewish destruction, Milgram had revived the image of Nazi evil in his work, and he had, moreover, made it clear that it was particularly the destruction of Nazi Jewry that galvanized his approach. In an article for a Jewish journal in England, *Patterns of Prejudice,* Milgram emphasized the significance of his findings for interpreting the Nazi extermination of European Jews.[24]

The analogy between his subjects' behavior and National Socialist genocide ran consistently throughout his 1974 monograph, *Obedience to Authority.* Not only did Milgram repeat the Nazi imagery of his first *JASP* article in his 1974 book, but he made it clear this time that his experiments had been designed explicitly to investigate the murder of European Jewry: "the Nazi extermination of European Jews is the most extreme instance of abhorrent immoral acts carried out by thousands of people in the name of obedience."[25] Milgram did address forthrightly in his book the concerns that his laboratory might not have replicated the Nazi experience. He noted, for example, that his experiments had not replicated "one essential feature of the situation in Germany . . . [the] vehement anti-Jewish propaganda [that] systematically prepared the German population to accept the destruction of the Jews."[26] Yet, he concluded that the same essential situation had "confronted both our experimental subject and the German subject and evoked in each a set of parallel psychological adjustments."[27] The psychologist did not need to rely on the example of Nazi Germany to demonstrate the philosophical or political significance of obedience. Nonetheless, he still consistently used the Nazi extermination of the Jews as an analogy for his obedient subjects.

In addition to his emphasis on the analogy to Nazi death camps, Milgram's reports of his study from 1962 through 1974 tended to emphasize the large numbers of subjects who had obeyed, while paying far less attention to the roughly 35–40 percent of people who had disobeyed or to the differences between obedient and disobedient individuals, or even to the variations in situation that he had developed so carefully. The fact that subjects had obeyed commands in surprising numbers was originally only one of three reported findings in Milgram's application to the National Science Foundation for continued funding in January 1962. In that report, Milgram also excitedly stated that obedience could be "intelligently" correlated with subjects' socioeconomic background, such as religion or education, and that different experimental situations had produced different rates of obedience.[28] During the next several years, however, the emphasis of Milgram's analysis changed. When he published his first article in 1963, the psychologist entirely eliminated all mention of individual and situational differences and instead emphasized only the stress experienced by subjects and the surprisingly large numbers of people who had obeyed.[29] In later articles, Milgram described more carefully the situational and personality differences among subjects, but he did not offer any theories to make sense of these differences, and he generally concluded these articles with his 1963 emphasis: the unexpected tendency of most subjects to continue shocking the "learner."[30] The high numbers of obedient subjects in New Haven were, in fact, so significant to Milgram that he decided to abandon his initial cross-cultural comparison of German and American obedience altogether.[31]

When Milgram published hi
shifted: the unexpected tendency
cal trait of human beings. Althou
and personality differences among
that these differences did not rema
thus less important than the genera
larly, although Milgram did describe
ferent situations that had led to dif
though his experiments had clearly
situation, his theory could only explai
dience. After working for years to expl
had arrived at an evolutionary hypothes
was based on their ability to function ii
the tendency to obey was "a fatal flaw r   ....u into us, and
which in the long run gives our species vmy a modest chance of survival."[34] With this genetic theory, by 1974, Milgram could explain very little
about the percent of subjects who had disobeyed, or about the sociological and situational differences among individuals that he had so excitedly noticed in 1962. The condition of the human species, in Milgram's 1974 analysis, was obedience.

THE PSYCHOLOGIST'S CENTRAL ARGUMENTS invite greater probing. Why did
Stanley Milgram emphasize the analogy between persons obeying orders at
Nazi concentration camps and his experimental subjects, even after the
comparison had drawn some criticism? And why did the psychologist
choose to stress the numbers of people who had obeyed, rather than paying
slightly more nuanced and sophisticated attention to disobedient, as well as
obedient, subjects?

There are no single answers to these questions. To be sure, Milgram's
decision to emphasize the Nazi analogy was probably motivated by a desire
to publicize his findings more widely by making them readily accessible
and relevant to a wide audience. Similarly, the bold claim that surprising
numbers of people will knowingly inflict harm on others because they are
given orders was more likely to captivate an audience than a careful delin-
eation of differences among obedient and disobedient subjects. Milgram's
dramatic personality certainly helps to explain his spectacular claims. He
enjoyed theater and the visual arts, developed films out of many of his experiments, and saw his psychological research as being on the border of
science and art.[35]

..t, however, were other components of Stanley

..ctual, and ethnic background. Milgram's liberal

..ie, may have had a powerful impact on his argument

..its had demonstrated an overwhelming, even universal,

..ig humans to obey.

..orter of liberal causes at the turn of the 1960s, Stanley Milgram

..letters to government officials supporting civil rights activists,

..ourned the death of John F. Kennedy by publicly calling for passage of the president's civil rights bill, and joked to a friend that he had dissociated himself from the Jewish religion since learning that conservative Republican presidential candidate Barry Goldwater was "only a generation removed from the talis [Jewish prayer shawl]."[36] Milgram connected his liberal beliefs with his research and believed that his obedience experiments had important significance for his political ideals, particularly that of peace. In his 1962 debriefing letter to subjects, for example, Milgram mentioned nuclear warfare as one of the consequences of obedience that the experiments might help to prevent: "Consider for example the possible day when a man in another country is told by a superior to drop a hydrogen bomb on the United States. Will he participate in this act of destruction? Or will he defy authority and refuse to drop the bomb?"[37] Similarly, in a 1963 interview with the *Yale Daily News,* the psychologist compared his subjects to flyers "being told to drop a bomb or push a button launching an atomic missile."[38] Milgram's concern for the liberal cause of peace seems to have influenced his interpretation of his laboratory experiments.

Just as his attraction to the peace movement may have encouraged Milgram to emphasize the blind obedience necessary to launch atomic weapons, his sympathies in the debate over Hannah Arendt's *Eichmann in Jerusalem* in 1963 may have encouraged Milgram to emphasize in his published works the tendency to obey, rather than the differences between the obedient and the disobedient. By asserting that Nazis such as Adolf Eichmann had perpetrated evil shallowly and thoughtlessly, as bureaucrats without any significant ideological hatred, Arendt created a great division among Jews and among intellectuals. Older, more established Jewish intellectuals, such as Irving Howe, were infuriated by Arendt's portrait of Eichmann because it seemed to exonerate Nazis and ignore antisemitism.[39] Younger, more leftist intellectuals, both Jews and non-Jews, however, applauded Arendt's position because it made it easier for them to find evil among American bureaucrats who allowed nuclear arms to proliferate and racial injustice to fester; Arendt's analysis made Americans seem just as culpable as Nazi bureaucrats.[40]

Milgram was in the latter camp. He was impressed by Arendt's conclusions and actively attempted to link his work with hers. In 1963, he eagerly wrote to Norman Podhoretz, then editor of *Commentary*, to encourage him to use the results of the obedience experiments as evidence for Arendt's claims in Podhoretz's forthcoming article on *Eichmann in Jerusalem*.[41] Clearly, Milgram supported Arendt's thesis, which dovetailed so well with the high levels of obedience he had found among his American subjects. It seems likely that as Milgram prepared his first article for publication in 1963, he became more excited by Arendt's profound vision of evil, and its relation to his own work, than by the prospect of cautiously delineating differences of class, religion, education, and personality among his own perpetrators.

Moreover, as the war in Vietnam heated up, Milgram, like other younger, more radical proponents of Arendt's Eichmann thesis, became more interested in demonstrating that Americans, just like people of all other nationalities, could be complicit in war crimes. Milgram's opposition to the war was reflected in his support for American men who refused to fight; in 1963, he supported War Resisters International, and in 1967, he donated money to the defense of the Fort Hood Three, three American soldiers who were court-martialed for refusing to fight in Vietnam.[42] In the late 1960s, Milgram's notes and lectures began including contrasts between his obedient subjects and Vietnam War resisters, or comparisons of his subjects to Green Berets who had been charged with murder for killing a double agent in Vietnam and, after 1969, to Lieutenant William Calley, the soldier held responsible for the massacre of hundreds of Vietnamese civilians at My Lai.[43]

By 1974, in *Obedience to Authority*, Milgram's entire epilogue was centered on the applicability of his findings to the war in Vietnam and to My Lai: "The catalogue of inhumane actions performed by ordinary Americans in the Vietnamese conflict is too long to document here in detail. . . . To the psychologist these do not appear as impersonal historical events but rather as actions carried out by men just like ourselves who have been transformed by authority."[44] A reading of Milgram's lectures, correspondence, and published work in the late 1960s and early 1970s suggests that the psychologist's growing frustration with the war in Vietnam may have encouraged him to read his experiments through a lens that emphasized an American, even a universal, tendency to obey, a lens that enabled him to critique the war in Vietnam. It is clear, at any rate, that Milgram did not choose to develop a more subtle discussion of sociological differences in his subjects' tendency toward obedience while he, like the rest of the nation, was engaged in passionate political debates over the Vietnam War.

To be sure, Milgram never openly linked his work to a particular political program, group, or label. Indeed, he rejected efforts by one interviewer to categorize his political thinking or the political meaning of the obedience experiments, noting that his work could be used to criticize authority in any political system, from democratic to fascistic.[45] Nonetheless, in both his published and his unpublished work, Milgram forcefully connected his obedience study to liberal positions, such as opposition to the Vietnam War, whereas he never connected the experiments to conservative perspectives, and he actively discouraged some leftist interpretations of his ideas. In one note comparing Adolf Eichmann and William Calley, for example, Milgram emphasized that this comparison was only a structural one, and he called "utter nonsense" the "radical assertion that the United States and Nazi Germany are virtually identical fascist states."[46] The psychologist clearly did not intend for his work to equate Nazi Germany and the United States, as many radicals were doing by the late 1960s, nor did he call for anarchy or Marxist revolution. Instead, he believed that a structural comparison of Nazi German and American authority might lead to constructive civil disobedience, reform of the United States Constitution, and an end to destructive military policies.[47] Political liberalism shaped Milgram's worldview, as well as his understanding of his experiments' meaning. In the midst of a tumultuous political era, in which liberals were deeply concerned with the dangers of nuclear proliferation and the expansion of the war in Vietnam, and in which Jewish intellectuals were struggling with changing interpretations of the Nazi destruction of European Jewry, Stanley Milgram interpreted the tendency of Americans to obey as the key finding of his research because it spoke directly to these emergent political and intellectual struggles.

In addition to the impact of Milgram's liberal political sympathies, Milgram's intellectual influences shaped the obedience study. The academic advisers with whom he worked, and the intellectual trends dominant while he attended graduate school at Harvard's Department of Social Relations from 1954 to 1960, were also fundamental in Milgram's design of the experiments and his understanding of their meaning, as well as his use of the Nazi camps as an analogy.

The most important of those advisers was Princeton psychologist Solomon E. Asch. Asch was a visiting professor at Harvard during Milgram's graduate studies, and he became Milgram's mentor and the central intellectual role model in the young psychologist's life. Asch had become famous in the psychological profession in the early 1950s by developing an admired experiment to test conformity. A naive subject was asked to take part in a study of visual perception along with six other subjects, who were really actors.

The subjects were asked to choose among three vertical lines the line that best matched a standard length. At first, all the subjects agreed on the lengths, but as the experiment progressed, the stooge subjects began to identify an obviously incorrect line, thus forcing the naive subject either to select the wrong line or to face being an outcast in the group. Naive subjects offered incorrect responses about one-third of the time in the face of this pressure, thereby demonstrating a powerful tendency toward conformity. Asch used his experiments as a springboard to discuss the larger philosophical relationship between the individual and society, and he compared his subjects to Germans who had lived near Nazi concentration camps and those who had marched under swastika banners.[48]

Milgram deeply admired Asch. In interviews and biographical statements, he testified that Asch's "quiet intellectual brilliance" and his deep philosophical concerns had made him "the single most important intellectual influence" in Milgram's life.[49] This influence was clearly visible in Milgram's dissertation: the young psychologist replicated Asch's conformity experiments in France and Norway, changing the experiments only slightly so that subjects were asked to gauge tones, rather than lines. Moreover, in designing his obedience experiments, Milgram used Asch's experiment as a direct model.[50] The similarity between the obedience and conformity paradigms was striking and quite obvious. Both used deception to place a naive subject into moral conflict: should he follow his own judgment, or that of others? Both Asch and Milgram, moreover, objectively measured the numbers of subjects who did not follow their own judgment and both psychologists further found philosophical and political significance in these numbers. Asch, like Milgram, did not explore closely the sociological or situational differences between conforming and nonconforming subjects; the fact that there existed so much conformity (or obedience) was the most significant finding for each psychologist.

Milgram saw both his own and Asch's work at the forefront of a new branch of psychology that he called "existential behaviorism," a blend of two very different strands of thought: existential philosophy and behaviorist psychology. Behaviorist psychology emphasized the objective measurement and manipulation of observable behavior, such as that of rats in mazes. Behaviorists such as B. F. Skinner sometimes envisioned human beings as laboratory animals who were easily manipulated and controlled. By contrast, existentialists such as Jean-Paul Sartre posited that human beings were absolutely free and that morality derived from recognizing the anxiety that freedom produced, choosing to act despite this anxiety, and taking responsibility for one's actions.

Although existentialism and behaviorism offered wholly different visions of the world, they shared two characteristics that made them attractive to Stanley Milgram. First, both were extremely popular in the 1950s, when Milgram came of age intellectually.[51] Second, both ultimately ignored individual thought processes and cultural differences: the observable behavior of each individual, in the end, was all that mattered to both existentialists and behaviorists. Just as existentialists believed that human nature "is constructed by the actions [a man] performs in the real world," Milgram explained in one unpublished note, behaviorists "focus on objective, visible, observable data, overt human actions."[52] By scientifically examining situations in which people were forced to make a moral choice, Milgram believed that existential behaviorists could provide objective answers to moral questions, thus providing a nonbiased, scientifically sound avenue to uncovering philosophical truth.

Existential behaviorism, moreover, offered an important methodological corrective to help improve other psychological subfields that interested Stanley Milgram in the 1950s: the study of national character and the exploration of stereotypes. Sparked in part by his parents' backgrounds as immigrants from eastern Europe and in part by historians and journalists like William Shirer, who believed that there was a correlation between German national traits and the rise of Nazism, Milgram was fascinated with the subject of national character, an inquiry that had gained popularity among psychologists in the 1950s.[53] Moreover, Milgram's adviser, Gordon Allport, was a gifted teacher whom the psychologist admired greatly, as well as one of the most famous scholars at the time associated with the study of prejudice. Allport's influence may have encouraged Milgram to think about the subject of stereotype, as may have Theodor Adorno's well-known and influential *Authoritarian Personality*, the study that correlated antisemitic prejudice with attitudes toward child rearing, among other things.[54] Early graduate papers on national character and national stereotypes testified to Milgram's interest in these subjects, as did Milgram's dissertation research conducted in Norway and France.[55]

These early works of Milgram, however, also suggest the psychologist's dissatisfaction with the field of national character and the study of stereotypes, and the ways that he hoped his own existential and behaviorist values might improve the subfields. Milgram believed that these psychologists' search for "attitudes" among subjects was of "limited utility." He was not impressed by works like Theodor Adorno's *Authoritarian Personality* because they catalogued only what people *said* they thought or felt, not what they actually *did* nor how they actually *behaved*: "The important things about a person [are] under his skin, can't be seen. . . . We don't really know how to measure what people are like, aside from how they act in situations."[56] It was only observable behavior that psychologists could properly quantify and use for their understandings of the world.

Milgram's interest in existential behaviorism, and his belief in its superority to studies of "attitudes," helps to explain his central concern with the large numbers of obedient subjects. The psychologist was not interested in exploring his subjects' responses to personality questionnaires, nor was he interested in correlating psychological or sociological data. It was observable behavior that was Milgram's chief interest. Moreover, it was also the dramatic difference between stated beliefs and actual behavior that galvanized Milgram's analyses. In his articles and book, Milgram continually emphasized the fact that psychiatrists, college students, and ordinary adults had all predicted far lower levels of obedience (both for themselves and for other people) than the ones he had elicited in his laboratory—indeed, these predictors had believed that 100 percent of all subjects would be disobedient.[57] This drastic difference between stated beliefs and the actual performance of subjects formed an important part of Stanley Milgram's rhetorical strategy in describing the obedience experiments, while it also signaled to him the intellectual significance of his large numbers of obedient subjects. Milgram's emphasis on existential behaviorism thus shaped the design of the obedience experiments as well as his reporting of the results.

Moreover, Milgram's advisers Allport and Asch, as well as the influential psychologist Adorno, were all in their own ways clearly influenced by the Nazi destruction of European Jewry. Allport's decision to focus on prejudice, Adorno's attention to authoritarianism and antisemitism, and Asch's attention to conformity—particularly illustrated by his quick but pointed comparison between his subjects and marching Nazi brownshirts—surely must have encouraged Milgram to believe that the recent catastrophe in Europe was a legitimate comparative framework for understanding human psychology. Indeed, a number of historians have noted several ways that the field of psychology in the United States was shaped by the destruction of European Jewry during World War II.[58]

It was not simply the lessons of his advisers or the trends of the profession, that encouraged Stanley Milgram to focus on the extermination of European Jewry. Milgram's own Jewish background was a crucial factor in his decision to develop and publicize his analogy between his subjects and Nazi camp guards. To be sure, Milgram rarely pointed out in his articles or books the connection between his Jewish background and his research.

Nonetheless, several times in private as well as in public, Milgram noted that his Jewish origins had encouraged him to develop the obedience experiments. For example, when Herbert Winer, a defiant subject in the obedience experiments, confronted Milgram angrily several days after his trial, Milgram made clear during the confrontation that his ethnic background had played a part in his work. "Milgram was very Jewish," Winer has said. "I was Jewish. We talked about this. There was obviously a motive beyond neutral research."[59] In an unpublished note, Milgram wrote: "My interest in [obedience] is purely personal, and concerns the fact that many of my friends and relatives were badly hurt by other men who were simply following orders."[60] And in a 1963 letter to an admiring reader of his article, Hannalore Lehnoff, Milgram remarked on her German background, adding, "My own interest in problems of obedience to authority is very much tied up with phenomena of the Nazi epoch. It was only an accident that I was on this side of the Atlantic when Hitler's insane orders were carried out with dispatch and efficiency."[61] Milgram's private statements thus suggest that his background as a second-generation Jew—particularly his personal connection to survivors and his existential unease at having survived World War II—led him to feel deeply about the problem of obedience in Nazi Germany.

Although he was more brief and circumspect in published materials, there too Milgram openly acknowedged the significance of his Jewish origins in developing his experiments and imagery. In the introduction to his 1977 book, *The Individual in a Social World,* Milgram noted that the problem of authority had been "forced upon members of my generation, in particular upon Jews such as myself, by the atrocities of World War II. . . . The impact of the holocaust on my own psyche energized my interest in obedience and shaped the particular form in which it was examined."[62] And in a 1970 *Esquire* interview, journalist Philip Meyer reported that Milgram's moral purpose in conducting his investigations of obedience was "colored by his own Jewish background."[63] Although Milgram rarely introduced his Jewishness into his published work, he told a number of admirers and interviewers that his ethnic background did have significance for his research.[64] Moreover, Milgram's wife, Alexandra, who has protected and managed her husband's work and legacy since his death of a heart attack in 1984, has stated that her husband's Jewish identity led to his "deep concern about the Holocaust" and to his "best-known research—obedience to authority."[65]

Unlike Stanley Elkins and Betty Friedan, Stanley Milgram seems to have had little experience with American antisemitism. It was not schoolyard violence or social snubs that shaped his understanding of Nazi concentration camps or his understanding of his own identity as a Jew. Elkins and Friedan were from slightly more established Jewish families who were less closely tied to the immigrant experience and who, moreover, lived in cities where Jews were clearly in a distinct minority. Understandably, American antisemitism was the significant factor that shaped what Elkins and Friedan thought it meant to be Jewish. As the child of Jewish immigrants living in a Jewish neighborhood in the Bronx, however, Stanley Milgram seems to have faced little significant antisemitism from other Americans: instead, he felt himself closely tied to the European Jewish milieu and personally affected by the murder of European Jews.

Born in New York City in 1933, Stanley Milgram was the child of two Jews born in Europe. His mother, Adele, had moved to the United States from Rumania with her family when she was about four or five, whereas his Hungarian Jewish father, Samuel, who was eleven years older than his wife, had emigrated as a young adult.[66] Stanley's sister Marjorie was a year and a half older than he; his brother, Joel, to whom he was very close, was five years younger than Stanley. During Stanley's childhood, the Milgrams lived in a neighborhood in the Bronx populated primarily by Jewish first-generation immigrants, most of them lower middle class; Samuel was a baker. Although some non-Jews lived in the neighborhood, and Joel has remembered one or two instances of antisemitism that the family encountered, that was not Stanley's brother's dominant memory of their childhood. Instead, his memories centered on the neighborhood as entirely Jewish, having little contact with or knowledge about the non-Jewish world. Stanley Milgram's unpublished journals, letters, and published works seem to echo Joel's memories: he recorded no significant recollections of discrimination or prejudice directed against him or his family in the United States.

Instead, the sense of being a product of two different European cultures seemed to have lasted in Stanley Milgram's memory and to have had a significant impact on his intellectual world. In several unpublished notes later in life, Milgram connected his intellectual interest in national character to his childhood experience as the child of immigrants: "To understand the difference between national cultures was . . . in my psychic system, to understand the difference between mother and father, the difference between the two sexes, the difference between two components of my personal identity."[67]

Probably even more importantly, Hitler's attempt to destroy European Jewry in World War II had a direct and personal impact on the Milgrams. Although Adele's immediate family members had emigrated to America before the war, much of Samuel's family was caught in Europe. As an adult, Stanley often remembered how his family had listened closely to the radio for news of the war in Europe, concerned for the safety of Samuel's family.[68] After the war, the Milgrams found out that Samuel's family had successfully hidden from the Nazis but that Adele's brother-in-law's relatives had been in the camps. After the war, these relatives came to stay with the Milgrams briefly. Joel, who was only seven years old at the time and who believes that his family purposely tried to protect him from the details, still remembers his "awe and fascination" during their stay: "I have memories as a child of reading the numbers on their arms."[69] As a thirteen-year-old in 1946, Stanley could not be as easily protected, and the recent events in Europe had even more significance for him. In his bar mitzvah speech, he testified, "As I come of age and find happiness in joining the ranks of Israel, the knowledge of the tragic suffering of my fellow Jews throughout wartorn Europe makes this also a solemn event and an occasion to reflect upon the heritage of my people—which now becomes mine."[70] This sensation of his own shared fate with murdered European Jews remained with Milgram throughout his adolescence and early adulthood. As a graduate student traveling through Europe in 1958, Milgram wrote home to one friend: "My true spiritual home is Central Europe. . . . I should have been born into the German-speaking Jewish community of Prague in 1922 and died in a gas chamber some twenty years later. How I came to be born in the Bronx Hospital I'll never quite understand."[71]

Stanley Milgram's understanding of what it meant to be Jewish was shaped by his experiences as the child of immigrants, growing up in a Jewish neighborhood peopled with immigrants and their children, and in a household where family members worried daily about the safety of their loved ones in the face of Nazi murder. His obedience experiments—in both their design and their reporting—bore the imprint of that concern. To be sure, Milgram's Jewishness was far from the only factor that determined the shape of the obedience experiments. But, like the political and intellectual concerns that influenced him early in life, the psychologist's ethnic and family background played a significant role.

THE SIGNIFICANCE OF STANLEY MILGRAM'S Jewish background is perhaps most intriguing when explored beside the well-publicized ethical storm that surrounded his experiments throughout their history, perhaps the most far-reaching and institutionalized legacy of Stanley Milgram's work. The ethical controversy over the obedience study offers a window into Milgram's personal conflict as a Jewish man who perceived himself both as an outsider, a victim of the Nazi destruction, and as an insider, a scientist who placed his concern for the pursuit of knowledge above the well-being of his subjects.

The ethics of conducting his experiments on human subjects was an issue for Stanley Milgram from the very beginnings of the obedience study, and this concern lasted throughout the rest of his life. Although Milgram was far from the only scientist deceiving his experimental subjects in the early 1960s, his experiments were quickly met with heated professional opposition, both because of his use of deception and because he had inflicted significant stress on his subjects.[72] Even before his first article on the obedience experiments was published, the psychologist's application for membership in the American Psychological Association (APA) was deferred for a year in 1962 because of ethical questions regarding his experiments.[73] And in 1964, only one year after Milgram's initial report of the study was published, Berkeley psychologist Diana Baumrind published an attack on Milgram's work in the *American Psychologist,* the journal published by the APA, criticizing him for "manipulat[ing], embarrass[ing], and discomfort[ing] subjects."[74] The journal allowed Milgram to respond several months later, and the interchange between the two became a foundation for serious debate throughout the 1960s and 1970s over the subject of ethics.

Although Diana Baumrind offered a number of substantial criticisms of Stanley Milgram's ethics, her opposition revolved around three major objections to his work. The first was that Milgram had involved men and women in experiments in which they lost their fundamental dignity as human beings because they were deceived and subjected to unusually high levels of stress. Ultimately, she argued, the experiments offered the potential of permanent harm, whereby subjects would suffer a loss of self-esteem and become cynical, losing all trust in even legitimate authority figures. Second, Baumrind scored Milgram for being indifferent to his subjects' pain, noting that his procedures for addressing their trauma were inadequate, "casual," and "indifferent," rather than sustained, "intense," and "careful" instances of debriefing. She suggested, moreover, that Milgram's "indifference" might be explained by the psychologist's own rationale for his subjects' destructive obedience: "They assume that the discomfort caused the victim is momentary, while the scientific gains resulting from the experiment are enduring."[75] Finally, Baumrind argued that, while medical researchers might justify the risk of harm to subjects because of the "concrete benefit to humanity" of their work, a social psychologist such as Stanley Milgram could not legitimate his experiments in the same way. Although Milgram was studying a significant human problem, she acknowledged, that of destructive obedience during World War II, his laboratory did not offer "a convincing parallel" with the "authority-subordinate relationships in Hitler's Germany."[76] Whereas Milgram's subjects experienced extreme tension because they were both concerned about the victim *and* respectful of the experimenter, SS officers perceived their victims as subhuman, she argued, and saw their work as part of a higher cause, thus experiencing no tension. All in all, Baumrind argued, experiments like Milgram's should not be conducted in the future, unless subjects were informed of the dangers of aftereffects and his debriefing had been proved to be effective.

Milgram responded to Baumrind's criticisms first by emphasizing that his subjects had in fact reported high levels of satisfaction: 92 percent of the questionnaires sent along with his debriefing report had been returned to him, he noted, and those responses indicated that roughly 84 percent of subjects were either glad or very glad to have participated in the experiments, and less than 2 percent were sorry to have done so.[77] Moreover, Milgram argued that, although subjects had experienced "momentary excitement," there was no lasting harm, noting that a psychiatrist had determined that there had been no long-term impact in the forty "worst cases," involving subjects who might have been expected to have been permanently harmed.[78] Addressing Baumrind's contention that the laboratory was not an adequate parallel for the Nazi death camp, Milgram explained that the death camp was not intended to be literally reproduced in the laboratory, as it could not be, but that the camps illustrated the problem of destructive obedience and that his experiments permitted scientists to understand that problem better by illuminating the power of legitimate authority and the loss of responsibility in a chain of command.[79] Finally, responding to Baumrind's charge that he had humiliated his subjects and denied them their human dignity, Milgram argued that he had in fact treated his subjects with greater respect than did his critic. Whereas Baumrind believed that "the experimenter *made* the subject shock the victim," Milgram explained, "I started with the belief that every person who came to the laboratory was free to accept or to reject the dictates of authority." His view of human dignity, the psychologist explained, included "in each man a capacity for *choosing* his own behavior."[80] Baumrind viewed the "subject as a passive creature," Milgram argued, whereas he saw "a person who comes to the laboratory" as "an active, choosing adult." Milgram concluded his work by noting that "every man must be responsible" for his actions and that he himself accepted the full responsibility for the obedience study.[81]

Milgram's intellectual existentialism clearly shaped his response to Baumrind. His emphasis on the moral necessity of choosing one's action illustrates his worldview, as does his emphasis on responsibility. Less obvious, but still distinguishable, are the ways that gender shaped Milgram's reply. Existentialism was a philosophical system that was itself gendered, placing value on traditionally male ideals of "action" and "responsibility" while assuming (as did most philosophical theories at the turn of the 1960s) that the universal actor was "every man."[82] Milgram's argument that Baumrind viewed the subject as a "passive creature" was surely designed to play on these gendered understandings of action and responsibility, suggesting that she was a tender woman who not only did not act herself but could not properly encourage men to take responsibility for their actions, instead treating them as children.

Interestingly, male graduate students who worked with Milgram defended him from Baumrind's criticism with much more vituperation and sexism. Leon Mann, in a letter to his adviser, Milgram, noted that the obedience study "is attracting the wrong sort of attention. Happily, the female who wrote that article was so hysterical and ridiculous, that you should have little trouble putting her in her place."[83] Another graduate student who had worked closely with Milgram on the obedience study, Alan Elms, replicated Milgram's portrait of Baumrind as a woman who could only treat men like children, but with far more personal and explicit attacks than Milgram had used: "she is a child psychologist and the volunteers are all children at heart, unable to resist the experimenter's wiles and therefore needing protection by someone who knows better, namely Dr. Baumrind."[84] The gendered suggestion that ethics was a female concern, one associated with softness, passivity, and even hysteria, certainly may have shaped the undercurrents of Stanley Milgram's response to Diana Baumrind's ethical concerns.

Although Milgram's work was by no means the only focus of ethical controversy in the 1960s, it was probably the best publicized in the argument over professional conduct during that era, in part because of the very visible debate between Baumrind and Milgram in the pages of *American Psychologist*.[85] Milgram and Baumrind's exchange over professional ethics flared at the APA convention in 1965, inspired articles and letters to the editor in psychological journals throughout the late 1960s and early 1970s, and eventually resulted in a revision of APA ethical guidelines in 1973.[86] Those guidelines coincided with new regulations from the federal government that limited the use of human subjects in psychology, along with medical research.[87] The continuing revision and the stringency of those guidelines help to explain why Milgram is probably still best remembered among re-search psychologists for his controversial method, rather than his findings.

Publicly, Milgram understandably expressed "astonishment," anger, and dismay that ethics had come to play such a large role in the reception of his work.[88] Milgram's personal files and unpublished notes, however, offer a very different portrait of the psychologist's responses to questions about the ethics of his obedience experiments, suggesting that the ethical attacks leveled at his work could not have been that surprising to him. These notes, moreover, suggest that Milgram considered his own Jewish identity to have been a mitigating factor that helped to explain his ethical behavior.

Milgram's private notes suggest that, as he conducted the obedience experiments, the psychologist was conflicted about the ethics of his work and wracked with unease about his own behavior. In January 1962, for example, he wrote: "Several of these experiments, it seems to me, are just about on the borderline of what ethically can and cannot be done with human subjects. Some critics may feel that at times they go beyond acceptable limits. These are matters that only the community can decide on, and if a ballot were held I am not altogether certain which way I would cast my vote."[89] Anticipating Diana Baumrind's comments by two years, in March 1962 Milgram wrote an unpublished note that compared his own inactivity in the face of his subjects' suffering to his obedient subjects' unresponsiveness to the "learner's" pain:

> Consider, for example, the fact—and it is a fact indeed, that while observing the experiment I—and many others—know that the naive subject is deeply distressed, and that the tension caused him is almost nerve shattering in some instances. Yet, we do not stop the experiment because of this.
>
> Remember also, that when the first group of 14 Yale students observed the experiment, they burst into laughter, were actually falling onto the floor with laughter. And no observer has ever thought to interrupt the experiment, although we know a man was suffering deeply.
>
> If we fail to intervene, although we know a man is being made upset, why separate these actions of ours from those of the subject, who feels he is causing discomfort to another. And can we not use our own motives and reactions as a clue to what is behind the actions of the subject.
>
> The question to ask then is: why do we feel justified in carrying through the experiment, and why is this any different from the justifications that the obedient subjects feel.
>
> I feel, though I cannot quite find the words for it, that the reactions of the observers—those who sit by "enjoying the show" are profoundly relevant to an understanding of the actions of the subject.[90]

Milgram thus intuited, and anguished over, the unattractive similarity between his own behavior and that of his subjects well before Diana Baumrind pointed it out.[91] Indeed, in a 1961 letter instructing graduate student Alan Elms to "deliver more people to the laboratory," Milgram noted the "resemblance" of his assistant's role to Mr. Eichmann's position." Although the psychologist quickly insisted that the subjects Elms was recruiting would have the opportunity to resist malevolent authority, the fact that Stanley Milgram made this connection between his own assistant's search for subjects and Adolf Eichmann's responsibility for transporting millions of Jews to their deaths suggests that the social psychologist understood, even at an unconscious level, the ways that his treatment of experimental subjects might have mirrored those same subjects' treatment of the "learner."[92]

Moreover, although Stanley Milgram continually justified his experiments in public by pointing to their social value, in some of his early private writings, he was far more skeptical of the trials' benefits to the world. In August 1962, he noted that the experiments might be used by those who sought *greater* obedience as well as by those who sought to resist unjust authority, and he also noted that it was his own personal scientific ambition, not his desire to help humankind, that really motivated his work: "Considered as a personal motive of the author the possible benefits that might redound to humanity withered to insignificance alongside the strident demands of intellectual curiosity. When an investigator keeps his eyes open throughout a scientific study, he learns things about himself as well as about his subjects, and the observations do not always flatter."[93] Given the degree of self-reflection and discomfort he had felt while conducting the experiments, it is small wonder, then, that Milgram's early notes regarding Diana Baumrind's article reflect little of the invective or anger that his graduate students displayed; instead, his unpublished notes from June 1964 feature a sketch of himself portrayed as a dog, along with the caption: "After reading Dr. Baumrind's article I feel bad."[94]

None of these notes are offered to suggest that Stanley Milgram was publicly dishonest about his understanding of his own moral accountability for the obedience experiments. Indeed, it is quite possible that subjects' questionnaires returned in 1963 eliminated most, if not all, of his ethical doubts. Nor are these notes described in order to reopen the subject of the psychologist's ethical responsibilities to his subjects. The purpose of uncovering these documents is to note the ways that Stanley Milgram struggled with his own power and authority in the obedience experiments. Unlike the public image he presented of an assured scientist comfortable with his status and his work, during the experiments, Milgram had privately questioned his right to conduct the trials.

The fact that Stanley Milgram questioned his own decision to continue the obedience experiments adds a particular poignance and significance to other unpublished notes in which the psychologist attempted to justify the ethics of the study by referring to his Jewish background. In a remarkable series of rough drafts of articles or chapters, probably written sometime in the mid-1960s, Milgram defended himself against ethical criticisms by noting that, as a Jew, he identified with neither the experimenter nor the subject in the obedience experiments but with the victim, the "learner" who was supposedly given painful shocks:

> Persons sometimes assume that the investigator identifies with the role of the experimenter. But the fact of the matter is that, in the present study, my deepest and most thoroughgoing identification is neither with the experimenter nor the subject, but with the victim.
>
> Under what conditions does one ask about destructive obedience? Perhaps under the same conditions that a medical researcher asks about cancer or polio; because it is important a threat to human welfare and has shown itself a scourge to humanity. Perhaps the need to understand and conquer the disease becomes more pressing when a member of the family has been hurt by it.
>
> The nightmare that engulfed Europe in 1933–45 claimed many victims; none was hit so hard as European Jewry. ~~It is only an accident of geography that I was not born in Prague and sent to Dachau with my coreligionists~~. . . . My only response, as a ~~survivor~~ remnant, and a student of human behavior, is to try to understand the elements in the ~~human~~ situation that allowed for the tragedy. And insofar as I see myself as part of that tragedy, it is in the role of ~~hounded, not the hound~~ victim.[95]

This haunted passage suggests the ways that Milgram struggled with the impact of Nazi annihilation; with his own understanding of himself as a potential Jewish victim, an innocent and accidental "survivor" of the murderous destruction of World War II; and with the public image that Diana Baumrind and others advanced, as well as the private image that he occasionally held of himself: an arrogant scientist who had misused subjects.

It is worth wondering why Milgram never overtly acknowledged any of his own struggles over the obedience experiments' ethics, and never published any of the passages that suggested that he identified with the Jewish victim rather than the cold, scientific experimenter. It is possible, after all, that Milgram's personal concern with the Jewish victims of the Holocaust might have elicited sympathy from readers, and that his public avowal of his own moral concerns while running the experiments might have made his arguments for the experiments' ultimate ethical responsibility more persuasive. Milgram may have believed that any acknowledgment that he had questioned his own actions would automatically jeopardize any claim to ethical behavior. He may also have believed that readers would interpret his Jewish identification as a "personal bias," as he indeed labeled his ethnic background, that might have clouded his judgment and allowed him to ignore the distress of his subjects.[96] It is unclear whether readers might have made these assumptions, but Milgram clearly did not feel comfortable taking such chances.

Stanley Milgram's unpublished notes on the ethics of his experiments suggest that he experienced significant personal ambivalence in being both an insider and an outsider. On the one hand, Milgram felt like an outsider, a Jew menaced and targeted by the Nazi Holocaust. Furious at the murder of his friends and family and at the mortal threat the Nazis had posed to himself, he wanted to understand the German perpetrators of the mass crime. Moreover, as the child of Jewish immigrants, Milgram was the first boy in his family from the Bronx to go to college; he was certainly not a member of an intellectual elite by birth.[97] At the same time, Milgram was unquestionably an intellectual insider. He had an appointment at Yale University and a National Science Foundation grant to permit him to explore his scientific and moral questions. Moreover, he had constructed a laboratory experiment that "marshal[ed] powerful forces" against participants and subjected hundreds of people to significant stress. Milgram recognized the existence of this power, and he felt uncomfortable about the ways he had wielded it:

At times I have concluded that, although the experiment can be justified, there are still elements in it that are ethically questionable, that it is not nice to lure people into the laboratory and ensnare them into a situation that is stressful and unpleasant to them. Therefore, while what has been done cannot be undone, I can at least resolve not to repeat the performance. There and then I decide, as a purely personal matter, not to do another experiment that requires illusion, or ensnarement, and certainly not to do an experiment that forces the subject into a moral choice and marshals powerful forces against his making the right choice.[98]

Stanley Milgram's ethical dilemma offers readers valuable insight into the ambivalence he felt as a young Jewish academic as he balanced between an understanding of himself as an outsider, a self-understanding imprinted during an era of antisemitism in the 1930s and 1940s, and his heady acceptance into an intellectual elite by the early 1960s.

CLEARLY, FOR SOME PSYCHOLOGISTS, Stanley Milgram had raised serious ethical concerns about the profession, and the early professional responses to his work centered on the morality of his research methodology.[99] For other psychologists, as well as many laypeople, however, Milgram's methods were less significant than the awful results and the frightening parallels that the scientist described. Particularly during the turn of the 1960s, the obedience experiments encouraged many lay readers and professional academics in psychology, sociology, and history to see their own lives through the lens of Nazi evil. Moreover, many Americans understood Milgram's experiments to have significant political meaning, and they frequently used the experiments to justify their own support for liberal causes.

From very early on, the obedience study received wide-ranging publicity, and it became a part of American—and even world—popular culture quickly. Mainstream newspaper writers, radio commentators, educators, and religious leaders were fascinated by the initial 1963 *JASP* report of Milgram's scientific experiments and immediately translated those experiments into larger lessons for their diverse lay audiences. Very soon after "Behavioral Study of Obedience" was printed in the *JASP* in October 1963, both the United Press International (UPI) wire service and the *New York Times* released stories on the experiments.[100] Once those stories were released, news outlets such as the *Sunday Times* of London, the *St. Louis Post Dispatch*, the *San Francisco Chronicle* and WOR Radio in New York widely publicized the experiments in articles, columns, editorials, and radio broadcasts within the last two months of 1963.[101] Throughout the next decade, even before Milgram finally published his monograph *Obedience to Authority* in 1974, journals as diverse as *Science Digest, Esquire*, and the *National Enquirer* published articles on the Milgram experiments.

The large majority of these articles emphasized the connections between Milgram's findings and the actions of Nazis during World War II. "What sort of people, slavishly doing what they are told, would send millions of fellow humans into gas chambers," asked the lead of the *New York Times* article.[102] *San Francisco Examiner* columnist George Dusheck compared Milgram's volunteers to former Nazis put on trial for their murder of Jews: "Like Eichmann and Major Zoepf, they were calmed by the knowledge they were obeying orders."[103] And a *New York Post* interview with Milgram was illustrated with a photograph of Adolf Eichmann and noted in its introduction that the "Nazi slaughter of the Jews" had set the stage for the Yale psychologist's finding.[104] Milgram's own decision to link his experiments to the Nazi era was significant in all these journalists' representations. Many reporters who made the connection between the Yale study and Nazism referred specifically to the psychologist's introduction noting that "gas chambers were built, death camps were guarded, daily quotas of corpses were produced."[105]

Many of the news reports further encouraged readers to interpret Milgram's findings by putting themselves into the experiments and seeing themselves as potential Nazis. Writers typically described the obedience study by making the reader into the naive subject. Articles outlined the experimental procedures slowly and carefully, omitting the crucial details that explained Milgram's deception until the very end and thus encouraging the reader to guess what her response would be: "If [the learner] gets it wrong you push a switch that buzzes and gives him an electric shock. . . . If at any point you hesitate, Mr. Williams calmly tells you to go on. If you still hesitate, he tells you again," Philip Meyer described ominously in *Esquire*.[106] "Soon the subject is screaming in agony. . . . Would you stop the experiment . . . or go right on through to the 30th switch?" challenged *Scholastic Teacher*.[107] Essays that did not so thoroughly re-create the experiments nevertheless still framed the experiments as representative of what "you," or "we," would do: "The experiment at Yale applies to each of us," warned Max Lerner in *McCall's,* while William Raspberry in the *Washington Post* claimed that the experiments "might give you some second thoughts about your moral superiority."[108]

Headlines further insisted that readers explore their own potential to behave like Nazis: *Esquire* titled its article on Milgram, "If Hitler Asked You to Electrocute a Stranger, Would You? Probably."[109] "You Might Do Eichmann's Job," *Pageant* magazine informed its readers.[110] "Could We Be Nazi Followers?" asked the headline of a *Science Digest* piece on the obedience study: "Does it take a madman or a monster to help send millions of men to their death on order, as in Nazi Germany? Or do the seeds of such slavish inhumanity exist in all of us?"[111] Newspaper articles thus sought to engage the reader by involving him in the experiments, and even by informing him that he could be a Nazi.

Newspaper and magazine articles sometimes put generic American symbols into Nazi situations, occasionally blending American iconography with that of Nazi Germany. For example, in order to illustrate a 1965 article reporting Milgram's findings and suggesting that American whites might have a "Nazi Germ," an African American newspaper, *Muhammad Speaks,* folded an image of stars and stripes into the prison uniforms worn by blacks who were drawn waiting in line to enter death camps guarded by white Americans and decorated with an American flag.[112] To illustrate its profile of Milgram in 1970, *Esquire* melded a portrait of Hitler into an Uncle Sam recruitment poster, with the message in German, "The Führer wants you," printed in bold Teutonic type.[113] These illustrations threw doubt on American emblems of liberty and democracy, such as the flag and Uncle Sam, by blending them with images of Hitler and death camps, symbols of Nazi Germany and evil.

Although these representations might today be seen as manifesting bad taste or a poor understanding of the Holocaust, there were few contemporary complaints about Milgram's reference to the Holocaust, even among Jews.[114] Instead, many Jews welcomed Milgram's perspective. Rabbis in Pennsylvania, New York, and Indiana used the experiments in their sermons. "May I express my sincere appreciation for your remarkable contribution to the phenomenon of 'evil,'" Rabbi Henry Enoch Kagan of Mount Vernon, New York, wrote to Milgram in 1965.[115] The editors of the Boston *Jewish Advocate,* similarly, were heartened by the psychologist's serious attention to the evils of the world, especially evils of such magnitude as Auschwitz or Hiroshima.[116] Far from being unhappy with the ways that Milgram made Nazi Germany relevant to contemporary American discourse, many Jews celebrated this relevance.

Unsurprisingly, perhaps, given the ways in which journalists described the experiments—and Nazi Germany—as a relevant template for understanding contemporary American life, Americans who read articles on Milgram's work absorbed it quickly into their own political belief systems. People involved in a wide range of protest and peace activities—from encouraging war resistance to exchanging hostages for peace to establishing alternative newspapers—wrote to Milgram to ask for additional information, to commend his work, and, most importantly, to link his results to their own activities.[117] Lawyer Kenneth MacDonald believed that Milgram's experiments could help him in his case challenging the loyalty oath for professors in Washington State.[118] College student Ellen S. Jaffe sent Milgram a clipped photograph of police dragging a civil rights demonstrator, telling him the picture explained "why it was possible to obtain your results in 'democratic' America.'"[119] Feminist psychologist Naomi Weisstein called Milgram a "brilliant, radical" social psychologist and used his findings to substantiate her claims that the psychological profession inaccurately categorized women as natural wives and mothers, ignoring the way that social expectations determined their lives.[120] And after California reinstated the death penalty, teacher Jeffrey P. Cook, who opposed capital punishment, wrote that he found himself "trapped" by authority, like Milgram's subjects, and called to the psychologist for "HELP!!"[121]

Readers most frequently associated Milgram's experiments with the two central political dilemmas of the late 1960s and early 1970s: Vietnam and Watergate. By the time Milgram had published an excerpt of his forthcoming book in *Harper's Magazine* in 1973, journalists such as Stanley Karnow and Robert Schneerson had seized on the obedience experiments as an explanatory guide to the massacre of hundreds of Vietnamese civilians at My Lai and the criminal activities in Nixon's White House: "Stanley Milgram . . . demonstrated in the laboratory what Lt. William Calley and his unit would later dramatize at Mylai—that man's behavior is almost invariably dominated by authority rather than by his own sense of morality."[122] Readers and viewers made the same associations. "As I sit here listening to the Watergate hearings," wrote oceanography professor Dale Krause, "your [work] continually comes to mind. . . . The Watergate affair is a real example of how people's behavior is conditioned by their acceptance of the correctness of their respected leaders' . . . orders."[123] Merrill G. Leonard told Milgram that "the most widespread example" of his obedience theory was "the many of us who knew that the Vietnam War was wrong from the very beginning; that it was unspeakably cruel from the beginning; and yet kept paying the taxes that made that war possible."[124]

Individuals who had personally protested the war or Watergate felt particularly vindicated by Milgram's work. "Thank you very much . . . very, very much," wrote legal secretary Mildred Spielmann, who had been indicted for helping her son emigrate to Canada to escape the draft, "You made [my friends] understand a bit better what I meant—what I could not express."[125] Arthur L. Murtagh, who had recently resigned from the FBI, compared his own rebellion against the "Watergate mentality" of the Bureau to the defiance of the "33% or so of your teachers who revolted against authority when it ran contrary to conscience and common sense."[126] People who were caught up in the Watergate scandals or angry with the government's maintentance of the Vietnam War and its suppression of dissent used Milgram's experiments to interpret the power of obedience in their own political lives.[127]

Social scientists were similarly eager to use Milgram's paradigm in protesting the Vietnam War and critiquing Watergate. The obedience experiments became reference points in two popular anthologies put together by social scientists, including Robert Jay Lifton, to protest the war.[128] Social pychologist Herbert Kelman used Milgram's analysis to explore American attitudes toward the My Lai massacre in a prizewinning, influential series of studies, and psychologists S. G. West, S. P Guan, and P. Chernicky replicated the Milgram paradigm with a twist: rather than asking subjects to shock a learner, experimenters asked them help commit a burglary of local political offices.[129] Milgram's obedience experiments thus served as a model and reference point for liberal critiques of the American government.

It is important to note that Milgram's thesis did not only serve as an interpretive guide to liberal American politics; it also encouraged ordinary Americans to act. The experiments, of course, had emphasized that verbal dissent was ineffectual: only active disobedience could help one avoid becoming a criminal. By illustrating the frightening tendency of people to become obedient perpetrators, Milgram inspired protest and political action. A number of Milgram's correspondents reported that he had motivated them to moral action and resistance against government policies. A student who had been a subject in a replication of Milgram's experiments at Princeton in 1964, for example, filed for conscientious objector status during the Vietnam War based on his experience as an obedient subject. Thanking Milgram for "your contribution to my life," the student told him, "You have discovered one of the most important causes of all the trouble in this world. . . . I am delighted to have acted, by refusing to serve in the Armed Forces, in a manner in which people must act if these problems are to be solved."[130] A professor testified that thinking about the obedience experiments had enabled him to break out of an "inner paralysis" that had prevented him from passing out leaflets protesting the American invasion of Cambodia.[131]

Moreover, the many organized protests of the New Left, from taking over administration buildings to forcing confrontations with National Guardsmen, may also have been inspired by Milgram's experiments. Thomas Bouchard, one of the students involved in the Berkeley Free Speech Movement in 1964, for example, asked Milgram for reprints of his papers in order to educate the judge who had convicted him and other students for their civil disobedience.[132] Richard Flacks, a sociologist who had been one of the earliest founders of Students for a Democratic Society (SDS), called Milgram's work, along with that of Solomon Asch and sociologist C. Wright Mills, "crucial in my own intellectual and moral development."[133] And Milgram himself remembered meeting "the President and articulate spokesman of the largest radical student organization, who greatly surprised me by telling me what a prominent part the 'obedience experiments' played in the mythology and thinking of his group."[134] Thus the New Left's radical activities, although obviously shaped by many factors, seem also to have been inspired by Stanley Milgram's experiments.

At the base of much of this political activism was the haunting image of Nazi Germany. Milgram received a large number of letters from ordinary people who were devastated by the demonstration that they could be as evil as Nazis. Geoffrey Davis, for example, saw himself as an Eichmann who had been willfully torturing women through his work in fertility control.[135] John Holt gloomily noted that Milgram's study had confirmed for him "that in their hearts most Americans, and indeed perhaps most people everywhere, have accepted a kind of Fascism."[136] After replicating Milgram's experiment for a science fair, high school student Harriet Tobin concluded that average American teenagers "were comparable to the Nazi youth groups who were completely dominated by Hitler's ideas and followed his orders without hesitation."[137] And school librarian Holly Beye Ruff was depressed and distraught over the "shockingly close parallel in the behavior of Americans in the 1960s and functionaries of the Nazi party in Hitler's Germany" that Milgram's work had pointed out.[138] Many of Milgram's readers thus came to see their own personal and political lives through the lens of Nazi Germany that the psychologist had affixed to his shocking experiments.

Of course, not all Americans found Milgram's work persuasive. Milgram received several letters from admirers who reported that they had tried to talk with friends, coworkers, and parishioners about the experiments, only to be greeted by skepticism.[139] Moreover, the psychologist also received a minority of letters from people who criticized his ethics or rejected the claim that his laboratory results could be applied to Nazi Germany or, in fact, to any real-world situation.[140]

These criticisms became more numerous in the early 1970s, as the liberal political moment of the turn of the 1960s was increasingly tempered by skepticism and disillusionment. Milgram received a mixed reception in the press when *Obedience to Authority* finally came out in 1974. His pronouncements about the inhumanity of man were no longer quite as fashionable among intellectuals or journalists. A number of reviewers, even positive ones such as Peter S. Prescott of *Newsweek,* noted that Milgram's claims about human nature were "perhaps fatuous and certainly unsubstantiated" by his results.[141] New York intellectual Daniel Bell, whose early radicalism had drifted to a more conservative stance by the early 1970s, claimed in the *New York Times* that Milgram had offered a "liberal platitude" about human evil that erased individual moral responsibility by suggesting that all people were guilty of destructive obedience.[142] Christopher Lehmann-Haupt, a book reviewer for the *New York Times,* questioned the representative nature of the subjects being tested and, along with many other reviewers, complained that Milgram had not paid any attention to the 35 percent of subjects who had been defiant, thus making unwarranted claims about humankind in general.[143] Moreover, fewer headlines or lead paragraphs forthrightly validated Milgram's claims by placing the reader into the experiment itself, asking questions like the *New York Times*'s "Is Eichmann in All of Us?"[144] More headlines, such as that in the *Chicago News*—"Zzap! But They Were Just Following Orders"—emphasized instead the experiments' infliction of pain or commented ironically on subjects' willingess to obey, thus distancing readers from the experiments, rather than enthusiastically making them potential subjects.[145] During the turn of the 1960s, a popular intellectual climate had prevailed that was favorable for a liberal worldview emphasizing all people's individual responsibility for pervasive social evil. However, by the middle of the 1970s, pronouncements about humankind, the malevolent social environment, and the need for civil disobedience had become less fashionable, and this shift in intellectual trends affected the reception of *Obedience to Authority*.

Certainly Milgram's liberal political sympathies had not gone completely out of style. Readers vigorously defended the psychologist from his harsh critics in several series of letters to the editor.[146] A good number of positive reviews still sung the book's virtues, labeling it "riveting" and "one of the most significant books I have read in more than two decades of reviewing."[147] *Obedience to Authority* was even nominated for the National Book Award in 1975.[148] In fact, Milgram received more positive publicity than he ever had before, through a variety of media channels such as the *Today Show,* the *Phil Donahue Show,* and *Sixty Minutes.*[149]

Almost all of the publicity surrounding *Obedience to Authority* in the mid-1970s tended to emphasize Stanley Milgram's initial connection between the obedience of subjects of his laboratory experiments and the actions of Nazis during World War II. The dramatic *Sixty Minutes* segment on Milgram, for example, first flashed stark images of Nazi death camps and the victims of the My Lai massacre, then broadcast a brief interview with Milgram, and then presented an extended clip from the film *Obedience* portraying an obedient subject in Milgram's experiment. The message of the segment was summed up by Milgram's familiar sound bite, which introduced the entire hour-long program: "If a system of death camps were set up in the United States of the sort we had seen in Nazi Germany, one would be able to find sufficient personnel for those camps in any medium-sized American town."[150] Even negative reviewers who were critical of Milgram's "empty pious sentiments" went out of their way to validate the psychologist's argument that Americans could perform Nazi-like actions.[151]

Although this image of Americans as potential Nazis remained a lasting message of the obedience experiments in the public consciousness, as the 1970s continued, the impact that this message had had on American liberal and left-wing political activism receded with the changing political tide. Instead, the Milgram experiments shaped American popular culture in two very different ways in the 1970s and 1980s: through the growing field of Holocaust studies and in debates over scientific ethics.

As the narrative of the Holocaust developed in the late 1960s and early 1970s, Milgram's work became an important aspect of its study, reorienting scholars' perspectives of German perpetrators. In the middle and late 1960s, scholars and educators became newly interested in studying and teaching about the Nazi destruction of European Jewry specifically, rather than subsuming this destruction within the narrative of World War II. The term "the Holocaust" became popular by the end of the 1960s, and in the 1970s, historical schools of interpretation began to generate debates about issues surrounding the Holocaust. Perhaps the most important of these debates was that of "intentionalism" versus "functionalism." The intentionalist school provided a new version of the interpretation of Nazism popular in the 1950s in works such as Adorno's *Authoritarian Personality;* intentionalists believed it was Hitler's insane antisemitism, a combination of psychological disease and ideological extremism, that had led directly to the murder of European Jews from 1933 on. In this interpretation, the delineations among perpetrators, bystanders, and victims were clear: perpetrators were absolutely guilty by intent, bystanders were guilty only of a passivity that allowed the government to continue as usual, and victims were not guilty at all.

The functionalist school, however, which has also been called the "structuralist" or "leftist" school, viewed the development of the Final Solution as an incremental process of radicalization that did have its origins in Hitler's orders but essentially escalated through local and bureaucratic efforts, rather than top-down orders from Hitler. In the structuralist interpretation, the responsibility apportioned to perpetrators and victims was more confusing: perpetrators were no longer viewed as antisemites determined to carry out Hitler's orders but in fact as bureaucrats interested in staking out and preserving their terrain, and victims became implicated in their own destruction.[152]

Milgram's work served as important background for the development of the functionalist school of Holocaust history.[153] His demonstration that the evils of the Nazi regime were not necessarily the result of a poisoned

German mind, but instead could have been the result of a more complex and horrifying bureaucracy, was liberating for a number of young scholars of the Holocaust in the late 1960s and 1970s, perhaps because the experiments seemed an objective means of legitimizing Hannah Arendt's thesis of the "banality of evil." Saul Friedländer, a current Holocaust scholar respected in the field, wrote excitedly to Milgram in 1966 that the obedience experiments had shaken the entire theory of "the authoritarian personality" and were of "the utmost importance" for his own work on National Socialism.[154] Although Friedländer ultimately did not rely on Milgram's thesis to make his arguments, many other scholars did. Throughout the 1970s, a host of journalists, sociologists, and psychiatrists, such as Henry Dicks and Gitta Sereny, who conducted interviews with Nazi war criminals and SS officers after the war, used Milgram's analysis to make sense of their own interview data.[155] Moreover, into the 1980s and 1990s, a number of well-respected Holocaust scholars, most of whom were functionalists, such as Zygmunt Bauman and Christopher Browning, continued to use Milgram's work in order to demonstrate the "ordinary" nature of Nazi perpetrators and to deemphasize the significance of "German national character" and murderous antisemitism in the Holocaust.[156] In the late 1990s, historian Daniel Goldhagen created a firestorm of controversy by emphasizing the significance of antisemitism and German culture among Nazi perpetrators, in opposition to the portrait of banal bureaucrats carrying out murder.[157] On the whole, however, by the turn of the twenty-first century, most recent sophisticated examinations of the Holocaust offered balanced approaches that integrated bureaucratic obedience and antisemitic ideology.[158] Thus, although it does not dominate Holocaust studies, Milgram's work, with its emphasis on the ordinary evils of bureaucracy, made a significant impact on Holocaust scholars that lasts to this day.

As Milgram's work became accepted in scholarly circles as a possible explanation for Nazi genocide, it similarly became an important aspect of secondary-school education about the Holocaust. Since Milgram's work presented the complexity of the Holocaust in a simple, dramatic fashion, with a potential for teaching students not only about history but also about their own moral behavior, it is understandable that secondary educators became excited by the obedience experiments. In the mid-1960s clinical psychologist Israel Charny, for example, wanted to include Milgram's obedience experiments in a Hebrew education seminar on Holocaust education, and he hoped Milgram might also suggest methods of "teaching humanistic, non-violent attitudes which hopefully could stand up in subsequent encounters with evil."[159] By the late 1970s, when Milgram's work had become part of an accepted scholarly explanation of the Holocaust, the obedience experiments frequently became a part of middle and high school curricula designed to teach about the event, often with an implicit liberal message. In one influential Holocaust curriculum, teachers were encouraged to show their students Milgram's film, *Obedience*: "One of his conclusions stands as a warning for us today: the more fragmented and bureaucratic our lives become the less responsible we feel for our actions."[160] To be sure, many teachers may have used this curriculum selectively. One scholar's recent research suggests that Stanley Milgram's work was not included in as many high school Holocaust classes as is usually assumed. Moreover, by the 1990s, this scholar reports, fewer Holocaust curricula made reference to the obedience study at all.[161] Nonetheless, just as Milgram influenced many scholars to deemphasize the role of antisemitic ideology in the Final Solution in the 1970s and 1980s, he similarly encouraged secondary educators during the same era to emphasize the ways in which ordinary people— even ordinary Americans like students themselves—might have been able to help perpetrate crimes like the Holocaust.

In addition to shaping Holocaust education in a way that emphasized Americans' capacity to behave similarly to Nazis, the Milgram experiments similarly shaped sociology and psychology education. One 1995 study of fifty college textbooks in sociology, psychology, and social psychology published since 1990 found that the vast majority of these books' authors devoted a disproportionate number of pages to the subject of the obedience study. Moreover, in 86 percent of these textbooks, the authors explicitly connected the results of the experiments to Nazi Germany, frequently offering pictures of the Holocaust to illustrate this connection to Milgram's work.[162] Stanley Milgram left a significant legacy in the field of psychology education, particularly among introductory college textbooks, thus allowing, once again, ordinary American students to view their own behavior through the lens of Nazi crime.

This lasting image of Americans as potential Nazis remained even as the substantial ethical criticism that Milgram had faced professionally became publicized in mainstream newspapers, television, and fiction. By the middle of the 1970s, popular representations of the obedience studies had begun to encourage ordinary Americans to question the morality of the experiments and even the sanity of the scientist himself. Nonetheless, even as significant criticism of Milgram's work became a part of the public understanding of the obedience study, the psychologist's parallel between American life and Nazi Germany continued to exert a powerful hold on many.

In 1974, many writers reporting Milgram's study or reviewing *Obedience to Authority* mentioned the ethical controversies as part of their articles, thus exposing lay readers to the existence of the debate and allowing them to question for themselves the ethical proprieties of the experiments.[163] Perhaps the most powerful critic was psychologist Lawrence Kohlberg, who specialized in the study of ethics and who, as a friend and colleague of Milgram at Yale, had conducted research with Milgram's subjects. Commenting in 1974 on a debate over Milgram's work in the *New York Times Book Review*, Kohlberg gently criticized Milgram for having treated his experimental participants as objects rather than as subjects of moral inquiry. Although Kohlberg called Milgram a victim, he also called him "another banal perpetrator of evil. Serving the authority [of] science under the banner of 'objectivity,' he himself inflicted pain on others for the greater social welfare." Kohlberg indicted himself as well as Milgram for their decision not to morally educate the participants in the obedience experiments.[164]

Kohlberg's comments had been anticipated even before 1974, as writers in mainstream media in the late 1960s had offered harsh criticisms of the psychologist's behavior and had even turned Milgram's comparison between his laboratory experiments and the Nazi camps against him. Psychologist Ray Bixler, for example, writing about professional ethics in the *Saturday Review* in 1966, noted that a Harvard scientist "enjoys telling his professional audiences that the cruelty exhibited in the Nazi concentration camps is latent in many Americans." After describing the obedience experiments, Bixler commented: "He has, I think, unwittingly assumed the role of a concentration camp doctor."[165] And in his 1970 article on Milgram in *Esquire*, Philip Meyer had carefully drawn out a comparison between Milgram's willingness to inflict temporary harm and his subjects' willingness, and had suggested that the psychologist, just like "you and me," and just like "the people with their fingers on the shock-generator switches," could have been a Nazi.[166] Milgram's analogy between death camp guards and his experimental subjects thus ironically offered his critics a powerful analogy for their own complaints, even encouraging at least some of them to see his own behavior as potentially Nazi.

By the middle of the 1970s, such criticism had multiplied and moved into popular culture. Emerging representations of the obedience experiments in popular culture emphasized the ethical controversy surrounding the study, portraying the experiments as morally questionable and conducted by a scientist and confederates who were obsessed by politics and psychologically disturbed. In 1973, for example, English playwright Dannie Abse wrote *The Dogs of Pavlov*, a play imagining a fictional replication of the

Milgram experiments from the perspective of the actor playing the "learner," Sally, and her boyfriend, Kurt, whom she tricks into becoming a subject. Although the play endorsed Milgram's belief that his experiments demonstrated the "incipient Nazi" in ordinary people, offering a highly unsympathetic portrait of an obedient subject as a sexist toady, Abse nonetheless ultimately portrayed the experimenter's confederate, Sally, as disturbed and manipulative, and shallowly sympathetic to the cause of the victimized. The play, moreover, concluded with the hero, Kurt, attacking the experimenter himself as an immoral fraud: "You play tricks on your victims. You reduce them to fools and in so doing you assert your own power."[167] It was the experimenter's lack of ethics that Abse's play emphasized in its harsh conclusion.

Similarly, television producer George Bellak produced a TV movie for CBS in 1976, called *The Tenth Level*, that legitimized Stanley Milgram's claims for the political significance of his work while it nonetheless portrayed him as a rather mad scientist and ended with a sharp attack on his ethics. The movie fictionalized Milgram as academic psychologist Stephen Turner, a somewhat quiet man who was consumed with Nazi concentration camp imagery, played by William Shatner. Because Turner was neither black nor Jewish but a "WASP," this obsession was pathological, a reflection of guilt and a need for martyrdom, according to Turner's friend Ben, a black psychologist played by Ossie Davis. With discordant horror-movie music in the background, the movie showed Turner's experiments going forward, particularly emphasizing the intense nervous reactions of subjects, but did not let viewers themselves know that the "learner" was not being shocked until the play was more than half over, thus emphasizing the film's portrait of the psychologist as crazy. After one subject, Barry, a student who had served in the army during Vietnam, had a breakdown during the experiment and destroyed the equipment, Turner was subjected to an ethical inquiry. Many of the subjects that viewers had seen breaking down earlier during the trials testified to the value of the experiment, including Barry: "Had I been over there in My Lai, I would have shot dogs, cats, women, children, old men, babies, I would have wasted them all," he told the ethics board. "I'm grateful to Dr. Turner, 'cause you see I know what is inside of me." Despite Barry's emotional admission, the last scene of the movie focused on a confrontation between Turner and his former lover, another psychologist on faculty, who demanded that he see the comparison between himself and his subjects: "You've been tested [like your subjects]," she charged "You had a choice, you could have stopped. . . . Your ends—which were knowledge—for that you knowingly inflicted pain." Turner had no answer to her angry charges, and the film ended with him sobbing on her shoulder.[168]

Thus, by the middle of the 1970s, popular audiences who were introduced to Stanley Milgram's obedience study were not simply encouraged to see the parallels between the experiments and Nazi Germany, nor did they tend only to see the political need for civil disobedience that many of Milgram's early lay audiences had perceived in the initial article with which he introduced his results. Instead, mainstream book reviews and cultural representations of the obedience study in the mid-1970s pushed audiences to question the ethics and perhaps even the sanity of the scientist himself. As a technical consultant, Stanley Milgram was able to have some impact in shaping his own image in *The Tenth Level,* and indeed Milgram seems to have approved of the conflicted scientist that Bellak portrayed.[169] Certainly, the television movie's portrait of a Protestant scientist strangely obsessed with the Nazi era contains a kernel of Stanley Milgram's private notes about his own justification as a Jew for carrying out his experiments. For the most part, however, Milgram's notes and letters suggest that the psychologist probably had little to do with this film, and that it certainly did not project the public image of his experiments that he had hoped for. Moreover, Milgram's letters to Dannie Abse justifying his ethics had little to no impact on *The Dogs of Pavlov,* although those letters were published along with the play. Thus, despite the psychologist's efforts, the controversy over Milgram's ethics became a significant part of his public image in the 1970s.

Importantly, however, even as ethical debate deflected some attention away from Milgram's analogy between his subjects and death camp guards, images of Nazis continued to recur in public representations of the obedience experiments. When journalists compared the psychologist himself to a Nazi, or artists created fictional portraits of scientists carrying out obedience experiments because they were obsessed with the Holocaust, the connection that Stanley Milgram had encouraged between American society and Nazi Germany remained a constant hovering presence. Perhaps even more significantly, television viewers who had seen *The Tenth Level* did not tend to write to the network or to *TV Guide* with ethical attacks against Milgram. Instead, many letter writers validated Milgram's comparison of Americans to Nazis, as well as the potential political message of his experiments.[170]

STANLEY MILGRAM'S EXPERIMENTS had important impact on and legacies for American intellectual and political thought. First, the psychologist's work both reflected and helped to spark the zeitgeist of the liberal turn of the 1960s. During that era, newspaper reports recognized the sensational nature of the experiments and highlighted their relevance for readers' own lives. Readers who read stories about the obedience experiments at this time were alternately horrified and energized, frequently finding in Milgram's research a greater understanding of the need for liberal commitments and civil disobedience to end segregation and war. Furthermore, many activists in early New Left groups, such as the Berkeley Free Speech Movement and Students for a Democratic Society, viewed their own civil disobedience as sanctioned and explained by Milgram's results.

In the late 1960s and early 1970s, Milgram's study continued to have significant political implications in the United States. To Americans who were fighting an unpopular, undeclared war featuring a widely publicized massacre carried out by American soldiers, and to Americans whose president had demanded that his subordinates steal and lie to protect and perpetuate his presidency, the obedience experiments expressed a profound political truth.[171] Moreover, since Milgram's analysis also offered a moral code of protest for individuals angered by the Vietnam War and Watergate, the obedience experiments offered Americans intellectual guidance and justification for their radical activism. All this activism had embedded within it the troubling vision of Nazi Germany; most of these actively protesting Americans were not only politically enraged by American society but also haunted by the possibility that if they did not act, they might, like Milgram's obedient subjects, be no better than German bureaucrats who had accomplished the mass murder of Jews simply by following orders. Stanley Milgram's analogy between Nazi death camps and American society thus encouraged liberal and left-wing opposition to the Vietnam War and to the Nixon administration's Watergate activities.

Nonetheless, ethical criticism of Milgram also intensified in the late 1960s and early 1970s. By the middle of the 1970s, that criticism had moved out of its mostly professional circle and into mainstream media outlets and fictional representations of the experiments in popular culture. Moreover, the enthusiasm and political urgency with which liberals and leftists had initially embraced Milgram's experiments had faded somewhat by the middle of the 1970s. More newspaper reporters and reviewers questioned Milgram's universalistic conclusions, and fewer insisted that readers probe their own capacities for evil.

Yet, Milgram's liberal use of Nazi imagery remained significant in American life. Throughout the 1970s, and even afterward, the comparison that the obedience experiments suggested between Nazi and American behavior remained powerful within American culture. Even critics of Milgram's ethics and theory seem to have been affected by this compelling analogy. Moreover, with its deep impact on Holocaust studies and on the field of psychology, Milgram's work continued to be featured prominently in high school and college textbooks and curricula for decades, thus ensuring that young adults throughout the 1970s and 1980s, and even afterward, would encounter the analogy between ordinary Americans and Nazis on a regular basis. Indeed, even in less formal and organized ways, the Milgram experiments continued to exert a hold on American popular culture, as politicians, attorneys, and journalists continued to use the Milgram experiments—and his analogies to Nazi Germany and Vietnam—throughout the 1970s and 1980s in order to urge opposition to genocide in Cambodia or to protest the United States' decision to prosecute the first Gulf War.[172] As psychologist Lee D. Ross has noted, Milgram's obedience study has become "part of our society's shared intellectual legacy—that small body of historical incidents, biblical parables, and classic literature that serious thinkers feel free to draw on when they debate about human nature or contemplate human history."[173] Milgram's analogy between American experimental subjects and Nazi bureaucrats has retained remarkable lasting power. Although Peter Novick has argued that Jews in the United States in the 1970s and 1980s used the Holocaust to encourage support for right-wing Israeli politics, he has not noted the way that an alternate discourse about the Holocaust, one that emphasized a liberal skepticism of authority, a criticism of technocratic bureaucracy, and that deemphasized the role of pathological antisemitism, exerted significant influence in American life not only in academic interpretations of the Holocaust but in ordinary Americans' understandings of their own behavior.

Exploring the significance of Milgram's Jewish background, as well as his political and intellectual influences, for the obedience experiments also sheds light on American Jewish history. Milgram's experience as the child of Jewish immigrants growing up in New York City illustrates the powerful personal meaning that Nazi destruction had for many American Jews in the 1940s and 1950s. Although young Stanley Milgram did not manifest his concern for the Jewish catastrophe in ways that Americans currently understand as "Holocaust consciousness"—that is, he did not link his concern for Nazi Germany openly to his Jewish identity, nor did he emphasize the significance of antisemitism or the uniqueness of the Holocaust in his intellectual work—he was deeply shaped by the knowledge that his own existence had been threatened by Nazi Germany and that "only an accident of geography" had saved him from extermination. Milgram's interest in German national character, and his sensitivity to the subject of the death camps even before the capture of Eichmann in 1960, suggest that there is more historical work to be done in exploring an early period of "Holocaust consciousness" among Jews at the turn of the 1960s, and even earlier. Finally, the ethical controversies surrounding Stanley Milgram's work offer a window into Jews' simultaneous position as insiders and as outsiders in the United States in the decades after World War II. Unpublished notes give us insight into both Milgram's sense of himself as a persecuted Jew who sought to understand the destruction of his people and Milgram's struggle with his own newfound power as a scientist who had federal funding and prestigious institutional backing for a coercive laboratory design that created significant stress for its volunteers.

| # Robert Jay Lifton and the Survivor

We may define the survivor as one who has come
into contact with death in some bodily or psychic
fashion and has himself remained alive.[1]

IN *Death in Life* (1967), psychiatrist Robert Jay Lifton devoted the lengthy
final chapter to a systematic comparison of survivors of Nazi concentration
camps and *hibakusha,* survivors of the atomic blast at Hiroshima.[2] Lifton
identified guilt, "psychic numbing," and scapegoating as among the numerous qualities that Nazi camp survivors and *hibakusha* shared and, thus,
as qualities that defined the psychological category of the "survivor." This
psychological category had significance for contemporary Americans, Lifton went on to argue, because "the holocausts of the twentieth century have
thrust the survivor ethos into special prominence, and imposed upon us all
a series of immersions into death which mark our existence."[3]

Few observers took exception to Robert Lifton's use of concentration
camp survivors or to the contemporary significance he ascribed to their experiences. In fact, almost all praised his work as groundbreaking and moving, and ultimately he won the National Book Award for his efforts. As Lifton used his portrait of the survivor throughout the next thirty years to
build a post-Freudian psychological theory and to criticize the Vietnam War
and nuclear proliferation, he attracted significantly more criticism, but his
initial analogy was rarely questioned, and much of his psychological theory
became part of the fabric of everyday American life.[4] For example, as the
basis for the psychiatric category "post-traumatic stress disorder" (PTSD),
Lifton's portrait of the survivor became a routine part of American psychiatric practice.

Although Lifton's work on the "survivor" has recently come under scrutiny, as critics from varying political perspectives have attacked the political
uses of post-traumatic stress disorder, very few historians or contemporary
critics have noted the ways that Lifton's work was built using an analogy
between the victims of Hiroshima and Dachau, nor have they paid attention

to the ways that the influential concept of post-traumatic stress disorder was grounded in part on the powerful image of the Nazi concentration camp survivor.[5] Scholars have thus neglected to examine a significant way in which the imagery of Nazi machinery has shaped the political, medical, and legal culture of the United States. Once again, while some leaders in the American Jewish community may have deployed the Holocaust in order to support right-wing Israeli policy, other American Jews actually used Holocaust imagery to bolster their backing for liberal and left-wing policies at home. Moreover, in the case of Lifton's "survivor," this Holocaust imagery had significant and lasting impact on the American public as a whole. The fact that Lifton's understanding of himself as a Jewish intellectual, moreover, helped to shape his decision to use Nazi concentration camps in developing the image of the "survivor" can further help historians to explore how secular Jews have constructed their ethnic identity, and how they have understood the impact of the Nazi destruction on them personally.

LIFTON INITIALLY COMPARED concentration camp and Hiroshima victims in a long footnote in the 1964 *Psychiatry* article "On Death and Death Symbolism." Although the bulk of this piece centered on *hibakusha,* Lifton noted in one extensive reference the fact that Japanese victims' psychology "strikingly resemble[d]" that of Nazi camp victims, particularly as both groups displayed depression, withdrawal, apathy, anger, and self-deprecation that might, at its greatest extremes, lead an individual to take on the appearance of a "living corpse."[6] Although he commented on significant differences between the two experiences, such as Nazi inmates' more direct understanding that their survival was at the expense of another person's death and atomic bomb survivors' greater fear of aftereffects, he concluded ultimately that the general psychological problems created by exposure to death needed to be explored more carefully by investigators.

In a more systematic and comprehensive fashion in the final chapter of *Death in Life,* "The Survivor," Robert Lifton compared these two groups again, this time strongly deemphasizing their differences and focusing on their similarities. Using his own extensive interviews with atomic bomb survivors, as well as Nazi camp survivors' testimony in works such as Bruno Bettelheim's *Informed Heart* and Elie Wiesel's *Night,* and contemporary studies of camp survivors conducted by psychiatrists such as William Niederland and Paul Chodoff, Lifton identified five qualities, or themes, common to both concentration camp survivors and *hibakusha.* Lifton believed that these themes, "death imprint, death guilt, psychic numbing, nurturance and contagion, and formulation," helped to make up a "general psychology of the survivor."[7]

Unlike the despairing portraits of dehumanized concentration camp inmates presented by Bruno Bettelheim, Robert Lifton's portraits of atomic bomb survivors were grim but not without hope. The most obvious and significant indication of Lifton's hopeful perspective was, in fact, his emphasis on victims as "survivors" rather than sufferers. Each of the five psychological themes Lifton identified represented individuals' constant, though impeded, efforts to carry on with their lives *after* undergoing an experience in which they were confronted by death. The "death imprint," for example, was the lasting anxiety that resulted after an individual was placed in a situation in which death was imminent. Individuals who experienced "psychic numbing" closed themselves off, or desensitized themselves, from the painful, death-filled world around them. The tendency of survivors to condemn themselves for having prioritized their own survival over that of others Lifton referred to as "death guilt." And "nurturance and contagion" referred to the paradoxical fears with which survivors approached relationships after their brushes with death, as they assumed that all help was counterfeit and that they would somehow infect everyone they touched with death. Although these portraits of survivors were by no means free of pain or anger, neither did they replicate the dehumanized, self-destructive tendencies of the victims portrayed by Bettelheim. By emphasizing the lasting marks that experiences with death left on individuals who had survived Nazi camps or atomic bombing, Lifton still nonetheless focused on the capacity of people to survive even the worst of circumstances and to continue to live.

Perhaps most hopeful was Lifton's belief that a survivor, by engaging in political activism, could rebuild his inner world through the process of "formulation." The psychiatrist posited that a survivor needed to formulate, or make sense of, both his death immersion and his "altered identity" by seeking moral order and justice in the world.[8] Although this search could devolve into a vengeful search for scapegoats, it could also develop into a valuable "survivor mission" that combined memories of love and harmony with a new sense of political purpose, as when survivors worked to establish a peace city in Hiroshima or participated in the formation of Israel. And even the search for scapegoats, Lifton insisted, was necessary and not inherently destructive: "[The survivor's] need to pass judgment on people and forces outside of himself" helped him "to avoid drowning in his own death guilt and symbolic disorder."[9] Thus, the psychiatrist emphasized political activism as a life-affirming process that could redeem ugly psychological tendencies, and he was hopeful that survivors could surmount their anxiety and live a productive life after their immersion in death.

In his subsequent works in the late 1960s and 1970s, Lifton drew out the implications of his analogy between Nazi camp and atomic bomb survivors to build a "death-oriented psychology of life" that considered the impact of twentieth-century holocausts on human psychology. In his "death-oriented psychology of life," Lifton theorized that human beings need to "maintain a *sense of immortality* in the face of inevitable biological death," that they have a "universal urge" to transcend death by developing continuous symbolic relationships with life; some of the activities that permitted such symbolic relationships were having children, writing books, or believing in life after death as a theological precept.[10] Death tested this "symbolic immortality" by threatening to sever all these relationships with the world. Death also tested the integrity and meaning of an individual's life, and finally it represented stasis, rather than the constant movement necessary to form identity. As individuals created their identities throughout their lives, they constantly battled these dangers: stasis, disintegration, and separation. After surviving a death immersion, or holocaust, that imposed all three of these threats, adults went through a three-step process that enabled them to "transform" themselves, to reshape and change their identities after having survived: first confrontation, then reordering, then renewal.

Holocaust and transformation were thus the two central themes at the heart of Robert Jay Lifton's "death-oriented psychology of life," and in essays and books throughout the late 1960s and 1970s, the psychiatrist made it clear that these themes, while universal, had special meaning at the end of the twentieth century because of the twin catastrophes of World War II.[11] "Auschwitz and Hiroshima" became Lifton's metaphor for the ways that twentieth-century holocaust had led to a "preoccupation with absurd death . . . and unlimited technological violence."[12] According to the psychiatrist, "Auschwitz and Hiroshima" represented a historical shift that "terminated man's sense of limits concerning his self-destructive potential, and thereby inaugurated an era in which he is devoid of assurance of living on eternally as a species."[13] In response to this shift, Lifton believed, young people transformed themselves by participating in a "New History" that was founded on spontaneity, community, mockery, rebellion, and transcendental experience. He envisioned a new "protean man," who constantly transformed his identity in response to social dislocation, as the absurd antihero of the post–World War II era.[14] For Robert Jay Lifton, twentieth-century holocaust introduced new fears of absurdity, dislocation, and loss of control, and these feelings allowed a new culture of young people to confront these fears and transform their identities to produce new selves with integrity and meaning.

Thus, for Lifton, the destruction wrought by Nazi Germany was not just a basis for an isolated typology of survivor psychology, but instead it had broad implications for human psychology in the twentieth century. The importance of Nazi Germany for general human psychology became apparent in the psychiatrist's later work in the 1980s and 1990s, as Lifton conducted an intensive and influential study on the psychology of Nazi doctors, as well as developing a book-length study comparing the "genocidal mentality" of Nazi doctors to that of American scientists, strategists, and military officers involved with the production and use of nuclear weapons.[15] Lifton has continued to draw on the example of Nazi violence as he has written in recent years about the apocalyptic rhetoric used to justify warfare in Afghanistan and Iraq, as well as the professional numbing employed by doctors witnessing torture in Guantanamo and Baghdad prisons.[16]

ROBERT JAY LIFTON'S BROAD EMPHASIS on human psychology, technological violence, and the late-twentieth-century human condition make it clear that his analysis of Nazi destruction and its significance in American life did not center on the subject of racial persecution or extermination. Although he did specifically refer to the continuing threat of antisemitism for Nazi survivors in his 1964 *Psychiatry* article, and moreover made a number of specific references to Jewish prisoners in *Death in Life*, the psychiatrist offered little analysis of racial discrimination or of the extermination of Jews in particular in these early works.[17] Lifton used Nazi destruction to understand problems of violence, technology, and alienation in American society, not to emphasize the subject of race or prejudice.

Nonetheless, Robert Jay Lifton's concern with Nazi Germany, and his decision to use camp survivors as a central part of his liberal critique of American nuclear politics, was still closely bound up with his Jewish origins. In *Death in Life*, Lifton called attention several times to his own ethnic background, and he intimated that that background had helped to shape his personal responses both to the atomic disaster and to the Nazi camps: "If my grandparents had not elected to emigrate from Eastern Europe, I might have been a concentration camp victim or survivor. Such accidents of history must be kept in mind."[18] In later work, Lifton called his Jewish heritage "part of the constellation" of his identity, explaining that his "relationship as a Jew to the Nazi persecutions" informed his writing about Hiroshima and made his analogy between the two events "an imperative personal task as well as a logical intellectual one."[19] Lifton left his meaning in both of these statements somewhat ambivalent, but he made clear that he experienced the same existential anxiety that Stanley Milgram had expressed privately, feeling his own existence as an American Jew to have been accidental and endangered. Closer examination of Lifton's Jewish background, and of his identity as a Jewish intellectual, will help to elucidate how that background might have shaped Lifton's anxiety, as well as his understanding of American politics and human behavior as he developed his concept of "the survivor."

Robert Jay Lifton was a third-generation Jew, born to a middle-class family in Brooklyn, New York, on May 16, 1926. Both of his parents, Ciel and Harold, were the American-born children of poor, Orthodox Jewish immigrants from Russia. Harold had used the New York City educational system to break out of his childhood poverty, eventually to become a successful small businessman who invested modestly in Broadway shows.[20] Harold had also rebelled against his parents' religiosity, labeling himself an atheist and abandoning most Jewish ritual as an adult.[21]

Despite Harold's rejection of the religion, Robert Jay Lifton has remembered that Jewishness was an important component of the Lifton household as he grew up in the 1930s. Harold and Ciel's friends were almost all Jewish, and Robert's social world too was Jewish; he lived in a predominantly Jewish neighborhood, made mostly Jewish friends, attended a Jewish summer camp, and in college at Cornell University joined a Jewish fraternity. Although they were "antireligion," Lifton has recently testified in an interview, "the message from my parents, especially my father, was very strongly one of Jewishness."[22] Having been sheltered within this mostly Jewish social world, Lifton has few memories of antisemitism affecting him or his family as a child or young man.[23]

Nonetheless, Lifton has remembered that being Jewish in the 1930s and the 1940s was accompanied by significant ambivalence. His family communicated to him, he believes, that the United States had enabled his comfort as a Jew, yet this stability could not be taken for granted. This ambivalence was in part economic, as Harold and Ciel swung widely between "love for the magnificent country that had enabled them to rise from poverty to real middle-class comfort" and a sense of financial vulnerability that became all too real during the Depression, as the family had to be taken in by Ciel's parents during a downturn in Harold's business. The elder Liftons combined their love for America and their pride in their class mobility, Robert has remembered, with a "sense of imminent threat that had to do with being Jews in a Gentile country."[24] In Lifton's memory, his parents themselves were torn between understanding themselves as

Jewish outsiders, always vulnerable and near persecution, and as part of the American mainstream, comfortable in their middle-class world and grateful to the country that had treated them so well.

This ambivalence was political as well as economic. Lifton's parents as well as his friends, neighbors, and teachers all communicated to the young Robert a significant sense of political danger as a Jew, even as they encouraged him to feel as American as anyone else and as they themselves felt strongly identified with the American political system. Much of the peril of being a Jew in Lifton's young world derived from the impending war in Europe and the threat it posed to Jews specifically. Although his parents tried to shelter him and his sister from the Nazi persecution of Jews in Europe, Lifton has said, "Still the message came across that we had to be on our guard and that dreadful things had happened to us."[25] Hitler was "the ultimate threat that loomed 'out there,'" he has remembered, serving as "destroyer, buffoon, evil incarnate, and fantasy target for our childhood games of violence."[26] As Lifton grew older, he and his father, who was "enormously interested in current events and current affairs," often talked about German aggression in Europe. Moreover, his teachers in junior and senior high school in Brooklyn, many of whom were themselves Jewish, made it clear to Lifton that the war had special meaning for Jews.[27] By the time the United States had entered the war, when Lifton was fifteen, he was "very aware that we Jews had a special stake in the war. It wasn't just an ordinary war. It threatened us."[28] Perceiving a sharp sense of "embattlement" in the Lifton household, among his parents' friends, from his teachers, and in their Brooklyn neighborhood, Lifton has remembered receiving a very strong, though unarticulated, "message that we didn't suffer directly, but really dreadful things were done to our people."[29]

At the same time, Lifton has remembered that this message had a "double sense" or "a double dimension." While his family quietly and unconsciously warned that as Jews "we had to watch our steps," at the same time he also noted that he felt "quite free and American." "As a kid, you just go out and play, and you go to school and you felt okay in New York, because everybody else or almost everybody else seemed to be Jewish," he recollected.[30] The sense of Jewish "embattlement" that he remembered from his family and friends went hand in hand with feelings of confidence and ease in his Brooklyn neighborhood, and indeed, with his parents' fervent belief that "only in America" could they have been "treated so well."[31]

Some of this sense of doubleness, of security and danger, was communicated through the Lifton family's confidence in American politics, and particularly in the Democratic party as a protector of Jews. Lifton remembered his elation at his first-grade teacher's announcement that Franklin Delano Roosevelt had won the presidential election in 1932, because his family had made it clear to him, even at that young age, that Roosevelt was "somebody good for the Jews."[32] He has recalled that his father "revered Roosevelt" and viewed him as "important for the Jews," a crucial part of Jewish survival.[33] The fact that, in a recent interview, Robert Lifton seamlessly linked discussion of the Holocaust to his family's support for Roosevelt indicates the degree to which his family had linked FDR to Jewish welfare.[34] The Liftons' support for Roosevelt was, on one hand, an acknowledgement of Jewish vulnerability in the 1930s, but it was also, on the other hand, an expression of confidence in the American political system.

As he grew up, then, Robert Jay Lifton saw political danger, as well as middle-class comfort and the protection of New Deal liberalism, as significant components of what it meant for him to be an American Jew. Lifton's understanding of his own fragility as an American Jew who was saved from concentration camps only through "an accident of history" makes sense when one understands the message of Jewish vulnerability that was communicated to him through his family and friends at a young age. Then, too, his later emphasis as a psychiatrist on human vulnerability in the face of twentieth-century technological disaster was clearly shaped by his amorphous but powerful sensitivity to Jewish victimization when he was an adolescent and young adult. At the same time, however, as a young man who experienced little personal antisemitism, who was a competent athlete and a successful student, able to attend college at Cornell University and medical school at New York Medical College, Robert Jay Lifton was a fairly confident middle-class American man who never felt himself personally to be a victim at all, and whose father's social mobility gave him genuine inspiration for the possibilities of human transformation.[35] His hopeful perspective on the possibilities of human survival after devastation seems to have been shaped by his own, and his family's, potential for growth, change, and success. Lifton's understanding of himself as both an insider and an outsider thus shaped both the form and the content of his comparison of Nazi concentration camp and Hiroshima survivors. *Death in Life*'s sensitivity to dehumanization and technological destruction was shaped by the psychiatrist's early understanding of himself as a potential Jewish victim, but his personal sense of comfort and freedom in the United States led him to dwell in his work not on Jewish victimization but instead on the possibilities for victims to survive and transform themselves.[36]

Of course, it was not Robert Lifton's experience as a Jew alone that shaped his comparison of Nazi concentration camp and Hiroshima survivors.

Being a Jew, as Lifton noted himself, was only one component of a larger constellation. Lifton's intellectual development during and after his academic training as a psychiatrist and his increasing interest in political activism also had significant impact on his later work.

Much of Lifton's early intellectual development revolved around his attraction to and his struggle with Freudian psychology, as Lifton searched for an understanding of individual identity that was flexible and cognizant of adult personality transformation. After entering medical school in part to fulfill his father's personal dream of becoming a doctor, Lifton gravitated to psychiatry because it offered the possibility of exploring human development and individual personality.[37] In an era when Freudianism dominated American psychiatry, Lifton was attracted to Freud's "hard brilliance and personal courage," but he was repelled by the mechanistic nature of some Freudian concepts, such as the belief that personality was essentially developed in the first six years.[38]

Robert Jay Lifton's interest in examining adult personality transformation was probably prompted, and certainly deepened, as he himself experienced significant cultural and identity change throughout his late twenties and thirties. Sent to Japan as an Air Force psychiatrist in 1952, Lifton and his wife, Betty Jean, embraced "the inner adventure of experiencing a new culture," and they allowed that new culture to shape their developing intellectual interests. Robert developed a new and lasting interest in Asian culture and personality, as well as in cross-cultural psychiatric study.[39] Moreover, while traveling to Hong Kong as part of a planned yearlong trip throughout Asia, a chance to interview people who had been subjected to thought reform in China led Lifton to abandon his planned career path of teaching and private practice and instead to become a research psychiatrist and writer who focused on the psychology of "extreme situations."[40] He stayed in Hong Kong for eighteen months researching the psychological mechanisms involved in the thought reform, or "brainwashing," that the Chinese government had employed on its citizens.

Exploring the psychological changes that had taken place among these adult men and women further pushed Lifton to struggle to understand adult personality change. When he returned to the United States to write up his findings, Lifton found himself newly inspired by the work of psychologist Erik Erikson. Erikson's central contribution to psychology was the development of the concept of "identity." Deemphasizing Freud's concept of the ego as the mechanism that operated automatically to defend against the forbidden wishes of the id, Erikson argued instead that ego was an actor in its own right, continually interacting with society. The psychologist believed that this interaction continued throughout life, and in his most famous book, *Childhood and Society* (1950), he described a "normal" life cycle model that consisted of eight stages during which the ego struggled with different conflicts, such as "guilt vs. initiative,"or "shame vs. autonomy," presented by the external world. A successful resolution of these conflicts resulted in a stable ego identity; if an individual did not successfully resolve a conflict, he was unstable and would continue to face this anxiety for the rest of his life.[41]

Erikson's concept of identity, particularly his vision of the ego interacting with society, helped make sense of the changing personalities of the Western and Chinese men and women subjected to thought reform that Robert Jay Lifton had studied, and it probably also offered insight into the personal changes that Lifton himself had undergone. The psychiatrist asked a colleague to introduce him to Erikson, and the two men soon developed a lifelong friendship and professional relationship.[42]

Lifton saw Erik Erikson as a mentor, from whom he learned a great deal and whose work served as a foundation for Lifton's own, more radical, ideas about adult transformation. For example, Lifton enthusiastically embraced the concept of identity formation in adolescence and urged Erikson to push the concept even further, to take more seriously radical identity formation as a constant process that lasted throughout life. He rejected Erikson's belief that one might ever be able to create a stable ego identity and insisted instead that identity was constantly being re-created, never fully stable.[43] And while Erikson sought to make sure that he remained a respected member of the psychoanalytic community, even as he revised and criticized elements of the Freudian canon, Lifton broke from orthodox psychoanalysis. In a 1961 book based on his research with men and women in Hong Kong, *Thought Reform and the Psychology of Totalism,* Lifton compared the conformity of psychoanalytic training to the thought reform of Communist China, and, by 1962, Lifton had abandoned his psychoanalytic training altogether.[44]

Thus, Lifton's intellectual development as an Air Force psychiatrist, as a researcher during his travels in Asia, and as a friend and admirer of Erik Erikson pushed him to move away from the standard Freudian framework of childhood development and from the traditional psychoanalytic community, and instead to emphasize adult personality transformation, particularly in the wake of "extreme situations" such as the thought reform of Chinese communism. Lifton's emphasis on the impact of "extreme situations" on adult identity was clearly crucial in shaping his later decision to explore the psychology of Hiroshima survivors, and indeed his use of Bruno Bettelheim's term "extreme situations" suggests that his sensitivity to these situations was subtextually connected to his sensitivity to the concentration camps, whose impact he would later compare with that of the atomic bomb.[45] Lifton's dedication to understanding adult personality transformation, moreover, later had particular importance as the psychiatrist worked with others in developing the concept of post-traumatic stress disorder because he was committed to "affirming the significance of stress and trauma to adults" within a psychiatric community that he believed still sometimes emphasized childhood trauma over adult interactions with society.[46]

In addition to his developing intellectual rebellion against Freudianism and his growing concern for adult identity transformation, Robert Jay Lifton's increasing political activism and radicalization also shaped his later use of Nazi camp imagery to criticize American nuclear and Vietnam policies.

Although Lifton's parents had adored Franklin Roosevelt and viewed his New Deal liberalism as "good for the Jews," they also possessed a certain measure of distrust for American capitalism and respect for radical politics, which they communicated to Robert. Mixed with pride in their upward mobility was an internalization of the "fragmentary elements of the Marxist imagery that permeated much of the literate Jewish life of that time."[47] Harold Lifton talked about reading Marx in college and believed that capitalism was "unscientific."[48] He had also made a number of close friends in the theater world, many of whom were politically radical. One of Harold's closest friends and former business partner was E. Y. "Yip" Harburg, most memorably the lyricist for *The Wizard of Oz*, who was blacklisted in the 1950s for his radical affiliations and socialist politics, though he was never a member of the Communist Party.[49] Although Robert Jay Lifton did not agree at first with all of his father's friends' radical sympathies, his love for them and exposure to their ideas helped to push him to "think more radically." By the time he became a medical student, he was spending a lot of time with Harold's friends on weekends and holidays. Prompted by such gatherings, he has said, "I began to articulate to myself and my own friends a kind of noncommunist radicalism."[50] That noncommunist radicalism, a variety of democratic socialism, would significantly shape Robert Jay Lifton's later intellectual framework.

His early years in Asia further pushed Lifton to adopt a more critical perspective on American politics. Betty Jean Lifton's reporting in Vietnam in 1954, just as the French were leaving and the Americans were entering the fight against the Vietcong, radicalized both her and her husband's perspective on American politics: "Partly because my wife and I had traveled in that whole area, we often would say we were against the Vietnam War before it started," Robert Lifton has noted. "We knew it was disastrous from the beginning, we knew it was wrong."[51] Moreover, the psychiatrist was exposed to the radicalism of Japanese students in 1960.[52]

Perhaps most significant, in the late 1950s, as a research associate in psychiatry at Harvard, Robert Lifton developed a close personal, social, and intellectual relationship with another mentor who was very different from Erik Erikson. Sociologist David Riesman encouraged Lifton to embrace his growing radicalism in his intellectual work and moreover helped direct the psychiatrist's leftist sentiment toward the burgeoning antinuclear movement.

Riesman is most famous for writing the groundbreaking book *The Lonely Crowd* (1950), about changing American character structure in the twentieth century. But Riesman was also a well-known figure in the peace movement at the turn of the 1960s. Despairing of the prevalent Cold War mentality in American liberalism, Riesman, along with other intellectuals including historian H. Stuart Hughes, established the peace organization Committees of Correspondence in 1960 at a meeting in Bear Mountain, New York.[53] Taking its name from the groups that formed to criticize the British Crown before the American Revolution, the Committees of Correspondence put out a newsletter intended to be an intellectual forum for criticism of the Cold War and for independent viewpoints on foreign policy. Riesman was the guiding force behind the Committees, which later came to be called the Councils of Correspondence; he produced the initial newsletters himself, then directed their production when he had found an editor, and was actively involved in searching for people to sponsor the organization.[54] Riesman was also the faculty adviser to an early student peace group, Tocsin, which combined intellectual debate on foreign policy and Cold War issues with demonstrations and political activism for peace; future Students for a Democratic Society (SDS) president Todd Gitlin began his political activism with Tocsin.[55] Riesman thus played an influential role in facilitating intellectual criticism of the Cold War in the early days of the antinuclear movement.

David Riesman involved Robert Jay Lifton in antinuclear politics in the 1950s, in the early days of their friendship before the Committees of Correspondence even began, encouraging him to join the small, informal peace group that Riesman held together at Harvard, composed of both faculty members and students in Tocsin.[56] In 1960, when Lifton traveled to Japan to conduct research for a cross-cultural study of American and Japanese youth, the two men carried on an intense correspondence that dwelt primarily on the dangers of the Cold War, Riesman's hopes for the Committees of Correspondence, and other aspects of foreign policy. Encouraged by Riesman, Lifton joined the Committees of Correspondence, wrote an article for their newsletter on the "strange psychology of shelter-building," and even directed Riesman to his father as a potential donor for the organization.[57]

David Riesman's own activism offered Robert Jay Lifton a model of intellectual and social engagement, as well as implanting within him a deep concern about nuclear politics, which remained with him throughout his life. "Riesman's antinuclearism taught me a lot about consistency in taking a stand and also about combining intellectual knowledge . . . with a stand in society," Lifton has remembered.[58] Although Riesman became more conservative and Lifton more radical as the political landscape of the 1960s shifted, the two men remained friends, and Lifton still traces his own antinuclear activism to the political and intellectual model that Riesman offered him: "It was . . . my friendship with Dave Riesman that I think brought me to Hiroshima."[59]

Lifton's radicalism never moved to the extreme left, as did the politics of a number of other antiwar activists by the late 1960s. The psychiatrist saw himself holding positions that he called variously "radical-liberal, radical, and nontotalitarian socialist," and he continuously described himself understanding the dangers of doctrinaire communism, even as he rejected the anticommunist position of liberals.[60] In a recent interview, Lifton continued to describe his politics as "radical-liberal" or "liberal-radical."[61]

Thus, by 1961, the date of publication of his *Thought Reform and the Psychology of Totalism,* Robert Jay Lifton had developed an intellectual position that rejected dogmatic Freudianism in order to emphasize adult personality change in response to dramatic historic upheavals, and he had also become more politically radical, with a growing commitment to finding ways to combine his democratic socialist principles with his intellectual work. In 1961, Lifton published an essay that suggested that these intellectual and political developments in his life had shaped his understanding of his Jewish background.

In the late 1950s, Lifton had developed friendships with members of the famous band of "New York intellectuals" such as Norman Podhoretz, Daniel Bell, and Nathan Glazer, and he became a member of that group, although he has rarely been publicly identified as a part of that circle.[62] In 1960, while Lifton was in Tokyo beginning his cross-cultural studies on Japanese and American youth, Podhoretz asked the psychiatrist to participate in a *Commentary* symposium on Jewish identity among "younger intellectuals," by responding to a series of questions such as "Do you think your experience as a Jew is importantly relevant to your experience as an American?"[63]

Lifton's responses drew on his intellectual attraction to Freud, as well as his political activism and his antinuclear position, to describe his perspective on his own Jewishness. As he did so, he clearly explicated the unconscious ambivalent messages his family had offered of Jews as both insiders and outsiders. He noted that, like Freud, he treasured the "special identity of the cultural outsider which the Jew still carries within himself," particularly because that identity offered the courage to oppose dominant thought as well as the courage "to reach beyond cultural prejudices." Yet, Lifton also warned that the identity of the cultural outsider featured a special danger: "[the] powerful urge to divest himself of this painful identity and become the arch-insider—a yearning that can be pursued, literally with a vengeance, as perhaps in the case of those cultural outsiders of various backgrounds who direct their energies more toward the build-up of American military power than toward the preservation of all human life."[64] The psychiatrist thus used his newer intellectual understandings of Freud and nuclear politics to interpret the "double sense" of Jewishness, as insider and outsider, that he had understood as a child and teenager growing up in the 1930s and 1940s.

Rather than emphasizing the ambivalence between the outsider and the insider, however, Lifton instead synthesized the two, noting that Jews' concerns about being cultural outsiders were, in fact, "very American after all, following the American pattern of the dramatic break with one's past." The psychiatrist argued powerfully, moreover, for a synthesis between the particular loyalties of Jews and the universal ideals of mankind. He noted that, rather than feeling a need to choose between "the senseless alternatives of either tribal exclusiveness or disembodied 'melting' into a hypothetical Anglo-Saxon community," he believed that the particular and the universal necessarily complemented one another: "In life, as in art, the particular is one's only connection with the universal. This applies even in relationship to barbarism: the Nazi atrocities were both a specifically Jewish and a broadly human tragedy." The significance of his Jewishness, Lifton argued, lay "primarily in the way in which it permits me to be related to humanity."[65] Thus, in his essay in the "Jewishness and the Younger Intellectuals" symposium, Robert Jay Lifton noted the ways that his political concern with nuclear politics and his intellectual attraction to Freud had shaped his understanding of his Jewishness. He also made clear that his Jewishness shaped his political and intellectual concerns, that he found his Jewish identity inseparable from his identity as an American and an intellectual, and that he viewed Nazi destruction as both a Jewish and universal concern. This essay helps to explain how the psychiatrist's ethnic, intellectual, and political background would all combine to lead him eventually to develop a powerful analogy comparing Nazi camp survivors to Hiroshima survivors.

THE CONNECTIONS THAT LIFTON MADE between his intellectual, political, and ethnic background became magnified and strengthened as he embarked on his career in what he called "advocacy research": scholarly investigation combined with open commitment to social or political ideals. Lifton came to view his scholarly work as inextricably intertwined with his political goals and his personal identity, and from *Death in Life* onward, he combined his work with strong personal and political statements. Although the psychiatrist's advocacy research inspired criticism and limited Lifton's fame among the general public, the psychiatrist's openness about his own politics and his optimistic hopes for political and personal transformation appealed to many politically active Americans. Their activism, as well as Lifton's own, cemented his analogy between Nazi concentration camps and American society.

Although Robert Jay Lifton did not describe his early work on Hiroshima as advocacy research, his months of work in the city marked the beginning of the psychiatrist's decision to combine his scholarship with active political commitment. Having traveled to Japan in 1960 to study Japanese youth in Kyoto and Tokyo, Lifton and his wife decided to visit the city of Hiroshima briefly in April 1962, drawn by their antinuclear politics. Shocked by evidence of the bomb's destruction, which he saw in the Hiroshima Peace Museum and learned about in discussions with survivors, and surprised that no one had conducted a psychological study of bomb survivors, Robert Lifton decided to postpone beginning his new position as Foundations Fund Research Professor of Psychiatry at Yale University so that he could stay in Hiroshima to carry out a "careful, objective study of the problem." Lifton's desire to be careful and objective, however, was linked with his feeling that he had "a kind of moral obligation to undertake the work," and with his hope that the study would be his "own form of contribution to the cause of peace."[66] In letters to David Riesman, Lifton combined his neutral, clinical observations of *hibakusha* with strong expressions of antinuclear political sentiment and a desire to use his psychological knowledge for political purposes: "we need some way of helping people to imagine [nuclear warfare's] true horror."[67] Although Lifton used the professional language of objectivity and realism in his correspondence, his goals were quite clearly political, suggesting he had found a way to take a stand in his professional life, as Riesman had.

When *Death in Life* was finally published five years later, in 1967, it displayed the same careful attempt to balance realism and objectivity on the one hand and political and moral commitment on the other that his letters had demonstrated. The book avoided all appearances of being a political document; the bulk of it was, in fact, quiet, measured, and nonjudgmental. A careful reader would find it obvious, however, that the book was an indictment of nuclear weaponry. Lifton referred to the "nuclear terror," to the "ethical issues" surrounding his work, to Americans' guilt for having dropped the bomb, and to the hope that Hiroshima "is a nuclear catastrophe from which one can still learn" how to prevent "the even more massive extermination it seems to foreshadow."[68] Just like his admission that his Jewish identity had shaped his concern with the Nazi concentration camps, Lifton's political antinuclearism was a quiet undercurrent, not a relentlessly repeated theme, in *Death in Life*. Although the book's writing style was emotionally restrained and even detached at times, Robert Jay Lifton's personal identity and political idealism were clearly a part of *Death in Life*.

This careful balance between objective reporting and political commitment led to critical success. *Death in Life* received, for the most part, extremely positive reviews and public acclaim. The book's sales were at first modest—his publisher estimated that only 5,800 hardback copies had been sold by March 3, 1969—but it became popular on campuses and among educated readers.[69] The psychiatrist went on to win the National Book Award in the sciences in April 1969, and in yet another example of his desire to blend his career as a psychiatrist with his political commitments, Lifton donated the money from the award to a fund for the survivors of Hiroshima and to the peace organizations Council for a Livable World and Physicians for Social Responsibility.[70]

The generally positive reception of Lifton's work was not affected by his comparison of the effects of Hiroshima to those of Nazi Germany. The analogy between *hibakusha* and concentration camp survivors created virtually no controversy or negative attention at all, and most reviewers, in fact, seem to have quietly appreciated it. Reviewers did not generally single out the concentration camp analogy for special attention, but instead many incorporated Lifton's camp imagery into their own writing, thus subtly legitimating the analogy.[71] A few critics who liked *Death in Life*, including Bruno Bettelheim himself, commented that the different experiences of camp survivors and atomic bomb survivors shed light on one another.[72] Several reviewers who criticized the book complained that Lifton's comparison was "distracting" or "superficial" or overly "theoretical," but none found it offensive or illegitimate.[73] On the whole, Lifton's survivor comparison became an accepted part of his overarching thesis, far more likely to be quietly and approvingly repeated than attacked, or even openly analyzed.

What reviewers tended to comment on more frequently was Lifton's combination of restrained reporting and political commitment. Jerome Frank praised Lifton in the *New York Times Book Review* for being "able to be compassionate without losing his objectivity," for example, while the *Christian Century* warned readers to "[p]repare to be torn apart by these 594 pages of cool reporting graced by occasional passages of philosophical depth."[74] In the *Atlantic*, historian Oscar Handlin approved of Lifton's "sober clinical language, which nevertheless does not obscure the author's emotional involvement in his findings."[75] Moreover, a good number of reviewers commented on Lifton's "carefully restrained writing," "rigorous" research, and "cool, scientific narrative," while also praising his work for its political message, claiming, for example, that the book's "greatest value is as an ultimate plea for sanity in public affairs."[76] For many reviewers, the balance that Lifton had achieved between emotional political commitment and objective reporting was perfect, and since it was so regularly commented on, this balance was one likely reason for the book's success.

Some reviewers, however, found Lifton's balance inadequate. These readers found Lifton too "objective," too attached to his psychoanalytic perspective and his stance as a scientist to understand or explain adequately the horrors of Hiroshima. Psychoanalysis, concluded Mary Ellman in *Commentary*, reduced all *hibakushas'* responses to illness, offering them no opportunity to "burst out" of their "dark . . . psychic space" and forcing them to remain "permanently marred people."[77] In the *New Yorker*, George Steiner complained that Lifton, working within the disciplines of American social science and without the imagination of an artist, had merely "provided statistical methodological support to the obvious."[78]

Most painful for Lifton, however, was a scathing review by Paul Goodman in the *New York Review of Books*. Goodman, like Mary Ellman and others, found Lifton's psychoanalytic perspective reductive, but more importantly, he attacked Lifton himself for being so detached from his subject as to be "demented," "fucked up," and "[p]olitically . . . idiotic." Lifton's attempt to be balanced by criticizing both American military research as well as the "over-reactions" and the paranoia of Japanese *hibakusha* protesters outraged Goodman: "Obviously the crazy people are more in touch with the reality than the doctor is. Why does not Dr. Lifton protest and strike?" he asked angrily. Goodman rejected as a "rationalization" Lifton's personal description of his own numbing as he conducted his research, and he accused the psychiatrist of "taking for granted," and ultimately sanctioning, the corruption of professionals engaging in evil tasks. Scientists, Goodman concluded, were responsible not only for nuclear weapons but for the growing "ecological and cultural calamity" of the world, and Robert Lifton, though "grave, judicious, and scrupulous," was nonetheless a member of their "monstrous" clan.[79]

Privately calling the review "bizarre but painful," Lifton asked his friends to write him supportive letters.[80] Others came to Lifton's defense too. In the *American Scholar,* Erik Erikson—a friend whom Lifton had not directly asked for support—noted that Lifton had been accused of being "too scrupulously clinical and interpretive and not enraged enough and exhortative" but asked the reader, "would you not rather be told plainly and tenderly what happened to the people over there."[81] And George Steiner called the "charges of moral indifference" against *Death in Life* "vulgar nonsense."[82]

Nonetheless, Goodman's attack obviously shook Lifton, as Lifton's private letters testify, and it is possible that this critique was one factor that encouraged Lifton to reconsider his cautious balancing of political commitment with objective reporting and to take instead a more aggressive political stand, an approach that marked most of his work in the late 1960s and 1970s. Certainly the escalating war in Vietnam and the spiraling radicalism of the late 1960s and the early 1970s also pushed Lifton to develop his concept of "advocacy research." The first evidence of this new approach to scholarship appeared in 1967, after Lifton traveled to Vietnam in the middle of a research trip to Asia and wrote an angry article about the war that condemned the "self-deception" of Americans in Vietnam.[83] Unable to sell the article to any major mainstream magazines, he eventually published the piece in the small journal *Trans-Action,* where it was well received, and even reprinted, by politically active readers.[84]

Although the destruction that Lifton saw during his trip to Vietnam angered him, it was the massacre at My Lai that led the professor to devote his professional work for the next four years to his political ideals. Lifton has written that, after reading an article on the murder of hundreds of Vietnamese civilians in My Lai in the *New York Times* in November 1969, he underwent "an abrupt change in my own relationship to the war, and in my life in general." Filled with "shame and rage," both at the United States government and at his own failure to do more to stop the war, he threw himself into antiwar activity, becoming "preoccupied" with the "issue of American war crimes in Vietnam" and eventually pushing aside his next major book on psychological theory—literally sweeping the papers off his desk—to devote himself to writing countless articles on Vietnam, organizing protests against the war, and finally writing a book on Vietnam veterans.[85] With this political radicalization, Lifton became more comfortable openly making his political opinions and his personal identity a part of the story: "articulated subjectivity, the use of the self as an investigative instrument, has become an increasingly important principle for me," he explained to readers, warning them he would not be a "phantom researcher."[86]

Robert Jay Lifton's combination of personal political commitment and intellectual scholarship took many different routes in late 1969 and the early 1970s, but these routes all focused on one central issue: the perpetration of war crimes or atrocities in Vietnam. Understandably, this central issue was marked by several different analogies to Nazi Germany: analogies to concentration camp survivors, analogies to the Nuremberg War Crimes trials of 1945 to 1946 and analogies to "good Germans," who had sat by and watched as innocent populations were murdered. Lifton tied together all these different analogies into his overarching theoretical portrait of the "survivor." In time, this theoretical portrait became increasingly popular and successful in American political and cultural life, both because Lifton's own intense political activism continually pushed his ideas into the mainstream and into radical protest circles and because his portrait of the survivor—and his use of the Nazi analogy—offered a hopeful vision of rebirth after trauma and of meaningful political action.

Not surprisingly, when he first saw news about My Lai in 1969, the analogy that Lifton drew on immediately was the comparison of *hibakusha* to concentration camp victims that he had already used to develop his concept of the survivor. As Lifton threw himself into reading all the material he could about the My Lai massacre, talking to returning GIs and veterans, meeting informally with groups of antiwar veterans, and conducting interviews with a veteran who had been at the massacre, he filtered this research through the concept of the "survivor."[87] In the two months after November 1969, Lifton prepared several different statements against the war for a variety of venues, thus offering both politicians and general readers his portrait of American Vietnam veterans as survivors. In December 1969, for example, during the initial uproar over My Lai, *U.S. News and World Report* advertised an interview with Robert Jay Lifton on its front cover, promising that a "prominent psychiatrist" would explain "Why Civilians Are War Victims." A month later, on January 27, 1970, Lifton testified at a U.S. Senate subcommittee hearing on wounded veterans in a statement reprinted in the magazine *Commonweal,* and in February, he spoke on My Lai at the Congressional Conference on War and National Responsibility. All these public statements dealt with the problem of veterans—and Americans in general—as survivors.

Vietnam veterans, Lifton explained, were survivors like *hibakusha* or concentration camp inmates for a number of reasons. As "soldier-survivors," he said, veterans had experienced the "death imprint" of being in war and thus surrounded by death daily, as well as the guilt of having survived friends.[88] Moreover, the particular experience of Vietnam, a guerrilla war fought by people of a different race and intimately involving civilians, led GIs to dehumanize the Vietnamese people and thus led to "an advanced stage" of "psychic numbing" and "extreme brutalization."[89]In this situation, the ordinary veteran tried to formulate his exposure to devastation by trying "to find some meaning in the death he has witnessed," but the frustration and dehumanization of the experience typically blocked his formulation and led him to find this meaning in a "perverted" way, through retaliation against defenseless citizens.[90] The war thus turned American soldiers into both victims and executioners.[91]

Once home, Lifton warned, veterans might experience delayed psychological disturbances such as depression and paranoia, just like concentration camp victims and *hibakusha*. This time lapse in manifesting psychological damage would hinder veterans' treatment, Lifton said, since U.S. law at the time limited veterans' medical benefits to conditions that arose no more than two years after discharge.[92] An even greater obstacle to veterans' treatment was the sense of betrayal, or the "suspicion of counterfeit nurturance," that veterans might feel in receiving help from a country that had sent them to war; "this kind of mistrust," Lifton warned, "could have disastrous consequences" for American society.[93] Thus, the psychiatrist found among Vietnam veterans all the five essential psychological manifestations of survivor psychology—death imprint, death guilt, psychic numbing, counterfeit nurturance, and formulation, or impaired formulation—and he additionally concluded that veterans experienced the same delayed psychological disturbances that plagued atomic bomb and concentration camp survivors.

This comparison of Vietnam vets to other types of survivors was not, of course, purely intellectual. Lifton linked his comparison to two pointed political conclusions. The first, as indicated by the psychiatrist's veiled warning that veterans' bitterness would be "disastrous" for American society, was that the war would lead to spiraling violence at home as young people, blacks, veterans, and "backlash-prone groups" experienced increasing alienation from society.[94] His second political conclusion was that all Americans were survivors of the war in Vietnam, not just veterans. All Americans were partaking "in the psychic numbing and brutalization experienced by GIs, even if indirectly and in less extreme form."[95] Body counts and burning villages on the six o'clock evening news were helping Americans get used to the war, "a form of callousness and numbing."[96] Moreover, like veterans, Americans in general were unable to formulate, or find a larger significance in, their "death immersion," and thus might bear "extensive and permanent" psychological scars.[97] Finally, and most importantly, the general American public shared the guilt for the atrocities in Vietnam, and Americans needed to examine that guilt honestly and publicly, and then to make "an honest decision to end that involvement [in Vietnam]."[98] Using the category of the "survivor" to analyze My Lai, therefore, allowed Robert Jay Lifton to combine his psychological theorizing with his political activism to end the war.

Lifton's sympathetic and overtly political approach to veterans as survivors attracted attention from a number of sources, including lawyers and academics, but the people most interested in Robert Jay Lifton's concept of the "survivor" were politically active veterans themselves.[99] Through antiwar networks, and through his public statements, Lifton drew the attention of a newly forming group, Vietnam Veterans Against the War (VVAW). In November 1970, Jan Barry, then president of VVAW, sent a letter to Lifton asking for the psychiatrist's help with two goals. The first was to help veterans with their "severe psychological problems" resulting from the war, and the second was to help protest the military policy "which results in war crimes and veterans' nightmares." Barry asked if VVAW might be able to obtain reprints and circulate among veterans Lifton's statement to the Senate subcommittee, and if Lifton might be willing to develop more statements for veterans.[100] Thus, although his name did not become a household word after he began publicizing his ideas about Vietnam to a mass audience, Lifton's work spoke to particular people, namely veterans and political activists, who wanted to use Lifton's ideas in their political and personal struggles.

Moreover, veterans' interest in Lifton's work led the psychiatrist to become actively engaged in the vets' antiwar struggle himself, to link his professional expertise with his political goals. When Lifton went, along with a professional and antiwar colleague, psychologist Chaim Shatan, to meet Jan Barry and other veterans in December 1970, Barry explained that veterans had been holding intense "rap sessions" in the VVAW offices about the war, their experiences, and American society. The vets wanted those sessions to become regular meetings, or "rap groups," in which psychological professionals, who might be able to help them therapeutically, participated. Veterans did not want the professionals to become their psychiatrists, however; they insisted that professionals join them as equals who held a particular brand of specialized knowledge, just as veterans themselves had their own specialized knowledge about the war. Then, too, vets did not want the rap groups to become private therapy for individual psychology; instead they wanted to discuss the political causes and ramifications of their suffering, and they also hoped that a vocal activist and prominent psychiatrist such as Lifton might help them make the proceedings public, in order to spur antiwar sentiment among Americans.[101] This blend of psychology and political activism was particularly attractive to Lifton, and the psychiatrist became a regular participant in one New York rap group throughout its life.

In addition to participating in rap groups, Lifton found other strategies for merging his political consciousness and his professional skills in the early 1970s. These strategies did not always focus on the concept of the survivor, however; some focused instead on analogies to the Nuremberg trials at the end of World War II. During the early 1970s, Lifton worked closely with antiwar activists who wanted to hold the leaders of the United States government and military, rather than individual soldiers or lower-level officers, responsible for war crimes committed in Vietnam, just as the Allies had prosecuted top generals and administrators at Nuremberg. Lifton thus concentrated at least some of his energies on an analogy that centered on the perpetrators, rather than the victims, of Nazi crime.

For example, the psychiatrist participated in three different "inquiries" into American war crimes in Vietnam in 1970 and 1971, inquiries that were, to a good degree, modeled after the Nuremberg War Crimes Tribunal. All these inquiries began with the Russell International War Crimes Tribunal, a proceeding organized in May 1967 in Stockholm by renowned intellectual and critic Bertrand Russell. Russell's trial was intended to echo that of the Nuremberg Tribunal, and it consistently made reference to the codes of war that had resulted from Nuremberg, the "Nuremberg principles" against wars of aggression, genocide, and indiscriminate slaughter.[102] After eight days of testimony from Vietnamese victims and some American veterans detailing hundreds of instances of torture and illegitimate warfare committed by Americans in Vietnam, Russell's tribunal declared the United States government and military guilty of "aggression in Vietnam."[103]

The Russell tribunal had little immediate impact in the United States in 1967. The phrase "American war crimes" sounded treasonous and unsubstantiated to most mainstream Americans, who were instead reading stories about North Vietnamese war crimes in American newspapers at that time. When My Lai became the major story in *Time, Newsweek,* and the *New York Times* in 1969, however, the notion of investigating American war crimes became more acceptable to people in the mainstream, and thus seemed a more fruitful avenue of protest for antiwar activists. In the wake of this shift in public opinion, in November 1969, the Bertrand Russell Peace foundation in New York, led by Ralph Schoenman, an American leftist who had served as Russell's personal secretary and general secretary of the Stockholm trial, issued a public call for American citizens to organize "citizens' commissions of inquiry" to document American war crimes, in much the same way the Russell tribunal had. Two radical organizers, Tod Ensign and Jeremy Rifkin, responded to this call, and guided by Schoenman, they eventually created a National Committee for a Citizens' Commission of Inquiry on U.S. War Crimes in Vietnam (CCI) that traveled first to Canada, then around the United States searching for veterans who would describe atrocities in which they had participated.[104]

Ensign and Rifkin's work led to a number of small, local hearings of veterans' testimony, as well as three major national war crimes inquiries: the National Veterans' Inquiry in Washington, D.C. on December 1–3, 1970; the Winter Soldier Investigation in Detroit, Michigan, on January 31–February 2, 1971; and the Dellums Committee Hearings on War Crimes in Vietnam in Washington, D.C. on April 26–29, 1971. Although the VVAW-sponsored Winter Soldier investigation eventually split from CCI, whereas the other hearings were directly sponsored by CCI, the content of all these inquiries was essentially the same: the sessions invited testimony from veterans who graphically described the atrocities that they had personally witnessed or committed in Vietnam. The message of all the inquiries, moreover, was identical: "to establish that the My Lai massacre was but the logical consequence of strategies and objectives developed for use in Indochina."[105] By encouraging veterans to talk about the massacres and tortures of which they had firsthand knowledge, but by also making certain that these veterans would not be prosecuted by the United States government for admitting to these activities, the Citizens' Commission hoped to shift veterans' focus from "concern for personal guilt to an analysis of institutional responsibility," and then to encourage the American people "to demand that responsibility for atrocities be placed where it truly belongs—on the civilian and military leadership of the U.S."[106] This focus on the responsibility of leadership, using the legal form of a hearing, was clearly an echo of the Nuremberg trials.

Robert Jay Lifton's participation in all these inquiries—both as an official observer and as a panelist speaker—indicates his support for this Nuremberg analogy.[107] Perhaps even more important than simply participating in these events, Lifton helped to found an anti-war group that partially funded the CCI hearings and that sponsored its own anti–war crimes public relations campaign. After participating in a February 1970 symposium "on war crimes and individual responsibility," organized through the American Friends Service Committee (AFSC), an important peace organization that united radical and moderate peace activists in the 1960s, Robert Jay Lifton became an active member and founder of the Education/Action Conference on U.S. Crimes of War in Vietnam. The conference sponsored workshops on war crimes, published a bibliography of books on American war crimes in Vietnam, and funded CCI hearings. Conference organizers hoped that eventually they would be able to educate Americans, not only to accept their government's responsibility for atrocities in Vietnam, but to take action to stop those atrocities by stopping the war.[108]

Perhaps most importantly for Lifton, the Education/Action Conference pushed him to coedit the volume *Crimes of War* with two other members of the organization steering committee, historian Gabriel Kolko and international law professor Richard Falk. Once again, Lifton was able to mesh his professional ambitions with his political ideals; *Crimes of War* was extremely successful and widely cited, becoming something of a classic in antiwar circles. The book was divided into three parts: Falk edited the section on the law of war crimes; Kolko, the section on the historical and political background of the war; and Lifton worked on the "psychological and ethical context." Despite these differences in approach, the introduction, written by all three men, emphasized the same essential argument put forth by CCI: the problem of war crimes was not to establish the individual guilt of the GI but instead the guilt of "those who have initiated, planned, and are continuing to carry out the vicious tactics of battle that have long been a daily part of this war."[109] With this argument at its core, it is understandable that the royalties of the book were donated to the Education/Action Conference and the book advance went to Tod Ensign, for the CCI hearings.[110] Thus, one of Lifton's more popular and successful publications in the 1970s was designed to charge American military and political leaders with responsibility for war crimes in Vietnam, and by extension, to compare those war crimes to those prosecuted at Nuremberg.

The same emphasis was true of another of Robert Jay Lifton's more influential works of the 1970s: a provocative review of two books on My Lai for the June 14, 1970, *New York Times Book Review*. In the review, Lifton focused on the "ultimate responsibility" of men at the very top of the chain of command, including the commanding general in Vietnam, the secretary of defense, and ultimately the president, "for creating the policies that legitimize this indiscriminate killing." The psychiatrist criticized the military for prosecuting participants at My Lai, calling the prosecutions "diversions from the murderous deceptions" at the heart of the Vietnam War, and he concluded that it was "criminal to send G.I.'s to fight in Vietnam."[111] Lifton's emphasis was thus on the ultimate perpetrators of the war; just as in Nuremberg, he argued, it was the military and political leaders, not the grunts in the field, who bore ultimate responsibility for the atrocities.

In Lifton's mind, however, the Nuremberg comparison was not simply limited to comparing American military and political leaders, perpetrators of war crimes, to those of Nazi Germany. Nuremberg also provided an essential analogy for ordinary citizens who viewed themselves as bystanders to atrocities; among the principles asserted by the Nuremberg judges was that "individuals have international duties which transcend the national obligations of obedience imposed by the individual state."[112] The image of "good Germans" who quietly sat by while millions of people were slaughtered, and who defended themselves after the war by insisting that they had not known, or that they had just been following orders, haunted Robert Jay Lifton, as it did many other American political activists in the 1960s and 1970s.[113] Unlike many other activists, however, Lifton helped to found a political group that explicitly used this image as a central organizing principle.

In addition to being a steering committee member for the Education/Action Conference, which was certainly concerned with educating Americans about their government's war crimes and motivating them to political action to stop the war, in 1972, Lifton also helped found and lead a group called Redress, which consistently referred to the "Nuremberg obligation" as one of the key principles for its activities.[114] Defining the "Nuremberg obligation" as the "obligation of individuals to prevent crimes of war," even if that meant "disobeying orders or breaking local laws," members of the group conducted a number of demonstrations and civil disobedience protests in 1972 and 1973, insisting throughout that they had an "active legal responsibility" to protest the commission of war crimes and that Nuremberg might even make them "criminally liable" if they failed to do so.[115]

Composed primarily of well-known professionals, intellectuals, and entertainers, Redress's activities included delivering petitions to the U.S. House of Representatives and Senate and then refusing to leave the congressional buildings, submitting instead to arrest and jail; submitting documents testifying to American war crimes to the United Nations; holding fund-raisers for the reconstruction of the Bach Mai hospital in Hanoi; and persuading members of the Philadelphia Orchestra to refuse to play at Richard Nixon's 1973 inauguration. References to the Nuremberg obligation were almost always prominent in the political literature and press releases surrounding these events.[116]

At times the imagery of "good Germans" became even sharper in Redress literature. For example, in explaining its May 25, 1972, act of civil disobedience inside the halls of the House of Representatives, Redress recalled Franklin Roosevelt's 1944 reminder to the German people that "their higher obligations to law and humanity took precedence over blind, sheeplike obedience to the orders and directives of the Nazi government."[117] When string bass player Wilfred Batchelder refused to play for Nixon's inaugural because he felt the orchestra was being asked to be "good Germans," the leaders of Redress, including Lifton, wrote to the *New York Times*, emphasizing the musician's reference to Nazi Germany and claiming that the musician "strengthen[ed] our determination to seek equivalent ways of living up to the Nuremberg obligation in our lives."[118]

Perhaps the most striking example of Redress's commitment to the Nuremberg principle was the organization's decision to link up with Project Nuremberg Obligation, a plan to send letters to about ten thousand American servicemen and women stationed in Vietnam, educating them about Nuremberg and about their right and responsibility to disobey orders, asking them to "honor America and resist illegal acts" and offering them support, counseling, and legal aid if they did decide to oppose the war while in service.[119]

Moreover, the Nuremberg obligation was not only at the center of the group's political rhetoric; it was also at the heart of its members' private consciences. Internal documents fretted over how the group might better fulfill its Nuremberg obligation. For example, was the conservative strategy of petitioning Congress better than more radical forms of civil disobedience?[120] Should the group postpone civil disobedience until November, in order to improve the chances of George McGovern in the 1972 election?[121] How could activists express the Nuremberg obligation, and help in the process of "deNazification," once the war was over?[122] One internal document, in fact, indicates that the group considered changing its name to Redress/ Nuremberg to express with more "clarity" the principles at the heart of the organization.[123] The Nuremberg obligation, Lifton wrote in 1973, is "the principle around which we act and build."[124]

Thus, the image of bystanders in Nazi Germany, expressed through the urgent moral imperative of the Nuremberg obligation, was tremendously important to Robert Jay Lifton's political and intellectual work in the 1970s, just as was the image of Nazi perpetrators in the Nuremberg-influenced war crimes inquiries he attended, and the image of Nazi victims in the "survivor" concept he wrote about. It is important to note, however, that all these images were very much linked for Lifton; sifting out and analyzing the various strains of Nazi analogies that infused his work is a useful task, but it should not obscure the fact that Lifton frequently combined all these analogies in his written work, and into his understanding of the Vietnam War.

The book review on My Lai in the *New York Times Book Review*, for example, certainly did emphasize the guilt of General William Westmoreland, the secretary of defense, and the president, but it also mentioned the "survivor's need to find meaning in his death encounter," and noted that it was "dangerously irresponsible to go on with business as usual" when confronted with evil.[125] Similarly, in *Crimes of War*, which was developed in part to protest the scapegoating of GIs and to blame instead military and political leaders for perpetrating war crimes, Lifton included several of his own essays about the survivor, as well as several other famous essays about bystanders' responsibility for evil.[126]

Lifton was able to incorporate all these images of perpetrators, bystanders, and victims into his political ideology because, for him, they all joined together as one interpretation of the Vietnam War and, in fact, one philosophical understanding of human nature and human identity. Americans in the late twentieth century, he believed, were living in a time of dislocation, technological absurdity, and Cold War ideological totalism. These factors led military and political leaders to numb themselves to the atrocities they perpetrated on people they had come to see as nonhuman. The same factors led ordinary Americans to stand by and let those atrocities take place in their name; ordinary GIs, moreover, as the actual people forced to be perpetrating war crimes, needed to numb themselves to the horror that they experienced every day. Only by accepting responsibility for these terrible circumstances and moving beyond guilt through some form of political action could any individual reclaim her identity from the numbing that separated her from life.

It is easier to describe the philosophical underpinnings of Robert Jay Lifton's political ideology than it is to gauge the impact of his political activism among ordinary Americans. To be sure, Lifton received letters from some people, particularly veterans and their families, who "wholeheartedly agree[d]" with his ideas or who felt he had given them a "significant moment of moral and psychological insight."[127] He also received angry letters from conservatives who attacked his "liberal propaganda," "intellectual dishonesty," and even his "latent exhibitionism."[128] Lifton's book review on My Lai for the *New York Times Book Review*, moreover, sparked some controversy; the *Book Review* printed several approving letters, one from a veteran, and two complaints that Lifton's review was overly political and that he overintellectualized the war.[129] In general, however, Lifton received far fewer letters from general readers than either Stanley Milgram or Betty Friedan received. Moreover, virtually none of Lifton's letters highlighted his use of Nazi analogies, so it is impossible to gauge how Lifton's Nazi analogy shaped the views of general readers.

There is, interestingly, little evidence that either Jews or Holocaust survivors protested Lifton's efforts to use the concentration camps for his left-liberal purposes, even as the Holocaust had become a mainstream term to define the Nazi destruction of the Jews.[130] Indeed, Lifton has remembered that one group of Holocaust survivors, including Elie Wiesel, actually asked the psychiatrist in the late 1960s if he would help them develop their own political protest connecting the events of My Lai to their suffering under the Nazis.[131] And a number of Jewish psychological professionals such as Chaim Shatan were drawn to Lifton's analogy between concentration camp survivors and Vietnam veterans.[132] The negative attention that one might expect the psychiatrist to have received in comparing American policies in Vietnam to Nazi concentration camps was not forthcoming from the organized Jewish community or from individual Jews in the late 1960s or even the early 1970s.

What Lifton did receive, however, was attention from and influence among antiwar activists. Members of the peace movement were impressed by Lifton's essays and consistently sought to reprint and distribute them.[133] James Simon Kunen, radical author of *The Strawberry Statement,* a book about the Columbia University uprising of 1968, used Lifton's concept of "psychic numbing" in his description of the 1970 National Veterans' Inquiry.[134] Vietnam Veterans Against the War dedicated their book, *The New Soldier,* "[t]o the survivors of the Indochina War," probably a product of Lifton's influence.[135] VVAW leaders may also have decided to concentrate their early political activities around the subject of war crimes as a result of discussions with Robert Lifton.[136]

Clearly Lifton had an impact on the antiwar movement in the 1960s and early 1970s. It is difficult to gauge, however, exactly how much he may have encouraged activists to think about the Nazi analogies that he employed. So many people at different times, and in different places, used the metaphor of Nazi Germany, particularly the two Nuremberg analogies, in the peace movement that it would be almost impossible to determine, for example, to what extent Lifton and Redress's focus on the Nuremberg obligation shaped other people's decisions to protest.[137] Certainly news articles about Redress actions were just as likely to emphasize the "radical chic" of the demonstrations—the presence of well-known actors such as Candice Bergen or Jon

Voight, for example—as they were to discuss with any clarity the moral significance of the Nuremberg obligation.[138] The most that can be said with certainty is that Lifton was a member of a core group of activists who worked very hard to educate Americans about the Nuremberg charters, and that they repeatedly and explicitly compared aspects of American society to Nazi Germany in all their educational and protest efforts.

The concept of the Vietnam veteran as a "survivor," and the analogy between Nazi and American destruction at the heart of that concept, however, is more particular to Lifton, and its impact on American society is not only traceable but quite evident in modern American culture. Although Robert Lifton had been publishing material on veterans as survivors since 1969, it was in 1973, with the publication of the monograph *Home from the War,* that the image began to become popular among ordinary Americans. The monograph was an analysis of Lifton's two years with a New York VVAW rap group. The psychiatrist focused on the portrait of these Vietnam veterans as survivors and suggested that through antiwar activities, such as rap groups, veterans were able to formulate their Vietnam experiences in an active way that allowed them to transcend their guilt and become reconnected to the world. With angry denunciations of the war borrowed from earlier articles and reviews, the book continued in Lifton's vein of "advocacy research," ending with a sharp attack on the traditional conservatism and pretension to objectivity of the psychiatric profession.[139]

Perhaps inevitably, given the strong political sentiments of the book, reviews of *Home from the War* varied more widely than had those of *Death in Life.* Harsh reviews in the *New York Times* and the *New York Times Book Review,* for example, attacked Lifton for his "circular form of reasoning" and his "moral arrogance," while *Time* magazine called his book "a polemic in which moralizing smothers analysis."[140] Even more sympathetic reviewers, who believed that Lifton's interviewing was "skillful and compassionate" and that his antiwar sentiments were appropriate, often complained that the psychiatrist's political biases had led him to focus on an "untypical" group of veterans and that he had allowed his political and psychological argument to "overwhelm and petrify rather than clarify our understanding of the veterans."[141] The book did receive praise, sometimes from reviewers in religious journals who likened Lifton's approach to personal transformation as akin to religious conversion, and Lifton was even nominated for a second National Book Award, but *Home from the War* was never as highly or as widely acclaimed as *Death in Life.*[142]

Once again, it was politically active veterans, and the psychologists who helped them, who were most persuaded by Robert Lifton's work and who worked to popularize the book and to use Lifton's ideas for their own political ends. It was this group, aided by Lifton's own political activism and his famous name and intellectual clout, that worked to cement the portrait of the survivor into American political and cultural discourse. .

Lifton, of course, was closely linked to antiwar veterans' activities through his relationship with VVAW and the rap groups. As time went on, he pushed his message of the veteran as survivor more into the mainstream, interviewing with journalists for stories on troubled Vietnam veterans and participating in a growing number of conferences designed to address the problems of the Vietnam vet.[143] Throughout the 1970s, psychologists, psychiatrists, and veterans around the country wrote to Lifton asking him for advice or help in starting rap groups, counseling Vietnam veterans, or presenting reports on the troubles of Vietnam veterans.[144] Since Lifton remained in touch with his friends from the VVAW, many of whom had gone on to begin their own projects or counseling efforts for veterans, he was able to offer help and advice, thus making him part of an expanding network of veterans and psychological professionals interested in improving care for Vietnam veterans.[145]

Moreover, Lifton's friend and colleague Chaim Shatan, who had joined him as a participant in the VVAW rap groups in 1970, began publishing articles on what he called "post-Vietnam syndrome," a constellation of guilt, rage, numbing, alienation, and feelings of being scapegoated that Shatan had observed in his work with veterans but that he had also developed using Lifton's concept of the survivor, relying indeed on pages in *Death in Life* recommended to him by Lifton himself.[146] Shatan's opinion piece "Post-Vietnam Syndrome," printed in the *New York Times* on May 6, 1972, sparked terrific interest in the syndrome among both veterans and nonveterans. Lifton received mail from veterans asking him for help with the syndrome, and the New York City VVAW office was besieged by interested phone callers immediately after the piece was published.[147]

Although Lifton's ideas were at the heart of Shatan's description of the syndrome, Lifton himself was initially uncomfortable with the concept of a syndrome, and he constantly distanced himself from it in his private letters and also in his published work. As a "standard psychiatric label," Lifton told one veteran, post-Vietnam syndrome (PVS) would "tend to obscure the psychological and ethical issues"; the psychiatrist was worried that Americans would dismiss veterans' problems as a medical syndrome rather than as an appropriate and healthy response to the evil they had encountered, and would thus "ignore the broader social ailments that produced Vietnam and the political and moral corruption that is so widespread throughout the society."[148]

The problem was that, without any sort of clinical diagnosis that described the psychological trauma that veterans were experiencing, veterans could not receive appropriate psychiatric care from the Veterans Administration (VA). First, as already discussed, the Veterans Administration provided free medical care for veterans only if their illness manifested within two years of discharge. Veterans' psychological problems, however, were frequently delayed beyond two years, thus making it simple for the VA to deny servicemen's claims. Second, the second edition of the *Diagnostic and Statistical Manual of Mental Disorders* (DSM-II), which was the standard diagnostic tool for psychiatrists and psychologists in current use in 1973, offered no diagnosis for stress or trauma of any sort. The first edition of the DSM, DSM-I, published in 1952, had offered a diagnosis of "gross stress reaction" to label soldiers who experienced mental breakdowns during combat, although the manual treated the condition as temporary and concluded that it would disappear after men left combat. In 1968, however, when the DSM-II was published, "gross stress reaction" was omitted, probably because the psychiatrists working on the edition had no firsthand experience with soldiers from World War II or Korea, and initial reports from Vietnam indicated that rates of psychiatric breakdown in combat had dropped precipitously. Psychiatrists in the early 1970s had no diagnostic category for diagnosing war-related stress, thus preventing many of them from helping Vietnam veterans in pain and ensuring that the VA would deny them benefits, since their illness was not considered to be combat-related.[149]

VVAW had attempted to push for changes in federal law in 1970 and 1971 that would permit VA benefits for time-delayed combat-related stress, but those efforts were unsuccessful. Thus, in June 1974, when *Psychology Today* reported that the American Psychiatric Association (APA) would begin revising the DSM a third time, politically active veterans and psychologists involved in veterans' issues jumped at the chance to put "post-Vietnam syndrome" in the DSM. The activists' successful lobbying of Robert Spitzer, the psychiatrist in charge of the DSM revision, led to an APA task force on Vietnam veterans. Despite his hesitations surrounding the concept of a syndrome, Robert Jay Lifton agreed in 1979 to become a part of the Vietnam Veterans Working Group, both because he wanted to emphasize the significance of adult trauma in a psychiatric profession that frequently downplayed adult experiences and because he knew that vets "were hurting" and that, without a diagnostic category in the DSM, many would not get the treatment they needed.[150]

It is difficult to determine how involved Lifton was in the activities of the Veterans Working Group. In *The Politics of Adjustment,* sociologist Wilbur

Scott put Lifton at the heart of the group. Working mainly from oral histories with many involved psychiatrists and veterans, but not with Lifton, Scott wrote that Lifton and Shatan were the ones who initially approached Robert Spitzer about creating the working group and that the two men, along with several other key veterans and psychiatrists, developed the recommendation that the APA include a new disorder, "post-traumatic stress disorder" (PTSD), in the DSM-III. Recent interviews with Robert Lifton have suggested that he did not spearhead the working group but that he was an active committee member who attended meetings and lent his prestigious name to the effort.[151] Documents in Lifton's collected papers seem to validate the psychiatrist's memory. There is very little of the accumulated paper trail surrounding the APA task force that one would expect in the Lifton papers had the psychiatrist been a founding member of the group or an active lobbyist. Moreover, the documents that are there suggest that one of Lifton's acquaintances in the veteran-psychologist network approached him about the task force, after others had done much of the lobbying, and that Lifton agreed to "do what I can to be helpful."[152]

Regardless of how involved Lifton actually was on the APA task force, what is significant is that his name was prominently listed as a member of the small task force committee and that, after the work of the task force had been completed, PTSD was accepted by the APA in 1980 as a legitimate psychiatric disorder taught in medical schools and accepted by judges and juries, insurance companies, and the federal government. Even if Robert Lifton was not actively involved in the rewriting of the DSM, his ideas were clearly a part of the manual: "psychic numbing" was one of the chief criteria used to diagnose PTSD, and "guilt about surviving when others have not, or about behavior required to achieve survival," was one of the secondary criteria.[153] Lifton's "survivor" had thus become a tangible diagnostic category, with reverberations in science, in politics, and in culture.

Importantly, too, the "survivor" concept that became part of the DSM-III was not limited to Vietnam veterans; it also referred to concentration camp victims. According to Wilbur Scott, Lifton was instrumental in having the APA task force consult with two psychiatrists, William Niederland and Henry Krystal, who specialized in the psychiatric treatment of Nazi victims. Lifton had referred to Niederland's work in *Death in Life,* and the two men maintained a relationship of mutual admiration and relied on one another's work. Krystal worked with Niederland, and Lifton had attended several of Krystal's conferences on concentration camp victims in the 1960s.[154] Thus it is highly likely that Lifton was instrumental in inviting Niederland and Krystal to participate in discussions of the APA task force on Vietnam veterans. Even if Lifton did not play this crucial organizational role, however, it is still significant that the task force continually referred to the trauma of death camp victims. A task force that was set up initially to respond to the political concerns of Vietnam veterans thus expanded its scope to include the traumas of different kinds of people who would not necessarily have had that kind of political leverage, such as concentration camp victims. Robert Lifton's analogy, and his broad definition of the survivor, clearly enabled this expansion.[155]

The concept of post-traumatic stress disorder expanded exponentially in the 1980s and the 1990s, in the wake of the DSM revision. Psychiatrists began to use PTSD to understand a variety of different traumas beyond the extreme situations of war or concentration camps, including rape, child abuse, and civilian disasters such as floods or toxic chemical spills. In 1985, the Society for Traumatic Stress formed in the United States, while the foundation of the International Society for Traumatic Stress Studies during the same year signaled international interest in the subject of trauma. The *Journal for Traumatic Stress* began several years later, providing one academic forum for the large quantity of research on the subject of trauma that had begun to proliferate.[156] A recent search on Pubmed found almost nine thousand citations for articles on post-traumatic stress disorder since 1964, with the numbers of articles increasing exponentially each year by the 1990s.[157] Then, too, when the DSM legitimized PTSD, it became a condition recognized by American legal institutions and insurance companies, thus transforming not only American medicine but also American legal culture. A Lexis-Nexis search of legal news from 2000 to 2005 found over eight hundred articles that addressed post-traumatic stress disorder in cases that spanned from workmen's compensation benefits to assault and from car accidents to insurance.[158] Beyond its professional significance, moreover, the term "survivor" has become a part of the mainstream lexicon as women who have experienced sexual violence and people who have been diagnosed with cancer, among other groups, embraced the word to define themselves. One 2000 television advertisement for a pharmaceutical company, for example, labeled each of the healthy men and women who appeared on the screen a "cancer survivor" and quoted bicyclist Lance Armstrong, who had cancer, saying: "I am not a victim. I am a survivor."[159]

Thus, Robert Jay Lifton's portrait of the survivor, with its explicit analogy between American warfare—first in Hiroshima, then in Vietnam—and Nazi concentration camps, became a tangible part of American medicine, politics, and culture with the inclusion of PTSD in the DSM-III. Of course, the power of this portrait was not Lifton's alone; it was the product of the struggles of many psychiatrists, psychologists, veterans, and survivors of both Hiroshima and Nazi concentration camps. But in some ways, that is precisely the point. Lifton was able to make concrete his vision of the survivor in American life because he was so active in political networks and so conscious of the political purpose of his work.

ROBERT JAY LIFTON'S USE of victims' experiences in Nazi concentration camps to analyze the social and psychological dangers of nuclear warfare and to attack the evils of the war in Vietnam clearly demonstrates that American Jews have not used the Holocaust solely to bolster their own Jewish identity or to gain support for Israeli politics. Instead, guided by his "radical-liberal" politics, Robert Lifton encouraged Americans to utilize Nazi camps in a variety of ways to criticize United States military and political leaders who were involved in the war on Vietnam and in the pursuit of nuclear dominance. Our contemporary understanding of Holocaust consciousness has obscured the variety of ways, by activists on the left as well as the right, in which the Nazi destruction of Jews has been used politically in American history. Moreover, the fact that neither Jews nor Holocaust survivors protested Lifton's efforts to use the concentration camp analogy for his left-liberal purposes further suggests that our understanding of Holocaust consciousness is one that has been developed during a particular historical moment, and that American Jews understood the event very differently thirty years ago than they do today.

It is true, to be sure, that Lifton is not a member of an organized Jewish group, nor is he a religiously active Jew. Nonetheless, he has openly discussed the significance of his Jewish background in his sensitivity to the subject of Nazi concentration camps and in his use of the camps for political purposes, and indeed a close examination of his published works, as well as of interview transcripts with him, does make clear that being Jewish has had an impact on his life and work. Historians of the Jewish experience in the United States need to take into account not only the experiences and activities of Jews affiliated with Jewish institutions or religious branches but also the wide variety of ways that secular and unaffiliated Jews have understood their ethnic and religious lives. Robert Jay Lifton is, of course, only one individual, but exploring the ways in which he interpreted and made sense of his Jewish background—particularly his sense of ambivalence between being an insider and an outsider—can help us to think anew about the significance of Jewishness for the large numbers of American Jews for whom being Jewish has meaning, although it is not expressed institutionally or religiously.

Finally, by developing a powerful analogy between concentration camp survivors and Hiroshima survivors, and then extending that analogy to Vietnam veterans, Robert Lifton established for many Americans—at least for those who were politically active—a valid and meaningful connection between life in the United States and the devastations of Nazi Germany. Although it is not clear to what extent Lifton's analogies between American life and Nazi camps shaped American mainstream thought in the late 1960s and early 1970s, it is clear that his analogy had impact on politically active veterans and psychological professionals and, because of that impact, changed American political, legal, and medical culture significantly in the late 1970s in ways that are still visible today. The diagnostic category of "post-traumatic stress disorder" in the DSM-III, influenced strongly by Lifton's analogy between concentration camp survivors and *hibakusha,* has had a dramatic impact on American society, allowing psychological professionals to diagnose and attach medical and legal significance to adult experiences of trauma that include, but extend well beyond, the experiences of concentration camp survivors and Vietnam veterans. To be sure, critics on the right have decried the way that post-traumatic stress disorder has contributed to a "culture of trauma" that erases individual responsibility and opens the door to frivolous lawsuits, and critics on the left have protested the ways that the psychiatric diagnosis medicalized and thus defanged the legitimate political anger of Vietnam veterans opposed to the war.[160] Nonetheless, throughout the 1980s and 1990s, the medical description of post-traumatic stress disorder, with origins in Robert Jay Lifton's powerful comparisons of Nazi concentration camp inmates, Hiroshima survivors, and Vietnam veterans, helped to shape the ways that Americans understood their politics, their bodies, and their minds.

Conclusion

THE EXAMPLES OF STANLEY ELKINS, Betty Friedan, Stanley Milgram, and Robert Jay Lifton help us to think anew about the history of the post–World War II era in the United States. They suggest that our conventional periodization of "the 1950s" and "the 1960s" is inadequate. They demonstrate at least some of the ways that being Jewish in America had substantial and lasting meaning in the late twentieth century, even when Jews chose not to practice Judaism or affiliate with Jewish organizational life, and even when they were viewed by others as "white," indistinguishable from all other whites. And perhaps most importantly, they remind us that the Nazi destruction of European Jewry—before it was labeled "the Holocaust"—had a substantial impact on American politics both much earlier and in very different ways than we have previously considered.

The Turn of the 1960s

The case of Stanley Elkins alone suggests that it is important to look beyond the conventional dichotomy between "the 1950s" and "the 1960s." Elkins's comparison of enslaved Africans to concentration camp inmates in 1959 was in many ways shaped by intellectual conventions and assumptions of the 1950s, such as the desire to disprove racial inferiority, to examine universal human nature, and to emphasize the impact of social institutions on the makeup of human personality. Yet, Elkins's liberal political convictions and his spiraling popularity between 1963 and 1965 suggest that he spoke particularly well to liberals who pushed for substantial civil rights reform, including affirmative action, in the early 1960s. It is not particularly helpful to see Elkins's work as a last gasp of the conservative social science of the

1950s, or as a weak prelude to the radicalism of black revolutionary hopes and ideals in the late 1960s. Instead, Elkins's work is much better understood as the product of the "turn of the 1960s," a distinctively liberal time when academics continued to hold intellectual assumptions from the 1950s, such as universalism, but when they stretched those assumptions and began to challenge some of the paradigms of the Cold War, such as the obligatory comparison of Nazi Germany to the Soviet Union, in an effort to push for liberal reform.

The works of Betty Friedan and Stanley Milgram reflect even better the enthusiastic liberalism at the turn of the 1960s. With *The Feminine Mystique* and "Behavioral Study of Obedience," both published in 1963, these two authors were clearly responding to, and helping to encourage, a spirit of reform that had become extremely popular and well publicized in the years since the publication of Elkins's *Slavery,* in the wake of successful direct action campaigns by both civil rights and peace activists. Neither work called openly for radical activism, and both relied on the language of universalism that dominated social science in the 1950s. Nonetheless, both works also used passionate rhetoric and connected their inquiries to contemporary political reform in ways that would have been unusual, even unimaginable, in the 1950s. Moreover, many of their readers in 1963 enthusiastically applauded Friedan's and Milgram's messages as being essential to liberal reform.

After 1965, the coalition of radicals and liberals that had sparked and championed the works of Elkins, Friedan, and Milgram splintered. There had been, to be sure, cracks in this coalition all along. But a series of key events between 1963 and 1965 crystallized underlying tensions between radicals and liberals and threatened their working coalitions. At the March on Washington in the summer of 1963, John F. Kennedy's liberal administration insisted that civil rights activist John Lewis moderate his angry speech criticizing the civil rights bill, infuriating Lewis and other radicals. In the summer of 1964, members of the Mississippi Freedom Democratic Party expressed outrage and disillusionment when liberals such as Hubert Humphrey encouraged them to compromise their goal of representing the state of Mississippi at the Democratic National Convention. And in 1965, Lyndon Johnson's decision to step up American intervention in Vietnam inspired the first major protests against the Vietnam War by members of the New Left.[1] Radicals in all these instances viewed liberals' reformist efforts as hypocritical and unsatisfactory, while liberals regarded radicals' intransigence as dangerously naive. The spirit of liberal reform that had characterized the turn of the 1960s thus came under substantial attack from the left by the latter half of the 1960s, as well as from a right that was growing in organizational strength and momentum.

Given this change in the political zeitgeist, by the late 1960s and early 1970s, Betty Friedan, Stanley Elkins, and Stanley Milgram all found their works, and the spirit of liberal reform they had reflected, under serious challenge. Radical African Americans and white leftists excoriated Stanley Elkins's images of passive black slaves, and radical feminists rejected Friedan as a conservative who had ignored the racial and class struggles of poor women of color. By the late 1960s, a growing number of social scientists had sharply attacked Milgram's ethics, and by the early 1970s, intellectuals and book reviewers had ridiculed his universalism. These writers' liberal works were by no means abandoned or forgotten after 1965, but in the latter half of the 1960s, and certainly by the early 1970s, their liberalism was much more sharply scrutinized and the controversies surrounding their works became an integral part of their popularization in American life.

To be sure, the success of Robert Jay Lifton's work after 1967 demonstrates that the divorce between liberals and radicals in the latter half of the 1960s was not complete or permanent. Lifton's analogy between concentration camp survivors and *hibakusha,* initially developed at the turn of the 1960s, appealed to many radicals as well as moderates in the late 1960s, and his image of the survivor helped to shape substantial changes in the medical and legal fields throughout the 1970s and beyond. Liberal reform thus continued to be an important goal for many throughout the 1970s, and radical activist groups, such as Vietnam Veterans Against the War, frequently mobilized to support this type of reform.

Nonetheless, because Lifton published his analogy later than did Elkins, Friedan, and Milgram, the liberal zeitgeist at the turn of the 1960s did not shape the reception of his work in the same way. Liberals and radicals in 1967 did not enthusiastically interpret Lifton's work as a call to action in the same way that many had viewed the works of Elkins, Friedan, and Milgram in 1963.[2] Even as radical VVAW activists warmed to Lifton's work, they were suspicious of his position as a liberal professional and an observer. Indeed, the psychiatrist reevaluated and ultimately changed his modes of research and writing in order to work successfully with radicals.[3] It was Lifton's own political activism, his sympathy for radical action throughout the late 1960s and early 1970s, as well as his willingness to reshape his work to address changing intellectual preoccupations and assumptions that pushed his work into the public eye and unified a growing body of radical Vietnam veterans and liberal psychiatrists behind the idea of the survivor in the late 1960s and 1970s. The liberal assumptions into which Elkins, Friedan, and

Milgram had tapped between 1957 and 1965 were no longer easily available to Lifton by 1967, nor did liberals and radicals immediately seize his message as justification for political action, as they had with the other writers. The work of Robert Jay Lifton thus demonstrates the lasting impact of liberal reform ideals from the turn of the 1960s as well as the peculiar nature of the time between 1957 and 1965, during which many Americans welcomed those ideals so enthusiastically and even unquestioningly.

During the present time, when "liberalism" has become a pejorative word connoting weakness, and when "moral values" have become associated with conservatives such as George W. Bush, it is worth reconsidering the turn of the 1960s as a distinct era in United States history. During that era, large numbers of North Americans viewed liberalism as a vigorous political ideology as well as a moral ideology, one committed not only to compassionate idealism but, crucially, to the preservation and dignity of universal humanity and to personal moral responsibility.

To be sure, this era must not be idealized. Liberal universalism at the turn of the 1960s blithely ignored crucial differences of gender, race, class, and ethnicity, and liberals' emphases on toughness and vigor exacerbated the Cold War, while giving fuel to the nation's imperial pretensions in Vietnam and elsewhere throughout the world. Nonetheless, leftists' and liberals' successful unity behind ideals of personal moral responsibility, universal human dignity, and political strength at the turn of the 1960s suggest that this era, understood anew as a separate and distinct moment in time, might offer lessons for the American left.

Jews as Insiders and Outsiders

The experiences of Stanley Elkins, Betty Friedan, Stanley Milgram, and Robert Jay Lifton offer us different lessons about American Jewish life. Elkins, Friedan, Milgram, and Lifton were, of course, not typical American Jews, nor does this monograph suggest that they were representative of American Jews in any way. Nonetheless, these men and women were members of an important population of American Jews that has not been understood adequately either by scholars or by lay or religious leaders: Jews who do not practice Judaism and who do not affiliate with Jewish organizations or institutions, yet continue to identify themselves as Jews. Estimates suggest that as many as one-half of all American Jews today may fall into this category.[4] Exploring the lives of four admittedly atypical Jews in the middle to late twentieth century allows us at least one window on the slippery, contradictory meanings of Jewishness in the United States after World War II.

Importantly, being Jewish meant something different to each one of these writers. For both Stanley Elkins and Betty Friedan, who had grown up as Jews respectively in Boston and Peoria, cities where they were an identifiable minority, being Jewish primarily meant exclusion and discrimination. Both experienced antisemitism personally as young people, and it dramatically shaped their later lives and perceptions of themselves as Jews. The fact that this antisemitism took place against a backdrop of spiraling persecution against Jews in Germany made it loom even larger in both Elkins's and Friedan's private lives.

Elkins and Friedan did not view their Jewishness in the same way, however. Gender played an important role in the different ways that Friedan and Elkins experienced and confronted antisemitism. For Elkins, being a young Jewish man meant confronting threats of physical violence, as well as images of male passivity and weakness. Friedan's life as a young Jewish woman, however, was marked by experiences of social exclusion, feelings of physical unattractiveness, and her mother's rage and shame at the family's second-class status. Moreover, Elkins's ability to overcome stereotypes of Jewish male weakness as a soldier in the U.S. Army led him to argue that only institutional structures could save individuals from oppression. Friedan's experiences fighting against her own isolation as a suburban housewife, however, led her to believe that individual Jews and individual women were capable of transcending their internalized oppression. These different means of confronting antisemitism affected audiences' responses to their works. While Elkins's pessimism infuriated African Americans who rejected his image of utterly passive slaves, Friedan's hopeful portrait of female victory over oppression empowered many of her readers and encouraged them to become politically active.

Despite these important differences, it was the painful experience of antisemitism that predominantly shaped both Elkins's and Friedan's understandings of Jewishness even at their earliest ages. For both Stanley Milgram and Robert Jay Lifton, however, who both grew up as members of a majority in predominantly Jewish neighborhoods in New York, personal experiences of antisemitism were uncommon or unmemorable.[5] Being Jewish to Milgram and Lifton meant, in part, living in these neighborhoods. Jewishness was woven into public, daily life for both young men, as their relatives, friends, neighbors, and schoolteachers were all predominantly Jewish and communicated to them that they were somehow different as Jews.

The Nazi catastrophe on the other side of the Atlantic was a large part of what made them different. During the war, family, friends, neighbors, and teachers all made it clear that Hitler was their personal enemy. Perhaps most substantially, once the war was over, the discomforting sense that it was "an accident of geography" that they were alive, that it was a quirk of fate that their relatives had chosen to immigrate years ago to the safe shores of the United States, dramatically shaped both Robert Jay Lifton's and Stanley Milgram's perceptions of what it meant to be Jewish.

Milgram's sense of geographical luck was directly shaped by his parents' recent immigrant roots. With close family members still trapped in Europe, Milgram's parents listened to the radio intently during the war; after the war, relatives who bore camp tattoos came to stay for a time in the Milgram household. Of all the members of this book's cohort, Stanley Milgram was probably most directly affected by the Nazi genocide, and his very personal and emotional descriptions of the camps in both his public and private writings suggest the significant impact that the Holocaust had on his identity as a Jew.

By contrast, Robert Jay Lifton was probably the least directly affected by the Nazi genocide as a young man. The product of a fairly comfortable middle-class Jewish household in Brooklyn, Lifton was separated by several generations from the European disaster, and mostly insulated from experiences of antisemitism as a young child growing up. As an athlete, fraternity member, and scholar, Lifton does not seem to have struggled a great deal with the stereotypical images of weak Jewish men that haunted Stanley Elkins, nor does he seem to have internalized any of the feelings of isolation or self-hatred that shaped Betty Friedan. In many ways, Jewishness seems to have affected Robert Lifton's internal life the least as a young man. Nonetheless, Lifton made clear in 1968 his own existential angst that only an "accident of history" had kept him alive. The psychiatrist was clearly shaped by his early education in his middle-class household and Brooklyn neighborhood; in the end, his understanding of the threat of the Nazi regime did not differ substantially from that of Stanley Milgram. Indeed, Betty Friedan and Stanley Elkins similarly expressed a shared sense of disquietude at their own good fortune as American Jews. The existential unease that American Jews experienced in the wake of the Holocaust cannot be minimized, and the impact of that unease on American Jewish history, and American history, should not be overlooked.[6]

Thus, although the four members of this cohort all experienced Jewishness differently, they all viewed themselves as outsiders: actual or potential victims of discrimination in the wake of an upsurge of world antisemitism and the mass murder of European Jews during World War II. These sensations were powerful, and they shaped all these authors' sensitivities to the stories of suffering in Nazi concentration camps.

At the same time, however, these writers were all ambitious thinkers who, in the years after World War II, were welcomed into elite intellectual settings as white men and women, indistinguishable from Catholics or Protestants. Of course, these intellectual enclaves were far less open to women. Betty Friedan's decision to leave academic psychology and move into journalism seems to have been, at least in part, due to gender discrimination, and her position as an intellectual throughout the turn of the 1960s was probably much more open to question because of her status as a woman. Nonetheless, all four of these Jewish thinkers trained in the social sciences were considered "white" and ultimately embraced as members of a new social and intellectual elite. As a graduate student at Columbia, for example, Stanley Elkins became close friends with Eric McKitrick, an Episcopalian who grew up in a privileged world surrounded by automobile executives in Flint, Michigan.[7] After moving to the elite New York suburb Grand View-on-Hudson, Friedan became part of a community organization that included intellectual leaders such as sociologists C. Wright Mills and William J. Goode.[8] The privileges that these Jewish men and women received—including access to the benefits of the GI Bill, elite higher education, and housing in wealthy suburbs—because they were white were substantial.[9]

As the biographical explorations of this book have suggested, however, understanding the meaning of being Jewish in the years after World War II cannot be limited to acknowledging the whiteness that publicly defined men and women such as Lifton, Elkins, Friedan, and Milgram. Stanley Milgram's heady experience of being a lead investigator in an NSF-funded psychological experiment at Yale University was substantially shaped by his fears of, and his rage at, the Nazi attacks on his family. Betty Friedan's self-representation as an ordinary white housewife from Peoria who had triumphed over her own oppression was framed by her understanding of, and her experiences with, Jewish self-hatred.

It was the intertwining of insider status and outsider memory that shaped Jewish life in the second half of the twentieth century. This intertwining sometimes resulted in insensitivity and blindness. Stanley Elkins's concern for Jewish weakness led him to silence the voices of enslaved African Americans, for example, while Stanley Milgram's preoccupation with the murders of Jews in Europe made him unwilling or unable to take full responsibility for his own substantial power over other people's lives in the Yale laboratory. Nonetheless, the combination of insider privilege and outsider fears also sensitized men and women such as Elkins,

Friedan, Milgram, and Lifton to the dangers of power and allowed them in some cases to become influential voices against oppression.

Of course, this cohort was by no means representative of the secular American Jewish population. Elkins, Friedan, Milgram, and Lifton were intellectuals who attained great fame in their fields, and their level of insider privilege was far greater than that experienced by most American Jews. Few American Jews published a best selling book, for example, or conducted scientific experiments that were publicized on *Sixty Minutes*. A large number of Jews did, however, experience newfound acceptance in the suburbs, the universities, and the white-collar professions that made up an expanding middle-class world of white privilege in the postwar United States. If Milgram's and Friedan's experiences are not representative, they can at least illuminate for us the significant social mobility experienced by Jews in the years after 1945. Then, too, the outsider experiences of men and women such as Friedan and Milgram may have been unusual; a minority of American Jewish families took in Holocaust survivors after the war, and, of course, very few Jews studied self-hatred with Kurt Lewin. Nonetheless, many American Jews experienced some form of discrimination in the 1930s and 1940s, and most if not all of them were conscious that their existence after World War II was an accident of geography, a lucky coincidence. Examining the ways that men and women such as Stanley Elkins, Betty Friedan, Stanley Milgram, and Robert Jay Lifton balanced their new arrival into the American intelligentsia with their Jewish fears of mass murder and destruction by using analogies involving Nazi concentration camps can offer us insight into at least some of the ways that being Jewish had meaning for newly successful, secular, unaffiliated Jews in the second half of the twentieth century.

Early Holocaust Consciousness

Finally, the works of Stanley Elkins, Betty Friedan, Stanley Milgram, and Robert Jay Lifton all demonstrate the existence of a Holocaust consciousness at the turn of the 1960s very different from that of our own era. For example, Elkins did not intend for his analogy between concentration camp inmates and African American slaves to have anything to do with race or racism. Americans today may have difficulty even imagining a comparison of American slavery and the Nazi Holocaust that does not emphasize state-sanctioned racism. Similarly, Friedan's intense emphasis on the psychological devastation of the Nazi concentration camp experience on its victims allowed her to compare those camps to American suburban homes. The American understanding of the Holocaust today much more heavily emphasizes the death camps' physical destruction of human life, making Friedan's claims today seem so solipsistic and narcissistic that she has publicly disclaimed them and her supporters have essentially forgotten them. And Stanley Milgram and Robert Jay Lifton argued that the psychological processes of Nazi concentration camp commandants and survivors might offer legitimate insight into the psyches of American soldiers who committed atrocities in the Vietnam War. Although Americans in the past ten years have been willing to compare genocides in Bosnia, Rwanda, or Darfur to the Nazi Holocaust, contemporary historical understandings of the Holocaust as genocide have tended to discourage most Americans from using the Holocaust to understand the actions of United States citizens or soldiers.

Our contemporary historical description of the Holocaust is clearly very different from the more universalistic and impressionistic psychological and sociological understandings of Nazi atrocity that shaped the works of men and women such as Elkins and Friedan. The early Holocaust consciousness of these men and women did not center on the Nazis' isolation, persecution, and destruction of millions of Jews but instead on the Nazis' use of bureaucracy and technology to dehumanize both the perpetrators and the victims enclosed within their vicious system. The political, intellectual, and cultural preoccupations of the turn of the 1960s as well as the limited historical scholarship on Nazi destruction during that era shaped this early Holocaust consciousness. It has been easy for scholars to overlook or dismiss early Holocaust consciousness because it lacked not only the label "the Holocaust" but also many of the crucial intellectual components that now define the Holocaust for scholars and lay audiences alike.

The fact that, for the most part, both Jewish and non-Jewish audiences at the turn of the 1960s enthusiastically embraced Friedan's portrait of the "comfortable concentration camp," or Elkins's descriptions of dehumanized slaves and camp inmates, suggests that this early Holocaust consciousness was widespread during the era, not simply a product of a small academic milieu. Then, too, this widespread enthusiasm for analogies that untied the Nazi destruction from its historical moorings helps us to see that our contemporary understanding of the Holocaust as a unique, incomparable, even sacred event has been a recent intellectual construction, not an inherent part of comprehending Nazi genocide.

Perhaps most importantly, the widely varied liberal political movements that employed these thinkers' understandings of Nazi destruction should make us think differently about the impact of the Holocaust on American life. It changes our understandings of American history and American politics, as well as our perceptions of Holocaust memory, to know that black activists and liberal policy makers, liberal and conservative housewives, radical student members of Students for a Democratic Society and the Berkeley Free Speech Movement, and activists in Vietnam Veterans Against the War all employed images of Nazi concentration camps as they grappled with political issues of the 1960s such as civil rights, feminism, nuclear proliferation, and My Lai.

Americans reshaped their political fears and reconsidered their political possibilities in the wake of the bureaucratic killing machine developed by Nazi Germany in the 1930s and 1940s. The dangers of political inaction in a mass society, for example, seemed overwhelming for many young Americans, both Jewish and non-Jewish, who had been raised to criticize "good Germans." By focusing primarily on domestic political experiences and memories to explain protest movements of the 1960s, we have overlooked the ways that the global experience of genocide shaped American political life and thought. Just as we have begun to consider in greater depth the ways that the Cold War and African decolonization affected the civil rights movement, and the ways that the Cuban Revolution affected the New Left, we need to think more closely and deeply about the ways that the Holocaust shaped American political thought and action in the second half of the twentieth century.[10]

Moreover, by focusing only on Jewish silence about the Holocaust in the 1950s and 1960s, or pointing to the ways that Jewish organizations have used the Holocaust in shaping American Jewish identity or supporting right-wing Israeli policy in the 1970s and 1980s, we neglect an important thread of liberalism in American political life. The extremity of Nazi destruction did not provoke repression or forgetfulness, nor did it discourage liberal reform; instead it provided a unifying rallying cry and a haunting warning for many activists at the turn of the 1960s, and even afterward.

As the above discussion should make clear, our current perspective on the Holocaust is markedly different from that of intellectuals at the turn of the 1960s. The Holocaust consciousness that shaped the works of Betty Friedan and Stanley Milgram changed slowly but dramatically in the United States throughout the decade of the 1960s. It is worth briefly exploring how this change took place. Beginning at the turn of the 1960s, mainstream intellectual life began to exhibit signs of a shifting perspective on Nazi destruction as more intellectuals began to publish works that emphasized the German persecution and murder of Jews.

Elie Wiesel's *Night,* for example, which has become a central text in Holocaust education in contemporary America, was published in the United States in 1960. The author's perspective as a religious Jew who lost his faith while in Nazi concentration camps won him high praise from critics, although he received very brief and limited attention in 1960.[11] In his *Kaddish* symphony (1961–1963), composer Leonard Bernstein similarly embraced his Jewish identity and openly addressed both Jewish ritual and Jewish extermination by the Nazis as the work's narrator sang a mourner's prayer for herself, afraid that "there may just be / No one to say it after me."[12] And Philip Roth's 1959 short story "Eli the Fanatic" described an assimilated suburban Jew who reclaimed his Jewish identity by identifying with Orthodox Jews who had moved into his neighborhood after surviving the Nazis' extermination efforts.[13] All these works focused attention on the Jewish victims of Nazi destruction and on Jewish religion, identity, and mourning in the wake of the catastrophe.

These works also, however, either intentionally or unintentionally invoked the universalistic interpretation of Nazi destruction during the turn of the sixties, blending together their image of holocaust as a component of Jewish identity with critiques of Nazi totalitarianism, mass conformity, psychiatric definitions of sanity, and a world in the throes of nuclear absurdity. Roth, for example, ridiculed the conformity of Eli's shaded suburb, Woodington, while he also sharply criticized the psychiatric definition of insanity that neighbors and doctors used to label and ultimately sedate Eli by the story's end: "The drug calmed his soul, but did not touch it down where the blackness had reached."[14] Nonetheless, the emphasis on Jewish identity in the works of Wiesel, Roth, and Bernstein suggested that another perspective on Nazi destruction, one that emphasized the German war against Jewish life, was emerging in mainstream American intellectual culture.

The controversy over Hannah Arendt's *Eichmann in Jerusalem* offers a partial explanation for, as well as an intriguing window onto, this changing intellectual landscape. While supporters of Arendt's book—both Jewish and non-Jewish—defended her universalistic portrait of responsibility in the Nazi destruction of European Jewry, many of her Jewish detractors rejected this universalism, decried her implication that Jews were responsible for their own deaths, and insisted on a more particular, a more sympathetically Jewish perspective on the Nazi annihilation. As young Jewish New Leftists championed Arendt for challenging American Jews to reject their "victim myth of the Jewish past," older Jewish liberals, socialists, and communists rose angrily to defend "the embattled dignity and honor of a people still too widely subject to the slings and arrows of outrageous misrepresentation."[15]

Similar controversies over the works of Raul Hilberg and Bruno Bettelheim emerged at precisely the same moment, as readers began to resist these scholars' portraits of Jews complicit in the Nazi bureaucracy. For example, in an essay in the Jewish magazine *Commentary*, historian Oscar Handlin harshly criticized Hilberg for his failure to note the existence of Jewish resistance to Nazi destruction and for "blaming the catastrophe on the victims."[16] And at a forum on the Nazi catastrophe at the University of Chicago in the early 1960s, professors and students began to attack Bettelheim publicly for publishing articles on Jewish passivity and "ghetto thinking."[17] During the turn of the 1960s, scholars' interpretations of the Nazi regime as a bureaucracy that implicated everyone in its mass destruction pushed many Jews to voice interpretations of the Nazi destruction of European Jewry that were more sympathetic to Jewish victims. These Jews' angry reactions ultimately helped to lead to a new perspective on Nazi destruction by the late 1960s and early 1970s that named the destruction "the Holocaust," emphasizing Hitler's "war against the Jews" as a fundamental, ineffable component of Jewish history and identity.

By the late 1960s, significant changes had begun to emerge in American mainstream Holocaust consciousness. Articles and books about the Nazi murder of six million Jews, such as Arthur Morse's *While Six Million Died,* Jean-François Steiner's *Treblinka,* and Lucy Dawidowicz's *War against the Jews* proliferated in the United States in the late 1960s and early 1970s.[18] The term "the Holocaust," with a capital H began to appear in popular literature and journalism without needing explanation.[19] Rather than being considered as an example of evil that might illuminate American politics or scholarship, the Nazi destruction of European Jewry became a historical narrative in itself for mainstream historians and journalists to explore.

In the wake of the 1967 Six-Day and the 1973 Yom Kippur wars, moreover, American Jews began more and more to view the Holocaust as a Jewish event, and to emphasize the connections between their own Jewish identities and the Holocaust. Some leaders of lay Jewish organizations began after the 1973 war to encourage Holocaust education in order to shore up what they believed was flagging Jewish identity and support for Israel.[20] These organizational leaders' efforts were matched and exceeded by the growth of mass movements for ethnic pride, which reshaped Jewish self-awareness in the United States and led many American Jews to understand the Holocaust as a component of their Jewish identy.

To be sure, not all Americans embraced this Jewish communal perspective on Nazi destruction in the late 1960s and early 1970s. Indeed, many radicals—both Jewish and non-Jewish—engaged in political protest during this era by using symbols of Nazism to equate that regime with the American state, as they began to talk more openly and more fearfully about the emergence of American fascism and the construction of American concentration camps.[21] Radical protesters who carried signs decrying "the United States of Amerika" or who shouted "Sieg Heil" at police officers were clearly not interested in exploring the Nazi destruction of European Jewry as a narrative in itself, nor were they interested in replicating the careful analogies of Stanley Milgram and Robert Lifton. These protesters' rhetorical equations of American democracy with Nazi fascism built on audiences' emotions regarding Nazism, rather than rational analysis of the two societies.[22] Nonetheless, this charged political rhetoric in the late 1960s and early 1970s may have been encouraged or even inspired by the willingness and openness of writers such as Lifton to place the subject of Nazi Germany into an American context.

By the late 1970s, however, this angry leftist rhetoric had fallen out of favor, as had the careful liberal analogies of Friedan and Milgram. By 1978, with the airing of the television miniseries *Holocaust*, the formation of an Office of Special Investigations to bring to justice Nazi war criminals living in the United States, and the establishment of a Presidential Commission on the Holocaust, the Holocaust had become a crucial component of American Jewish identity and communal life.[23] Moreover, as Holocaust denial garnered substantial notoriety in academia and in the press at the very same time, some Jewish scholars began to criticize any efforts to compare American life to the Holocaust as "stealing the Holocaust"; such comparisons, for these scholars, were evidence of ignorance or antisemitism or both.[24] In the conservative political and cultural climate ushered in by the Reagan revolution of the 1980s, efforts to draw liberal lessons from the Holocaust were generally met with contemptuous scorn, or at the very least with substantial challenges.[25] For example, when, in 1990, Robert Lifton published *Genocidal Mentality*, a book that compared the psychology of Nazi leaders to that of American leaders engaged in nuclear weapons construction and diplomacy, reviews signaled far more skepticism for his use of such a comparison than they had before, and far less tolerance in general for broad uses of Nazi imagery that transcended the historical context of the Holocaust.[26] It was this environment that shaped the Holocaust consciousness with which most of us are familiar, the Holocaust consciousness that called for a boycott of the Jewish Museum in New York (see page 1). In this environment, the concentration camp analogies of authors such as Betty Friedan and Stanley Elkins became incomprehensible and even disgusting for modern audiences who actually considered them. More frequently, Americans simply forgot about Friedan's and Elkins's comparisons altogether, and their origins in early Holocaust consciousness became invisible.

Although analogies like those of Friedan and Elkins had been substantially forgotten by the 1990s, it would be a mistake to believe that early Holocaust consciousness had no significant impact on our contemporary understandings of politics, or even on our contemporary definitions of the Holocaust. Although the early Holocaust consciousness I have described in this book was a product of a distinct moment in time—the turn of the 1960s—this perspective was by no means limited to that era.

In academic discussions of the Holocaust, the ideas of some members of this book's intellectual cohort, particularly Robert Jay Lifton and Stanley Milgram, have had substantial and lasting impact. As described in chapter 3, Milgram's experiments have shaped the development of Holocaust scholarship, changing the nature of scholarly debate and pushing scholars to grapple with the bureaucratic, technological nature of murder during the Holocaust alongside the antisemitism of many perpetrators. Even through the present, Holocaust scholars have continued to engage with Milgram's ideas, testifying to the lasting significance of his work in Holocaust studies.[27] Perhaps just as crucially, in 1986, Robert Jay Lifton's book exploring the psychology of Nazi doctors became an important part of Holocaust scholarship, one that encouraged readers to view Nazi evil as a product of both antisemitism and technocratic numbness. *Nazi Doctors* is still cited and regarded as something of a classic in Holocaust literature.[28] Early Holocaust consciousness has helped to reframe and redirect our contemporary understandings of the Holocaust.

Then, too, both Lifton's and Milgram's analogies between American political life and Nazi concentration camps have continued to have substantial political and intellectual resonance. As described in chapter 4, Lifton's vision of the "survivor" has continued to have broad impact in American medical and legal culture through its translation into the diagnosis of post-traumatic stress disorder. Then, too, in the wake of revelations of prisoner abuse at Abu Ghraib prison in Baghdad in 2004, Robert Jay Lifton's understandings of survivors and of atrocities once again became the subject of radio, television, and print interviews, as the psychiatrist published articles that put his descriptions of Iraq as an "atrocity-producing situation" at the center of public discourse.[29] Stanley Milgram's obedience experiments similarly were revived by journalists seeking to understand the problems of moral responsibility and conscience in a brutal bureaucracy.[30] Although neither Lifton's portrait of "survivors" nor Milgram's of "obedience" dominated

American discussion about Abu Ghraib the way they arguably did during the discussion about My Lai, they nonetheless still played a significant role in the way Americans understood their political dilemma.

Early Holocaust consciousness thus did not reflect only the preoccupations of academic American Jews at the turn of the 1960s. Instead it reflected an alternative stream of American intellectual thought, one that throughout the past half century has used the imagery of the Nazi extermination of European Jewry to bolster a liberal or left-wing critical perspective on American political life.

Unfortunately, this alternative stream of Holocaust consciousness has been marginalized, so much so that it has been forgotten by many liberals and left-wing Americans, both Jewish and non-Jewish. The thorough disrepute into which Betty Friedan's and Stanley Elkins's concentration camp analogies have fallen offers evidence of this marginalization. To be sure, it would be ridiculous to suggest that we revive Friedan's or Elkins's ideas in toto. Given contemporary, more historically accurate and sympathetic understandings of concentration camp inmates and survivors, as well as enslaved African Americans and suburban housewives, we could not responsibly support African American civil rights or women's rights today with Stanley Elkins's or Betty Friedan's portraits of Nazi concentration camps.

But the intellectual openness with which Friedan and Elkins, and their readers, approached the Nazi destruction of European Jewry as a part of world history that might have important lessons for the United States is certainly worth reconsidering and reviving. Indeed, American politics would be substantially strengthened by a revived political liberalism that took the lessons of Stanley Milgram and Robert Jay Lifton seriously and encouraged today's Americans to see themselves, as well as their elected leaders, as being responsible for political evils committed in their name today.

By treating the Holocaust as an exclusively Jewish subject, one that is somehow so unique that it cannot be compared to other historical phenomena, we impoverish our political and intellectual landscape. Similarly, by overlooking the fact that American Jews themselves were emotionally and intellectually affected by the ravages of the Holocaust and that they grappled with their fears of extermination and subjugation by calling for liberal reforms of American evils such as racial and gender inequality, we have forgotten important components of American, Jewish, and even world history and foreclosed real possibilities for American politics and thought.

To be sure, there is no shortage of political rhetoric on both the right and the left today that uses the Holocaust as a metaphor for any evil, from abortion to meat eating to environmental destruction. This rhetoric casually equates Nazism with any contemporary behavior in an effort to label and isolate that behavior. These rhetorical strategies are very different from efforts at the turn of the 1960s to use the Nazi camps in social-scientific analogies in order to understand the psychological and social processes of obedience, oppression, and survival and to call for political change on the basis of those processes. It is this sort of understanding that could be revived, and that might make American intellectual life—and American politics—richer and deeper.

NOTES

Introduction

1. For more on the exhibit itself, including photographs and reproductions of the artwork, see Norman L. Kleeblatt, ed., *Mirroring Evil: Nazi Imagery/Recent Art* (New York: The Jewish Museum; New Brunswick, N.J.: Rutgers University Press, 2001). For editorials, articles, and letters to the editor about the exhibit and its protesters, see, for example, Menachem Z. Rosensaft, "The Case against 'Mirroring Evil,'" *Jewish Week,* 8 March 2002, 31; Michael Berenbaum, "Must Facing Evil Itself Be Offensive?" *Jewish Week,* 8 March 2002, 30; Rabbi Haskel Lookstein and Stephen J. Lubofsky, letters to the editor, *Jewish Week,* 15 March 2002, 7; Daniel Belasco, "Jewish Museum's 'Nazi Art' Fracas," *Jewish Week,* 18 January 2002, 1; Nacha Cattan, "Supporters Turn Backs on Museum over 'Nazi' Exhibit," *Forward,* 22 March 2002, 8; Daniel Belasco, "Hot Issues, Cool Art," *Jewish Week,* 22 March 2002, 51.

2. For the absence of either the name, "the Holocaust," or the discrete narrative of the "war against the Jews," before the late 1960s, see, for example, Gerd Korman, "The Holocaust in American Historical Writing," *Societas* 2 (Summer 1972): 259–65; Leon Jick, "The Holocaust: Its Use and Abuse Within the American Public," *Yad Vashem Studies* 14 (1981): 303–18; and Jeffrey Shandler, *While America Watches: Televising the Holocaust* (New York: Oxford University Press, 1999), 23. There is debate over whether the term "Holocaust" is limited to Jews. For good description of this debate, Edward T. Linenthal, *Preserving Memory: The Struggle to Create America's Holocaust Museum* (New York: Penguin Books, 1995), 53–55, 112–22, 228–50. Most Holocaust scholars today use the Holocaust to refer specifically to the extermination of about 6 million Jews, but most also acknowledge that many millions of other people, including Poles, homosexuals, Jehovah's Witnesses, communists, Russian POWs, the handicapped, and members of the Roma and Sinti tribes (Gypsies) were killed by the same Nazi machinery.

3. My decision to label the works of Stanley Elkins, Betty Friedan, Stanley Milgram, and Robert Jay Lifton "social scientific" may seem somewhat problematic for readers, because the term "social scientist" does not necessarily define each of these men and women perfectly: Friedan never received her

Ph.D. in psychology, Lifton's training was medical rather than social scientific, and the historical profession in which Stanley Elkins trained has never clearly defined itself as either a social science or a humanity. Nonetheless, all of these men and women's analogies between Nazi and American life were grounded in the social sciences.

4. "Letters," *Newsweek* 25, No. 18 (30 April 1945): 8; "Letters," *Time* 46, no. 25 (17 December 1945): 4.

5. See Michael Staub, *Torn at the Roots: The Crisis of Jewish Liberalism in Postwar America* (New York: Columbia University Press, 2002), 19–44.

6. This is not to say that these sorts of analogies were non-existent before 1957. In the 1945 essay "The Responsibility of Peoples" as well as in the series of other essays in the journal *Politics,* New York intellectual Dwight Macdonald compared Nazi horrors to Allied terror bombing and ultimately to the atomic bombing of Hiroshima and Nagasaki. Macdonald emphasized that, in Germany and the United States, the growth of rationalized mass society had eroded individuals' sense of responsibility for their governments' actions and had thus enabled these horrors. See Robert Westbrook, "The Responsibility of Peoples: Dwight Macdonald and the Holocaust," in *America and the Holocaust: Holocaust Studies Annual, Volume 1,* eds. Sanford Pinsker and Jack Fischel (Greenwood, Fla.: Penkevill Publishing, 1984), 35–68; and Westbrook, "Horrors—Theirs and Ours: The *Politics* Circle and the Good War," *Radical History Review* 36 (1986): 9–25.

7. Erving Goffman, *Asylums: Essays on the Social Situation of Mental Patients and Other Inmates* (Garden City, N.Y.: Anchor Books, 1961).

8. Lawrence Kohlberg, "Stage and Sequence: The Cognitive-Developmental Approach to Socialization," in *Essays on Moral Development, Volume II: The Psychology of Moral Development: The Nature and Validity of Moral Stages* (San Francisco: Harper and Row, 1984), 54–60. The author's notes indicate that the first half of this essay, which includes Eichmann's testimony, was initially prepared and presented as a paper for the Social Science Research Council in November 1963. See also Kohlberg, "Moral and Religious Education and the Public Schools: A Developmental View," in *Religion and Public Education,* ed. Theodore R. Sizer (Boston: Houghton Mifflin, 1967), 164–83.

9. Arthur Miller, *After the Fall* (New York: Bantam Books, 1964), 1.

10. Edward Lewis Wallant, *The Pawnbroker* (New York: McFadden-Bartell, 1962; orig. pub. Harcourt, Brace, and World, 1961); *The Pawnbroker,* dir. Sidney Lumet (Allied Artists, 1964).

11. *Dr. Strangelove or: How I Learned to Stop Worrying and Love the Bomb,* dir. and prod. Stanley Kubrick (Columbia, 1964).

12. See, for a call for analysis of the early 1960s as a distinct moment, David Hollinger, *Science, Jews, and Secular Culture: Studies in Mid-Twentieth Century American Intellectual History* (Princeton, N.J.: Princeton University

Press, 1996), 3–7. A number of works on the 1960s have treated the early 1960s as an era distinct from the later 1960s, although this treatment has not been central to their arguments. See, for example, Morris Dickstein, *Gates of Eden: American Culture in the Sixties* (New York: Basic Books, 1977); Margot A. Henriksen, *Dr. Strangelove's America: Society and Culture in the Atomic Age* (Berkeley: University of California Press, 1997); James J. Farrell, *The Spirit of the Sixties: The Making of Postwar Radicalism* (New York: Routledge, 1997); Arthur Marwick, *The Sixties: Cultural Revolution in Britain, France, Italy, and the United States, c. 1958-c. 1974* (New York: Oxford University Press, 1998); and Doug Rossinow, *The Politics of Authenticity: Liberalism, Christianity, and the New Left in America* (New York: Columbia University Press, 1998).

13. My work follows a trend among historians of finding continuity between these two eras. For an important historical work advancing this argument of continuity, see Joanne Meyerowitz, ed., *Not June Cleaver: Women and Gender in Postwar America, 1945–1960* (Philadelphia: Temple University Press, 1994).

14. See Abbott Gleason, *Totalitarianism: The Inner History of the Cold War* (New York: Oxford University Press, 1995); Les K. Adler and Thomas G. Paterson, "Red Fascism: The Merger of Nazi Germany and Soviet Russia in the American Image of Totalitarianism," *American Historical Review* 75, no. 4 (April 1970): 1046–64. For a good example of one influential book during this era that praised American democracy while uniting the evils of Nazi Germany and the Soviet Union, see Arthur Schlesinger, *The Vital Center: The Politics of Freedom* (Boston: Houghton Mifflin, 1949).

15. See Staub, *Torn at the Roots*, 19–44; Deborah Lipstadt, "America and the Memory of the Holocaust, 1950–1965," *Modern Judaism* 16, no. 3 (October 1996): 199–207.

16. For Little Rock, see Mary Ann Dudziak, *Cold War Civil Rights* (Princeton, N.J.: Princeton University Press, 2000), 115–51; for Sputnik, see, for example, John A. Douglass, "A Certain Future: Sputnik, American Higher Education, and the Survival of a Nation," in *Reconsidering Sputnik: Forty Years Since the Soviet Satellite*, ed. Roger D. Launius, John M. Logsdon, and Robert W. Smith (Amsterdam: Harwood Academic Publishers, 2000), 338.

17. Ellen Schrecker, *Many Are the Crimes: McCarthyism in America* (New York: Little, Brown, 1998), 296–97; Alan Barth, "The Supreme Court's June 17th Opinions," *New Republic* 137, nos. 1–2 (1 July 1957): 9.

18. In the *Nation*, D. F. Fleming reported that it was still "dangerous" to question the concept of "totalitarianism," but he nonetheless openly called for such questioning. See Fleming, "NEEDED: A Purge of Obsessions," *Nation* 188, no. 8 (21 February 1959): 164.

19. A number of articles and books published at the turn of the 1960s emphasized the paranoia, hysteria, and atavism of the conservative movement. See,

for example, Daniel Bell, ed., *The Radical Right,* 3rd ed. (New Brunswick, N.J.: Transaction Publishers, 2002; originally published 1962); Betty E. Chmaj, "Paranoid Patriotism: The Radical Right and the South," *Atlantic* 210, no. 5 (November 1962); "Thunder on the Far Right: Fear and Frustration . . . Rouse Extremists to Action Across the Land," *Newsweek* 58, no. 23 (4 December 1961): 18–22, 27–28, 30. For more recent historical treatments of the rising conservative movement during this era, see, for example, Mary Brennan, *Turning Right in the Sixties: The Conservative Capture of the GOP* (Chapel Hill: University of North Carolina Press, 1995); Lisa McGirr, *Suburban Warriors: The Origins of the New American Right* (Princeton, N.J.: Princeton University Press, 2001); David Farber and Jeff Roche, eds., *The Conservative Sixties* (New York: Peter Lang, 2003).

20. My analysis of liberalism's rise from the last third of the 1950s through the middle of the 1960s is in accord with Godfrey Hodgson's description of a "liberal consensus" during approximately the same era. Hodgson emphasizes the conservative compromise of liberals during this era, however, while I emphasize their initial support for progressive reform. See Godfrey Hodgson, *America in Our Time* (Garden City, N.Y.: Doubleday, 1976), 67–98. A number of historians have questioned Hodgson's thesis, as well as the significance of Northern liberalism during the postwar era, noting the prevalence of white flight and racial hostility in northern cities and suburbs in the 1940s and 1950s. See, for example, Arnold R. Hirsch, *Making the Second Ghetto: Race and Housing in Chicago, 1940–1960* (New York: Cambridge University Press, 1983); Thomas Sugrue, *The Origins of the Urban Crisis: Race and Inequality in Postwar Detroit* (Princeton, N.J.: Princeton University Press, 1996); and Gary Gerstle, "Race and the Myth of the Liberal Consensus," *Journal of American History* 82, no. 2 (September 1995): 579–86. These authors make important contributions to the literature with their discussions of northern racism in housing and employment in the postwar era; their work does not, however, invalidate the existence of growing unified sentiment among liberals by the early 1960s that legal racism in the South needed to end. Their criticisms of the "liberal consensus," moreover, do not focus on the limited time period between the middle of the 1950s and the middle of the 1960s.

21. Stanley Elkins, *Slavery: A Problem in American Institutional and Intellectual Life,* 3rd ed. (Chicago: University of Chicago Press, 1976; originally published 1959), 21.

22. "Angry Battler for Her Sex," *Life* 55 (1 November 1963): 87. For an excellent description of the idealism and enthusiasm of liberals during this era, see Maurice Isserman and Michael Kazin, *America Divided: The Civil War of the 1960s,* 2nd ed. (New York: Oxford University Press, 2004), 53–57.

23. Michel W. Kildare, "Helping the Sit-Ins," *Nation* 190, no. 14 (2 April 1960): n.p. For a few more examples of this sort of identification between

liberals and radicals, see Gene Grundt, "Unfair to Whites," *Nation* 190, no. 17 (23 April 1960): n.p.; Allen Klein, "If We Want Peace," *Nation* 188, no. 11 (14 March 1959): n.p.; Michael Wales, "People or Cattle?" *Nation* 197, no. 18 (30 November 1963): n.p.; Alex Morisey, "Easy Way Out" and D. H. Lane, "Admission of Fear," both in *Saturday Review* 42, no. 3 (17 January 1959): 53.

24. Thomas J. Bouchard, Jr., to Stanley Milgram, 3 August 1965, in Stanley Milgram papers, manuscripts and archives, Yale University Library, New Haven, Conn., Series III, Box 56, Folder 29; Stanley M. Elkins, interview by author, tape recording, Northhampton, Mass., 21 November 1997. For historical accounts that have suggested a shared political world between liberals and activists in the early 1960s, see Rossinow, *Politics of Authenticity,* 23–51; Todd Gitlin, *The Sixties: Years of Hope, Days of Rage* (New York: Bantam Books, 1987), 54–67, 133–35; and Peter Levy, *The New Left and Labor in the 1960s* (Urbana: University of Illinois Press, 1994), 7–44.

25. Ella J. Baker, "Bigger Than a Hamburger," in *Eyes on the Prize Civil Rights Reader,* ed. Clayborne Carson, David J. Garrow, Gerald Gill, Vincent Harding, and Darlene Clark Hine (New York: Penguin Books, 1991), 121; Alma Sothman, "Deadly Hesitation," *Saturday Review* 42, no. 3 (17 January 1959): 53; Women Strike for Peace, founding statement, quoted in Amy Swerdlow, *Women Strike for Peace: Traditional Motherhood and Radical Politics in the 1960s* (Chicago: University of Chicago Press, 1993), 88.

26. David Riesman, *The Lonely Crowd: A Study of the Changing American Character* (New Haven, Conn.: Yale University Press, 1950); William Whyte, *The Organization Man* (New York: Simon and Schuster, 1956); C. Wright Mills, *Power Elite* (New York: Oxford University Press, 1956); Mills, *White Collar: The American Middle Classes* (New York: Oxford University Press, 1951).

27. Vance Packard, *The Hidden Persuaders* (New York: D. McKay, 1957); Daniel J. Boorstin, *The Image; or, What Happened to the American Dream?* (New York: Athenaeum, 1962; originally published 1961); Elkins, *Slavery.*

28. For discussion of this universalism in the post-World War II era, and the shift towards the valuation of ethnic groups in the late 1960s and 1970s, see David Hollinger, "How Wide the Circle of the 'We'? American Intellectuals and the Problem of the Ethnos since World War II," *American Historical Review* 98, no. 2 (April 1993): 317–37.

29. Edward Steichen, *The Family of Man: The Greatest Photographic Exhibition of All Time* (New York: Published for the Museum of Modern Art by the Maco Magazine Corp., 1955); Alfred C. Kinsey, Wardell B. Pomeroy, and Clyde E. Martin, *Sexual Behavior in the Human Male* (Philadelphia: W. B. Saunders, 1948). Hollinger uses these examples to illustrate the universalism of the post-World War II era in "How Wide the Circle of the 'We'?"

30. John Howard Griffin, *Black Like Me* (Boston: Houghton Mifflin, 1961); *Black Like Me,* dir. Carl Lerner (Hilltop, 1964); Harper Lee, *To Kill a Mockingbird*

(Philadelphia: J. B. Lippincott, 1960); *To Kill a Mockingbird*, dir. Robert Mulligan (Brentwood Productions, 1962); *A Patch of Blue*, dir. Guy Green (Metro-Goldwyn Mayer, 1965); Leonard Bernstein, *West Side Story: A Musical* (New York: Random House, 1958); *West Side Story*, dir. Robert Wise and Jerome Robbins (Mirisch Productions, 1961).

31. This does not mean, however, that there were no connections between Nazi antisemitism and American racism before 1967. Some prominent Jews between the 1930s and the 1960s did make these connections. See Stuart Svonkin, *Jews Against Prejudice: American Jews and the Fight for Civil Liberties* (New York: Columbia University Press, 1997); Michael Staub, "'Negroes Are Not Jews': Race, Holocaust Consciousness, and the Rise of Jewish Neoconservatism," *Radical History Review* 75 (Fall 1999): 3–27.

32. For the significance of categories such as "maturity," "normality," "sanity," and "adjustment" in the early 1950s, see, for example, Barbara Ehrenreich, *The Hearts of Men: American Dreams and the Flight from Commitment* (New York: Anchor Press, 1983); Ellen Herman, *The Romance of American Psychology* (Berkeley: University of California Press, 1995).

33. Paul Goodman, *Growing Up Absurd* (New York: Vintage Books, a division of Random House, 1960); Goffman, *Asylums*.

34. Joseph Heller, *Catch-22* (New York: Simon and Schuster, 1961); Ken Kesey, *One Flew Over the Cuckoo's Nest* (New York: Viking Press, 1962).

35. Dickstein, *Gates of Eden*, 91–127. See also Henriksen, *Dr. Strangelove's America*, 241–69.

36. *Dr. Strangelove.*

37. *The Manchurian Candidate*, dir. John Frankenheimer (Metro Goldwyn Mayer—United Artists, 1962).

38. Quoted in Henriksen, *Dr. Strangelove's America*, 329–30.

39. Kurt Vonnegut, Jr., *Mother Night* (New York: Dell, 1961).

40. Morris Dickstein notes this difference between literature of the early and late 1960s. See Dickstein, *Gates of Eden*, 126–27, 213–16.

41. See, for example, David T. Bazelon, *Power in America: The Politics of the New Class* (New York: New American Library, 1967), 307–32; Barbara and John Ehrenreich, "The Professional-Managerial Class," in *Between Labor and Capital*, ed. Pat Walker (Boston: South End Press, 1979); Jean-Christophe Agnew, "A Touch of Class," *democracy* (Spring 1983): 59–72.

42. See, for more on anti-Jewish discrimination, as well as on changing policies in the postwar era, Stephen Steinberg, *The Academic Melting Pot: Catholics and Jews in American Higher Education* (New York: McGraw-Hill, 1974), 5–31; Marcia Graham Synnott, *The Half-Opened Door: Discrimination and Admissions at Harvard, Yale, Princeton, 1900–1970* (Westport, Conn.: Greenwood Press, 1979); Leonard Dinnerstein, *Anti-Semitism in America* (New York: Oxford University Press, 1994), 83–86; Dan A. Oren, *Joining the Club: A History of Jews and Yale* (New Haven, Conn.: Yale University Press, 1985); Andrew S.

Winston, "'The Defects of His Race': E. G. Boring and Antisemitism in American Psychology, 1923–1953," *History of Psychology* 1, no. 1 (February 1998): 27–51; Lewis S. Feuer, "The Stages in the Social History of Jewish Professors in American Colleges," *American Jewish History* 71, no. 4 (June 1982): 437–38; 458–59; Peter Novick, *That Noble Dream: The "Objectivity Question" and the American Historical Profession* (New York: Cambridge University Press, 1988), 365–66; and Everett Carll Ladd, Jr., and Seymour Martin Lipset, "Jewish Academics in the United States: Their Achievements, Culture and Politics," in *American Jewish Year Book 1971*, vol. 72, ed. Morris Fine and Milton Himmelfarb (New York: The American Jewish Committee; Philadelphia: Jewish Publication Society of America, 1971). Although they generally did not face quotas, Catholics also faced significant distrust and discrimination from Protestant elites in the first half of the twentieth century, and Catholics also entered the New Class in growing numbers after World War II. Although they represented 25 percent of the nation's population, only about 15 percent of university professors were Catholic before 1945; by 1975, the number had grown closer to 20 percent. See Novick, *That Noble Dream*, 174, n. 10; Steinberg, *Academic Melting Pot*, 33–55; 104; Everett Carll Ladd, Jr., and Seymour Martin Lipset, *The Divided Academy: Professors and Politics* (New York: McGraw-Hill, 1975), 170–71.

43. For more on these postwar social and ideological changes as they shaped Jewish life, see Karen Brodkin, *How Jews Became White Folks and What That Says about Race in America* (New Brunswick, N.J.: Rutgers University Press, 1998); and Matthew Frye Jacobson, *Whiteness of a Different Color: European Immigrants and the Alchemy of Race* (Cambridge, Mass.: Harvard University Press, 1998), 187–99.

44. Carl Bridenbaugh, "The Great Mutation," *American Historical Review* 68 (1963): 322–23, 328, cited in Ladd and Lipset, "Jewish Academics," 96; Novick, *That Noble Dream*, 339–40; and Edward S. Shapiro, *A Time for Healing: American Jewry since World War II* (Baltimore: Johns Hopkins University Press, 1992), 105–6. Contemporaries universally understood Bridenbaugh's speech to have been directed hostilely toward Jews. See Novick, *That Noble Dream*, 339–40.

45. For some examples of these works, see Henry Cohen, "Jewish Life and Thought in an Academic Community: A Case Study of Town and Gown," *American Jewish Archives* 14 (November 1962): 107–28; Edwin Wolf 2nd, "Wanted: Jewish Intellectuals for Jewish Community Life," *Jewish Digest* 8 (February 1963): 2–8; Judah Pilch, "The Intellectual as Layman in Jewish Education," *Reconstructionist* 31 (28 May 1965): 7–14; and Eugene B. Borowitz, "Believing Jews and Jewish Writers: Is Dialogue Possible?" *Judaism* 14 (Spring 1965): 173. For a good discussion of this literature, see Norman L. Friedman, "The Problem of the 'Runaway Jewish Intellectuals': Social Definition and Sociological Perspective," *Jewish Social Studies* 31, no. 1 (January

1969): 3–19. In 1963, the B'nai B'rith Hillel Foundation instituted a National Hillel Faculty Program to reach out to "alienated" Jewish professors. See Friedman, "'Runaway Jewish Intellectuals,'" 8–9.

46. Allan Mazur, "Resocialized Ethnicity: A Study of Jewish Social Scientists" (Ph.D. diss., Johns Hopkins University, 1969). I am indebted to Thomas Blass for making me aware of Milgram's participation in Mazur's study, and to Allan Mazur for confirming that participation. Thomas Blass, personal e-mail communication with author, 15 November 2004; Allan Mazur, personal e-mail communication with author, 29 December 2004.

47. Hollinger, *Science, Jews, and Secular Culture*, 17–41.

48. Novick, *That Noble Dream*, 337–41.

49. For brief mentions of Jews in concentration camps, see Elkins, *Slavery*, 105, 113, 114.

50. Goffman, *Asylums*, 35, 44.

51. Sylvia Plath, "Daddy," in *Ariel* (London: Faber and Faber, 1965), 50.

52. Vonnegut, *Mother Night*, 22.

53. For other examples of non-Jewish writers who developed more brief comparisons between American life and Nazi Germany, albeit comparisons that foregrounded racial oppression, see James Baldwin, *The Fire Next Time* (New York: Dial Press, 1963), and Lee, *To Kill a Mockingbird*, 282. For one non-Jewish writer who compared American and Nazi behavior without addressing the fact that Jews were murdered in the Holocaust, see Thomas Merton, "A Devout Meditation in Memory of Adolf Eichmann," in *Raids on the Unspeakable* (New York: New Directions Publishing, 1964), 45–49.

54. See Michael Rogin, *Blackface, White Noise: Jewish Immigrants in the Hollywood Melting Pot* (Berkeley: University of California Press, 1996); Michael Alexander, *Jazz Age Jews* (Princeton, N.J.: Princeton University Press, 2001); and Naomi Seidman, "Fag Hags and Bu Jews: Toward a (Jewish) Politics of Vicarious Identity," in *Insider/Outsider: American Jews and Multiculturalism*, ed. David Biale, Michael Galchinsky, and Susannah Heschel (Berkeley: University of California Press, 1998).

55. See, for example, the cases of Marie Syrkin and Hayim Greenberg in Carole S. Kessner, ed., *The "Other" New York Jewish Intellectuals* (New York: New York University Press, 1994).

56. For a work that persuasively suggests this approach, see Ezra Mendelsohn, "Should We Take Notice of Berthe Weill?" *Jewish Social Studies* (new series) 1, no. 1 (Fall 1994): 22–39.

57. The sociological literature on the subject of American Jewish identity is too immense to list exhaustively. For a few prominent examples, see Charles S. Liebman, *The Ambivalent American Jew* (Philadelphia: Jewish Publication Society of America, 1973); Marshall Sklare and Joseph Greenblum, *Jewish Identity on the Suburban Frontier: A Study of Group Survival in the Open Society* (New York: Basic Books, 1967); Sklare, *America's Jews* (New York: Random House,

1971); and Steven M. Cohen, *American Modernity and Jewish Identity* (New York: Tavistock, 1983).

58. See, for example, Laurence J. Silberstein, *Mapping Jewish Identities* (New York: New York University Press, 2000); Laurence J. Silberstein and Robert L. Cohn, eds., *The Other in Jewish Thought and History* (New York: New York University Press, 1994); David Theo Goldberg and Michael Krausz, eds., *Jewish Identity* (Philadelphia: Temple University Press, 1993).

59. Daniel and Jonathan Boyarin's conceptualization of Jewish identity as "partially given" and the result of "bodies . . . marked as different and often as negatively different to the dominant cultural system," rather than radically individualistic and voluntary, has influenced my thinking greatly. See Boyarin and Boyarin, "Diaspora: Generation and the Ground of Jewish Identity," *Critical Inquiry* 19 (Summer 1993): 704.

60. For ideas about "descent," see Susan A. Glenn, "In the Blood? Consent, Descent, and the Ironies of Jewish Identity," *Jewish Social Studies* 8, nos. 2 and 3 (Winter/Spring 2002): 139–52.

61. For a recent perspective that criticizes American Jewish intellectuals for their emphasis on black civil rights and their lack of attention to Jewish life, see Seth Forman, *Blacks in the Jewish Mind: A Crisis of Liberalism* (New York: New York University Press, 1998). For a perspective that describes Jewish vicarious identification as racist efforts to become "white," see Rogin, *Blackface, White Noise*. For a recent perspective that sees vicarious identification as "Jewish liberalism" and a by-product of the Jewish experience of exile, see Alexander, *Jazz Age Jews*. For some other perspectives on American Jews' identification with African Americans, see Hasia R. Diner, *In the Almost Promised Land: American Jews and Blacks, 1915–1935* (Westport, Conn.: Greenwood Press, 1977) and Jeffrey Melnick, *A Right to Sing the Blues: African Americans, Jews, and American Popular Song* (Cambridge, Mass.: Harvard University Press, 1999). Note that there is an extensive historiography on Jewish liberalism. This historiography has informed my project, but I have not specifically intervened in this literature. See, for example, Marc Dollinger, *Quest for Inclusion: Jews and Liberalism in Modern America* (Princeton, N.J.: Princeton University Press, 2000); Steven M. Cohen, *The Dimensions of American Jewish Liberalism* (New York: American Jewish Committee, 1989); "Forum: Jews and American Liberalism: Studies in Political Behavior," *American Jewish Historical Quarterly* 65, no. 2 (December 1976); Lawrence Fuchs, *The Political Behavior of American Jews* (New York: Free Press, 1956).

62. My view of Jewish intellectuals as insiders and outsiders is obviously indebted to Biale, Galchinsky, and Heschel, *Insider/Outsider*.

63. Jonathan D. Sarna, "The Cult of Synthesis in American Jewish Culture," *Jewish Social Studies* (new series) 5, nos. 1 and 2 (Fall 1998/Winter 1999): 52.

64. Sarna, "Cult of Synthesis." Although Sarna describes the "cult of synthesis" losing much of its public power in the 1960s and 1970s, when the cultural

meaning of the United States itself became more fractured, he also notes that the coalescence of Americanness and Jewishness did not disappear but instead became submerged and internalized within American Jews' identities and values.

65. See, for example, Gitlin, *Sixties*, 24–26; Maurice Isserman and Michael Kazin, "The Failure and Success of the New Radicalism," in *The Rise and Fall of the New Deal Order*, ed. Steve Fraser and Gary Gerstle (Princeton, N.J.: Princeton University Press, 1989), 219–20; and Henriksen, *Dr. Strangelove's America*, 270–86.

66. See, for example, Stephen Whitfield, "The Holocaust and the American Jewish Intellectual," *Judaism* 28, no. 4 (1979): 391–407; Whitfield, *In Search of American Jewish Culture* (Hanover, N.H.: University Press of New England for Brandeis University, 1999), 168–96; Leon A. Jick, "The Holocaust: Its Use and Abuse within the American Public," *Yad Vashem Studies* 14 (1981): 303–18; Shapiro, *Time for Healing*, 212–17; Lipstadt, "America and the Memory of the Holocaust," 195–214; Peter Novick, *The Holocaust in American Life* (Boston: Houghton Mifflin, 1999); and Alan Mintz, *Popular Culture and the Shaping of Holocaust Memory in America* (Seattle: University of Washington Press, 2001).

67. See Novick, *Holocaust in American Life*, esp. 279–81.

68. Deborah Lipstadt, for example, mentions a range of examples in which the Holocaust became a significant part of American public discourse between 1950 and 1965. Yet, she essentially discounts the significance of these cultural artifacts, because "the Holocaust did not emerge as a factor in the construct of American Jewish identity." See Lipstadt, "America and the Memory of the Holocaust," 208.

69. See Svonkin, *Jews against Prejudice*; Shandler, *While America Watches*; Staub, "'Negroes Are Not Jews'"; Staub, *Torn at the Roots*; Eli Lederhendler, *New York Jews and the Decline of Urban Ethnicity, 1950–1970* (Syracuse, N.Y.: Syracuse University Press, 2001), esp. 36–62; Rona Sheramy, "'Resistance and War': The Holocaust in American Jewish Education, 1945–1960," *American Jewish History* 91, no. 2 (June 2003): 287–313; Lawrence Baron, "The Holocaust and American Public Memory, 1945–1960," *Holocaust and Genocide Studies* 17, no. 1 (Spring 2003): 62–88; and Hasia Diner, "Post-World-War-II American Jewry and the Confrontation With Catastrophe," *American Jewish History* 91, nos. 3 and 4 (September and December 2003): 439–67.

70. See, for example, "The Gieseking Affair," *Newsweek* 33, no. 6 (7 February 1949): 21–22. Lawrence Baron addresses both Frank and Poliakov, as well as a host of other literary and social-scientific representations of Nazi destruction during the 1940s and 1950s. See Baron, "Holocaust and American Public Memory." Hasia Diner describes the organized Jewish community's memorialization of Nazi destruction, including religious responses to the catastrophe. See Diner, "Post-World-War-II American Jewry."

71. See, for example, "The Atlantic Report on the World Today," *Atlantic* 205, no. 3 (March 1960): 4–8; Terence Prittie, "The German Conscience," *Atlantic* 206, no. 5 (November 1960): 108–13; Terrence Prittie, "The Generation of Nazis," *New Republic* 142, no.3 (18 January 1960): 9–10; "Neo-Nazi Outrages," *New York Times*, 31 December 1959, 20.

72. For descriptions of newspaper coverage of Eichmann, see "The Rush of History," *Time* (21 April 1961): 45. For television coverage, documentaries, and dramas, see Shandler, *While America Watches*, 97–100, 104–7, 121–27; for film, see Howard Thompson, review of *Operation Eichmann*, *New York Times* (14 May 1961), 40; for books about Eichmann, see Norbert Muhlen, "The U.S. Image of Germany, 1962, as Reflected in American Books," *Modern Age* 6, no. 4 (Fall 1962): 421.

73. Charles Y. Glock, Gertrude J. Selznick, and Joe L. Spaeth, *The Apathetic Majority: A Study Based on Public Responses to the Eichmann Trial* (New York: Harper and Row, 1966), cited in Baron, "Holocaust and American Public Memory," 78–79.

74. Leon Uris, *Exodus* (Garden City, N.Y.: Doubleday, 1958); Baron, "Holocaust and American Public Memory," 76; "A People's Return to the Promised Land," *Life* 49 (pt. 3), no. 24 (12 December 1960): 70–77; Gideon Bachmann, review of *Exodus*, *Film Quarterly* 14, no. 3 (Spring 1961): 58.

75. William L. Shirer, *The Rise and Fall of the Third Reich: A History of Nazi Germany* (New York: Simon and Schuster, 1960). See, for example, Hugh Trevor-Roper, "Light on Our Century's Darkest Night," *New York Times Book Review*, 16 October 1960, 1; Naomi Bliven, "The Thousand-Year Civilization," *New Yorker* 36, no. 37 (29 October 1960): 174–77; Bernard Levin, "Sic Semper Tyrannis," *Spectator*, 15 November 1960, 789–90; Gavriel Rosenfeld, "The Reception of William L. Shirer's *The Rise and Fall of the Third Reich* in the United States and West Germany, 1960–1962," *Journal of Contemporary History* 29, no. 1 (January 1994): 95–128.

76. *Judgment at Nuremberg*, dir. Stanley Kramer (United Artists, 1961).

77. Rolf Hochhuth, *The Deputy*, trans. Richard and Clara Winston (New York: Grove Press, 1964; originally published as *Der Stellvertreter* [Reinbek bei Hamburg: Rowoholt Verlag GmbH, 1963]; Robert C. Doty, " 'The Deputy' Is Here: Rolf Hochhuth's Controversial Play Has Had an Embattled History," *New York Times* (23 February 1964), X1; "'Deputy' Opening Picketed by 150," *New York Times*, 27 February 1964, 26; "Hochhuth's 'Deputy' Debated by Interfaith Panel in Brooklyn," *New York Times*, 18 November 1963, 34; Richard F. Shepard, " 'Deputy' Debate Heats Tempers," *New York Times*, 5 March 1964, 37; "Spellman Attacks 'The Deputy' as 'an Outrageous Desecration,'" *New York Times*, 3 March 1964, 31.

78. Muhlen, "U.S. Image of Germany," 423–24; Philip T. Hartung, "Who Shall Judge?" *Commonweal* 75, no. 12 (15 December 1961): 19; Francis Russell, "Judgment in Nuremberg," *National Review* 12, no. 14 (10 April 1962): 254, 256; Bosley Crowther, "Hollywood's Producer of Controversy," *New York Times Magazine*, 10 December 1961, 76, 79–80, 82, 84–85.

79. Shirer, *Rise and Fall of the Third Reich*, 94. For conservatives' criticism of Shirer's position on Germany, see Felix Morley, "Those Incorrigible Germans," *Modern Age* 5, no. 2 (Spring 1961): 192–93; Muhlen, "U.S. Image of Germany," 420–21.

80. For another, more veiled, criticism of U.S. willingness to ignore German war crimes for Cold War expediency, see Gellhorn, "Is There a New Germany?" 69.

81. Richard F. Shepard, "'Deputy' Author Hopes His Play Will Be 'Factually' Received," *New York Times*, 25 February 1964, 23; Doty, "'The Deputy' Is Here," XI.

82. John Gillett, "Judgment at Nuremberg," *Sight and Sound* 31, no. 1 (Winter 1961/1962): 41. For similar comments, see Bosley Crowther, review of *Judgment at Nuremberg*, *New York Times*, 20 December 1961, 36; "Tube," *Variety*, 18 October 1961, cited in *Filmfacts* 4, no. 47 (22 December 1961): 301.

83. See also, for example, the coverage of the Eichmann trial in Gellhorn, "Eichmann and the Private Conscience" and "Our Moral Duty," *New Republic* 146, no. 1 (1 January 1962), 5.

84. Hannah Arendt, *Eichmann in Jerusalem: A Report on the Banality of Evil* (New York: Penguin Books, 1994; originally published by Viking Press, 1963), 276

85. Arendt, *Eichmann* in Jerusalem, 125–26.

86. Elisabeth Young-Bruehl, *Hannah Arendt: For Love of the World* (New Haven, Conn.: Yale University Press, 1982), 348.

87. *Intermountain Jewish News*, 19 April 1963, 4, cited in "'Eichmann in Jerusalem'—Can One Know the 'Whole' Truth?" *Newsweek* 61, no. 24 (17 June 1963): 94–95; Young-Bruehl, *Hannah Arendt*, 348; Lipstadt, "America and the Memory of the Holocaust," 206; and Novick, *Holocaust in American Life*, 134, n.37.

88. See, for examples of reviews and articles, "'Eichmann in Jerusalem'—Can One Know the 'Whole' Truth?"; Frederic S. Burin, review of *Eichmann in Jerusalem*, *Political Science Quarterly* 79, no. 1 (March 1964): 122–25; and Michael A. Musmanno, "Man with an Unspotted Conscience," *New York Times Book Review*, 19 May 1963, 1, 4. For running opinion pieces and letters to the editor, see "Letters to the Editor: 'Eichmann in Jerusalem,'" *New York Times Book Review*, 23 June 1963, 4–5, 22; and *New York Times Book Review*, 14 July 1963, 28–30; "Letters from Readers: Arendt on Eichmann," *Commentary* 37, no. 2 (Feburary 1964): 6–14; and "Letters from Readers: Of Banality and Romanticism," *Commentary* 37, no. 5 (May 1964): 16–18.

89. Robert Hayden to the Editor, *New York Times Book Review*, 23 June 1963, 5. For similar comments, see Rosalie L. Colie to the Editor, *New York Times Book Review*, 23 June 1963, 5; Irving J. Weiss to the Editor, *New York Times Book Review*, 14 July 1963, 29–30; Stephen Spender, "Death in Jerusalem," *New York Review of Books* 1, no. 2 (Spring-Summer 1963): 8.

90. See, for example, Rachelle Marshall to the Editor, *Commentary* 37, no. 2 (February 1964): 12; Werner M. Feig to the Editor, *Commentary* 37, no. 2 (February 1964): 8; Spender, "Death in Jerusalem," 10; Lore Segal, "Memories of a Brownshirt Girlhood," *New Republic* 153 (21 August 1965): 26–28.

91. Arendt, *Eichmann in Jerusalem*, 273. Margot Henriksen highlights Arendt's concern with nuclear weaponry in *Dr. Strangelove's America*, 280.

92. P. Richman to the Editor, *New York Times Book Review*, 23 July 1963, 29. See also, for example, John Gross, "Arendt on Eichmann," *Encounter* 21, no. 5 (November 1963): 65–67.

93. Raul Hilberg, *The Destruction of the European Jews* (Chicago: Quadrangle Books, 1961). See, for praise, Gerhard L. Weinberg, review of Hilberg, *Destruction of the European Jews*, *American Historical Review* 67, no. 3 (April 1962): 694–95; Jack Raymond, "Yesterday and Today," *New York Times Book Review*, 19 November 1961, 22.

94. Bruno Bettelheim, *The Informed Heart: Autonomy in a Mass Age* (Glencoe, Il: Free Press, 1960); Bettelheim, "Individual and Mass Behavior in Extreme Situations," *Journal of Abnormal and Social Psychology* 38 (October 1943): 417–52. For the influence of Bettelheim's initial article, see Richard Pollak, *The Creation of Dr. B.: A Biography of Bruno Bettelheim* (New York: Simon and Schuster, 1997), 362–63; 124–25.

95. Bettelheim, "Individual and Mass Behavior," 452. See also Bettelheim, *Informed Heart*, 177–78, 191–92, 194, 198–200, 209–12, 230, 234–35.

96. Recent scholars have briefly addressed political and intellectual uses of the Holocaust in the late 1950s and early 1960s. Michael Staub, for example, describes liberal uses of Nazi camps to support the civil rights movement; see Staub, "'Negroes Are Not Jews,'" 6–9; and Staub, *Torn at the Roots,* 45–111. Lawrence Baron notes that literature on Nazi destruction sparked Americans' interest in the psychology of dehumanization and in civil rights. See Baron, "Holocaust and American Public Memory," 69–71. And Alan Mintz suggests the existence of, but does not explore, an earlier phase of Holocaust consciousness shaped by social and political commitment. See Mintz, *Popular Culture,* 208.

Chapter 1. "One of the Lucky Ones": Stanley Elkins and the Concentration Camp Analogy in *Slavery* (pp. 24–57)

1. For some discussions of tensions between blacks and Jews over the Holocaust and slavery, see Wendy Zierler, "'My Holocaust Is Not Your Holocaust': 'Facing' Black and Jewish Experience in *The Pawnbroker, Higher Ground* and the *Nature of Blood*," *Holocaust and Genocide Studies* 18, no. 1 (Spring 2004): 46–67; Emily Miller Budick, *Blacks and Jews in Literary Conversation* (New

York: Cambridge University Press, 1998), 161–217; Jeffrey Melnick, *A Right to Sing the Blues: African Americans, Jews, and American Popular Song* (Cambridge, Mass.: Harvard University Press, 1999), 200–206; Paul Gilroy, *Black Atlantic* (Cambridge, Mass.: Harvard University Press, 1993); Lawrence Mordekhai Thomas, *Vessels of Evil: American Slavery and the Holocaust* (Philadelphia: Temple University Press, 1993); Jack Salzman, Adina Back and Gretchen Sullivan Sorin, eds., *Bridges and Boundaries: African Americans and American Jews* (New York: George Braziller in association with The Jewish Museum, 1992); and Ethan Goffman, *Imagining Each Other: Blacks and Jews in Contemporary American Literature* (Albany: State University of New York Press, 2000). Anna Deveare Smith's performance, *Fires in the Mirror*, offers an excellent dramatic representation of these tensions. See Smith, *Fires in the Mirror: Crown Heights, Brooklyn, and Other Identities* (New York: Anchor Books/Doubleday, 1993).

2. For recent discussions of the Elkins controversy in American historiography, see August Meier and Elliott Rudwick, *Black History and the Historical Profession, 1915–1980* (Urbana: University of Illinois Press, 1986), 247–60; Peter Novick, *That Noble Dream: Objectivity and the American Historical Profession* (New York: Cambridge University Press, 1988), 352–53; 480–91; Daryl Michael Scott, *Contempt and Pity: Social Policy and the Image of the Damaged Black Psyche, 1880–1996* (Chapel Hill: University of North Carolina Press, 1997), 113–18; Peter Ling, "The Incomparable Elkins," *Rethinking History* 1 (Spring 1997): 67–74; and Richard H. King, "Domination and Fabrication: Re-thinking Stanley Elkins's Slavery," *Slavery and Abolition* 22, no. 2 (August 2001): 1–28. Not all historians have rejected Elkins: King has called for a re-evaluation of Elkins's work, Bertram Wyatt Brown has urged that historians retain some of Elkins's concepts, and Nell Painter has called it a "pity" that Elkins's comparison between slaves and camp victims was tainted by his use of the concept "Sambo." See King, "Domination and Fabrication"; Brown, "The Mask of Obedience: Male Psychology in the Old South," *American Historical Review* 93, no. 5 (December 1988): 1228–52; Painter, "The Shoah and Southern History," talk given at Princeton University Center for Arts and Cultural Policy Studies, 11 October 2002.

3. Most texts on the 1960s do not mention Elkins. See, for example, Maurice Isserman and Michael Kazin, *America Divided: The Civil War of the 1960s*, 2nd ed. (New York: Oxford University Press, 2004); James Farrell, *The Spirit of the Sixties: The Making of Postwar Radicalism* (New York: Routledge, 1997); Terry Anderson, *The Movement and the Sixties* (New York: Oxford University Press, 1995); David Farber, *The Age of Great Dreams: America in the 1960s* (New York: Hill and Wang, 1994); Todd Gitlin, *The Sixties: Years of Hope, Days of Rage* (New York: Bantam Books, 1987). Texts on African American culture in the 1960s have addressed Elkins, though they have not generally focused on the positive reception of *Slavery* in the early 1960s.

See, for example, William L. Van Deburg, *New Day in Babylon: The Black Power Movement and American Culture, 1965–1975* (Chicago: University of Chicago Press, 1992); Albert Stone, *The Return of Nat Turner: History, Literature, and Cultural Politics in Sixties America* (Athens: University of Georgia Press, 1992).

4. For brief mentions of Jews in concentration camps, see Stanley Elkins, *Slavery: A Problem in American Institutional and Intellectual Life*, 3rd ed. (Chicago: University of Chicago Press, 1976), 105, 113, 114.

5. The book also contained a fourth, historiographical essay surveying the literature of the field.

6. Elkins, *Slavery*, 82.

7. Elkins made clear that he was aware of the stereotype's power to offend: in a footnote, he described a 1951 controversy at Queens College over Samuel Eliot Morison's use of the name "Sambo." See Elkins, *Slavery*, 82–83.

8. Elkins, *Slavery*, 23, 104.

9. Elkins, *Slavery*, 98.

10. Elkins, *Slavery*, 98. Although he used Herskovits's research extensively, Elkins made clear that he absolutely rejected the anthropologist's argument for the survivals of African culture in African American culture. See Elkins, *Slavery*, 93–94, n.16.

11. Elkins, *Slavery*, 109–12. Elkins's descriptions were heavily influenced by Bruno Bettelheim. See Bettelheim, "Individual and Mass Behavior in Extreme Situations," *Journal of Abnormal and Social Psychology* 38 (October 1943): 417–52.

12. Elie Cohen, *Human Behavior in the Concentration Camp* (New York: Norton, 1953), 177. Italics in original. Quoted in Elkins, *Slavery*, 112.

13. Elkins, *Slavery*, 113.

14. Elkins, *Slavery*, 114–15.

15. This Freudian framework was not unusual. Many of the influential works that Elkins relied on used Freud to explain the altered behavior of Nazi camp inmates. See, for example, Bettelheim, "Individual and Mass Behavior in Extreme Situations"; Cohen, *Human Behavior;* and Hilde O. Bluhm, "How Did They Survive?" *American Journal of Psychotherapy* 2 (1948): 3–32.

16. Elkins, *Slavery*, 105, 90.

17. Elkins, *Slavery*, 105.

18. Elkins, *Slavery*, 97–98; see also 93–96.

19. Elkins, *Slavery*, 130.

20. Olga Lengyel, *Five Chimneys: The Story of Auschwitz* (Chicago: Ziff-Davis, 1947); Ella Lingens-Reiner, *Prisoners of Fear* (London: Victor Gollancz, 1948). See Elkins, *Slavery*, 106, n. 42. It is worth noting that Elkins also used the works of other men on concentration camps, such as Elie Cohen, David Rousset, and Eugen Kogon. Those men mostly offered portraits of male dehumanization similar to that of Bettelheim; when they did not, Elkins did not address

their differences. See for example, Cohen, *Human Behavior*; David Rousset, *The Other Kingdom* (New York: Reynal and Hitchcock, 1947); and Eugen Kogon, *The Theory and Practice of Hell* (New York: Farrar, Straus, 1946).

21. Elkins, *Slavery*, 110; for inability to imagine providing for families, see 108, n. 47; for loss of status in work or profession, see 108, n. 48; for sexual impotence, see 107, 111.

22. Elkins, *Slavery*, 115.

23. Meier and Rudwick note that "some historians have theorized that his *Slavery* (1959) was really a way of addressing the problem posed by the limited Jewish resistance to Nazi tyranny." See Meier and Rudwick, *Black History*, 141. Daryl Michael Scott also suggests that Elkins's concentration camp analogy may have been the result of his Jewish background. See Scott, *Contempt and Pity*, 114.

24. Scott, *Contempt and Pity*, 114.

25. Meier and Rudwick, *Black History*, 141.

26. John A. Garraty, *Interpreting American History: Conversations with Historians, Part I* (New York: Macmillan, 1970), 1–198.

27. Stanley M. Elkins, interview by author, tape recording, Northhampton, Mass., 21 November 1997. I conducted two interviews with Stanley Elkins. At the time of the first interview, I did not intend to ask the historian many questions about being Jewish, and Jewishness was not the subject of my study. The historian himself returned consistently to stories about his own Jewish past as I asked questions about the intellectual background of *Slavery*. After reflecting on this interview, I changed the direction of my study and conducted a second interview with Elkins that focused on his Jewish background.

28. For discussions of Jewish neighborhoods, see Gerald H. Gamm, "In Search of Suburbs: Boston's Jewish Districts," in *The Jews of Boston: Essays on the Occasion of the Centenary (1895–1995) of the Combined Greater Jewish Philanthropies of Greater Boston* (Boston: Combined Greater Jewish Philanthropies of Greater Boston, 1995), esp. 148–50; Hillel Levine and Lawrence Harmon, *The Death of an American Jewish Community: A Tragedy of Good Intentions* (New York: Free Press, 1992), 12–13, 51.

29. Stanley M. Elkins, telephone interview by author, tape recording, 2 February 1998.

30. Elkins, telephone interview by author, 2 February 1998. Elkins's negative appraisal of his Jewish education and participation in Jewish ritual may have been shaped by the fact that his son became an Orthodox rabbi.

31. Elkins, telephone interview by author, 2 February 1998.

32. Elkins, telephone interview by author, 2 February 1998.

33. Elkins, telephone interview by author, 2 February 1998.

34. Elkins, telephone interview by author, 2 February 1998.

35. John F. Stack, Jr., *International Conflict in an American City: Boston's Irish, Italians, and Jews, 1935–1944* (Westport, Conn.: Greenwood Press, 1979), 54–57, 91.

36. See Stephen H. Norwood, "Marauding Youth and the Christian Front: Anti-semitic Violence in Boston and New York During World War II," *American Jewish History* 91, no. 2 (June 2003): 233–67; Stack, *International Conflict*, 54–57, 92–94; Levine and Harmon, *Death of an American Jewish Community*, 22–23; Nat Hentoff, *Boston Boy* (New York: Alfred A. Knopf, 1986), 16–17, 21.
37. Elkins, telephone interview by author, 2 February 1998.
38. Elkins, telephone interview by author, 2 February 1998.
39. Stanley M. Elkins, interview by author, tape recording, Northhampton, Mass., 21 November 1997.
40. Elkins, telephone interview by author, 2 February 1998.
41. Warren Rosenberg, *Legacy of Rage: Jewish Masculinity, Violence and Culture* (Amherst: University of Massachusetts Press, 2001), offers a good synopsis of this historical trajectory. See, for more details, Paul Breines, *Tough Jews: Political Fantasies and the Moral Dilemma of American Jewry* (New York: Basic Books, 1990); Sander Gilman, *The Jew's Body* (New York: Routledge, 1991); and Daniel Boyarin, *Unheroic Conduct: The Rise of Heterosexuality and the Invention of the Jewish Man* (Berkeley: University of California Press, 1997). David Biale convincingly suggests that Jews did bear arms, despite legal prohibitions. See Biale, *Power and Powerlessness in Jewish History* (New York: Schocken Books, 1986), 72–77.
42. See, for more detail on this construction, Boyarin, *Unheroic Conduct*; Barbara Breitman, "Lifting Up the Shadow of Antisemitism: Jewish Masculinity in a New Light," in *A Mensch among Men: Explorations in Jewish Masculinity*, ed. Harry Brod (Freedom, Calif.: Crossing Press, 1988), 105–7.
43. See, for example, Gail Bederman, *Manliness and Civilization: A Cultural History of Gender and Race in the United States, 1880–1917* (Chicago: University of Chicago Press, 1995).
44. See, for example, Breines, *Tough Jews*, 102–67; Rosenberg, *Legacy of Rage*, 21–24; David Biale, "Zionism as an Erotic Revolution," in *People of the Body: Jews and Judaism from an Embodied Perspective*, ed. Howard Eilberg-Schwartz (New York: State University of New York Press, 1992), 283–307.
45. Elkins, telephone interview by author, 2 February 1998.
46. Elkins, telephone interview by author, 2 February 1998.
47. Deborah Dash Moore has offered a similar portrait of American Jewish soldiers fighting back against Nazism in World War II in *GI Jews: How World War II Changed a Generation* (Cambridge, Mass.: Harvard University Press, Belknap Press, 2004).
48. See, for example, Carl Degler, *In Search of Human Nature: The Decline and Revival of Darwinism in American Social Thought* (New York: Oxford University Press, 1991), 206, 215–16.
49. Oscar Handlin, *The Uprooted* (New York: Grosset and Dunlap, 1951). For the significance of Elkins's class with Handlin, see Elkins, telephone interview by author, 2 February 1998.

50. For Elkins's work with Merton, see Elkins, interview by author, 21 November 1997. For discussion of Merton's structural perspective, his support for functionalism, and the "tough-minded" postwar mind-set of sociologists who emphasized social structure over individual action, see Anthony Giddens, "R. K. Merton on Structural Analysis," in *Robert K. Merton: Consensus and Controversy*, ed. Jon Clark, Celia Modgil and Sohan Modgil (London: Falmer Press, 1990), 97–110.

51. Stanley M. Elkins, interview by author, 21 November 1997.

52. Stanley M. Elkins, interview by author, 21 November 1997.

53. Stanley M. Elkins, interview by author, 21 November 1997.

54. For other interviews in which Elkins emphasized the significance of his time in the army for the argument in *Slavery*, see Michael Rogin, *Blackface, White Noise: Jewish Immigrants in the Hollywood Melting Pot* (Berkeley: University of California Press, 1996) 248; and Meier and Rudwick, *Black History*, 140. See also Elkins, "Slavery and Ideology," in *Slavery*, 3rd ed., 250. Originally published in *The Debate Over* Slavery, ed. Ann J. Lane (Urbana: University of Illinois Press, 1971). In this essay, Elkins offers a fundamentally different portrait of the army, noting that his experience in the army "may have 'made men of us' [but] in other more pervasive respects it turned us into boys." When asked about this contradiction, Elkins had trouble reconciling the two positions, but suggested that the army had made them "men but not independent men." See Elkins, interview by author, 21 November 1997.

55. Elkins, interview by author, 21 November 1997.

56. See, for example, Leonard Dinnerstein, *Antisemitism in America* (New York: Oxford University Press, 1994), 150–74; Edward S. Shapiro, *A Time for Healing: American Jewry since World War II* (Baltimore: Johns Hopkins University Press, 1992), 28–59.

57. Elkins, telephone interview by author, 2 February 1998.

58. For McKitrick as an elite Gentile, see "Memorial Resolution: Eric L. McKitrick (1919–2002)," *Anglican and Episcopal History* 71, no. 4 (2002):, 470–72; and Elkins, telephone interview by author, 2 February 1998.

59. Elkins, telephone interview by author, 2 February 1998. See, for virtually identical sentiments, Elkins, interview by author, 21 November 1997.

60. Paul Breines criticizes Zionism as a form of "Jewish toughness" that uses images of "Jewish gentleness" to maintain its emotional resonance and moral legitimacy. Stanley Elkins's attraction to Israel did not reflect this "Jewish toughness," I do not think, so much as it reflected his identity as an American Jewish intellectual who sought to attack racist ideology and to integrate into American life. My argument is still somewhat consistent with that of Breines, who argues that images of Jews in the American military were not those of "tough Jews" but instead Jews assimilating into American culture. See Breines, *Tough Jews*, 120–21.

61. Elkins, telephone interview by author, 2 February 1998.

62. Elkins, telephone interview by author, 21 November 1997.

63. King, "Domination and Fabrication," 20, n.5. August Meier and Elliott Rudwick state that Elkins's interest in slavery came first, and his awareness of the concentration camp parallel later. See Meier and Rudwick, *Black History*, 141. But in his interviews with both King and myself, Elkins stated that he had read the Bettelheim article before he became interested in slavery.

64. Elkins, telephone interview by author, 2 February 1998.

65. When I followed up this statement by asking him whether he was conscious of the contrast between his power as a soldier and the lack of power of Nazi victims before or after he wrote the book *Slavery*, Elkins first said it was before. He then said, "You know, I'm not sure. There's a tendency to read back." Elkins, telephone interview by author, 2 February 1998.

66. Elkins, interview by author, 21 November 1997.

67. Elkins, telephone interview by author, 2 February 1998.

68. Elkins, interview by author, 21 November 1997.

69. Elkins, *Slavery*, 82–83, n.1; 158.

70. See Scott, *Contempt and Pity*, 93–118.

71. Scott, *Contempt and Pity*, 74–75, 82–83.

72. See, for an example of this elitist liberalism, Arthur Schlesinger, *The Vital Center: The Politics of Freedom* (Boston: Houghton Mifflin, 1949).

73. Scott, *Contempt and Pity*, 116; Meier and Rudwick, *Black History*, 140–41.

74. David Hollinger, "The Defense of Democracy and Robert K. Merton's Formulation of the Scientific Ethos," in *Science, Jews, and Secular Culture: Studies in Mid-Twentieth-Century American Intellectual History* (Princeton, N.J.: Princeton University Press, 1996), 84–85. Originally published in *Knowledge and Society* 4 (1983): 1–15.

75. Ulrich B. Phillips, *American Negro Slavery: A Survey of the Supply, Employment, and Control of Negro Labor as Determined by the Plantation Regime* (Baton Rouge: Louisiana State University Press, 1966; originally published by D. Appelton and Company, 1918). Elkins noted that, by 1929, Phillips had stopped arguing that black inferiority was a result of biological traits and argued instead that it was the result of a "primitive culture." See Elkins, *Slavery*, 17.

76. Elkins, *Slavery*, 21.

77. Occasionally, southern conservatives compared federal troops to Nazi soldiers. See, for example, William D. Workman, "New Orleans Tragedy and Pathos Are Part of Vicious NAACP Plan,"*Augusta Chronicle and Augusta Herald*, 26 December 1960, in Michigan State University Special Collections, Vertical File, "Citizens' Council, Radicalism." More typically, southerners linked U.S. troops enforcing desegregation with generic totalitarian military forces or with more specific Soviet or Chinese Communist troops. See, for example, William J. Simmons, *The Mid-West Hears the South's Story*, pamphlet (Greenwood, Miss.: Educational Fund of the Citizens' Councils, 3 February

1958), 14–16, in Vertical File, "Citizens' Council, Radicalism"; Senator Harry Byrd, speech, cited in Numan V. Bartley, *The Rise of Massive Resistance: Race and Politics in the South in the 1950s* (Baton Rouge: Louisiana State University Press, 1969), 109.

78. Stanley Elkins, "The Two Arguments on Slavery," in *Slavery*, 3rd ed., 267–69. Originally published as "The Slavery Debate,"*Commentary* 60, no. 6 (December 1975): 40–54.

79. Elkins, interview by author, 21 November 1997.

80. Elkins, interview by author, 21 November 1997. Daryl Michael Scott reports that, in his interview with the historian, Elkins had misgivings about Moynihan's political use of *Slavery*. Elkins also expressed those misgivings to me, saying that his book had not been intended to explain the contemporary situation of African Americans, but Elkins also reiterated his support for Moynihan's goals and his belief that Moynihan was "grossly mistreated." Elkins's 1975 *Commentary* essay seems to suggest that Elkins did indeed support Moynihan's programs: "Moynihan's conception had much to be said for it," he wrote, noting that even Moynihan's critics would have supported the policies that Moynihan proposed.

81. See Meier and Rudwick, *Black History*, 250, for sales data. Stanley Elkins remembered that it sold 1,600 copies during the first four years. See Elkins, interview by author, 21 November 1997. Meier and Rudwick interpret the initial reception of *Slavery* by historians as "almost entirely negative." I believe, however, that they did not plumb deeply enough the variety of responses, even from within the same reviews. See Meier and Rudwick, *Black History*, 141.

82. See, for primarily positive reviews of Elkins, Sidney Mintz, review of Stanley Elkins's *Slavery*, *American Anthropologist* 63 (June 1961): 579–87; John William Ward, "New Ways to Ask New Questions," *American Scholar* 30, no. 3 (Summer 1961): 440–44; John Hope Franklin, "Slavery and Personality: A Fresh Look," *Massachusetts Review* 2 (Autumn 1960): 181–83. See, for more negative evaluations, David Donald, review of Stanley Elkins's *Slavery*, *American Historical Review* 65 (July 1960): 921–22; Oscar Handlin, review of Stanley Elkins's *Slavery*, *New England Quarterly* 34, no. 2 (June 1961): 253–55; and Abraham Barnett, review of Stanley Elkins's *Slavery*, *Library Journal* 84 (15 November 1959): 3581.

83. See Donald, review of *Slavery*, 921; and Robert F. Durden, review of Stanley Elkins's *Slavery*, *South Atlantic Quarterly* 60, no. 1 (Winter 1961): 95.

84. Donald, review of *Slavery*, 922.

85. Barnett, review of *Slavery*, 3581. Historians Eugene Genovese and Earl Thorpe both noted that concentration camp literature suggested that there might have been exceptions to the infantilization in the camps. See Genovese, "Problems in the Study of Nineteenth-Century American History," *Science and Society* 25, no. 1 (Winter 1961): 45, n.6; and Thorpe, "Chattel Slavery and Concentration Camps," *Negro History Bulletin* (May 1962): 175, n.23.

86. Nathan Glazer, "The Differences Among Slaves," *Commentary* 29, no. 3 (March 1960): 454–48,

87. Morris Fine and Milton Himmelfarb, eds., *American Jewish Year Book,* vols. 60–63 (New York: American Jewish Committee, 1959–1962).

88. "The Question of Sambo: A Report of the Ninth Newberry Library Conference on American Studies," *Newberry Library Bulletin* 5 (December 1958): 23. Elkins presented an early version of his work at the Newberry conference, summarized in this report, and it was here that scholars Daniel Boorstin, Norman A. Graebner, and Stow Persons pointed out the concrete differences between the two systems. Elkins referred to the criticisms of "The Question of Sambo" in one of his appendixes, and several reviewers pointed to those criticisms briefly but did not draw on them. Oscar Handlin also pointed out concrete differences between the two experiences, but he emphasized the different cultural experiences of twentieth-century Europeans and seventeenth-century Africans before their incarceration. See Handlin, review of *Slavery,* 253–55. The attendees of the Newbury conference, as well as Handlin, made the analysis of the differences between slavery and concentration camps only a part of their arguments. Historian Earl Thorpe wrote the only extensive analytic attack on Elkins's analogy during these early years. See Thorpe, "Chattel Slavery and Concentration Camps," 171–76.

89. Elkins, interview by author, 21 November 1997.

90. See, for example, George Shepperson, review of Stanley Elkins's *Slavery* and Orville Taylor's *Negro Slavery in Arkansas, History* 45 (1960): 297–98; Durden, review of Elkins's *Slavery,* 94; Robert F. Gordon, "Slavery and the Comparative Study of Social Structure," *American Journal of Sociology* 66 (September 1960): 184–85.

91. Ward, "New Ways," 443–44.

92. For "extended metaphor," see Elkins, *Slavery,* 305.

93. See, for one overt expression of this assumption, "The Peculiar Institution,"*Times Literary Supplement,* 25 March 1960, 190; for a more muted expression of southern offense at Elkins's analogy, see Avery Cravens's comments in "The Question of Sambo," 25–26. Other than Earl Thorpe's review in the *Negro History Bulletin,* no initial review stated that African Americans might be offended by Elkins's comparison (although several suggested that the use of "Sambo" would be offensive to African Americans).

94. Stanley Crouch, "Aunt Medea," in *Notes of a Hanging Judge: Essays and Reviews, 1979–1989* (Oxford: Oxford University Press, 1990), cited in Budick, *Blacks and Jews,* 165.

95. For "ingenious," see Handlin, review of *Slavery,* 255; for "original," see Shepperson, review of *Slavery* and *Negro Slavery in Arkansas,* 297; Franklin, "Slavery and Personality," 183.

96. For "provocative," and "daring," see Mintz, review of *Slavery,* 586: Gordon, "*Slavery* and the Comparative Study," 184.

97. See Meier and Rudwick, *Black History,* 250, for sales data and academic interest. Michael Harrington, review of Stanley Elkins's *Slavery, Village Voice,* 21 November 1963, 7, 16; William Styron, "New Editions," *New York Review of Books* 1, no. 1 (25 February 1963): 43; and Styron, "Overcome," *New York Review of Books* 1, no. 3 (26 September 1963): 18–19. In a piece devoted to the best books of 1963 in *Book Week,* Norman Podhoretz listed Elkins's *Slavery* as one of the books he had "enjoyed or found especially worthwhile" that year. See "A Cornucopia of 1963 Favorites," *Book Week* (1 December 1963), 18. *Book Week* was a book review supplement to a number of major American newspapers, including the *Washington Post* and the *New York Herald Tribune;* see *Dictionary Catalog of Research Libraries of the New York Public Library, 1911–1971,* vol. 86, p. 228.

98. Howard Zinn, *The Southern Mystique* (New York: Knopf, 1964), 36, 265; Charles Silberman, *Crisis in Black and White* (New York: Random House, 1964), 74–93. See also Thomas F. Pettigrew, *A Profile of the Negro American* (Princeton, N.J.: D. Van Nostrand, 1964).

99. See Morris Fine and Milton Himmelfarb, eds., *American Jewish Year Book,* vols. 64–66 (New York: American Jewish Committee, 1963–1965); Marion Gans, Miriam Leikind, and Bess Rosenthal, eds., *Index to Jewish Periodicals* 1 (Cleveland, Ohio: College of Jewish Studies Press, 1964); Leikind, ed., *Index to Jewish Periodicals* 2–3 (Cleveland, Ohio: College of Jewish Studies Press, 1965–67).

100. "A View of Ourselves," *Jewish Advocate* (Boston), 14 January 1965, 10.

101. Elkins, interview by author, 21 November 1997; Elkins, telephone interview by author, 2 February 1998.

102. Harrington, review of *Slavery,* 7.

103. Silberman, *Crisis,* 75. The title of the chapter that contains descriptions of the concentration camp analogy is "The Problem of Identification."

104. Styron, "New Editions," 43. See also Styron, "Overcome," 19.

105. Harrington, review of *Slavery,* 7.

106. Stanley Elkins noted this rebelliousness as the source of his book's popularity among young white southern liberals and included Styron within this group. Elkins, interview by author, 21 November 1997.

107. For the appeal of *Slavery* to young black students, see Meier and Rudwick, *Black History,* 250.

108. Glazer's review became the introduction of the Grosset and Dunlap paperback edition of *Slavery* in 1963. For Glazer's introducing *Slavery* to Moynihan, see Elkins, interview by author, 21 November 1997. See also Godfrey Hodgson, *The Gentleman from New York: Daniel Patrick Moynihan, a Biography* (Boston: Houghton Mifflin, 2000), 90. In 1963, Glazer and Moynihan worked together on *Beyond the Melting Pot.* See Nathan Glazer and Daniel Patrick Moynihan, *Beyond the Melting Pot: The Negroes, Puerto Ricans, Jews, Italians, and Irish of New York City* (Cambridge, Mass.: MIT Press, 1963).

109. Elkins, interview by author, 21 November 1997.

110. Daniel Patrick Moynihan, "The Negro Family: The Case for National Action," in *The Moynihan Report and the Politics of Controversy*, ed. Lee Rainwater and William L. Yancey (Cambridge, Mass.: The MIT Press, 1967); originally published by the Office of Policy Planning and Research, United States Department of Labor, March 1965.

111. Moynihan borrowed the word "pathology" from liberal black psychologist Kenneth Clark. See Daniel Patrick Moynihan, *Miles to Go: A Personal History of Social Policy* (Cambridge, Mass.: Harvard University Press, 1996), 178.

112. For his staff's research, see Hodgson, *Gentleman*, 90. Moynihan actually quoted from the works of two men who had popularized Elkins's work, Nathan Glazer and Thomas Pettigrew, but Moynihan explicitly gave Elkins credit for the concentration camp analogy in the text of his report.

113. Pettigrew, *Profile of the Negro American*, 13–14, cited in Moynihan, "Negro Family," 16, in *Moynihan Report*, ed. Rainwater and Yancey, 62.

114. Silberman specifically places his work in this context. See Silberman, *Crisis*, 36–58. Daryl Michael Scott calls this school of theory "the immigrant model." Scott, *Contempt and Pity*, 138–39.

115. Oscar Handlin, *The Newcomers* (Cambridge, Mass.: Harvard University Press, 1959), 119, cited in Silberman, *Crisis*, 39.

116. The term "affirmative action" was first used to describe a policy of racial equal employment established in a 1961 executive order signed by John F. Kennedy. Moynihan did not use the term "affirmative action" to describe the federal programs he advocated, but his emphasis on economic equality for African Americans, rather than simply formal legal equality, made his report, and the 1965 speech he cowrote, significant milestones in the history of affirmative action. See Terry Anderson, *The Pursuit of Fairness: A History of Affirmative Action* (New York: Oxford University Press, 2004), 60, 87–90.

117. Lyndon Johnson, "To Fulfill These Rights," 4 June 1965, in *Moynihan Report*, ed. Rainwater and Yancey, 126. The speech was drafted by Richard N. Goodwin and Daniel P. Moynihan.

118. Moynihan was not alone in his use of black "exceptionalism" to argue for race-based programs to aid African Americans. See Scott, *Contempt and Pity*, 137–59. See also Hamilton Cravens, "American Social Science and the Invention of Affirmative Action, 1920s–1970s," *Prospects* 26 (2001): 361–89.

119. Daryl Michael Scott has commented, in fact, that Elkins's and Frazier's theories did not blend well with each other because Elkins argued that slavery created emasculated black men whereas Frazier portrayed hyperaggressive black men. Scott argues persuasively that Moynihan was "intellectual paperhanging," insisting on using Frazier because the sociologist's black identity gave Moynihan cover from charges of racism. Scott does not address, however, why Moynihan felt compelled to use Elkins. See Scott, *Contempt and Pity*, 154–55.

120. Moynihan, "Negro Family," 16, in *Moynihan Report*, ed. Rainwater and Yancey, 62.

121. For a discussion and examples of this trend, see Michael Staub, *Torn at the Roots: The Crisis of Jewish Liberalism in Postwar America* (New York: Columbia University Press, 2002), 108–9.

122. Rowland Evans and Robert Novak, "Inside Report: The Moynihan Report," syndicated column, Publishers Newspaper Syndicate, 18 August 1965, republished in *Moynihan Report,* ed. Rainwater and Yancey, 376–77. For other suggestions that Jews were being used as a "model minority" to be compared to African Americans, see Laura Carper, "The Negro Family and the Moynihan Report," *Dissent* (March–April 1966), republished in *Moynihan Report,* ed. Rainwater and Yancey, 466–67; Rabbi Jay Kaufman, "'Thou Shalt Surely Rebuke Thy Neighbor,'" in *Black Antisemitism and Jewish Racism* (New York: Richard W. Baron, 1969), 43–76, esp. 68–75.

123. "The American Negro Family," *America* 113 (30 October 1965): 492. See also "Moynihan Report," *New Republic* 153 (11 September 1965): 8; and "The Negro Family: Visceral Reaction," *Newsweek* 66 (6 December 1965): 39.

124. See James Farmer, "The Controversial Moynihan Report," *Amsterdam News* (18 December 1965), reprinted in *Moynihan Report,* ed. Rainwater and Yancey, 409–11; and William Ryan, "Savage Discovery: The Moynihan Report," *Nation* 201 (22 December 1965): 380–84, reprinted in *Moynihan Report,* ed. Rainwater and Yancey, 457–66. Although he does not use it in this article, Ryan is generally credited with developing the phrase "blaming the victim" in his later book, inspired by the Moynihan report. See Ryan, *Blaming the Victim* (New York: Pantheon Books, 1971). For other critics, see Benjamin F. Payton, "New Trends in Civil Rights," *Christianity and Crisis* 25, no. 21 (13 December 1965): 268–71, reprinted in *Moynihan Report,* ed. Rainwater and Yancey, 395–402.

125. William H. Grier and Price M. Cobbs, *Black Rage* (New York: Bantam Books, with arrangement by Basic Books, 1968), 20–21, 31. Other examples of psychiatrists who similarly adapted Elkins's thesis about slavery to their own theories about modern black psychological problems, although they did not use the concentration camp analogy, are James P. Comer, "Individual Development and Black Rebellion: Some Parallels," *Midway: A Magazine of Discovery in the Arts and Sciences* 9, no. 1 (Summer 1968): 33–48; and Alvin F. Poussaint, "A Negro Psychiatrist Explains the Negro Psyche," in *Majority and Minority: The Dynamics of Racial and Ethnic Relations,* ed. Norman Yetman (Boston: Allyn and Bacon, 1971), 348–56. Originally published in *New York Times Magazine,* 20 August 1967, 52–53+.

126. They do say that there is "nothing comparable to this outright abandonment of reality" among modern blacks but state that this unreality must have been common among slaves. Grier and Cobbs, *Black Rage,* 145.

127. Charles A. Pinderhughes, "Questions of Content and Process in the Perception of Slavery," in *Debate Over* Slavery, ed. Lane, 104.

128. The publication page of Grier and Cobbs, *Black Rage*, lists five printings in 1968 and five in 1969, as well as publication by the Negro Book Club, Library of Urban Affairs, and United Features Syndicate.

129. For sales numbers, see Elkins, interview by author, 21 November 1997.

130. Ernest Kaiser, "Negro History: A Bibliographical Survey," *Freedomways* 7, no. 4 (1967): 341. See Yuri Suhl, *They Fought Back: The Story of the Jewish Resistance in Nazi Europe* (New York: Crown Publishers, 1967); Jean-François Steiner, *Treblinka* (New York: Simon and Schuster, 1968); John Hersey, *The Wall* (New York: Alfred A. Knopf, 1950). Other scholars relied on Kaiser's research to make the same point. See, for example, Roy Simon Bryce-Laporte, "Slaves as Inmates, Slaves as Men: A Sociological Discussion of Elkins's Thesis," in *Debate Over* Slavery, ed. Lane, 279.

131. Lucy Dawidowicz, *The War against the Jews, 1933–1945* (New York: Holt, Rinehart, and Winston, 1975), 220, cited in John Blassingame, "Redefining the Slave Community: A Response to the Critics," in *Revisiting Blassingame's* The Slave Community: *The Scholars Respond*, ed. Al-Tony Gilmore (Westport, Conn: Greenwood Press, 1978), 136.

132. John Blassingame, *The Slave Community* (New York: Oxford University Press, 1972), 226.

133. Kaiser, "Negro History," 341.

134. Kenneth Stampp, "Rebels and Sambos: The Search for the Negro's Personality in Slavery," *Journal of Southern History* 37 (August 1971): 377. For similar statements, see also Mina Davis Caulfield, "Slavery and the Origins of Black Culture: Elkins Revisited," in *Americans from Africa: Slavery and Its Aftermath*, ed. Peter I. Rose (New York: Atherton Press, 1970), 176, 182; Mary Agnes Lewis, "Slavery and Personality," in *Debate Over* Slavery, ed. Lane, 79; Eugene Genovese, "Rebelliousness and Docility in the Negro Slave," in *Debate Over* Slavery, ed. Lane, 64–66; George M. Fredrickson and Christopher Lasch, "Resistance to Slavery," *Debate Over* Slavery, ed. Lane, 230–31. Genovese, Fredrickson, and Lasch all pointed out the greater space that slavery permitted to enable African American humanity, but they also built on Elkins's comparison rather than rejecting it completely. Harvey Wish was one of the earliest historians to make this argument: slave culture, Wish argued, "*did* show an impressive zest for life and a level of existence undoubtedly higher than that of the inmates of a twentieth-century concentration camp." See Harvey Wish, ed., *Slavery in the South: First-Hand Accounts of the Ante-Bellum American Southland* (New York: Farrar, Straus, and Giroux, 1964), xix.

135. Louis R. Harlan, *The Negro in American History*, pub. no. 61 (Baltimore: American Historical Association, 1965), 9–10.

136. Robert F. Madgic, Stanley S. Seaberg, Fred H. Stopsky, and Robin W. Winks, *The American Experience: A Study of Themes and Issues in American History* (Menlo Park, Calf.: Addison-Wesley, 1979), cited in Stone, *Return of Nat Turner*, 353–55.

137. Early works on blacks and Jews included *Black Anti-Semitism and Jewish Racism;* Robert Weisbord and Arthur Stein, *Bittersweet Encounter: The Afro-American and the American Jew* (Westport, Conn.: Negro Universities Press, 1970); and *Negro and Jew: An Encounter in America: A Symposium Compiled by Midstream Magazine,* ed. Shlomo Katz (New York: Macmillan, 1967).

138. See Budick, *Blacks and Jews,* 61–88; Rogin, *Blackface, White Noise,* 247–48; 267.

139. Elkins, *Slavery,* 89.

140. Budick notes this statement as offensive. See Budick, *Blacks and Jews,* 78. See also William Issel, "History, Social Science, and Ideology: Elkins and Blassingame on Ante-Bellum American Slavery," *History Teacher* 9, no. 1 (1975), 63.

141. See Harold Cruse, "My Jewish Problem and Theirs," in *Black Anti-Semitism and Jewish Racism,* 161, cited in Budick, *Blacks and Jews,* 231, n.32.

142. Michael Rogin makes this charge of all Jews involved in an alliance with African Americans for civil rights, and he specifically includes Elkins in this category. See Rogin, *Blackface, White Noise,* 17, 262–63. Harold Cruse, again, offers a good example of an African American scholar in the late 1960s who charged Jewish intellectuals, like historians in the Communist Party, with silencing blacks by speaking for them. See Cruse, "My Jewish Problem," 179–83.

143. For Holocaust scholars in the 1970s critical of Elkins's portrait of debased victims, see Terrence Des Pres, *The Survivor: An Anatomy of Life in the Death Camps* (New York: Pocket Books, 1977; originally published New York: Oxford University Press, 1976), 177–90; Gerd Korman, "The Holocaust in American Historical Writing," *Societas* 2 (Summer 1972): 268. Holocaust theologian Richard L. Rubenstein noted Elkins's analogy with approval, though he detailed differences between slavery and the Holocaust. See Rubinstein, *The Cunning of History: The Holocaust and the American Future* (New York: Harper and Row, 1975), 36–47.

144. William Styron, *Sophie's Choice* (New York: Random House, 1979). For evidence that Styron's understanding of both slavery and the Nazi concentration camp system, as well as his belief that significant connections existed between the two institutions, was shaped by the portraits offered in Elkins's *Slavery,* see Styron, "Introduction," in Rubenstein, *Cunning of History* (New York: Harper and Row, 1975; reprint, with new introduction, New York: Harper and Row, 1978), vii–ix; James L. W. West III, *William Styron, a Life* (New York: Random House, 1998), 341–42; Ben Forkner and Gilbert Schricke, "An Interview with William Styron (April 1974)," *Southern Review* 10 (October 1974): 923–34, reprinted in *Conversations with William Styron,* ed. James L. W. West III (Jackson: University Press of Mississippi, 1985), 190–202, see esp. 197–99.

145. For Jewish intellectuals' criticisms of *Sophie's Choice,* see Alvin H. Rosenfeld, "The Holocaust According to William Styron, "*Midstream* 25, no.10 (December 1979): 43–49; and Irving S. Saposnik, "Bellow, Malamud, Roth

... and Styron? Or One Jewish Writer's Response," *Judaism* 31, no. 3 (1982): 322–32. For an influential earlier criticism of Styron's *New York Times* opinion piece on the Holocaust, see Cynthia Ozick, "A Liberal's Auschwitz," in *The Pushcart Prize: Best of the Small Presses,* ed. Bill Hudson (New York: Pushcart Book Press, 1976), 149–53. For a more recent attack on Styron's portrait of the Holocaust in *Sophie's Choice,* see D. G. Myers, "Jews without Memory: *Sophie's Choice* and the Ideology of Liberal Anti-Judaism," *American Literary History* 13, no. 3 (2001): 499–529.

Chapter 2. The "Comfortable Concentration Camp": The Significance of Nazi Imagery in Betty Friedan's *Feminine Mystique* (pp. 58–82)

1. Betty Friedan, *The Feminine Mystique* (New York: Dell, 1964; originally published by W. W. Norton, 1963), 294.
2. Friedan, *Feminine Mystique,* 325.
3. See, for example, Betty Friedan, "The Fraud of Femininity," *McCall's* (March 1963), 81; Friedan, "Is Home Her Concentration Camp?" *San Francisco Examiner,* 24 October 1963, 25; Barbara Haines, "Author Urges Housewives to Develop New Interests," *Columbus Dispatch,* 4 December 1963, in Betty Friedan papers, M-62, Schlesinger Library, Radcliffe Institute, Harvard University, Cambridge, Mass. (hereafter BF-S papers), Series I, Box 1, Folder 90; Dusty Vineberg, "Best-Selling Author Busy Defending Book," *Montreal Star,* 30 December 1963, 8, in BF-S papers, Series I, Box l, Folder 90; and Cyndi Beer, "Brainy Women Should Work, Says Author," *Citizen Journal* (Columbus, Ohio), 4 December 1963, in BF-S papers, Series I, Box 1, Folder 90.
4. See bell hooks, *Feminist Theory: From Margin to Center* (Boston: South End Press, 1984), 2–3.
5. See Daniel Horowitz, *Betty Friedan and the Making of the Feminine Mystique: The American Left, the Cold War, and Modern Feminism* (Amherst: University of Massachusetts Press, 1998), 205. Horowitz does, however, sympathetically note that Friedan's Jewish background may have made the comparison natural. Although I do not wholly agree with his evaluation of Friedan's concentration camp analogy, I am nonetheless deeply indebted to Horowitz's work, which pays serious attention to Friedan's Jewish roots, seeing in them the origins of her left-wing politics.
6. Betty Friedan, *Life So Far* (New York: Simon and Schuster, 2000), 132.
7. Betty Friedan, interview by author, tape recording, Washington, D.C., 15 May 2001.
8. See, for Friedan's experience of domestic violence, Judith Hennessee, *Betty Friedan: Her Life* (New York: Random House, 1999), 64, 74–75, 92–94, 109–113, 119, 121–22; Friedan, *Life So Far,* 87, 145–47, 166, 224–25, 227–28; Horowitz, *Betty Friedan,* 153–55. Hennessee and Horowitz, as

well as Friedan, hesitate in describing her experience as domestic violence, because Friedan used violence against her husband as well.

9. Jennifer Moses, "She's Changed Our Lives," *Present Tense* 15, no. 4 (May/June 1988): 30.

10. Bruno Bettelheim, *The Informed Heart* (New York: Free Press, 1960), 109.

11. Bettelheim, *Informed Heart*, 130.

12. Bettelheim, *Informed Heart*, 131–34; 168–69.

13. Bettelheim, *Informed Heart*, 170, 169–75.

14. Bettelheim, *Informed Heart*, 250–51.

15. Friedan, *Feminine Mystique*, 295–96.

16. Friedan, *Feminine Mystique*, 296.

17. Friedan, *Feminine Mystique*, 297.

18. Friedan, *Feminine Mystique*, 297.

19. Concentration camps imprisoned and tortured people of many different ethnic groups, including political prisoners, Jehovah's Witnesses, and the like. Gas chambers in extermination camps were reserved primarily—though not used exclusively—for the extermination of Jews. See, for example, Konnilyn Feig, *Hitler's Death Camps* (New York: Holmes and Meier, 1979); Francois Furet, ed., *Unanswered Questions: Nazi Germany and the Genocide of the Jews* (New York: Schocken Books, 1989). For the conflation of gas chambers with concentration camps, see Friedan, *Feminine Mystique*, 297, 298; for "exterminated," see Friedan, *Feminine Mystique*, 295–96; for "genocide," see Friedan, *Feminine Mystique*, 351.

20. See Friedan's discussion of Freud's Jewish upbringing and her brief mention of Jews as a restrictive ethnic group that inculcated female passivity, Friedan, *Feminine Mystique*, 100, 283, 340.

21. Moses, "She's Changed Our Lives," 30. For Friedan beginning in the 1970s to address her Jewish background in her work, see Joyce Antler, *The Journey Home: How Jewish Women Shaped Modern America* (New York: Schocken Books, 1997), 259, 267.

22. See, for example, the cases of Marie Syrkin and Hayim Greenberg in Carole S. Kessner, ed., *The "Other" New York Jewish Intellectuals* (New York: New York University Press, 1994).

23. Friedan, interview by author, 15 May 2001.

24. For the sake of convenience and consistency throughout this chapter, I have chosen to use Betty Friedan's married last name, and to spell her first name without the final "e" that initially accompanied her given name. I have maintained this policy throughout the text and the footnotes, varying the policy only when I have cited material that Friedan actually published under the name Bettye Goldstein.

25. See "Jewish Roots: An Interview with Betty Friedan," *Tikkun* 3, no. 1 (January/February 1988): 25; Amy Stone, "Friedan at 55," *Lilith* 1, no. 1 (Fall 1976): 11–12; Horowitz, *Betty Friedan*, 19; Friedan, *Life So Far*, 16, 23–24, 28, 32, 35, 53;

Marcia Cohen, interview with Amy Adams, 13 July 1985, 3–4, in Schlesinger Library, Radcliffe Institute, Harvard University, Marcia Cohen collection, Folder "Betty Friedan." See also Horowitz, *Betty Friedan,* 23; Hennessee, *Betty Friedan,* 6, 13; Friedan, *Life So Far,* 24–25. See Leonard Dinnerstein, *Anti-Semitism in America* (New York: Oxford University Press, 1994), 91–92, for discussion of the upsurge in antisemitism in social clubs in the 1920s.

26. For nose job, see Hennessee, *Betty Friedan,* 10. For description of Miriam's insistence that Betty's sorority rejection was not because she was Jewish, see "Jewish Roots," 25; Friedan, *Life So Far,* 24. See also Betty Friedan, "A Good Woman Driver," n.d., BF-S papers, Series III, Box 13, Folder 463.

27. Harry Goldstein, interview with Marcia Cohen, n.d., in Marcia Cohen collection, Schlesinger Library, Radcliffe Institute, Harvard University, Cambridge, Mass., cited in Hennessee, *Betty Friedan,* 9.

28. See Horowitz, *Betty Friedan,* 38–39; Friedan, *Life So Far,* 36–37.

29. See, for Lewin's efforts to rescue friends and family, and for his Zionism, Alfred J. Marrow, *The Practical Theorist: The Life and Work of Kurt Lewin* (New York: Basic Books, 1969), 103, 139–40.

30. Kurt Lewin, "Bringing Up the Jewish Child," in *Resolving Social Conflicts: Selected Papers on Group Dynamics* (New York: Harper and Brothers, 1948), 182; originally published in *Menorah Journal* 28 (1940); 29–45. See also Lewin, "When Facing Danger," in *Resolving Social Conflicts,* 159–68; originally published in *Jewish Frontier* (September 1939); and Lewin, "Psycho-Sociological Problems of a Minority Group," in *Resolving Social Conflicts,* 145–58; originally published in *Character and Personality* 3 (1935): 175–87.

31. Kurt Lewin, "Self-Hatred among Jews," in *Resolving Social Conflicts,* 193. Originally published in *Contemporary Jewish Record* 4 (1941): 219–32. Lewin actually borrowed the concept of the "marginal man" from the influential sociological work of Robert Park and the Chicago School in the 1930s. See Daryl Michael Scott, *Contempt and Pity: Social Policy and the Image of the Damaged Black Psyche, 1880–1996* (Chapel Hill: University of North Carolina Press, 1997), 22–26.

32. Lewin, "Self-Hatred," 193.

33. Friedan, interview by author, 15 May 2001.

34. Betty Friedan, "B.G.," n.d., BF-S papers, Series II, Carton 6, Folder 276.

35. "Jewish Roots," 26.

36. "Jewish Roots," 26. See also Friedan, *Life So Far,* 53.

37. "Jewish Roots," 26; see Stone, "Friedan at 55," 12, for Friedan's comment on herself as an antisemitic Jew. For more on Friedan's understanding of herself as an antisemitic Jew, see Friedan, *Life So Far,* 39.

38. Betty Friedan, "The Scapegoat," 1 October 1941, BF-S papers, Series II, Carton 6, Folder 271. See also Bettye Goldstein, "The Scapegoat," *Smith College Monthly* (October 1941): 5, 26–30; Betty Friedan, "Notes for a Short Story—Lila," 1941, BF-S papers, Series II, Carton 6, Folder 271.

39. Stone, "Friedan at 55," 12; Friedan, *Life So Far,* 52–53.

40. See, for example, Friedan, "A Good Woman Driver," and Betty Friedan, "The Swimming Pool," n.d., BF-S papers, Series III, Box 13, Folder 463.

41. Friedan, "A Good Woman Driver," 463.

42. Betty Friedan, "Women and Jews: The Quest for Selfhood," *Congress Monthly* 52, no. 2 (February/March 1985): 8; "Jewish Roots," 26.

43. Stone, "Friedan at 55," 12; Friedan, *Life So Far,* 36–37; "Jewish Roots," 26.

44. Friedan, *Life So Far,* 39.

45. Betty Friedan, unpublished rough draft of *Feminine Mystique,* n.d., BF-S papers, Series III, Box 17, Folder 454. See also Friedan, unpublished rough draft of *Feminine Mystique,* n.d., 809–11, BF-S papers, Series III, Box 16, Folder 585.

46. Friedan, *Feminine Mystique,* 292, 288, 297.

47. Lewin, "Self-Hatred," 193.

48. See, for example, Betty Friedan, *The Second Stage* (New York: Summit Books, 1981), 93.

49. For "impotent rage," see Paul Wilkes, "Mother Superior to Women's Lib," *New York Times Magazine,* 29 November 1970, 29. For Friedan's descriptions of Miriam as a domineering mother, see, for example, Friedan, *Second Stage,* 93; and Betty Friedan, *It Changed My Life: Writings on the Women's Movement* (New York: W. W. Norton, 1985), 6–19.

50. Joyce Antler has analyzed the importance of Miriam Goldstein as the model for the domineering mother image in *The Feminine Mystique.* Antler focuses on the image of the "Jewish mother" inherent in Friedan's work, rather than the connections between antisemitic Jews and domineering mothers. See Antler, *Journey Home,* 266.

51. "Jewish Roots," 26.

52. Bettelheim, *Informed Heart,* 263.

53. Betty Friedan, unpublished notes, "Bett 258," n.d., in BF-S papers, Series III, Box 15, Folder 548; Friedan, rough draft of *Feminine Mystique,* n.d., 660, BF-S papers, Series III, Box 15, Folder 589.

54. Friedan, *Feminine Mystique,* 63.

55. See Horowitz, *Betty Friedan.*

56. See Horowitz, *Betty Friedan,* 237–48, for clear discussion of his argument, as well as acknowledgment that Friedan did authentically feel trapped; see also Daniel Horowitz, "Rethinking Betty Friedan and *The Feminine Mystique:* Labor Union Radicalism and Feminism in Cold War America," *American Quarterly* 48, no. 1 (March 1996): 20–21.

57. Betty Friedan, unpublished notes, "Women's Search for Fulfillment," May 1960, BF-S papers, Series III, Box 12, Folder 454.

58. Betty Friedan, rough draft of *Feminine Mystique,* n.d., 1601–4, BF-S papers, Series III, Box 13, Folder 505.

59. Friedan, *Life So Far,* 132–33.

60. Bettelheim, *Informed Heart*, 112.

61. Betty Friedan, "original FM postscript," 775, 778, BF-S papers, Series III, Box 15, Folder 575; Bettelheim, *Informed Heart*, 111.

62. See Betty Friedan, unpublished note, "At end, say—" May 1960, BF-S papers, Series III, Box 12, Folder 454; Bettelheim, *Informed Heart*, 104.

63. Betty Friedan, unpublished note, "Self—," n.d., BF-S papers, Series III, Box 14, Folder 516. For Bettelheim's discussion of personal growth in camps, see *Informed Heart*, 126. For Friedan's discussion of growth during her "moratorium" as a housewife, see Betty Friedan, "original FRIEDAN, FM postscript," 778, BF-S papers, Series III, Box 15, Folder 575, and Friedan, unpublished notes, n.d., 1652–53, BF-S papers, Series III, Box 16, Folder 590.

64. Bettelheim, *Informed Heart*, 269; see also 40–41, 107.

65. Bettelheim, *Informed Heart*, 262.

66. Bettelheim, *Informed Heart*, 267–68; for Bettelheim's extended discussions of Jews whose attachment to possessions led to their extermination, see Bettelheim, *Informed Heart*, 256–59.

67. See David Riesman, Nathan Glazer, and Reuel Denney, *The Lonely Crowd: A Study of the Changing American Character* (New Haven, Conn.: Yale University Press, 1950); and William Whyte, *The Organization Man* (New York: Simon and Schuster, 1956). Paul Goodman offered a similar analysis of men in the modern industrial era but expanded his analysis to include young men and Beats. See Goodman, *Growing Up Absurd* (New York: Vintage Books, 1960).

68. See, for emasculation and inability to fight back, Bettelheim, *Informed Heart*, 198–200; for regression to childishness and passivity, Bettelheim, *Informed Heart*, 131–36, 151–53, 209–12; for loss of position as breadwinners and patriarchs, Bettelheim, *Informed Heart*, 163–65, 194–95, 270.

69. Friedan, *Feminine Mystique*, 275, 280.

70. Friedan, *Feminine Mystique*, 297.

71. Jennifer Kalish does quote Friedan's concentration camp analogy to demonstrate that the feminist participated in this discourse of male autonomy, but she does not analyze the analogy, nor does she emphasize the ways that Friedan critiqued this discourse and used it for her own purposes. See Jennifer Kalish, "Spouse-Devouring Black Widows and Their Neutered Mates: Postwar Suburbanization—A Battle over Domestic Space," *UCLA Historical Journal* 14 (1994): 147–49.

72. For the Cold War use of domesticity to fight the USSR, as well as for images of suburban air-raid shelters, see Elaine Tyler May, *Homeward Bound* (New York: Basic Books, 1988), esp. ix–xi.

73. Friedan, *Feminine Mystique*, 53–54.

74. See, for a description of the impact of McCarthyism and therapy on Friedan, Horowitz, *Betty Friedan*, 145–52, 161–65.

75. See, for Friedan's attraction to existential and humanistic psychological perspectives, especially that of Maslow, Friedan, *Feminine Mystique*, 299–325;

and Horowitz, *Betty Friedan*, 205–9. For the impact of humanistic psychology on participants in other 1960s protest movements, see Ellen Herman, "Being and Doing: Humanistic Psychology and the Spirit of the 1960s," in *Sights on the Sixties*, ed. Barbara L. Tischler (New Brunswick, N.J.: Rutgers University Press, 1992), 87–101; and Herman, *The Romance of American Psychology: Political Culture in the Age of Experts* (Berkeley: University of California Press, 1995), 213–15, 292–303. For the Jewish origins of humanistic psychology, see Andrew R. Heinze, *Jews and the American Soul: Human Nature in the 20th Century* (Princeton, N.J.: Princeton University Press, 2004), 261–90.

76. Several pages of rough drafts of *The Feminine Mystique* did compare the situation of women to that of African Americans in the 1950s. These pages did not address the problems of working-class or poor black women but instead compared the problem of women, who were presumably white and middle-class, to that of blacks, who were presumably male. See Betty Friedan, rough draft of *Feminine Mystique*, n.d., 313–15, BF-S papers, Series III, Box 17, Folder 624; Friedan, rough draft of *Feminine Mystique*, nd, 308–9, BF-S papers, Series III, Box 15, Folder 581. Friedan has written that she eliminated these pages at the suggestion of her editor. See Friedan, *Life So Far*, 135.

77. Friedan, *Feminine Mystique*, 356.

78. Friedan, *Life So Far*, 152–53. In a 1970 interview, Friedan quoted herself slightly differently: "George, you made me feel Jewish for trying to sell that book. Go —— yourself!" See Wilkes, "Mother Superior," 142.

79. Hennessee, *Betty Friedan*, 76–78.

80. Joan Cook, "'Mystique' View Backed by Many, Author Finds," *New York Times*, 12 March 1964, in BF-S papers, Series I, Box l, Folder 91. For local panel discussions, see, for example, letter to Betty Friedan, St. Louis, Missouri, 2 January 1964 in BF-S papers, Series IV, Box 32, Folder 1086; "The Masculine Mystique," *Lamplighter* (November 1963), 3, in BF-S papers, Series III, Box 18, Folder 670. For a list of some of Friedan's television and radio appearances, see "F. Myst," W. W. Norton papers, Rare Books and Manuscripts, Butler Library, Columbia University, Series II, Box 230, Folder "Betty Friedan correspondence 1963."

81. See Barbara Ehrenreich, *The Hearts of Men: American Dreams and the Flight from Commitment* (New York: Anchor Press, 1983), 37–38, for more discussion of this discourse among some "male rebels," such as Phillip Wylie. See also Kalish, "Spouse-Devouring Black Widows," 128–54, for discussion of misogyny and gender battles among 1950s male intellectuals.

82. See, for discussion of American reception of de Beauvoir, Sandra Dijkstra, "Simone de Beauvoir and Betty Friedan: The Politics of Omission," *Feminist Studies* 6, no. 2 (Summer 1980), 290–303; for feminism as epithet, see Cynthia Harrison, *On Account of Sex: The Politics of Women's Issues, 1945–1968* (Berkeley: University of California Press, 1988), ix.

83. Eva Moskowitz, "'It's Good to Blow Your Top': Women's Magazines and a Discourse of Discontent, 1945–1965," *Journal of Women's History* 8, no. 3 (Fall 1996): 66–98.

84. Friedan, *Feminine Mystique*, 21.

85. *Clinical Psychology* (Summer 1963), in BF-S papers, Series III, Box 18, Folder 669; Eleanor T. Smith, review of *Feminine Mystique, Library Journal* 88, no. 1 (1 January 1963): 114; Anne Scott, review of *Feminine Mystique, South Atlantic Quarterly* 62, no. 4 (Autumn 1963): 617; A. C. Higgins, review of *Feminine Mystique, Social Forces* 42, no. 3 (March 1964): 396; Miriam Allen de Ford, "Are Women Human?" *The Humanist* 23, no. 3 (May/June 1963), 101.

86. Review of *Feminine Mystique, Kirkus Reviews,* in BF-S papers, Series III, Box 18, Folder 668.

87. Review of *Feminine Mystique, Times Literary Supplement,* 31 May 1963, 391; Mary Lyons, "The Feminine Rebellion," *Brooklyn Heights Press,* 18 July 1963, in BF-S papers, Series I, Box 1, Folder 90.

88. See, for example, Anne's Reader Exchange: "Hard Sell on a Soft Job?" *Washington Post,* 10 March 1963 in BF-S papers, Series III, Box 18, Folder 668; "Speaking of Books," *St. Louis Jewish Light,* 16 October 1963, in BF-S papers, Series III, Box 18, Folder 670; Adeline McCabe, "Mrs. America: Buried Alive?" *State Tribune* (Cheyenne, Wyo.), 13 October 1963 in BF-S papers, Series III, Box 18, Folder 670; review of Friedan, *Feminine Mystique, Together* (June 1963), in BF-S papers, Series III, Box 18, Folder 668; Virgilia Peterson, review of Friedan, *Feminine Mystique, Book Find News,* no. 307, n.d., in BF-S papers, Series III, Box 18, Folder 668.

89. Cynthia Seton, "Skirting the Issue: The Feminine Mystique," *Journal Record* (Amherst, Mass.), 11 July 1963, in BF-S papers, Series III, Box 18, Folder 668.

90. Nancy Scott, review of *Feminist Mystique, People's World,* 1963, in BF-S papers, Series III, Box 18, Folder 669; Anne Vogel, review of *Feminist Mystique, Peace News,* 25 October 1963 in BF-S papers, Series III, Box 18, Folder 669. See also Sylvia Fleis Fava, review of *Feminine Mystique, American Sociological Review* 26, no. 6 (December 1963): 1053–54; Evelyn Reed, "A Study of the Feminine Mystique," *International Socialist Review* (Winter 1964): 24–27; Jane Marcinowski, review of *Feminine Mystique, Mainstream* 16, no. 6 (June 1963): 55–57.

91. See, for example, Lars I. Granberg, "Wise Men Never Try," *Christianity Today,* 14 February 1964, in BF-S papers, Series III, Box 18, Folder 668; "The Masculine Mystique," *Lamplighter* (November 1963), 3, in BF-S papers, Series III, Box 18, Folder 670; and Julius J. Nodel, "Is the Feminine Mystique a Feminine Mistake?" sermon, Temple Shaare Emeth, St. Louis, Mo., 15 November 1963, 4–6, in BF-S papers, Series III, Box 15, Folder 522.

92. Jean Libman Block, "Who Says U.S. Women Are 'Trapped'?" *This Week,* 6 October 1963, in BF-S papers, Series III, Box 19, Folder 688.

93. Lucy Freeman, review of *Feminine Mystique, New York Times Book Review,* 7 April 1963, 46.

94. See also Kate Aitken, "Canadian Women Not Deluded," *Toronto Globe and Mail*, 2 May 1964, in BF-S papers, Series I, Box 1, Folder 91.

95. Review of *Feminine Mystique, Psychiatric Quarterly Supplement*, pt. 1, [date illegible] in BF-S papers, Series III, Box 18, Folder 668.

96. Patricia Krebs, "More Feminine Image Maneuvers," *Post-Dispatch* (St. Louis, Mo.), 2 June 1963, in BF-S papers, Series III, Box 18, Folder 670. See also Louise Lux, "Housewives Raked Over Coals," *Bulletin* (Philadelphia, Pa.), 21 February 1963, in BF-S papers, Series III, Box 18, Folder 668; and Alden Hoag, "To Herd Women by a New Dogma," *Herald* (Boston, Mass.), 11 March 1963, in BF-S papers, Series III, Box 18, Folder 668.

97. Mary Engel, "Cherchez L'Homme," *Contemporary Psychology* 8, no. 11 (November 1963): 424.

98. Friedan compared women's "sex-directed education" to black segregation. See Friedan, *Feminine Mystique*, 171.

99. See, for example, Nodel, "Is the Feminine Mystique a Feminine Mistake?" and "Speaking of Books," *St. Louis Jewish Light*, 16 October 1963.

100. See Marion Gans, Miriam Leikind, and Bess Rosenthal, eds., *Index to Jewish Periodicals*, June 1963-May 1964, vol. 1 (Cleveland, Ohio: College of Jewish Studies Press, 1964); Morris Fine and Milton Himmelfarb, eds., *American Jewish Yearbook 1964*, vol. 65 (New York: American Jewish Committee, 1964).

101. Nodel, "Is the Feminine Mystique a Feminine Mistake?" 5.

102. Letter to Betty Friedan, Itasca, Ill., 12 May 1963, in BF-S papers, Series III, Box 19, Folder 686.

103. Letter to Betty Friedan, Indianapolis, Ind., 1 June 1963, in BF-S papers, Series III, Box 19, Folder 686. This woman offered few details of her life during the war, making it unclear whether she was in hiding or interned in concentration camps; she made clear only that she was Jewish, that her high school education was interrupted in Europe "thanks to Hitler and the rest," and that she came to the United States in 1951.

104. Letter to Betty Friedan, Larchmont, N.Y., 14 January 1964, in BF-S papers, Series III, Box 19, Folder 689.

105. See, for example, letter to Betty Friedan, n.d., in BF-S papers, Series III, Box 19, Folder 681; letter to Betty Friedan, Portland, Maine, 11 August 1969, in BF-S papers, Series III, Box 19, Folder 703. Some Jewish letter-writers did take exception to Friedan's portrait of Jews as an ethnic group that particularly restricted women. See, for example, letter to Betty Friedan, 30 March 1965, in BF-S papers, Series III, Box 19, Folder 695.

106. See, for example, letter to Betty Friedan, St. Louis, Mo., 2 January 1964, in BF-S papers, Series IV, Box 32, Folder 1086; Mildred Young, "Housekeeper—What Else," *Dallas Times Herald*, 30 October 1963, in BF-S papers, Series I, Box 1, Folder 90; "Author Explodes Feminine Myths," *Dallas Morning News*, 30 October 1963, in BF-S papers, Series I, Box 1, Folder 90; "Women Urged to Find a New Image," *Newsday* (Long Island, N.Y.), 20 November 1963, in BF-S papers,

Series I, Box 1, Folder 90; "Stop Enslaving Selves," *Boston Sunday Globe*, 8 December 1963, in BF-S papers, Series I, Box 1, Folder 90; "Betty Friedan's 'The Feminine Mystique' Offers Enchanting Panacea to Our Women," *Detroit Jewish News*, 7 June 1963, 32, in BF-S papers, Series I, Box 1, Folder 90.

107. Letter to Betty Friedan, Minneapolis, Minn., 5 October 1963, in BF-S papers, Series III, Box 19, Folder 688.

108. Letter to Betty Friedan, 15 August 1963, in BF-S papers, Series III, Box 19, Folder 687; letter to Betty Friedan, Riverton, Wyo., 3 June 1964, in BF-S papers, Series III, Box 19, Folder 683; letter to Betty Friedan, Ridgewood, N.J., 13 March 1963, in BF-S papers, Series III, Box 19, Folder 685.

109. Letter to Betty Friedan, 23 March 1967, in BF-S papers, Series III, Box 19, Folder 701; letter to Betty Friedan, Sioux City, Iowa, 12 March 1964, in BF-S papers, Series III, Box 19, Folder 690.

110. Letter to Betty Friedan, 6 May 196[?] [year unreadable], in BF-S papers, Series III, Box 19, Folder 680; for recommendations about required reading, see letter to Betty Friedan, Winona, Minn., 24 July 1967, in BF-S papers, Series III, Box 19, Folder 701; letter to Betty Friedan, Appleton, Wis., 27 September 1967, in BF-S papers, Series III, Box 19, Folder 701; letter to Betty Friedan, San Jose, Calif., 14 July 1963, in BF-S papers, Series III, Box 19, Folder 687; for lending *Feminine Mystique* to friends, see letter to Betty Friedan, 10 April 1963, in BF-S papers, Series III, Box 19, Folder 685; letter to Betty Friedan, Woodland Hills, Calif., 8 November 1963, in BF-S papers, Series III, Box 19, Folder 698; and letter to Betty Friedan, Durham, N.C., 14 September 1963, in BF-S papers, Series III, Box 19, Folder 688.

111. Letter to Betty Friedan, Brooklyn, N.Y., 2 June 1964, in BF-S papers, Series III, Box 19, Folder 683.

112. Letter to Betty Friedan, Towson, Md., 30 July 1963, in BF-S papers, Series III, Box 19, Folder 687.

113. Letter to Betty Friedan, Los Angeles, Calif., 19 August 1963, in BF-S papers, Series III, Box 19, Folder 687.

114. For other examples of Friedan's letter-writers approving of or adopting the concentration camp analogy, see letter to Betty Friedan, Lynchburg, Va., 5 May 1964, in BF-S papers, Series III, Box 22, Folder 800; letter to Betty Friedan, Los Angeles, Calif., 28 August 1963, in BF-S papers, Series III, Box 19, Folder 695; letter to Betty Friedan, Decatur, Ga., 12 November 1963, in BF-S papers, Series III, Box 19, Folder 681; and letter to Betty Friedan, St. Gall, Switzerland, 22 April 1967, in BF-S papers, Series III, Box 19, Folder 701. For a letter writer impressed by the concentration camp analogy but offering criticism of Friedan's logic, see letter to Betty Friedan, New Haven, Conn., 13 December 1963, in BF-S papers, Series III, Box 19, Folder 681.

115. Letter to *McCall's*, Empire, Ore., 1 April 1963, in BF-S papers, Series III, Box 21, Folder 751; letter to *McCall's*, Dearborn, Mich., 28 March 1963, in BF-S papers, Series III, Box 21, Folder 750.

116. Letter to *McCall's*, Helena, Mont., n.d., in BF-S papers, Series III, Box 21, Folder 752.

117. Letter to *McCall's*, Abington, Pa., 12 March 1963, in BF-S papers, Series III, Box 21, Folder 748.

118. Letter to *McCall's*, 6 March 1963, in BF-S papers, Series III, Box 21, Folder 747.

119. The *Ladies' Home Journal* excerpt does not refer to "comfortable concentration camps." See Betty Friedan, "Have American Housewives Traded Brains for Brooms?" *Ladies' Home Journal* (Winter 1963): 24, 26.

120. Letter to *McCall's*, 5 March 1963, in BF-S papers, Series III, Box 21, Folder 746; letter to *McCall's*, 1 March 1963, in BF-S papers, Series III, Box 21, Folder 745.

121. Letter to *McCall's*, Newark, N.J., n.d., in BF-S papers, Series III, Box 21, Folder 752.

122. Letter to *McCall's*, Los Angeles, Calif., 23 February 1963, in BF-S papers, Series III, Box 21, Folder 742. See, for similar examples, letter to *McCall's*, Yardley, Pa., 6 March 1963, in BF-S papers, Series III, Box 21, Folder 747; letter to *McCall's*, Ann Arbor, Mich., n.d., in BF-S papers, Series III, Box 21, Folder 752; letter to *McCall's*, Dearborn, Mich., 28 March 1963, in BF-S papers, Series III, Box 21, Folder 750; letter to *McCall's*, Rocky Mount, Va., 4 April 1963, in BF-S papers, Series III, Box 21, Folder 751.

123. Betty Friedan, "Women's Lib" speech at Fordham University, April 1970, reprinted in Glenda F. Hodges, "Betty Friedan's Role as Reformer in the Women's Liberation Movement, 1960–1970," (Ph.D. diss., Bowling Green State University, 1980). The text notes "(LAUGHTER)" after Friedan's comment.

124. The collection of newsclippings on Friedan from the late 1960s and early 1970s in the feminist's archives do not mention her concentration camp analogy. See BF-S papers, Series I, Box 1, Folders 93, 94, and 95. For substantial profiles of Friedan from the early 1970s that do not mention the concentration camp analogy, see Wilkes, "Mother Superior," and Lyn Tornabene, "The Liberation of Betty Friedan," *McCall's* (May 1971), 84, 136–40, 142, 146. See, for an exception to this generalization, Denise DeClue, "'It Changed My Life': Friedan Looks Back," *Times-Picayune* (New Orleans), 1976, in BF-S papers, Series I, Box 1, Folder 104.

125. For examples of positive evaluations of *The Feminine Mystique* from a radical perspective, see, for example, "Radical Critique Ground Breaking Attack," in *Feminist Revolution* (Redstockings, 1975), 169; "The Minot Meanies: Feminism in North Dakota," *Ain't I a Woman* 1, no. 12 (19 February 1970): 11; Karen Lindsey, review of *Man's World, Woman's Place, Everywoman* 2, no. 12; "Read," *It Ain't Me Babe* 1, no. 1 (15 January 1970): 7; "The Ladies Home Urinal," *Goodbye to All That*, no. 2 (29 September 1970); Gloria Hull, "History/ My History," in *Changing Subjects: The Making of Feminist Literary Criticism,* ed. Gayle Greene and Coppelia Kahn (New York: Routledge, 1993), 52,

quoted in Wini Breines, "What's Love Got to Do With It?" *Signs* 27, no. 4 (Summer 2002): 1112, n.19.

126. Roxanne Dunbar, "Who Is the Enemy?" *No More Fun and Games*, no. 2 (February 1969): 53; Robin Morgan, "Introduction," in *Sisterhood Is Powerful* (New York: Vintage Books, 1971), xxiv–xxvi; Zillah Eisenstein, *The Radical Future of Liberal Feminism* (Boston: Northeastern University Press, 1986; originally published New York: Longman Press, 1981), 177–200; Sheila Van Hyning, letter to the editor, *Up from Under* 1, no. 1 (May/June 1970): 3; Diane Levine, review of *Feminine Mystique, Tooth and Nail* 1, no. 1 (16 September 1969): 7.

127. See, for example, letter, Glen Ridge, N.J., 4 August 1964; and letter, Folcroft, Pa., 29 May 1964, in BF-S papers, quoted in May, *Homeward Bound*, 193–95.

128. See, for example, hooks, *Feminist Theory*, 2–3; Paula Giddings, *When and Where I Enter: The Impact of Black Women on Race and Sex in America* (New York: Bantam Books, 1984), 299; Some Red Witches, "The Sharks Are Coming with Betty Friedan as Pilot Fish," *It Ain't Me Babe* 1, no. 11 (6 August 1970), 12.

129. Kathie Sarachild, "The Power of History," in *Feminist Revolution*, 20; Brooke, "What's Wrong with Sex Role Theory," in *Feminist Revolution*, 70.

Chapter 3. "An Accident of Geography": Stanley Milgram's Obedience Experiments (pp. 83–123)

1. Stanley Milgram, "Behavioral Study of Obedience," *Journal of Abnormal and Social Psychology* 67, no. 4 (1963): 371.

2. Thomas Blass, *The Man Who Shocked the World: The Life and Legacy of Stanley Milgram* (New York: Basic Books, 2004). Blass's exploration of the obedience experiments' impact is detailed and valuable; as a psychologist rather than a historian, however, Blass does not examine the experiments or their impact in their historical context.

3. Omer Bartov has noted that Stanley Milgram's biases may have shaped his interpretation of his subjects in ways that Holocaust scholars have overlooked. See Bartov, *Germany's War and the Holocaust: Disputed Histories* (Ithaca, N.Y.: Cornell University Press, 2003), 181–91.

4. Peter Novick, *The Holocaust in American Life* (Boston: Houghton Mifflin, 1999), 136–37, 245.

5. For reference to students helping Milgram with experimental procedure, see John W. Hadden to Stanley Milgram, 12 February 1974, Stanley Milgram Papers, Manuscripts and Archives, Yale University Library, New Haven, Conn. (hereafter Milgram papers), Series III, Box 61, Folder 111. For NSF funding, see Milgram, "Behavioral Study," 371.

6. Stanley Milgram, *Obedience to Authority* (New York: Harper and Row Publishers, 1974), 16–19.

7. Milgram, *Obedience to Authority*, 16, 22–23.

8. Milgram, *Obedience to Authority*, 36, 11.

9. Milgram, *Obedience to Authority*, 21.

10. Milgram, "Behavioral Study," 375.

11. Milgram, "Report to Memory Project Subjects," 6, in Milgram papers, Series II, Box 45, Folder 159; Milgram, *Obedience to Authority*, 195.

12. William Shirer, *The Rise and Fall of the Third Reich* (New York: Simon and Schuster, 1960), 92–93, e.g.

13. Stanley Milgram, "Obedience: Experimental Studies," unpublished note, n.d., Milgram papers, Series III, Box 70, Folder 290. See, for Milgram's particular interest in Shirer's work, Philip Meyer, "If Hitler Asked You to Electrocute a Stranger, Would You? Probably," *Esquire* 73, no. 2 (February 1970): 73, in Milgram papers, Series I, Box 21, Folder 339. For other evidence of Milgram's interest in German national character as an origin of Nazism, see Milgram, "German Leaders and German Followers," unpublished note, n.d., Milgram papers, Series III, Box 70, Folder 280; and Milgram, "Spring Cleaning Auf Deutschland," unpublished note, May 1960, Milgram papers, Series I, Box 23, Folder 283. Milgram intended to continue working on German national character later in his career. See Stanley Milgram to Gordon W. Allport, 10 October 1960, Milgram papers, Series II, Box 29, Folder 68.

14. Stanley Milgram, "Obedience: Experimental Studies," unpublished note, n.d., Milgram papers, Series III, Box 70, Folder 290.

15. Stanley Milgram, unpublished note, n.d., Milgram papers, Series III, Box 70, Folder 289.

16. For examples of other unpublished notes that address the Nazi destruction of Jews as a fundamental component of Milgram's thinking in designing and understanding his experiment, see Stanley Milgram, "Obedience: Structural Conditions," n.d., Milgram papers, Series II, Box 46, Folder 164; Milgram, "Binding Factors," n.d., Milgram papers, Series II, Box 46, Folder 168; and Milgram, untitled notes, n.d., Milgram papers, Series II, Box 46, Folder 164. Although they are not dated, these notes, particularly the untitled notes, seem to have been written while he was in the midst of conducting the experiments.

17. Stanley Milgram to Henry Riecken, 21 September 1961, in Milgram papers, Series II, Box 43, Folder 127.

18. "Report to Memory Project Subjects," in Milgram papers, Series II, Box 45, Folder 159.

19. "Content Analysis of Free Responses of Subjects in Questionnaire," n.d., in Milgram papers, Series II, Box 47, Folder 179. See also "Responses to questionnaire by obedience subjects," n.d., in Milgram papers, Series II, Box 44, Category 2, Subject 0230, for example.

20. See Alan C. Elms and Stanley Milgram, "Personality Characteristics Associated with Obedience and Defiance toward Authoritative Command," *Journal of Experimental Research in Personality* 1 (1966): 282–89.

21. Milgram, "Behavioral Study," 371.

22. C.P. Snow, "Either-Or," *Progressive* (February 1961), 24, cited in Milgram, "Behavioral Study," 371.

23. Diana Baumrind, "Some Thoughts on the Ethics of Research: After Reading Milgram's 'Behaviorial Study of Obedience,'" *American Psychologist* 19, no. 6 (June 1964): 423; Stanley Milgram, "Some Conditions of Obedience and Disobedience to Authority," *Human Relations* 18, no. 1 (1965); reprinted in Milgram, *Individual in a Social World* (New York: McGraw-Hill, 1977), 136. In "Technique and First Findings of a Laboratory Study of Obedience to Authority," *Yale Scientific Magazine* (November 1964), 9–11, 14, Milgram did not offer any political or philosophical significance at all.

24. Stanley Milgram, "The Compulsion to Do Evil," *Patterns of Prejudice* 1 (1967): 3–7.

25. Milgram, *Obedience to Authority*, 2.

26. Milgram, *Obedience to Authority*, 27.

27. Milgram, *Obedience to Authority*, 177.

28. Stanley Milgram, "Obedience to Authority: Experiments in Social Psychology," application for research grant, National Science Foundation, 25 January 1962, 2, 14–15, in Milgram papers, Series II, Box 43, Folder 128. For other early reports of correlations between obedience and socioeconomic background, see Milgram, "Cognitive Adjustments in Obedience," February 1962, in Milgram papers, Series II, Box 46, Folder 164.

29. Milgram, "Behavioral Study," 376–77.

30. Stanley Milgram, "Some Conditions of Obedience," 154–58; Elms and Milgram, "Personality Characteristics," 288.

31. See, for example, Meyer, "If Hitler Asked You," 73.

32. Milgram, *Obedience to Authority*, 205.

33. John Laurent has persuasively argued that the changes in Milgram's interpretations were due to changing fashions in psychology, from behaviorism in the early 1960s to sociobiology in the early 1970s. See Laurent, "Milgram's Shocking Experiments: A Case in the Social Construction of 'Science,'" *Indian Journal of the History of Science* 22, no. 3 (1987): 251–54.

34. Milgram, *Obedience to Authority*, 188.

35. See, for example, John Sabini, "Stanley Milgram (1933–1984)," *American Psychologist* 41, no. 12 (December 1986): 1379; Carole Tavris, "A Man of 1,000 Ideas," *Psychology Today* (June 1974), 74–75.

36. Stanley Milgram to Nicholas deKatzenbach, 14 February 1965, Milgram papers, Series I, Box 1a, Folder 14; Stanley Milgram to the Editors, *Harvard Crimson* (25 November 1963), cited in Blass, *Man Who Shocked the World*, 136–37; Stanley Milgram to Leon Mann, 29 October 1964, Milgram papers, Series I, Box 18, Folder 263.

37. "Report to Memory Project Subjects," 6.

38. John H. Garabedian, "Experiments Warn of Blind Obedience," *Yale Daily News*, 31 October 1963, 1. Milgram also seems to have compared his subjects to the flyers who dropped atomic bombs on Hiroshima and Nagasaki. See "Obedience to Authority Is a Habit, Yale Psychological Testing Reveals," *New Haven Register*, 21 May 1963, 1. Both in Milgram papers, Series I, Box 21, Folder 335.

39. See, for example, Irving Howe, "'The New Yorker' and Hannah Arendt," *Commentary* 36 (October 1963): 318–19; Norman Podhoretz, "Hannah Arendt on Eichmann," *Commentary* 36 (September 1963): 201–8; letters, *Commentary* 37 (February 1964): 6–14.

40. See, for example, James Weinstein, "Nach Goldwasser Uns?" *Studies on the Left* 4, no. 3 (Summer 1964): 59–63; Norm Fruchter, "Arendt's Eichmann and Jewish Identity," *Studies on the Left* 5, no. 1 (Winter 1965): 22–42.

41. Stanley Milgram to Norman Podhoretz, 14 August 1963, Milgram papers, Series I, Box 1a, Folder 8.

42. "Three American Heroes," advertisement, *New York Times*, 26 March 1967, E5, in Milgram papers, Series I, Box 2, Folder 29. The clipped advertisement includes a notation from Milgram: "I sent in $10.00."

43. See, for example, Stanley Milgram, "Eichman and Calley," unpublished note, n.d., Milgram papers, Series III, Box 61, Folder 116; Milgram, "The Green Beret Case," unpublished note, October 1969, Milgram papers, Series III, Box 62, Folder 130; Milgram, "The Psychological Analysis of Destructive Obedience," lecture presented at Wright Institute conference titled "The Legitimation of Evil," 21 February 1970, Milgram papers, Series III, Box 71, Folder 320; Milgram, course outline, "Authority and the Individual," 20 February 1974, Milgram papers, Series IV, Box 98, Folder 83.

44. Milgram, *Obedience to Authority*, 180.

45. Maury Silver, "On Being a Social Psychologist: An Interview with Stanley Milgram," unpublished interview, in Milgram papers, Series I, Box 23, Folder 282.

46. Milgram, "Eichman and Calley," 1.

47. Milgram, "Eichman and Calley"; Milgram, "Moreover, this is less a solution . . . ," unpublished note, n.d.; and Milgram, "Since 1963 the country has witnessed . . . ," unpublished note, n.d., both in Milgram papers, Series III, Box 62, Folder 129.

48. Solomon E. Asch, "Group Forces in the Modification and Distortion of Judgments," in *Conformity, Resistance, and Self-Determination*, ed. Richard Flacks (Boston: Little, Brown, 1973), 46–48. Excerpted from Asch, *Social Psychology* (Englewood Cliffs, N.J.: Prentice-Hall, 1952).

49. Stanley Milgram, "Introduction: The Individual and the Group," in *Individual in a Social World*, 195–96; Milgram, unpublished interview fragment, n.d., Milgram papers, Series I, Box 23, Folder 282; and Carole Tavris, "The Frozen World of the Familiar Stranger," *Psychology Today* 8, no. 1 (June 1974): 77.

50. Stanley Milgram, interview with Richard Evans, in Richard Evans, ed. *The Making of Social Psychology: Discussions with Creative Contributors* (New York: Gardner Press, distributed by Halsted Press, 1980), reprinted in Milgram, *Individual in a Social World*, 127.

51. For a good examination of the popularity of existentialism in the 1950s in the United States, see George Cotkin, *Existential America* (Baltimore: Johns Hopkins University Press, 2003). For the popularity of behaviorism after World War II, see, for example, Jeroen Jansz and Peter Van Drunen, eds., *A Social History of Psychology* (Oxford: Blackwell Publishing, 2004), 114–15; Ellen Herman, *The Romance of American Psychology: Political Culture in the Age of Experts* (Berkeley: University of California Press, 1995), 36, 241; Morton Hunt, *The Story of Psychology* (New York: Doubleday, 1993), 262–79; Laurent, "Milgram's Shocking Experiments," 251–52; Albert R. Gilgen, *American Psychology since World War II: A Profile of the Discipline* (Westport, Conn.: Greenwood Press, 1982), 97–110. Thomas Blass importantly notes that Milgram's mentor, Solomon Asch, had influentially tempered Skinner's mechanistic vision of behaviorism with a more complex portrait of human behavior that was observable and measurable, but rationally chosen, rather than passively induced. See Blass, *Man Who Shocked the World*, 27. It is worth noting that behaviorism faced important competition and criticism by the 1960s. See, for example, Ernest R. Hilgard, *Psychology in America: A Historical Survey* (Chicago: Harcourt Brace Jovanovich, 1987), 221–26.

52. Stanley Milgram, "A Methodological Introduction: The New Behaviorism in Social Psychology," unpublished note, n.d., Milgram papers, Series III, Box 70, Folder 290. For further evidence of existential philosophy's influence on Milgram, see Milgram, unpublished note, "Obedience-Analysis, Philosophy," n.d., Milgram papers, Series II, Box 46, Folder 167: "The relevance of existential philosophy to [the obedience] experiment is clear. A man defines his being by what he does. Our focus is on the actions of the subject and far less so on his explanations, rationalizations, excuses."

53. For the significance of his parents' immigrant roots in Milgram's study of national character, see Stanley Milgram, "Social Influence," unpublished note, n.d., Milgram papers, Series III, Box 71, Folder 293. For the state of national character study in the 1950s, see Alex Inkeles and Daniel J. Levinson, "National Character: The Study of Modal Personality and Sociocultural Systems," in *Handbook of Social Psychology*, ed. Gardner Lindzey, Vol. 2 (Cambridge, Mass.: Addison-Wesley, 1954), 977–1020; and David Potter, *People of Plenty* (Chicago: University of Chicago Press, 1954), 36–42.

54. See Gordon Allport, *The Nature of Prejudice* (Reading, Mass.: Addison-Wesley Publishing, 1987; originally published 1954); T. W. Adorno, Else Frenkel-Brunswik, Daniel J. Levinson, and R. Nevitt Sanford, *The Authoritarian Personality* (New York: Harper and Brothers, 1950), 384–89. For Allport's significance as Milgram's mentor, see Blass, *Man Who Shocked the World*, 15–16.

55. See Stanley Milgram, "Analysis and Measurement of National Stereotypes," unpublished graduate paper, Harvard University, 1955, in Milgram papers, Series III, Box 68, Folder 248a; and Stanley Milgram, "National Character," unpublished graduate paper, Harvard University, May 1956, in Milgram papers, Series III, Box 68, Folder 249.

56. Stanley Milgram, "I do not believe that radical situationism . . . ," unpublished note, n.d., in Milgram papers, Series III, Box 70, Folder 289.

57. See, for example, Milgram, "Behavioral Study," 375; Milgram, *Obedience to Authority*, 44–48. At least one psychologist has thrown doubt on Milgram's results by questioning the predictions of these subjects and by developing studies that elicited predictions of much higher levels of obedience by offering different, more specific descriptions of the experiment. See Don Mixon, *Obedience and Civilization: Authorized Crime and the Normality of Evil* (London; Winchester, Mass.: Photo Press, 1989). For a good description of Mixon's studies, see Arthur G. Miller, *The Obedience Experiments: A Case Study of Controversy in Social Science* (New York: Praeger, 1986), 173.

58. See, for example, Robert M. Farr, *The Roots of Modern Social Psychology, 1872–1954* (Oxford: Blackwell Publishers, 1996), 153–54; Herman, *Romance of American Psychology*, 38–40, 57–61; Gilgen, *American Psychology since World War II*, 47–48.

59. Ian Parker, "Obedience," *Granta* 71 (Autumn 2000): 109. Winer's comment came during an interview with Parker; this article contains no footnotes, however.

60. Stanley Milgram, "Conditions of Obedience and Disobedience to Authority," unpublished note, n.d., Milgram papers, Series III, Box 70, Folder 291.

61. Stanley Milgram to Hannalore Lehnoff, 4 November 1963, Milgram papers, Series III, Box 55, Folder 12.

62. Milgram, *Individual in a Social World*, 92–93.

63. Meyer, "If Hitler Asked You," 73. See also Barbara Yuncker, "Where Conscience Ends," *New York Post*, 23 February 1964, 28, in Milgram papers, Series I, Box 21, Folder 335. Yuncker quoted Milgram saying that he had "reasons both intellectual and personal" for conducting his research. She noted that he refused to discuss the personal but gave an illustration of an Oslo medical student whose parents had been killed by the Germans, "one of many whom I met who had suffered terribly from indiscriminate blind obedience."

64. A number of secondary observers of Milgram's work have noted that Milgram's Jewish background played a part in the development of his obedience experiments. See, for example, Miller, *Obedience Experiments*, 16–17; Blass, *Man Who Shocked the World*, 62; and Blass, "The Roots of Stanley Milgram's Obedience Experiments and Their Relevance to the Holocaust," *Analyse and Kritik* 20 (1998): 49.

65. Alexandra Milgram, "My Personal View of Stanley Milgram," in *Obedience to Authority: Current Perspectives on the Milgram Paradigm,* ed. Thomas Blass (Mahwah, N.J.: Lawrence Erlbaum, 2000), 3.

66. For an evocative description of Stanley Milgram's childhood, especially the Bronx neighborhood in which he grew up, see Blass, *Man Who Shocked the World,* 1–13. Briefly, during World War II, the Milgram family moved to Camden, N.J.; in 1949, the family moved to Richmond Hills, Queens. For additional information used to construct a biographical portrait of Milgram, see Joel Milgram, interview with author, tape recording, Wayland, Mass., 22 January 1999; and Alexandra Milgram, "My Personal View of Stanley Milgram."

67. Stanley Milgram, "Social Influence," unpublished note, n.d., in Milgram papers, Series III, Box 71, Folder 293. See also "As I review the facts," unpublished note, n.d., in Milgram papers, Series III, Box 71, Folder 293.

68. Alexandra Milgram, "My Personal View of Stanley Milgram," 3.

69. Joel Milgram, interview with author, tape recording, Cambridge, Mass., 19 January 1999.

70. Stanley Milgram, bar mitzvah speech, quoted in Blass, *Man Who Shocked the World,* 8; and "Roots of Stanley Milgram's Obedience," 49.

71. Stanley Milgram to John Shaffer, 9 November 1958, quoted in Blass, *Man Who Shocked the World,* 46.

72. In 1963, 37 percent of all articles in *JASP* reported experiments that used deception. See James H. Korn, *Illusions of Reality: A History of Deception in Social Psychology* (Albany: State University of New York Press, 1997), 23.

73. See Jane D. Hildreth to Stanley Milgram, 23 November 1962, in Milgram papers, Series I, Box 1a, Folder 4. One of Milgram's colleagues at Yale brought the experiments to the APA's attention. See Blass, *Man Who Shocked the World,* 112–13.

74. Baumrind, "Some Thoughts," 422.

75. Milgram, "Behavioral Study," 378, quoted in Baumrind, "Some Thoughts," 422.

76. Baumrind, "Some Thoughts," 423.

77. Stanley Milgram, "Issues in the Study of Obedience: A Reply to Baumrind," *American Psychologist* 19 (1964): 848–52, reprinted in Arthur G. Miller, ed., *The Social Psychology of Psychological Research* (New York: The Free Press, 1972), 12–21. Note that, in Miller's book, there is a typographical error that suggests that only 74 percent of subjects were glad or very glad to have been in the study; in the table of data reprinted in Miller's book the responses do not add up to 100 percent. For the correct data, see Milgram, *Obedience to Authority,* 214.

78. Milgram, "Issues in the Study," 117. For the full psychiatrist's report, see "Statement by Paul Errera, M.D. Assistant Professor of Psychiatry, Yale University, Based on Interviews with Forty 'Worst Cases' in the Milgram

Obedience Experiments, June 20, 1963," in Milgram papers, Series II, Box 45, Folder 162. Errera's statement was published in Jay Katz, *Experimentation with Human Beings: The Authority of the Investigator, Subject, Professions, and State in the Human Experimentation Process* (New York: Russell Sage Foundation, 1972). Errera's report does not include "a description of the selection process, a description of the population as compared to the overall sample and an accounting of those who did not keep their return appointments."

79. Milgram, "Issues in the Study," 118–19.

80. Milgram, "Issues in the Study," 119–20. Italics are all Milgram's in the original.

81. Milgram, "Issues in the Study," 120.

82. For a brief hint at existentialism's emphasis on heroes, rather than heroines, see Cotkin, *Existentialist America*, 251.

83. Leon Mann to Stanley Milgram, 5 July 1964, in Milgram papers, Series I, Box 18, Folder 263. It is worth noting that, in his response, Milgram rejected Mann's assertion, "I do not think it is a matter of 'putting Baumrind in her place' but of patiently explaining the facts." See Stanley Milgram to Leon Mann, 9 July 1964, in Milgram papers, Series I, Box 18, Folder 263.

84. Alan C. Elms, *Social Psychology and Social Relevance* (Boston: Little, Brown, 1972), 151.

85. Among other social scientists whose ethics came under harsh scrutiny at this time were experimenters at Harvard who gave hallucinogenic drugs to students and a psychology graduate student at Washington University in St. Louis who posed as a gay man and a public health worker in order to elicit information about the sexual practices of homosexuals who had encounters in public places. See Miller, *Obedience Experiments*, 267, n. 11.

86. For the controversy at the APA convention, see Harry Kaufmann, "The Price of Obedience and the Price of Knowledge," *American Psychologist* 22, no. 4 (April 1967): 321–22. For articles and letters to the editor, see Herbert Kelman, "Human Use of Human Subjects: The Problem of Deception in Social Psychological Experiments," *Psychological Bulletin* 67, no. 1 (January 1967): 1–11; Gary E. Stollak, "Obedience and Deception Research," *American Psychologist* 22, no. 8 (August 1967); Zick Rubin, "Jokers Wild in the Lab," *Psychology Today* 4, no. 7 (December 1970): 18–24; Diana Baumrind, "Principles of Ethical Conduct in the Treatment of Subjects: Reaction to the Draft Report of the Committee on Ethical Standards in Psychological Research," *American Psychologist* 26, no. 10 (October 1971): 887–96; Kenneth Gergen, "The Codification of Research Ethics: Views of a Doubting Thomas," *American Psychologist* 28 (October 1973): 907–12.

87. For a brief chronological discussion of APA and government regulations on research, see Korn, *Illusions of Reality*, 137–57.

88. Milgram, *Individual in a Social World*, 98. See also Stanley Milgram, fragment of interview with unknown interviewer, n.d., 11, in Milgram papers, Series I, Box 23, Folder 282.

89. Stanley Milgram, "Obedience: *Ethics* of Experimentation," unpublished note, January 1962, in Milgram papers, Series II, Box 46, Folder 165.

90. Stanley Milgram, "Extending the Field of Observation," unpublished note, March 1962, in Milgram papers, Series II, Folder 46, Box 163.

91. Other critics since Baumrind have made this connection. See, for example, Steven Patten, "The Case That Milgram Makes," *Philosophical Review* 86 (1977): 350–64; and Patten, "Milgram's Shocking Experiments," *Philosophy* 52 (1977): 425–40.

92. Stanley Milgram to Alan Elms, 27 June 1961, in Milgram papers, Series II, Box 43, Folder 127.

93. Stanley Milgram, "Ethics of Experimentation," unpublished note, August 1962, Milgram papers, Series II, Box 46, Folder 173.

94. Stanley Milgram, "After reading," unpublished note, June 1964, in Milgram papers, Series I, Box 17, Folder 246.

95. Stanley Milgram, unpublished note, n.d., Milgram papers, Series III, Box 62, Folder 126. This folder contains several copies of rough drafts with similar versions of this passage. Milgram's reference to "persons" who "sometimes assume" his identification with the experimenter suggests that he wrote this note after Baumrind's criticism was published; his reference to the obedience experiment as "the present study," however, suggests that it was his most current work and thus that this draft was written sometime in the mid-1960s, not in the mid-1970s.

96. Stanley Milgram, "Ethical Issues-4," unpublished note, n.d., Milgram papers, Series III, Box 62, Folder 126.

97. Psychologist Philip Zimbardo, who went to high school with Stanley Milgram, has expressed much more openly than Milgram the sentiment of being an outsider in psychology because of his non-Protestant, city upbringing. It is unclear that Milgram felt this as strongly. See Zimbardo, "Behaviorism with Minds and Matters," in *Reflections on 100 Years of Experimental Social Psychology,* ed. Aroldo Rodrigues and Robert V. Levine (New York: Basic Books, 1999), 138–42.

98. Stanley Milgram, "An Experimenter's Dilemma," unpublished note, n.d., in Milgram papers, Series III, Box 62, Folder 126.

99. For an example of laymen criticizing the ethics of Milgram's experiments early in the 1960s, see "Experiment at Yale," *St. Louis Post-Dispatch,* 2 November 1963, in Milgram papers, Series III, Box 55, Folder 9.

100. It is unclear how either UPI or the *New York Times* were initially alerted to the story. Milgram's unpublished notes state that he discouraged both from publishing their articles. Many other mainstream news outlets, including *Life* magazine, ABC, and *Reader's Digest,* asked Milgram to talk or write about the experiments for them; he apparently declined them all. See Stanley Milgram, "Other Contacts on the Obedience Article," unpublished note, n.d., Milgram papers, Series II, Box 46, Volume 165.

101. See "Experiment at Yale," *St. Louis Post-Dispatch;* "Danger: Shock," *San Fran-cisco Chronicle,* November 1963, in Milgram papers, Series I, Box 21, Folder 335; Cyril Connolly, "War on Torturers," *Sunday Times* (London), 3 November 1963, in Milgram papers, Series I, Box 21, Folder 335; and "Other Contacts on the Obedience Article."

102. Walter Sullivan, "Blind Obedience Is High in Tests," *New York Times,* 26 Oc-tober 1963, C28, in Milgram papers, Series I, Box 21, Folder 335.

103. George Dusheck, "A Nazi Jolt Close to Home," *San Francisco Examiner,* 3 February 1967, 27, in Milgram papers, Series I, Box 21, Folder 337.

104. Yuncker, "Where Conscience Ends," 28.

105. See, for example, Sullivan, "Blind Obedience"; "Danger: Shock," *San Fran-cisco Chronicle;* "Experiment Perilous," *Scholastic Teacher,* 15 November 1963, 2-T, in Milgram papers, Series I, Box 21, Folder 335; "Could We Be Nazi Fol-lowers?" *Science Digest* (January 1964), 81–82.

106. Meyer, "If Hitler Asked You," 128.

107. "Experiment Perilous," *Scholastic Teacher.*

108. Max Lerner, "Are the Experts Destroying Our Judgment?" *McCall's* (Novem-ber 1967), 26, in Milgram papers, Series I, Box 21, Folder 337; William Rasp-berry, "The Psychology behind 'Just Following Orders,'" *Washington Post,* 21 November 1973, A19, in Milgram papers, Series I, Box 21, Folder 340.

109. Philip Meyer, "If Hitler Asked You" 128.

110. "You Might Do Eichmann's Job," *Pageant* (1966), cited in Blass, *Man Who Shocked the World,* 159.

111. "Could We Be Nazi Followers?" For other examples of articles beginning with similar questions, see "Obedience to Authority Is a Habit," *New Haven Register* (see n.38 above); and "Experiment Found Plenty of Sadists," *Roch-ester* (Minn.) *Bulletin,* 14 November 1963, 23, in Milgram papers, Series I, Box 21, Folder 335.

112. Ossie Sykes, "Could Nazi-Germ in U.S. Whites Bring About Gas Chamber 'Solution'?" *Muhammad Speaks,* 9 September 1965, 9, in Milgram papers, Series I, Box 21, Folder 336.

113. Meyer, "If Hitler Asked You" 72.

114. There are no reports of complaints of Milgram's work being tasteless or trivializing the Holocaust in either the *American Jewish Year Book* or the *Index to Jewish Periodicals* between 1963 and 1973. See Morris Fine and Mil-ton Himmelfarb, eds., *American Jewish Year Book* , vols. 64–74 (New York: American Jewish Committee; Philadelphia: Jewish Publication Society of America, 1963–73); Marion Gans, Miriam Leikind, and Bess Rosenthal, eds., *Index to Jewish Periodicals,* June 1963-May 1964, vol. 1 (Cleveland, Ohio: College of Jewish Studies Press, 1964); Miriam Leikind, ed., *Index to Jewish Periodicals* (Cleveland Heights, Ohio: College of Jewish Studies Press, 1965–73). In the *Jewish Spectator* in 1974, Trude Weiss-Rosmarin

criticized Milgram's *Obedience to Authority* because he gave credence to Hannah Arendt's interpretation of Adolf Eichmann in *Eichmann in Jerusalem,* and thus seemed to excuse the Nazi for his murderous behavior. She did not criticize Milgram for trivializing the Holocaust or for universalizing a Jewish experience. See Trude Weiss-Rosmarin, "Did Eichmann 'Obey'?" *Jewish Spectator* 39 (19 September 1974): 12–14.

115. Henry Enoch Kagan to Stanley Milgram, 19 September 1965, in Milgram papers, Series I, Box 2, Folder 117; Sue Snyderman to Stanley Milgram, 4 March 1965, in Milgram papers, Series III, Box 55, Folder 14; Eugene Glick to Stanley Milgram, 14 September 1963, in Milgram papers, Series III, Box 55, Folder 13.

116. "A View of Ourselves," *Jewish Advocate* (Boston), 14 January 1965, 10, in Milgram papers, Series I, Box 21, Folder 335.

117. See, for example, Steven R. James to Stanley Milgram, 23 February 1964, Milgram papers, Series I, Box 1a, Folder 10; Devi Prasad to Stanley Milgram, 2 June 1964, Milgram papers, Series III, Box 55, Folder 13; David Weller to Stanley Milgram, 16 November 1973, Series III, Box 61, Folder 106; Henry J. Korn to Stanley Milgram, 22 February 1975, Milgram papers, Series III, Box 61, Folder 112.

118. Kenneth MacDonald to Stanley Milgram, 2 December 1963, Milgram papers, Series III, Box 55, Folder 12.

119. Ellen S. Jaffe to Stanley Milgram, 2 November 1963, Milgram papers, Series I, Box 1a, Folder 9.

120. Naomi Weisstein to Stanley Milgram, 23 May 1968, Milgram papers, Series I, Box 3, Folder 41; Naomi Weisstein, "'Kinde, Kuche, Kirche' as Scientific Law: Psychology Constructs the Female," in *Sisterhood Is Powerful,* ed. Robin Morgan (New York: Vintage Books, 1970), 240–41.

121. Jeffrey P. Cook to Stanley Milgram, 27 December 1973, Milgram papers, Series III, Box 61, Folder 106.

122. Stanley Karnow, "Calley Defense Not New," *Washington Post,* 29 March 1971, A19, in Milgram papers, Series I, Box 21, Folder 339; see also Robert Schneerson, "Conscience and Congress: The Dilemmas of Obedience," *Harper's Magazine* 247, no. 1483 (December 1973): 61; Raspberry, "Psychology behind 'Just Following Orders.'"

123. Dale C. Krause to Stanley Milgram, 27 June 1973, Milgram papers, Series I, Box 6, Folder 86.

124. Merrill G. Leonard to Stanley Milgram, 19 November 1973, Milgram papers, Series III, Box 61, Folder 106.

125. Mildred H. Spielmann to Stanley Milgram, 4 April 1974, Milgram papers; Series III, Box 61, Folder 111.

126. Arthur L. Murtagh to Stanley Milgram, 20 November 1973, Milgram papers, Series III, Box 61, Folder 106.

127. See also Walter Lautz to Stanley Milgram, 16 August 1973, Milgram papers, Series I, Box 6, Folder 86; Janine Brittin to Stanley Milgram, 4 December 1973, Milgram papers, Series III, Box 61, Folder 106; Esther Mattson to Stanley Milgram, 28 March 1974, Milgram papers, Series III, Box 61, Folder 111; Darrell Wolfe to Letters Department, *TV Guide,* 26 August 1976, Milgram papers, Series III, Box 64, Folder 163.

128. See Nevitt Sanford and Craig Comstock, *Sanctions for Evil* (San Francisco: Jossey-Bass, 1971), xi, 211, 305, 331; Richard Falk, Gabriel Kolko, and Robert J. Lifton, eds., *Crimes of War* (New York: Random House, 1971), 460.

129. See Herbert C. Kelman and Lee H. Lawrence, "Assignment of Responsibility in the Case of Lt. Calley: Preliminary Report on a National Survey," *Journal of Social Issues* 28, no. 1 (1972): 177–212; Herbert C. Kelman, "Violence without Moral Restraint: Reflections on the Dehumanization of Victims and Victimizers," *Journal of Social Issues* 29, no. 4 (1973): 25–61; and S. G. West, S. P. Guan, and P. Chernicky, "Ubiquitous Watergate: An Attributional Analysis," *Journal of Personality and Social Psychology* 32 (1975): 55–65.

130. Cited in Stanley Milgram to Dannie Abse, 21 February 1972, published in Dannie Abse, *The Dogs of Pavlov* (London: Valentine, Mitchell, 1973), 43–44. Also published in Milgram, *Obedience to Authority,* 200. It is impossible to view this subject's letter independently or compare this subject's experience with that of other subjects, because Milgram's correspondence with subjects has been restricted from public viewing until 2039.

131. Stanley Milgram, unpublished note, n.d., Milgram papers, Series III, Box 61, Folder 116. The professor is not identified; it is possible that this professor's testimony, which Milgram calls "a first person account," was in fact written by Milgram himself. Since the account, however, refers to Milgram in the third person, I have assumed that Milgram received this testimony from a colleague or neighbor.

132. Thomas J. Bouchard, Jr., to Stanley Milgram, 3 August 1965, Milgram papers, Series III, Box 56, Folder 29.

133. Richard Flacks, *Conformity, Resistance, and Self-Determination: The Individual and Authority* (Boston: Little, Brown, 1973), 12. For Flacks's history in SDS, see James Miller, *"Democracy Is in the Streets": From Port Huron to the Siege of Chicago* (New York: Simon and Schuster, 1987).

134. The "largest radical student organization" was most likely SDS. Stanley Milgram, unpublished note, n.d., Milgram papers, Series III, Box 62, Folder 129.

135. Geoffrey Davis to Stanley Milgram, 6 June 1974, Milgram papers, Series III, Box 61, Folder 111.

136. John Holt to Stanley Milgram, 5 December 1973, Milgram papers, Series III, Box 61, Folder 106.

137. Harriet Tobin to Stanley Milgram, 23 March 1964, Milgram papers, Series I, Box 1a, Folder 10.

138. Holly Beye Ruff to Stanley Milgram, 15 November 1963, Milgram papers, Series III, Box 55, Folder 12.

139. See, for example, Holly Beye Ruff, "Milgram's Experiment in Blind Obedience," *Capsule* 2, no. 4 (February 1964): 1–2, in Milgram papers, Series III, Box 55, Folder 13; Edna G. Lichtenstein to Milgram, n.d. (1965), Milgram papers, Series III, Box 56, Folder 29; and Gene Bridges to Stanley Milgram, 17 September 1964, Milgram papers, Series I, Box 1a, Folder 12.

140. See, for ethical criticisms, Charles A. Miller to Stanley Milgram, 25 November 1973; Lorelei Krakowski to Stanley Milgram, 17 November 1973, both in Milgram papers, Series III, Box 61, Folder 106. See, for criticisms of applicability, Thomas Thorsen to Stanley Milgram, 23 November 1973; Ronald Karr to Stanley Milgram, 20 November 1973, both in Milgram papers, Series III, Box 61, Folder 106; and Hans Dolezalek to Stanley Milgram, 14 January 1970, Milgram papers, Series I, Box 4, Folder 53.

141. Peter S. Prescott, "People in Shock," *Newsweek* 83, no. 4 (24 January 1974): 74, 76.

142. Daniel Bell, "Is Eichmann in All of Us?" *New York Times*, 26 May 1974, sec. 2, p. 1.

143. Christopher Lehmann-Haupt, "But Why Do People Disobey?" *New York Times*, 3 January 1974, 33, in Milgram papers, Series III, Box 63, Folder 149. See also Steven Marcus, review of *Obedience to Authority*, *New York Times Book Review*, 13 January 1974, 2, in Milgram papers, Series III, Box 63, Folder 149; review of *Obedience to Authority*, *Science Digest* (May 1974), 95, 100, in Milgram papers, Series III, Box 63, Folder 149; Karl Hess, "When Push Comes to Shove," *Washington Post Book World*, 3 February 1974, 1, 4, in Milgram papers, Series III, Box 63, Folder 149; "Punishment-Block," *Times Literary Supplement*, 7 June 1964, 602.

144. Bell, "Is Eichmann in All of Us?" See also Robert Kirsch, "Have You Guts to Defy Authority?" *Jersey Journal*, 13 March 1974, 12, in Milgram papers, Series I, Box 21, Folder 340.

145. Abe Peck, "Zzzap! But They Were Just Following Orders," *News* (Chicago), 2 February 1974, in Milgram papers, Series III, Box 63, Folder 150. See also, for example, Hans J. Eysenck, "Doing as They Were Told," *Guardian*, 8 June 1974, 21; Prescott, "People in Shock"; Michael Rogers, "Obedience as Shocking Behavior," *Rolling Stone*, 11 April 1974, 74–75, in Milgram papers, Series III, Box 63, Folder 149; Robert Kirsch, "'But I Was Only Following Orders,'" *Los Angeles Times Calendar*, 10 March 1974, 58–60, in Milgram papers, Series III, Box 63, Folder 149.

146. See letters to the editor, *New York Times Book Review*, 24 February 1974, 42–44, in Milgram papers, Series I, Box 21, Folder 340; letters to the editor, *New York Times Book Review*, 24 March 1974: 42–43; and "Mailbag: Is Eichmann in All of Us," *New York Times*, 30 June 1974, sec. 2, pp. 10, 32, in Milgram papers, Series I, Box 21, Folder 340.

147. Rogers, "Obedience as Shocking Behavior," 74–75; Kirsch, "'But I Was Only Following Orders,'" 58–60. Thomas Blass found that about half of the sixty-two reviews he surveyed generally approved of *Obedience to Authority,* about one-third disapproved, and a remaining 20 percent were ambivalent. See Blass, *Man Who Shocked the World,* 296–99.

148. Blass, *Man Who Shocked the World,* 219–20.

149. See, for appearances on radio and television, letters in Milgram papers, Series III, Box 63, Folder 145.

150. *Sixty Minutes,* 31 March 1974, Museum of Television and Radio, New York, N.Y.

151. See, for example, Marcus, review of *Obedience to Authority,* 1–3; and Marcus, reply, "Letters to the Editor: Authority," *New York Times Book Review,* 24 February 1974, 43–44.

152. See, for discussion of intentionalism versus functionalism, Michael Marrus, *The Holocaust in History* (Hanover, N.H.: University Press of New England for Brandeis University Press, 1987), 34–46. Saul Friedländer offers the characterizations "liberal" and "structuralist," and notes the changing responsibility between perpetrators and victims, in describing the same debate. See Friedländer, *Memory, History and the Extermination of the Jews of Europe* (Bloomington: Indiana University Press, 1993), 24–28.

153. Neil Lutsky has claimed that Milgram's work was more significant for intentionalists than for functionalists, since intentionalists emphasized the power of top-down orders to be followed unquestioningly by subordinates, while functionalists emphasized more active efforts to murder on the part of local bureaucrats. Lutsky's argument is interesting and plausible, but ultimately I believe it is mistaken. Milgram's work has primarily been used by scholars who have identified with functionalism, such as Christopher Browning, and the implications of his work have been excoriated by scholars identified with intentionalism, such as Lucy Dawidowicz. By claiming that the ideological intentions of the murderers were not as important as the mundane bureaucratic realities under which they operated, Milgram offered an intellectual paradigm for functionalists, not intentionalists. For Lutsky's argument, see "When Is 'Obedience' Obedience? Conceptual and Historical Commentary," *Journal of Social Issues* 51, no. 3 (1995): 63. For the characterizations of Browning and Dawidowicz, see Marrus, *Holocaust in History,* 35–37, 43–46. For Dawidowicz's rejection of Milgram's ideas, see "How They Teach the Holocaust," *Commentary* 90, no. 6 (December 1990): 30–31.

154. Saul Friedländer to Stanley Milgram, 4 January 1966, Milgram papers, Series III, Box 55, Folder 14.

155. See Henry Dicks, *Licensed Mass Murder: A Socio-Psychological Study of Some SS Killers* (New York: Basic Books, 1972), 230, 261–63; Gitta Sereny, *Into That Darkness: From Mercy Killing to Mass Murder* (New York: Vintage Books, 1983; originally published New York: McGraw Hill, 1974), 283;

Hans Askenasy, *Are We All Nazis?* (Secaucus, N.J.: L. Stuart, 1978); and John Steiner, "The SS Yesterday and Today: A Sociopsychological view," in *Survivors, Victims, and Perpetrators: Essays on the Nazi Holocaust*, ed. J. E. Dimsdale (Washington, D.C.: Hemisphere Publishing, 1980), 405–56.

156. Christopher R. Browning, *Ordinary Men: Reserve Police Battalion 101 and the Final Solution in Poland* (New York: Harper Collins, 1992), 171–74; Zygmunt Bauman, *Modernity and the Holocaust* (Ithaca, N.Y.: Cornell University Press, 1989), 151–67.

157. See Daniel J. Goldhagen, *Hitler's Willing Executioners: Ordinary Germans and the Holocaust* (New York: Knopf; distributed by Random House, 1996). For some works on the controversy over Goldhagen, see Robert R. Shandley, *Unwilling Germans? The Goldhagen Debate* (Minneapolis: University of Minnesota Press, 1998); Norman G. Finkelstein and Ruth Bettina Birn, *A Nation on Trial: The Goldhagen Thesis and Historical Truth* (New York: Metropolitan Books, 1998); and Geoff Eley, ed., *The "Goldhagen Effect": History, Memory, Nazism—Facing the German Past* (Ann Arbor: University of Michigan Press, 2000).

158. See, for example, Omer Bartov, "Introduction," in *The Holocaust: Origins, Implementation, Aftermath*, ed. Bartov (New York: Routledge, 2000), 4–6.

159. Israel W. Charny to Stanley Milgram, 14 September 1965, Milgram papers, Series I, Box 2, Folder 16. Other evidence of secondary educators who used the experiments to teach the Holocaust and attendant moral principles may be found in Stanley Milgram to Oscar Cohen, 26 July 1974, Milgram papers, Series I, Box 7, Folder 92; and Diane Englander to Stanley Milgram, 15 March 1974, Milgram papers, Series I, Box 6, Folder 90.

160. See Margaret Stern Strom and William S. Parsons, *Facing History and Ourselves: The Holocaust and Human Behavior* (Watertown, Mass.: International Educations, 1982): 156–57. Conservative Holocaust scholar Lucy Dawidowicz complained about the impact of Milgram's liberal message in Holocaust education, though she did not mention the psychologist by name. See Dawidowicz, "How They Teach the Holocaust," 30–31.

161. See Anne Saltzman, "The Role of the Obedience Experiments in Holocaust Studies: The Case for Renewed Visibility," in *Obedience to Authority*, ed. Blass, 125–43.

162. See Arthur G. Miller, "Constructions of the Obedience Experiments: A Focus upon Domains of Relevance," *Journal of Social Issues* 51, no. 3 (1995): 38–43.

163. See, for example, H. J. Eysenck, "Doing as They Were Told," *Guardian*, 8 June 1974, 21; R. J. Herrnstein, "Measuring Evil," *Commentary* 57 (June 1974): 88; A. Lawrence Chickering, "Authority: Garbling the Issues," *The Alternative: An American Spectator* 8, no. 8 (May 1975): 6; Alan Astrow, "Milgram Dispute Survives," *Yale Daily News*, 1 May 1974, 1, 9, 12, in Milgram papers, Series I, Box 21, Folder 340; Marcus, review of *Obedience to Authority*; and Bell, "Is Eichmann in All of Us," 13. Several of these reviewers did

ultimately validate Milgram's ethics, but they generally made clear that it was a substantial issue to be addressed in considering the book. Thomas Blass found that roughly half (47 percent) of the sixty-two reviewers he surveyed mentioned the ethical issues associated with *Obedience to Authority*. See Blass, *Man Who Shocked the World*, 298–99.

164. Lawrence Kohlberg, "More Authority," *New York Times Book Review*, 24 March 1974, 42–43.

165. Ray H. Bixler, "'Ostracize Them!' A Challenge to Professional Societies," *Saturday Review* 49 (2 July 1966): 47.

166. Meyer, "If Hitler Asked You," 132.

167. Abse, *Dogs of Pavlov*, 111, 122.

168. *The Tenth Level*, dir. George Bellak (CBS television movie, 1976). In author's possession.

169. Stanley Milgram, "The 10th Level: Notes," unpublished document, n.d., in Milgram papers, Series III, Box 64, Folder 164. For Milgram's work on the film as a consultant, see Stanley Milgram to Arthur Asa Berger, 20 January 1975, in Milgram papers, Series I, Box 14, Folder, "Berger, Arthur Asa." For descriptions of some other, later, popular cultural representations of the obedience experiments, including the French film *I comme Icare* and the Peter Gabriel rock song "We Do as We're Told (Milgram's 37)" see Blass, *Man Who Shocked the World*, 262–64.

170. See, for example, Catherine Brooks to Letters Department, *TV Guide*, 27 August 1976; Peter Bono to *TV Guide*, 27 August 1976; Darrell Wolfe to Letters Department, *TV Guide*, 26 August 1976, all in Milgram papers, Series III, Box 64, Folder 163.

171. See Kenneth J. Gergen, "Social Psychology as History," *Journal of Personality and Social Psychology* 26, no. 2 (1973): 315, for a brief comment on the significance of historical context in the reception of Milgram's work.

172. See, for example, "We Must Stop the Cambodian Holocaust," *Congressional Record*, 96th Congress, 1st session, vol. 125, no. 136 (10 October 1979); and Saul Jay Singer, "Obey—but at What Cost?" *Sun* (Baltimore), 17 July 1991, 15A.

173. Lee D. Ross, "Situationist Perspectives on the Obedience Experiments," *Contemporary Psychology* 33, no. 2 (1988): 101.

Chapter 4. Robert Jay Lifton and the Survivor (pp. 124–58)

1. Robert Jay Lifton, *Death in Life* (New York: Basic Books, 1967), 479.

2. Lifton also referred to survivors of the plagues of the Middle Ages, but to a much more minor extent. The sixty-two-page chapter includes only three examples from the Middle Ages, while the rest of the chapter is taken up essentially with a point by point comparison of *hibakusha* and Nazi camp victims.

3. Lifton, *Death in Life*, 479.

4. It is important to note that Lifton does not believe that his comparison of concentration camp survivors to *hibakusha* is an "analogy." He believes that the word "analogy" connotes a comprehensive equation between the two subjects being compared, and he firmly rejects any suggestion that he is making such an effort at equation when he compares Nazi camp survivors to other survivors. I do not believe that the word "analogy" necessarily connotes equation—indeed, I believe exactly the opposite—and I do not at all intend to suggest that Lifton is equating Nazi camp survivors and *hibakusha*, or camp survivors and Vietnam veterans. In my view, Lifton, like Friedan, Ellkins, and Milgram, developed a social scientific analogy that used likenesses between society in Nazi Germany and in the United States in order to highlight universal psychological and sociological tendencies. These analogies were very different from radicals' brief metaphorical references that literally equated American policemen with Nazi SS troops in the late 1960s, for example. Because this book uses the word "analogy" to describe systematic comparisons being made by social scientists at the turn of the 1960s, I have continued to use that word to describe Lifton's work in this chapter and throughout this text. For Lifton's feelings about the word "analogy," see Robert Jay Lifton, telephone interview by author, 6 July 2004. For an essay that has influenced my understanding of the concept of "analogy," see Dedre Gentner, "Are Scientific Analogies Metaphors?" in *Metaphor: Problems and Perspectives,* ed. David S. Miall (Atlantic Highlands, N.J.: Humanities Press, 1982), 106–32.

5. For criticisms of Lifton and PTSD from the right, see, for example, B. G. Burkett and Glenna Whitley, *Stolen Valor: How the Vietnam Generation Was Robbed of Its Heroes and Its History* (Dallas: Verity Press, 1998), 138–61; Sally Satel, "Returning from Iraq, Still Fighting Vietnam," *New York Times,* 5 March 2004, A26. For criticism from the left, see Jerry Lembcke, *The Spitting Image: Myth, Memory, and the Legacy of Vietnam* (New York: New York University Press, 1998), 101–26. For criticisms less easily politically categorized, see Eric T. Dean, *Shook Over Hell: Post-Traumatic Stress, Vietnam, and the Civil War* (Cambridge, Mass.: Harvard University Press, 1997), 183, 200; Ben Shephard, *A War of Nerves: Soldiers and Psychiatrists in the Twentieth Century* (Cambridge, Mass.: Harvard University Press, 2001), 358–67, 395–96; and David H. Marlowe, *Psychological and Psychosocial Consequences of Combat and Deployment with Special Emphasis on the Gulf War* (Rand Corporation, 2000), http://www.rand.org/publications/MR/MR1018.11/, accessed 11 March 2005. Ben Shephard does make note of the significance of the Holocaust in the development of post-traumatic stress disorder, but he does so very briefly, and he specifically argues that the Holocaust played little part in Lifton's work. See Shephard, *War of Nerves,* xxii–xxiii, 359–61.

6. Robert Jay Lifton, "On Death and Death Symbolism," in Lifton, *History and Human Survival* (New York: Random House, 1970), 171–72; originally published in *Psychiatry* 27 (1964).

7. Lifton, *Death in Life*, 479.
8. Lifton, *Death in Life*, 525.
9. Lifton, *Death in Life*, 531.
10. Lifton, "On Death and Death Symbolism," 173. Italics are Lifton's.
11. Robert Jay Lifton, *The Life of the Self* (New York: Basic Books, 1976), 59, 114–15.
12. Robert Jay Lifton, *The Broken Connection* (New York: Simon and Schuster, 1979), 4–5; see also Lifton, *Death in Life*, 541.
13. Robert Jay Lifton, "The Young and the Old—Notes on a New History," in *History and Human Survival*, 337–38; originally published in *Atlantic Monthly* (September 1969 and October 1969).
14. Robert Jay Lifton, "Protean Man," in *History and Human Survival*, 311–31; originally published in *Futurible* (Paris) series (Sedeis January 1967), and in *Partisan Review* (Winter 1968), 13–27.
15. Robert Jay Lifton, *The Nazi Doctors: Medical Killing and the Psychology of Genocide* (New York: Basic Books, 1986); Robert Jay Lifton and Eric Markusen, *The Genocidal Mentality: Nazi Holocaust and Nuclear Threat* (New York: Basic Books, 1990).
16. Robert Jay Lifton, *Superpower Syndrome: America's Apocalyptic Confrontation with the World* (New York: Thunder's Mouth Press/Nation Books, 2003), 35–39, 192–94; Robert Jay Lifton, "Doctors and Torture," *New England Journal of Medicine* 351, no. 5 (29 July 2004): 415–16.
17. For specific references to Jewish prisoners, see Lifton, *Death in Life*, 495, 502, 513, and 530.
18. Lifton, *Death in Life*, 540. For another explicit reference to himself as an American Jew, see Lifton, *Death in Life*, 321–22.
19. Robert Jay Lifton, "Introduction: On Becoming a Psychohistorian," in *History and Human Survival*, 19–20.
20. Lifton, *Life of the Self*, 86–87; for Harold Lifton's investing in Broadway plays, see Betty Jean Lifton, *Twice Born: Memoirs of an Adopted Daughter* (New York: McGraw-Hill, 1975), 51; and Robert Jay Lifton to Harold Lifton, 12 May 1961, in Robert Jay Lifton papers, New York Public Library (hereafter RJL-NYPL), Chronological Correspondence, Box 1, "Copies of Outgoing Correspondence, 1961–2."
21. Robert Jay Lifton, interview by author, tape recording, New York, N.Y., 27 January 2000; Robert Jay Lifton, *The Protean Self* (Chicago: University of Chicago Press, 1993), 38.
22. Lifton, interview by author, 27 January 2000.
23. For little personal antisemitism, see Lifton, interview by author, 27 January 2000.
24. Lifton, *Life of the Self*, 86.
25. Lifton, interview by author, 27 January 2000.
26. Lifton, *Life of the Self*, 87.

27. Lifton, interview by author, 27 January 2000.

28. Lifton, interview by author, 27 January 2000.

29. Lifton, interview by author, 27 January 2000.

30. Lifton, interview by author, 27 January 2000.

31. Lifton, *Life of the Self,* 87.

32. Lifton, interview by author, 27 January 2000.

33. Lifton, *Life of the Self,* 87.

34. Lifton, interview by author, 27 January 2000.

35. For Lifton's rejection of any description of himself as a victim, see Lifton, interview by author, 27 January 2000; for his father's social mobility as inspiration for human transformation, see Lifton, *Life of the Self,* 87; for Lifton's athletic and academic trajectory, see Robert J. Lifton, "Autobiography," n.d., in RJL-NYPL, General Correspondence, Box 2, Folder 6.

36. For Lifton's preference for addressing the category of the survivor as "a step away from remaining merely a victim," while still acknowledging the terror that victims had undergone, see Robert Jay Lifton, interview by author, tape recording, New York, N.Y., 29 March 2000.

37. For the impact of his father's desire to be a doctor, see Lifton, interview by author, 27 January 2000; for Lifton's gravitation to psychiatry, see Lifton, *Life of the Self,* 88.

38. For Freud's courage and brilliance, see Robert Jay Lifton essay in "Jewishness and the Younger Intellectuals" Symposium, *Commentary* 31 (April 1961), 307–8; see also Lifton, "Introduction," in *History and Human Survival,* 14; Lifton, *Life of the Self,* 53–54; for Lifton's rejection of Freudian mechanisms and Freud's emphasis on childhood experiences, see Lifton, *Life of the Self,* 66–68.

39. Lifton, "Autobiography," 7–8; see also Betty Jean Lifton, *Twice Born,* for more in-depth description of her experience in Japan.

40. Lifton, *Protean Self,* 7–8.

41. Erik Erikson, *Childhood and Society,* 2nd. ed. (New York: W. W. Norton, 1962; originally published 1950), 247–74; Lawrence J. Friedman, *Identity's Architect: A Biography of Erik H. Erikson* (New York: Scribner, 1999).

42. See Lifton, "Introduction," in *History and Human Survival,* 14–15.

43. For Lifton's description of intellectual differences between himself and Erikson, see Lifton, *Life of the Self,* 68–75.

44. Robert Jay Lifton, *Thought Reform and the Psychology of Totalism* (New York: W. W. Norton, 1961), 446–54; Friedman, *Identity's Architect,* 356–63.

45. For Lifton calling himself a psychiatrist who focused on "extreme situations," see, for example, Lifton, *Home from the War: Vietnam Veterans: Neither Victims nor Executioners* (New York: Simon and Schuster, 1973), 16; for Lifton's belief that his use of this term signaled his subtextual concern with concentration camps, see Lifton, interview by author, 27 January 2000.

46. Lifton, interview by author, 29 March 2000.

47. Lifton, *Life of the Self,* 86.

48. Lifton, *Life of the Self,* 87; Lifton, interview by author, 27 January 2000.

49. For Harburg's politics, see Harold Meyerson and Ernie Harburg, *Who Put the Rainbow in The Wizard of Oz? Yip Harburg, Lyricist* (Ann Arbor: University of Michigan Press, 1993), 272–73; for his friendship and partnership with Harold Lifton, see Meyerson and Harburg, *Who Put the Rainbow,* 22, 27.

50. Lifton, interview by author, 27 January 2000.

51. Lifton, interview by author, 27 January 2000; see also Lifton, interview by author, 29 March 2000; Lifton, *Home from the War,* 15. For Betty Jean Lifton's descriptions of her experiences in Vietnam, see Betty Jean Lifton, "Waiting for the Herky Bird," *New Journal* 1, no. 7 (4 February 1968): 3–4; and Lifton, "An Outsider at Someone Else's Feast," *New Journal* 1, no. 13 (12 May 1968): 10–11.

52. Robert Jay Lifton, "Young Demonstrators," in *History and Human Survival,* 81–111; originally published in *American Scholar* 3 (1961): 332–44. For Lifton's general sense that his time in Asia had radicalized his politics, see Lifton, "Recollections of Partisan Review Discussion Group at William Phillips House, May 2, 1971," 3–4, unpublished document in RJL-NYPL, General Correspondence 14, Folder 5.

53. Charles DeBenedetti, *An American Ordeal: The Antiwar Movement of the Vietnam Era* (New York: Syracuse University Press, 1990), 45.

54. See correspondence between Lifton and Riesman in RJL-NYPL, Series I, Box 15, Folders 4–8; Box 16, Folders 1–3.

55. Todd Gitlin, *The Sixties: Years of Hope, Days of Rage* (New York: Bantam Books, 1987), 87–104.

56. Lifton, interview by author, 27 January 2000.

57. Lifton, interview by author, 27 January 2000.

58. Lifton, interview by author, 27 January 2000.

59. Lifton, interview by author, 27 January 2000; Michael S. Kimmel, "Prophet of Survival," *Psychology Today* 22, no. 6 (June 1988): 46.

60. Lifton, "Introduction," in *History and Human Survival,* 20; for Lifton describing the dangers of communism while also rejecting American anticommunism, see Lifton, "Young Demonstrators," in *History and Human Survival,* 87–100, esp. 89, 91–92.

61. Lifton, interview by author, 27 January 2000.

62. Lifton, interview by author, 27 January 2000; see also Lifton, "Recollections of Partisan Review Discussion."

63. "Jewishness and the Younger Intellectuals," 311.

64. Lifton, in "Jewishness and the Younger Intellectuals," 339.

65. Lifton, in "Jewishness and the Younger Intellectuals," 338–40.

66. Robert Jay Lifton to Harold Lifton, 17 April 1962, in RJL-NYPL, Chronological Correspondence, Box 1, "Copies of Outgoing Correspondence, 1961–62."

67. Robert Jay Lifton to David and Evelyn Riesman, 28 July 1962, in RJL-NYPL, General Correspondence, Box 15, Folder 1. See other letters in this folder for similar expressions of objectivity and political concern.

68. Lifton, *Death in Life*, xv, 8, 327, 499, 541.

69. For publisher's statistics, see Jane C. Seitz to Lily Finn, 3 March 1969, in RJL-NYPL, Publishing Correspondence, Box 2, "Random House, 1969–71"; for a statement on the fame but the generally modest sales of Lifton's books, see Robert Jay Lifton to Stuart Fletcher, 27 August 1976, in RJL-NYPL, Chronological Correspondence, Box 5, "Correspondence, 1974–78."

70. Robert Jay Lifton, "Appendix: Acceptance Speech for the 1969 National Book Award in the Sciences," in *History and Human Survival*, 375.

71. See, for example, Kenneth Lamott, "Community of Death and Guilt," *Nation* 206 (6 May 1968): 604–5; Robert Coles, "Us Unmistakably," *Kenyon Review* 30, no. 4 (1968): 561–62; George Adelman, review of *Death in Life*, *Library Journal* 93, no. 2 (15 January 1968): 196; and Saul Maloff, "The Great Dying," *Newsweek* 71, no. 8 (19 February 1968): 96.

72. Bruno Bettelheim, review of *Death in Life*, *Political Science Quarterly* 84, no. 1 (March 1969), 145–46; "Survival Guilt," *Times Literary Supplement*, 17 November 1968, 1253; J. Bronowski, "The Psychological Wreckage of Hiroshima and Nagasaki," *Scientific American* 218, no. 6 (June 1968): 134.

73. Abraham Kardiner, review of *Death in Life*, *American Journal of Sociology* 74, no. 3 (November 1968): 316; George Steiner, "White Light in August," *New Yorker* 44, no. 24 (3 August 1968): 79; Geoffrey Gorer, "Surviving the Atom Bomb," *Listener* 80, no. 2057 (29 August 1968): 276–77.

74. Jerome Frank, "After the Event," *New York Times Book Review*, 31 March 1968, 10; "This Week," *Christian Century* 85, no. 5 (31 January 1968): 146.

75. Oscar Handlin, "Reader's Choice," *Atlantic* 221, no. 3 (March 1968): 133.

76. Adelman, review of *Death in Life*, 196; Ardath W. Burks, review of *Death in Life*, *American Historical Review* 74, no. 3 (February 1969): 1063; and Maloff, "Great Dying," 96. See also "Survival Guilt," 1253; and David Riesman, "Return to Hiroshima," *Dissent* 15, no. 3 (May–June 1968): 269.

77. Mary Ellmann, "After the Bomb," *Commentary* 45, no. 5 (May 1968): 88. For other critiques of Lifton's psychoanalytic perspective as reductive, see Ira Morris, "Under the Mushroom Cloud," *Saturday Review* 51 (3 February 1968): 26; and Alasdair Macintyre, "One Man's View of Hiroshima," *Observer Review*, 8 September 1968, 26.

78. Steiner, "White Light," 78–79. Steiner did call Lifton's work "lucid, authoritative," but he also ultimately called it a "disappointment" and devoted much of his review to this disappointment.

79. Paul Goodman, "Stoicism and the Holocaust," *New York Review of Books* 10 (28 March 1968): 15–19.

80. Robert Jay Lifton to Phillip Rieff, 12 April 1968, in RJL-NYPL, General Correspondence, Box 15, Folder 3; Robert Jay Lifton to John Simon, 11 March

1968, in RJL-NYPL, General Correspondence, Box 15, Folder 1; Diana Trilling to Robert Jay Lifton, 17 April 1968, in RJL-NYPL, Chronological Correspondence, Box 2, "Correspondence, 1968."

81. Erik Erikson, "Recommended Summer Reading," *American Scholar* 37, no. 3 (Summer 1968): 527.

82. Steiner, "White Light," 78.

83. Robert Jay Lifton, "America in Vietnam—the Counterfeit Friend," in *History and Human Survival*, 210, 215. Originally published as "America in Vietnam—the Circle of Deception," *Trans-Action* 5 (1968): 10–19.

84. For inability to sell the article to major journals, see Robert Jay Lifton to Philip Rieff, 5 October 1967, in RJL-NYPL, General Correspondence, Box 15, Folder 3, and Bryant Wedge to Robert Jay Lifton, 6 November 1967, in RJL-NYPL, Chronological Correspondence, Box 2, "Correspondence 1966–67"; for positive reception, see Elizabeth Jay Hollins to Robert Jay Lifton, n.d., in RJL-NYPL, Vietnam Files, Box 1, "Letters to President, Senators, media, 1968," and Mark O. Hatfield to Robert Jay Lifton, 29 May 1968, in RJL-NYPL, Chronological Correspondence, Box 2, "Correspondence 1968"—2; for reprints, see Isidore Ziferstein to Robert Jay Lifton, 21 July 1969, in RJL-NYPL, Chronological Correspondence, Box 3, "Correspondence 1969"—3.

85. Lifton, *Home from the War,* 16; for description of sweeping papers off the desk, see Lifton, interview by author, 27 January 2000.

86. Lifton, *Home from the War,* 21.

87. Lifton, *Home from the War,* 17–18.

88. Congress, Senate, Committee on Labor and Public Welfare, *Hearings Before the Subcommittee on Veterans' Affairs . . . on the Examination of the Problems of the Veterans Wounded in Vietnam,* 91st Congress, 27 January 1970, 492–96. Reprinted in *Commonweal* 91, no. 20 (20 February 1970): 554–56.

89. "Interview with Prominent Psychiatrist: Why Civilians are War Victims," *U.S. News and World Report* 67, no. 24 (15 December 1969): 26.

90. "Why Civilians Are War Victims," 26.

91. Congress, *Hearings before the Subcommittee on Veterans' Affairs,* 496.

92. Congress, *Hearings before the Subcommittee on Veterans' Affairs,* 498–99.

93. Congress, *Hearings before the Subcommittee on Veterans' Affairs,* 504, 506.

94. Robert Jay Lifton, "My Lai and the Malignant Spiral," paper presented at the Congressional Conference on War and National Responsibility, Washington, D.C., 20–21 February 1970, 3, in RJL-NYPL, Vietnam Files, Box 2.

95. Lifton, "My Lai and the Malignant Spiral," 2.

96. "Why Civilians Are War Victims," 28.

97. Lifton, "My Lai and the Malignant Spiral," 2.

98. "Why Civilians Are War Victims," 28.

99. See Robert C. Williams and Allen E. Falk to Robert Jay Lifton, 26 February 1970, in RJL-NYPL, Chronological Correspondence, Box 4, "Correspondence

1970"—3; Craig K. Comstock to Robert Jay Lifton, 23 May 1970, in RJL-NYPL, Chronological Correspondence, Box 4, "Correspondence 1970"—2.

100. Quoted in Lifton, *Home from the War*, 75.

101. For discussion of the formation of rap groups, see Lifton, *Home from the War*, 75–76; Lifton, "Experiments in Advocacy Research," in *Science and Psychoanalysis, Vol. 21: Research and Relevance*, ed. Jules H. Masserman (New York: Grume and Strattion, 1972), 262–64; Wilbur J. Scott, *The Politics of Readjustment: Vietnam Veterans since the War* (New York: Aldine de Gruyter, 1993), 14–18; Andrew E. Hunt, *The Turning: A History of Vietnam Veterans Against the War* (New York: New York University Press, 1999), 86–88; and Gerald Nicosia, *Home to War: A History of the Vietnam Veterans' Movement* (New York: Crown Publishing, 2001), 158–75.

102. See International War Crimes Tribunal, *Against the Crime of Silence: Proceedings of the Russell International War Crimes Tribunal* (New York: Bertrand Russell Peace Foundation, 1968), for the complete proceedings of the Russell tribunal.

103. William J. Bosch, *Judgment on Nuremberg* (Chapel Hill: University of North Carolina Press, 1970), 190–92.

104. For connections between the Bertrand Russell tribunal and the Citizens' Commission of Inquiry, see Tod Ensign, "Organizing Veterans through War Crimes Documentation," *Vietnam Generation* 5, nos. 1–4 (1994): 145–47; James Simon Kunen, *Standard Operating Procedure: Notes of a Draft-Age American* (New York: Avon Books, 1971), 17–27; and Hunt, *Turning*, 58.

105. Tod Ensign, Jeremy Rifkin, Mike Uhl, and Bob Johnson for the Citizens' Commission of Inquiry, introduction to *The Dellums Committee Hearings on War Crimes in Vietnam* (New York: Vintage Books, 1972), viii.

106. Ensign, Rifkin, Uhl, and Johnson, *Dellums Committee Hearings*, x; xiii; for legal research on veterans' rights, see Ensign, "Organizing Veterans," 145.

107. For evidence of Lifton's participation, see Jan Crumb to Robert Jay Lifton, 20 January 1971, in RJL-NYPL, Vietnam Files, Box 4, "Vietnam Vets 1971–76"; Lifton, *Home from the War*, 75; and National Committee for a Citizens' Commission of Inquiry on U.S. War Crimes in Vietnam, press release, 16 November 1970, in RJL-NYPL, Vietnam Files, Box 1, "Citizens Commission. . . ."

108. American Friends Service Committee, "Draft Proposal for NARCOW," May 1971, in RJL-NYPL, Vietnam Files, Box 1, "Citizens' Commission. . . ." See also Gabriel Kolko, "Memo on the New Organization," 4 May 1970, in RJL-NYPL, Vietnam Files, Box 1, "Citizens' Commission. . . ."

109. Richard Falk, Gabriel Kolko, and Robert Jay Lifton, "Editors' Statement," in *Crimes of War* (New York: Random House, 1971), xi.

110. Robert Jay Lifton to Tod Ensign, 27 July 1970, in RJL-NYPL, Vietnam Files, Box 1, "Citizens' Commission. . . ."

111. Robert Jay Lifton, review of Seymour Hersh, *My Lai 4*, and Richard Hammer, *One Morning in the War*, *New York Times Book Review*, 14 June 1970, 2–3, 23.

112. *Trial of the Major War Criminals before the International Military Tribunal, Nuremberg, Germany: 14 November 1945–1 October 1946*, 42 vols. (Nuremberg: International Military Tribunal, 1947–49), vol. 1, 223, cited in Bosch, *Judgment on Nuremberg*, 15.

113. See, for example, Todd Gitlin, *Sixties*, 24–26; Maurice Isserman and Michael Kazin, "The Failure and Success of the New Radicalism," in *The Rise and Fall of the New Deal Order, 1930–1980*, ed. Steve Fraser and Gary Gerstle (Princeton, N.J.: Princeton University Press, 1989), 219–20.

114. See, for example, "Call to Action," n.d., in RJL-NYPL, Subject Files, Box 3, "Redress 1973"; and "Redress Without Tears—Some Thoughts on Who and What We Are," in RJL-NYPL, Subject Files, Box 3, "Redress 1973."

115. "Redress Resolution on Ending the War," n.d., in RJL-NYPL, Subject Files, Box 3, "Redress"—1; "Dear Fellow Americans," n.d., in RJL-NYPL, Subject Files, Box 3, "Redress"—2; and "Redress: A Statement of Defense," n.d., in RJL-NYPL, Subject Files, Box 3, "Redress—May 24, 1972."

116. In addition to all the above-listed documents, see Redress press release, "Anti-war group plans to petition Congress next month," 25 January 1973, in RJL-NYPL, Subject Files, Box 3, "Redress 1973"; "In Defense: USA vs. Benjamin J. Spock, et al.," 25 May 1972, in RJL-NYPL, Subject Files, Box 3, "Redress—May 24, 1972 Protest"; and "The Reasons Why," in RJL-NYPL, Subject Files, Box 3, "Redress"—1.

117. "Redress: A Statement of Defense," n.d., in RJL-NYPL, Subject Files, Box 3, "Redress—May 24, 1972."

118. Robert Jay Lifton, Andre Gregory, Richard Falk, and Joseph Papp to Editor, *New York Times*, 16 January 1973, in RJL-NYPL, Subject Files, Box 3, "Redress 1973"; published as "The President and His Inauguration," *New York Times*, 19 January 1973, 32. For similar emphasis on Batchelder's "good Germans" comment, see "Eugene Ormandy and Van Cliburn still urged to withdraw from inaugural concert," 17 January 1973, in RJL-NYPL, Subject Files, Box 3, "Redress 1973."

119. Minutes of Redress Steering Committee Meeting, 21 August 1972, in RJL-NYPL papers, Subject Files, Box 3, "Redress"—1; "Dear Fellow Americans," n.d., in RJL-NYPL, Subject Files, Box 3, "Redress"—2.

120. Minutes of Redress Steering Committee Meeting, 21 August 1972, in RJL-NYPL, Subject Files, Box 3, "Redress"—1

121. "On Elections and the Nuremberg Obligation," n.d., in RJL-NYPL, Subject Files, Box 3, "Redress"—1;

122. "Anti-War Programs for the Post-War Period," in RJL-NYPL, Subject Files, Box 3, "Redress 1973."

123. "Redress Without Tears—Some Thoughts on Who and What We Are," in RJL-NYPL, Subject Files, Box 3, "Redress 1973."

124. "Redress Without Tears—Some Thoughts on Who and What We Are," in RJL-NYPL, Subject Files, Box 3, "Redress 1973." Lifton did not actually sign

this document, but its language is clearly his, and it is written in the same style as other memos that Lifton wrote for himself and others.

125. Lifton, review of *My Lai 4* and *One Morning in the War*, 2, 23.

126. See, for example, Lifton, "Absurd Technological Death"; Edward M. Opton, Jr., and Robert Duckles, "It Didn't Happen and Besides, They Deserved It"; Karl Jaspers, "German Guilt"; and Hannah Arendt, "On Responsibility for Evil," in Falk, Kolko, and Lifton, *Crimes of War*, 559–75, 441–44, 476–85, and 486–501.

127. Robert E. Anneheim to Robert Jay Lifton, 17 September 1969, in RJL-NYPL, Chronological Correspondence, Box 3, "Correspondence 1969"—3; Frederick J. Marchant to Robert Jay Lifton, 5 April 1973, in RJL-NYPL, Vietnam Files, Box 4, "Vietnam Vets Correspondence, 1971–76." See also William G. Wickland to Robert Jay Lifton, 13 February 1973, in RJL-NYPL, Publications Correspondence, Box 4, "1973"; Andy Brambilla to Robert Jay Lifton, 13 April 1974, in RJL-NYPL, Vietnam Files, Box 4, "Vietnam Veterans Correspondence 1978–79."

128. Robert Costello to Robert Jay Lifton, n.d. [1972], in RJL-NYPL, Subject Files, Box 3, "Redress correspondence"; George E. Rubin to Robert Jay Lifton, 4 August 1972, in RJL-NYPL, Subject Files, Box 3, "Redress correspondence"; and Chauncey M. Depuy to Robert Jay Lifton, 25 May 1972, in RJL-NYPL, Subject Files, Box 3, "Redress correspondence."

129. See "Letters: My Lai," *New York Times Book Review*, 9 August 1970, 28–30.

130. There is no notice in the *American Jewish Year Book* of protests against or concerns with Robert Jay Lifton's *Death in Life*. See Morris Fine and Milton Himmelfarb, eds., *American Jewish Year Book 1967*, vol. 68 (New York: American Jewish Committee; Philadelphia: Jewish Publication Society of America, 1967); Fine and Himmelfarb, eds., *American Jewish Year Book 1968*, vol. 69 (New York: American Jewish Committee; Philadelphia: Jewish Publication Society of America, 1968). The *Index to Jewish Periodicals* for 1968 cites two articles about Lifton; one was Mary Ellman's review of *Death in Life* in *Commentary*—a somewhat critical review but with no criticism of the comparison of camp survivors to *hibakusha*. See Ellman, "After the Bomb." The other cited article enthusiastically used Lifton's concept of a "protean man" to analyze recent television shows. See Neil Compton, "TV Specials," *Commentary* 45, no. 6 (June 1968): 69–71; and Miriam Leikind, ed., *Index to Jewish Periodicals*, vol. 5, nos. 3–4, January–June 1968 (Cleveland Heights, Ohio: College of Jewish Studies Press, 1969), 149.

131. Lifton, interview by author, 27 January 2000.

132. Shephard, *War of Nerves*, 361.

133. See, for example, Robert Jay Lifton to Tod Ensign, 27 July 1970, in RJL-NYPL, Vietnam Files, Box 1, "Citizens' Commission"; and Robert Jay Lifton, "Have Americans Become Murderers?" Promoting Enduring Peace reprint no. 164, n.d., in RJL-NYPL, Vietnam Files, Box 3.

134. Kunen, *Standard Operating Procedure,* 19.

135. John Kerry and the Vietnam Veterans Against the War (edited by David Thorne and George Butler), *The New Soldier* (New York: Macmillan, 1971), n.p.

136. Scott, *Politics of Readjustment,* 12. Lifton believes that the VVAW leaders' decision to focus on war crimes was the result of discussions between him and them, but he does not believe that he was the prime source of their decision. See Lifton, interview by author, 29 March 2000. Douglas Brinkley has suggested that John Kerry, one of VVAW's early leaders, was influenced by Lifton's description of veterans as victims. See Brinkley, *Tour of Duty: John Kerry and the Vietnam War* (New York: Harper Collins, 2004), 407–8. Lifton is not certain that he had this influence on Kerry. See Lifton, telephone interview by author, 6 July 2004.

137. Robert Jay Lifton to Robert Coles, 6 June 1972, in RJL-NYPL, General Correspondence, Box 3, Folder 1; "Some Answers to Questions That Have Been Asked about the Redress Emergency Action . . . " in RJL-NYPL, Subject Files, Box 3, "Redress—May 24, 1972."

138. See, for example, Marjorie Hunter, "Prominent Foes of War Seized in Capitol Protest," *New York Times,* 25 May 1972; "Galaxy of Sit-ins Arrested at Capitol," *New York Post,* 25 May 1972, in RJL-NYPL, Subject Files, Box 3, "Redress 1973"; and Robert Buchanan, "112 Celebrity-Led War Foes Arrested in Capitol Protest," *Evening Star* (Washington, D.C.), 28 June 1972, in RJL-NYPL, Subject Files, Box 3, "Redress"—1.

139. See, for example, Lifton, *Home from the War,* 37, 41–42, 411–42.

140. Christopher Lehmann-Haupt, "Presumptuous Psychohistory," *New York Times,* 6 August 1973, 29; Richard Locke, review of *Home from the War, New York Times Book Review,* 24 June 1973, 27; Laurence I. Barrett, "War of Words," *Time* 102 (9 July 1973): 62.

141. Richard H. King, "Victims and Executioners," *Psychology Today* 7, no. 3 (August 1973): 17; J. Glenn Gray, "Back," *New York Review of Books* 20, no. 11 (28 June 1973): 22; James S. Gordon, "The Death Immersion," *New Republic* 169, nos. 4–5 (28 July and 4 August 1973): 31. See also Fred Weinstein, "Personal Conflict and Advocacy Research," *American Scholar* 42, no. 4 (Autumn 1973): 696–700.

142. See, for example, Don Browning, "Psychiatry and Pastoral Counseling: Moral Context or Moral Vacuum," in *Christian Century* 91, no. 5 (6 February 1974): 158–61; Robert Hassenger, review of *Home from the War, America* 129, no. 5 (1 September 1973): 128–29.

143. See, for example, "Veterans Battle Emotional Strain," *New York Times,* 1 May 1973, 13; Catherine Breslin, "Vietnam Veterans: A Shocking Report on Their Damaged Lives," *Redbook* 141 (May 1973): 141; Timothy J. Renwick to Robert Jay Lifton, 21 August 1979, in RJL-NYPL, Vietnam Files, Box 4, "Vietnam Veterans Correspondence 1978–79"; and Mark S. Hanson to Robert Jay Lifton, 8 May 1973, in RJL-NYPL, Vietnam Files, Box 4, "Vietnam Veterans Correspondence, 1971–76."

144. See, for example, Richard L. Killmer to Robert Jay Lifton, 3 August 1971, in RJL-NYPL, Vietnam Files, Box 4, "Correspondence 1971–72"; Donald A. Bloch to Robert Jay Lifton, 17 December 1971, in RJL-NYPL, Vietnam Files, Box 4, "Correspondence 1971–72"; and Fred Mager to Robert Jay Lifton, 22 June 1970, in RJL-NYPL, General Correspondence, Box 19, Folder 3.

145. Robert Jay Lifton to J. Stephen Frye, 3 January 1978, in RJL-NYPL, Vietnam Files, Box 4, "Vietnam Veterans Correspondence, 1978–79."

146. Chaim Shatan, "The Grief of Soldiers," *American Journal of Orthopsychiatry* 43, no. 4 (July 1973): 640–53; Chaim Shatan to Robert Jay Lifton, 4 February 1972, in RJL-NYPL, Vietnam Files, Box 4, "Correspondence 1971–72."

147. Chaim Shatan, "Post-Vietnam Syndrome," *New York Times* 6 May 1972, 35; Ralph Yehle to Robert Jay Lifton, 25 April 1972, in RJL-NYPL, Vietnam Files, Box 4, "Correspondence 1971–72"; Alf Hill to Robert Jay Lifton, 4 February 1973, in RJL-NYPL, Vietnam Files, Box 4, "Vietnam Veterans Correspondence, 1971–76"; see Scott, *Politics of Adjustment*, 43–44, for increase in public interest after Shatan's piece was published.

148. Robert Jay Lifton to Robert J. Boudewijn, 2 April 1973, in RJL-NYPL, Vietnam Files, Box 4, "Vietnam Veterans Correspondence, 1971–76;" Robert Jay Lifton, "A Re-examination," *New York Times*, 20 August 1973, 31. See also Robert Jay Lifton to Sarah Oakes and Stuart Bird, 26 February 1973, in RJL-NYPL, General Correspondence, Box 19, Folder 7; and Lifton, *Home from the War*, 420.

149. Scott, *Politics of Adjustment*, 32–35.

150. Scott, *Politics of Adjustment*, 58–60. Lifton, interview by author, 29 March 2000.

151. Scott, *Politics of Adjustment*, 58–60. Lifton, interview by author, 29 March 2000; Lifton, telephone interview by author, 6 July 2004.

152. Robert Jay Lifton to Charles Figley, 9 November 1979, in RJL-NYPL, Chronological Correspondence, Box 5, "Correspondence 1979"—5; and Stephen M. Sonnenberg to Donald G. Langsley, 9 October 1979, in RJL-NYPL, Chronological Correspondence, Box 5, "Correspondence 1979"—5.

153. The Task Force on Nomenclature and Statistics of the American Psychiatric Association, *Diagnostic and Statistical Manual of Mental Disorders, Third Edition, Draft* (Washington, D.C.: American Psychiatric Association, 1978), N:3–5.

154. See, for example, Henry Krystal to Robert Jay Lifton, 2 March 1965, in RJL-NYPL, General Files, Box 11, Folder 1; William G. Niederland to Lifton, 17 April 1964, in RJL-NYPL, General Files, Box 13, Folder 5; and Lifton to Niederland, 12 February 1965, in RJL-NYPL, General Files, Box 13, Folder 5.

155. Gerald Nicosia has briefly described other points of contact between Nazi camp survivors and psychological professionals hoping to revise the DSM-II, including Chaim Shatan. See Nicosia, *Home to War*, 181.

156. Shephard, *War of Nerves*, 385; Paul Lerner and Mark S. Micale, "Trauma, Psychiatry, and History: A Conceptual and Historiographical Introduction," in

Traumatic Pasts: History, Psychiatry, and Trauma in the Modern Age, 1870–1930, ed. Lerner and Micale (New York: Cambridge University Press, 2001), 3.

157. Pubmed, www.ncbi.nlm.nih.gov, accessed 25 April 2005.

158. Lexis-Nexis, http:/lexis-nexis.com/universe, accessed 13 March 2005.

159. Advertisement, Bristol-Myers Squibb Company.

160. For criticism from the right, see Satel, "Returning From Iraq." For criticism from the left, see Lembcke, *Spitting Image,* 101–26.

Conclusion (pp. 159–74)

1. These key events in 1960s history have been described in a number of texts. For the conflict between John Lewis and the Kennedy administration at the March on Washington, see, for example, Clayborne Carson, *In Struggle: SNCC and the Black Awakening of the 1960s* (Cambridge, Mass.: Harvard University Press, 1981), 91–95; Todd Gitlin, *The Sixties: Years of Hope, Days of Rage* (New York: Bantam Books, 1987), 144–46. For the disillusionment of the Mississippi Freedom Democratic Party, see, for example, Carson, *In Struggle,* 123–29; Gitlin, *Sixties,* 151–62. For New Left protests against the Vietnam War in 1965, see, for example, James Miller, *Democracy Is in the Streets: From Port Huron to the Siege of Chicago* (New York: Simon and Schuster, 1987), 230–34; Terry Anderson, *The Movement and the Sixties* (New York: Oxford University Press, 1995), 131–51. It should be noted that as early as 1962, some New Leftists were arguing that it was liberals, not conservatives, who represented the left's most dangerous enemies. See Editors, "The Ultra-Right and Cold War Liberalism," *Studies on the Left* (Winter 1962). The breakup of the coalition between radicals and liberals was a gradual process, not a cataclysmic event.

2. Paul Goodman's angry review of *Death in Life* suggests the scrutiny that liberal perspectives faced in the late 1960s. See Paul Goodman, "Stoicism and the Holocaust," *New York Review of Books* 10 (28 March 1968): 15–19.

3. For Lifton's description of veterans' responses to his work, and his own reevaluation of his research processes, see Lifton, *Home from the War: Vietnam Veterans, Neither Victims nor Executioners* (New York: Simon and Schuster, 1973), 86–90.

4. Egon Mayer, Barry Kosmin, and Ariela Keysar, *American Jewish Identity Survey 2001* (New York: Graduate Center of the City of New York, 2001; reissued New York: Center for Cultural Judaism, 2003), 6.

5. There was antisemitic violence against Jews in New York city, but it occurred predominantly in Jewish neighborhoods that abutted heavily Irish neighborhoods and does not appear to have affected either Lifton's or Milgram's childhood communities. See Stephen H. Norwood, "Marauding Youth and the Christian Front: Antisemitic Violence in Boston and New York during World War II," *American Jewish History* 91, no. 2 (June 2003): 236–37.

6. Peter Novick calls this existential unease a form of "survivor guilt," but he does not address it in detail, and his discussion of this guilt is limited to his description of the immediate postwar years. See Novick, *The Holocaust in American Life* (Boston: Houghton Mifflin, 1999), 75.

7. Stanley M. Elkins, telephone interview by author, tape recording, 2 February 1998.

8. Daniel Horowitz, *Betty Friedan and the Making of the Feminine Mystique* (Amherst: University of Massachusetts Press, 1998), 166–79.

9. For the significance of "whiteness" for Jews in the postwar years, see, for example, Karen Brodkin, *How Jews Became White Folks and What That Says about Race in America* (New Brunswick, N.J.: Rutgers University Press, 1998); and Matthew Frye Jacobson, *Whiteness of a Different Color: European Immigrants and the Alchemy of Race* (Cambridge, Mass.: Harvard University Press, 1998), 187–99.

10. On civil rights, the Cold War, and African decolonization, see, for example, Penny M. Von Eschen, *Race against Empire: Black Americans and Anticolonialism, 1937–1957* (Ithaca, N.Y.: Cornell University Press, 1997); Mary Ann Dudziak, *Cold War Civil Rights: Race and the Image of American Democracy* (Princeton, N.J.: Princeton University Press, 2000). On Cuba and the New Left, see Van Gosse, *Where the Boys Are: Cuba, Cold War America, and the Making of a New Left* (New York: Verso, 1993). For one recent effort to consider the impact of the Holocaust on American political science, see Ira Katznelson, *Desolation and Enlightenment: Political Knowledge after Total War, Totalitarianism, and the Holocaust* (New York: Columbia University Press, 2003).

11. Elie Wiesel, *Night* (New York: Hill and Wang, 1960).

12. Leonard Bernstein, *Kaddish: Symphony No. 3*, vocal score, ed. Abraham Kaplan and Ruth Mense (New York: Amberson Enterprises and G. Schirmer, 1963), quoted in David Schiller, "'My Own Kaddish': Leonard Bernstein's Symphony No. 3," in *Key Texts in American Jewish Culture*, ed. Jack Kugelmass (New Brunswick, N.J.: Rutgers University Press, 2003), 188–89.

13. Philip Roth, "Eli, the Fanatic," in *Goodbye, Columbus and Five Short Stories* (New York: Bantam Books, 1980; originally published Boston: Houghton Mifflin, 1959), 179–216.

14. Roth, "Eli the Fanatic," 216. David Schiller has argued that Bernstein's imagery of extermination was shaped not only by the composer's Jewishness but also by his liberal political activism in the antinuclear group SANE. See Schiller, "'My Own Kaddish'," 186–89. And Wiesel's reviewers tended to praise his book for its insight into the "inhuman degradation" of the concentration camp, "one of the distinctive institutions of the twentieth century," more than they concentrated on Wiesel's religious imagery or on the extermination of European Jewry. See, for example, "Individual Loss," *Times Literary Supplement* (19 August 1960), 523; review of *Night, New Yorker* 37, no. 5 (18 March 1961): 175.

15. Norm Fruchter, "Arendt's Eichmann and Jewish Identity," *Studies on the Left* 5, no. 1 (Winter 1965): 23, 42; Morris U. Schappes, "On Arendt's Eichmann and Jewish Identity," *Studies on the Left* 5, no. 4 (Fall 1965): 67. For more on the conflict over Arendt's *Eichmann in Jerusalem* as generational, see Elisabeth Young-Bruehl, *Hannah Arendt: For Love of the World* (New Haven, Conn.: Yale University Press, 1982), 360–62. For aspects of the conflict over Arendt influenced by gender, see Jennifer Ring, *The Political Consequences of Thinking* (Albany: State University of New York, 1997), 109–56.

16. Oscar Handlin, "Jewish Resistance to the Nazis," *Commentary* 34 (November 1962): 398–99, 405. For positive reception of Handlin's essay, see "Letters from Readers," *Commentary* 35 (March 1963): 253–56; for Hilberg's work coming under increasing attack as the *Eichmann in Jerusalem* controversy developed, see Young-Bruehl, *Hannah Arendt*, 347, 360; Raul Hilberg, *The Politics of Memory: The Journal of a Holocaust Historian* (Chicago: Ivan R. Dee, 1996), 147–57.

17. For Bettelheim's portrait of Jewish passivity and "ghetto thinking," see Bruno Bettelheim, *The Informed Heart: Autonomy in a Mass Age* (Glencoe, Ill.: Free Press, 1960), 252–65. For the University of Chicago forum, see Richard Pollak, *The Creation of Dr. B.: A Biography of Bruno Bettelheim* (New York: Simon and Schuster, 1997), 358–61; for Bettelheim's work being criticized along with Arendt's *Eichmann in Jerusalem*, see Young-Bruehl, *Hannah Arendt*, 347–48, 360. Criticisms of Bettelheim became sharper in the late 1970s with the publication of Terrence Des Pres, *The Survivor: An Anatomy of Life in the Death Camps* (New York: Oxford University Press, 1977), 185–95. And in the 1980s and 1990s, many psychological professionals and Holocaust studies scholars rejected Bettelheim's work. See, for example, Lawrence L. Langer, *Versions of Survival* (Albany: State University of New York Press, 1982), 33–53; George Kren, "The Survivor and Psychoanalysis," in *Healing Their Wounds: Psychotherapy with Holocaust Survivors and Their Families,* ed. Paul Marcus and Alan Rosenberg (New York: Praeger, 1990), 5–9; Paul Marcus and Alan Rosenberg, "Bruno Bettelheim's Work on the Nazi Concentration Camps: The Limits of His Psychoanalytic Approach," in "Bruno Bettelheim's Contribution to Psychoanalysis," a special issue of *Psychoanalytic Review* 81, no. 3 (Fall 1994): 537–664; Robert Krell, "Psychiatry and the Holocaust," in *Medical and Psychological Effects of Concentration Camps on Holocaust Survivors, Vol. 4, Genocide: A Critical Bibliographic Review,* ed. Robert Krell and Marc I. Sherman (New Brunswick, N.J.: Transaction Publishers, 1997). Psychoanalyst Paul Marcus has recently made efforts to revive the value of Bettelheim's ideas; see Marcus, *Autonomy in the Extreme Situation: Bruno Bettelheim, the Nazi Concentration Camps and the Mass Society* (Westport, Conn.: Praeger, 1999).

18. Jean-François Steiner, *Treblinka* (New York: Simon and Schuster, 1967); Arthur Morse, *While Six Million Died: A Chronicle of American Apathy* (New

York: Random House, 1968); and Lucy S. Dawidowicz, *The War against the Jews, 1933–1945* (New York: Holt, Rinehart, and Winston, 1975).

19. See, for example, Nora Levin, *The Holocaust: The Destruction of European Jewry, 1933–1945* (New York: T. Y. Crowell, 1968); Christopher Lehmann-Haupt, "Holocaust Melodrama," *New York Times,* 22 May 1967, 41; Jack Kuper, *Child of the Holocaust* (Garden City, N.Y.: Doubleday, 1967); Eliot Fremont-Smith, "Books of the Times: Moral Trauma and the Holocaust," *New York Times,* 12 February 1968, 37.

20. See Novick, *Holocaust in American Life,* 153–55.

21. Radicals had considered the possibility that America might be turning toward fascism during the turn of the 1960s, but they had also pointed out the differences between contemporary American democracy and the fascist state. See, for example, James Weinstein, "Nach Goldwater Uns?" and Staughton Lynd, "Reply," in *Studies on the Left* 4, no. 3 (Summer 1964): 59–64. By 1968, radical disillusionment and anger had escalated, and the equation of the U.S. government with a fascist state became a standard assumption among leftists. See Gitlin, *Sixties,* 340, 361; Roxanne Dunbar, "Who Is the Enemy," *No More Fun and Games,* no. 2 (February 1969): 58; "'Fascism' Decried at Black Panther Conference," *New York Times,* 21 July 1969, 48; William Hedgepeth, "America's Concentration Camps: The Rumors and the Realities," *Look* (28 May 1968), 85–90; Herbert H. Levine, "Watergate: Surreptitious Entry," *Nation* 217, no. 7 (10 September 1973): 199–202.

22. For protesters at the Democratic National Convention in Chicago in 1968 shouting "Sieg Heil," see Gitlin, *Sixties,* 335; David Farber, *Chicago '68* (Chicago: University of Chicago Press, 1988), 193. For radicals using the Germanic spelling "Amerika," see Anderson, *Movement and the Sixties,* 200. It is worth noting that conservatives and liberals during the late 1960s used similar rhetoric to equate radicals with fascists. See, for example, "Revolutionary Adventurism," *New York Times,* 8 May 1969, 46; "The New Fascists," *New York Times,* 17 December 1969, 54; Anthony Ripley, "'Squares' Picket at S.D.S. Offices," *New York Times,* 27 June 1969, 42. See also comments by Bruno Bettelheim comparing leftist protesters to Nazi brown shirts, in *Chicago Daily News,* 31 January 1969, as cited in Pollak, *Creation of Dr. B.,* 307–8.

23. For the valuable argument that 1978 was a crucial year in American Holocaust consciousness, see Edward Linenthal, *Preserving Memory: The Struggle to Create America's Holocaust Museum* (New York: Penguin Books, 1995), 11–13.

24. For Holocaust denial gaining more attention and legitimacy in the late 1970s and 1980s, see Deborah Lipstadt, *Denying the Holocaust: The Growing Assault on Truth and Memory* (New York: Macmillan International, 1993). For "stealing the Holocaust," see, for example, Yehuda Bauer, "Whose Holocaust?" *Midstream* 26, no. 9 (November 1980): 42–46; and Edward Alexander, "Stealing the Holocaust," *Midstream* 26, no. 9 (November 1980): 46–50.

25. For an example of scorn, see Lucy Dawidowicz, "How They Teach the Holocaust," *Commentary* 90, no. 6 (December 1990): 25–32.

26. See, for example, Sheila Tobias, "The Seeds of Our Own Destruction?" *New York Times Book Revew* 27 May 1990, 19; Hans Bethe, "Changing Nuclearthink," *Issues in Science and Technology* 7, no. 1 (Fall 1990): 97–98; Review of *The Genocidal Mentality, Orbis: A Journal of World Affairs* 34, no. 3 (Summer 1990): 454–55; Chaim Bermant, "From One Holocaust to the Next: The Genocidal Tendency," *Independent* (London), 7 April 1991, 29; Murray Polner, review of *Genocidal Mentality, Washington Monthly* 22, no. 3 (April 1990): 59–60; K. Jonassohn, review of *Genocidal Mentality, Ethics* 10, no. 4 (July 1991): 901–2. For another example of an extended analogy between the Holocaust and American society during this later era in Holocaust consciousness, see Mary Daly, *Gyn/Ecology* (Boston: Beacon Press, 1978), 293–312. Daly's work grappled with recent interpretations of the Holocaust as Jewish by specifically rejecting an analysis of Nazi atrocity that would emphasize Jews or antisemitism. See Daly, *Gyn/Ecology*, 311–12.

27. See, for example, Omer Bartov, *Germany's War and the Holocaust: Disputed Histories* (Ithaca, N.Y.: Cornell University Press, 2003), 181–91.

28. The Web of Science indicates that at least ten scholarly articles on the Holocaust since 2000 have cited Lifton's *Nazi Doctors*. See Web of Science, http://isi01.isiknowledge.com/portal.cgi. For my suggestion that Lifton's work has become a classic in Holocaust literature, note the respectful way that Holocaust scholar Omer Bartov uses Lifton's language describing doctors "transformed from healers to killers" as Bartov introduces a recent scholarly article on psychiatry and Nazi "euthanasia." See Bartov, ed, *The Holocaust: Origins, Implementation, Aftermath* (New York: Routledge, 2000), 44.

29. Robert Jay Lifton, "Conditions of Atrocity," *Nation* 278, no. 21 (31 May 2004): 4–5; Robert Jay Lifton, "Doctors and Torture," *New England Journal of Medicine* 351, no. 5 (29 July 2004): 415–16; Associated Press, "Abu Ghraib Docs Accused of Abuse," 20 August 2004, accessed 15 November 2004, at http://www.foxnews.com/story/0,2933,129496,00.html; "Heart of Darkness," *Newshour with Jim Lehrer*, 11 May 2004, accessed 15 November 2004 at http://www.pbs.org/newshour/bb/middle_east/jan-june04/prisoners_5-11. html.

30. See, for example, Marianne Szegedy-Maszak, "Sources of Sadism," *U.S. News and World Report* 136, no. 18 (24 May 2004): 30; John Schwartz, "Simulated Prison in '71 Showed a Fine Line between 'Normal' and 'Monster,'" *New York Times*, 6 May 2004, A20; James O. Goldborough, "Americans and Abu Ghraib," *San Diego Union Tribune*, 13 May 2004, accessed 18 November 2004 at http://www.signonsandiego.com/uniontrib/20040513/ news_lz1e13 golds.html; and Richard L. Cravatts, "The Dark Psychology of Abu Ghraib," *Washington Dispatch* 20 May 2004, accessed 18 November 2004 at http://www.washingtondispatch.com/article_9095.shtml.

death guilt, 126
death imprint, 126, 143
Death in Life (Lifton), 124–28, 131, 138–41, 152, 155, 238n2
de Beauvoir, Simone, 74–75
dehumanization. *See* personality disintegration
Democratic Party, 41, 130–31, 160
Deputy, The (Hochhuth), 19–20
Destruction of the European Jews, The (Hilberg), 22, 45–46
Diagnostic and Statistical Manual of Mental Disorders (DSM), 154–55
Diary of a Young Girl (Frank), 2, 18
Dicks, Henry, 116
Dogs of Pavlov, The (Abse), 118–20
Donald, David, 43
Dr. Strangelove (Kubrick), 4, 10
Dunbar, Roxanne, 81
Dusheck, George, 108

Eichmann, Adolf: Arendt on, 20–22, 92; as compliant bureaucrat, 80, 89, 108–9, 169; Milgram on, 94, 105; war crimes trial of, 3, 19
Eichmann in Jerusalem (Arendt), 20–22, 45–46, 92, 169
Eisenhower, Dwight D., 72
Elkins, Stanley M.: antisemitism experiences of, 30–37, 73, 163–65; elision of Judaism in *Slavery*, 13, 15, 25, 40; Holocaust/slavery analogy in *Slavery*, 2–3, 30–31, 38–40, 43–56, 159, 192n63; as Jewish writer, 12–13, 16–17, 25, 30, 40, 57, 190n27; liberalism of, 6, 40–43, 159, 161, 194n80; military experience, 30, 34–38, 163, 192n54, 193n65; *Slavery* intellectual climate, 8; *Slavery* overview, 24–29, 197n119; *Slavery* reception, 42–57, 163, 194n81; upbringing, 30–33; view of Nazism, 9, 34–35
Ellman, Mary, 140
Elms, Alan, 89, 103, 105
Ensign, Tod, 146–47
environmentalism: Bettelheim argument for, 38–39; bureaucracy as

moral abdication, 20–23, 56, 115–16; concentration camp inmate passivity and, 22, 39, 67, 170; impact of Milgram experiments and, 172; individual vs. institutional guilt, 26; Iraq War as an "atrocity-producing situation," 172–73; Lifton's *Nazi Doctors* and, 172; as response to Jewish state, 37–38; as response to Nazi race theory, 35–36; slavery and, 39–42. *See also* infantilism; personality disintegration
Erikson, Erik, 132–33, 141
ethics, 101–8, 115, 117–19, 218n85, 224n163
ethnicity: acculturation theory and, 48–49; American multiculturalism and, 17; in Elkins Holocaust/slavery analogy, 13, 25, 28, 55–56; ethnic martyrdom, 44–45, 57; ethnic pride movements, 170; Handlin depiction of immigrants, 35; Japanese American internment, 21; New Class and, 11–12; persecution-of-Jews imagery, 9. *See also* race
Evans, Roland, 50
existential behaviorism, 72, 95–97, 103, 215n52
Exodus (novel, Uris; film, Preminger), 19

Falk, Richard, 147, 150
Family of Man, The (Steichen), 9
Farmer, James, 50
Federal Housing Administration, 11
Feminine Mystique, The. See Friedan, Betty
feminism: acceptance of term in U.S., 74–75; class bias and, 80–81; Milgram obedience experiments and, 110–11; social restructuring vs. New Deal–like assistance and, 73; subversion of masculine liberalism in Friedan, 71, 205n71; women's responses to *The Feminine Mystique*, 77–81. *See also* Friedan, Betty; gender
Flacks, Richard, 112

Lifton, Robert Jay *(continued)*
124, 128, 134–35, 138–57, 161–62,
236n136; *Crimes of War*, 147, 150;
Death in Life, 124–28, 131, 138–41,
152, 155, 238n2; "death-oriented
psychology of life," 126–27; *Genocidal
Mentality*, 171; Hiroshima/Holocaust
analogy, 2, 124–27, 133–34, 137–42,
149–52, 156–58, 161; *Home from the
War*, 152; influence on PTSD concept,
153–57; as Jewish writer, 12–13, 17,
125, 128–32, 136–37, 157; liberalism
of, 6, 130–31, 134–35, 150–51; *Nazi
Doctors*, 172, 242n28; "On Death and
Death Symbolism," 125, 128; on "survivor" concept, 124–26, 142–45,
155–56, 172, 229nn35–36
Lonely Crowd (Riesman), 8, 71, 135
Lumet, Sidney, 4
Lutsky, Neil, 224n153

MacDonald, Dwight, 176n6
Manchurian Candidate, The (Franken-
heimer), 10
Mann, Abby, 19–20
Mann, Leon, 103, 218n83
Marxism, 134
masculinity. *See* gender
Maslow, Abraham, 72
mass society: Bettelheim on mass dehu-
manization, 70–71; bureaucratic be-
havior and, 20–21; suburban homes
as "comfortable concentration
camps," 58–61, 67–68, 72–82; "turn
of the 1960s" depiction of, 8
McCarthyism, 4, 5, 72, 134
McKitrick, Eric, 37, 165
Meier, August, 30
mental asylums, 3
Merton, Robert K., 35–36, 41
Meyer, Philip, 98, 109, 118
Milgram, Alexandra, 98
Milgram, Stanley: Allport influence
on, 96–97; antisemitism experiences of, 98–99, 163–65, 238n5;
Arendt influence on, 92–93; Asch
influence on, 94–95, 97, 215n51;

"Behavioral Study of Obedience,"
83, 87, 89–91; family Holocaust experiences, 99–100, 164–65; Hiro-
shima/obedience analogy, 214n38;
Holocaust/obedience analogy, 84,
87–91, 98, 101–2, 105–10, 113–23,
216n63, 220n114; Jewish reaction
to, 110, 116–17; as Jewish writer,
12–13, 17, 84, 89, 97–99, 106–8,
122–23, 219n97; liberalism of, 6, 8,
92–94, 114, 160–61, 161; *Obedience*
(film), 87, 114, 117; obedience experiments, 2–3, 10, 85–87, 109, 216n57,
219n100; *Obedience to Authority*, 87,
89–91, 93, 108, 113–14, 118,
224n163; professional ethics issues
with, 101–8, 115, 117–19, 224n163;
Skinner behaviorism and, 215n51;
upbringing, 98–100
Miller, Arthur, 4
Mills, C. Wright, 8, 112, 165
moral responsibility: "culture of
trauma" and, 158; Eichmann as bureaucrat and, 20–22, 80, 89, 92, 94,
108–9, 169; of elected officials, 173;
Friedan analogy and, 80; individual
vs. institutional guilt, 26; Lifton analogies and, 142, 149–51; moral passivity, 148–51; My Lai massacre and,
147–48; obedience and, 20–23, 56,
92, 98, 102–3, 115–16; post-Vietnam
syndrome and, 153–54; social theory
and, 224n152–53; "turn of the 1960s"
changing views on, 114
Morgan, Robin, 81
Morse, Arthur, 170
Moskowitz, Eva, 75
Mother Night (Vonnegut), 10, 14
Moynihan, Daniel Patrick, 43, 47–54,
56, 194n80, 197n116
"Muscle-Jews," 34
My Lai massacre, 93, 111, 141–42,
144–47, 150–51. *See also* Vietnam War
Myrdal, Gunnar, 35, 39–40

national character, 96, 122–23
National Committee for a Citizens'

Commission of Inquiry on U.S. War Crimes in Vietnam (CCI), 146–47
National Organization for Women (NOW), 80
National Science Foundation, 85, 88, 107
National Veterans' Inquiry, 146, 151
Nazi Doctors (Lifton), 172, 242n28
Nazism: alienation/conformity vs. persecution of Jews, 9; German Officer Corps' code of obedience, 89; mass society and, 8; racial ideology and, 27; traditional German personality traits and, 87–88, 96, 122–23
"Negro Family, The" (Moynihan), 47–54, 56
Neilson, William Allen, 63, 65
New Class, 11–12
Niederland, William, 125, 155
Night (Wiesel), 125, 169, 239n14
1960s. *See* "turn of the 1960s"
Nixon, Richard, 121, 148–49
Nodel, Julius, 76
Novak, Robert, 50
Novick, Peter, 84, 122
nuclear disarmament, 7–8, 21, 92, 135–36, 239n14
Nuremberg Obligation, 149–52
Nuremberg War Crimes trials, 142, 145–49

obedience. *See* Milgram, Stanley
Obedience (film, Milgram), 87, 114, 117
Obedience to Authority (Milgram), 87, 89–91, 93, 108, 113–14, 118, 224n163
"On Death and Death Symbolism" (Lifton), 125, 128
One Flew Over the Cuckoo's Nest (Kesey), 10
Organization Man (Whyte), 8, 71

Packard, Vance, 8
passivity. *See* environmentalism; infantilism; moral responsibility
Patch of Blue, A (Green), 9
patriarchy, 27, 29
Patterns of Culture (Benedict), 35

Pawnbroker, The (novel, Wallant; film, Lumet), 4
Peculiar Institution (Stampp), 39–40, 42
personality, 87–88, 90–91, 96, 98, 122–23
personality disintegration: Bettelheim on, 22, 70–71; Elkins on, 27–28; Milgram obedience experiments and, 101; self-interest as motivation for study of, 69–70; of women, 60–61, 65–66. *See also* infantilism; psychology
Persons, Stow, 195n88
Phillips, Ulrich B., 42–43, 193n75
Physicians for Social Responsibility, 139
Pinderhughes, Charles, 51
Plath, Sylvia, 14
Podhoretz, Norman, 45, 93, 136
Poliakov, Leon, 18
post-traumatic stress disorder (PTSD), 124–25, 155–56, 158
post-Vietnam syndrome (PVS), 153–54
Power Elite (Mills), 8
Prescott, Peter S., 113
prisons, 3
Project Nuremberg Obligation, 149–51
psychiatry. *See* psychology
"psychic numbing," 126, 155
psychoanalysis. *See* Freudian theory
psychology: Asch conformity experiments, 94–95, 215n51; behaviorism, 95, 213n33, 215n51; black psychology, 51–52; brainwashing, 132; Clark racism experiments, 41; critique of sanity, 9–10; "damage liberalism" and, 40–41; *Diagnostic and Statistical Manual of Mental Disorders,* 154; existential behaviorism, 72, 95–97, 103, 215n52; Freudian theory, 27–28, 132–34, 136–37, 140; group dynamics, 63–64; Holocaust effect on, 97; Jewish self-hatred, 63–66; mental asylums, 3; Milgram experiments, 2; "Negro Family, The" ("Moynihan Report") and, 47–54; post-traumatic stress disorder, 124–25, 155–56, 158; post-Vietnam syndrome, 153–54;

psychology *(continued)*
    professional ethics issues in, 101–8,
    115, 117–19, 218n85; theories of slav-
    ery and, 27–28; thought reform,
    132–33, 150. *See also* infantilism; per-
    sonality disintegration

race: affirmative action, 48–49,
    197n116; African American view of
    Milgram experiments, 109–10; as
    biological concept, 35, 42; black/Jew-
    ish tension, 54–55; black psychology,
    51–52; elided Jewishness as white-
    ness, 165; as factor in persecution,
    26, 28; Holocaust as sanctioned ra-
    cism, 166; Jewish identity and, 16–17,
    40; Nazi ideology and, 27, 35; "Negro
    Family, The" ("Moynihan Report"),
    47–54, 197n116; psychology of preju-
    dice, 96–97; racism in post-WWII
    liberalism, 178n20; savagery vs. civil-
    ization and, 54–55, 193n75; socio-
    economic distress and, 48–49; treat-
    ment in Friedan, 73, 206n76;
    treatment in Lifton, 128. *See also* eth-
    nicity; "Sambo" stereotype; slavery
Raspberry, William, 109
Redress, 148–49, 151
Redstockings, 81
religion: anti-Catholic prejudice,
    180n42; B'nai Brith Anti-Defamation
    League, 21, 32, 110; Catholic condem-
    nation of the Holocaust, 19; Catholi-
    cism as influence on slavery, 25–26;
    individual vs. institutional guilt, 26;
    Milgram Biblical analogy, 89; secular
    intellectuals and, 12, 16–17. *See also*
    Judaism
resistance theory, 52–53, 199n134
Riesman, David, 8, 71, 135–36, 138
Rifkin, Jeremy, 146
Rise and Fall of the Third Reich, The
    (Shirer), 19–20, 87–88
Rogin, Michael, 54, 200n142
role theory, 28
Roosevelt, Franklin D., 130–31, 134, 149

Ross, Lee D., 122
Roth, Philip, 169
Rudwick, Elliott, 30
Russell, Bertrand, 145
Ryan, William, 50, 54

"Sambo" stereotype: infantilism and,
    24; race vs. environment and, 26, 28;
    reception of Elkins and, 43, 195n88,
    195n93; socioeconomic distress and,
    48–49; "turn of the 1960s" political
    reception of, 40; as voicing planta-
    tion owners, 55. *See also* race
SANE (antinuclear group), 239n14
Sartre, Jean-Paul, 95
"Scapegoat, The" (Friedan), 64–65
"scapegoat" process, 64–66
Schiller, David, 239n14
Schoenman, Ralph, 146
Schwerner, Michael, 15
Scott, Daryl Michael, 30, 40–41,
    197n119
Scott, Wilbur, 154–55
Second Sex (de Beauvoir), 74–75
Sedgwick, Eve Kosofsky, 15
Sereny, Gitta, 116
Seton, Cynthia, 75
sexism. *See* gender
Sexual Behavior in the Human Male
    (Kinsey, Pomeroy, and Martin), 9
sexuality, 27, 29, 34
Shatan, Chaim, 144, 151, 153, 155
Shirer, William, 19–20, 87–88, 96
Silberman, Charles, 45–47
Six-Day War, 18, 22, 170
Skinner, B. F., 95, 215n51
Slave Community, The (Blassingame),
    53
slavery, 24–29, 197n119, 199n134. *See
    also* Elkins, Stanley M.
Slavery (Elkins). *See* Elkins, Stanley M.
Snow, C. P., 89
sociobiology, 213n33
sociology, 8, 35–36, 48, 63–64
Sophie's Choice (Styron), 55–56
Soviet Union, 8

World War II: as fight against totalitarianism, 5–6; Japanese American internment, 21; Jewish American soldiers in, 34–36; occupation of Germany, 3; war-related stress in, 154

Yom Kippur War, 18, 170

Zimbardo, Philip, 219n97
Zinn, Howard, 45, 47
Zionism, 34, 37–38, 192n60
Zoepf, Wilhelm, 108